RIVAL BYZANTIUMS

This is a comprehensive comparative view of the way the phenomenon of Byzantium has been treated by the historiographies of the polities that have emerged from its remains – Bulgaria, Greece, Romania, Serbia and Turkey – from the Enlightenment to the present day. Synthesising a sprawling mass of material largely unknown to academic audiences, it highlights the important place Byzantium's representations occupy in the identity building and historical consciousness in that part of Europe. The diverse interpretations of the Byzantine phenomenon across and within these historiographic traditions are scrutinised against the backdrop of shifting geopolitical and cultural contexts, in constant dialogue and competition with each other and in communication with extra-regional, western and Russian, academic currents. The book will be of value to medieval historians, Byzantinists and historians of historiography as well as students of and specialists in modern politics, cultural and intellectual history.

DIANA MISHKOVA is Professor of History and Academic Director of the Centre for Advanced Study in Sofia. She is the author of *Beyond Balkanism: The Scholarly Politics of Region Making* (2018) and *Domestication of Freedom: Modernity and Legitimacy in Serbia and Romania in the Nineteenth Century* (2001), and the editor of many collective volumes, including *European Regions and Boundaries: A Conceptual History* (2017), *Entangled Histories of the Balkans*, vols. II and IV (2014, 2017) and *We, the People: Politics of National Peculiarity in Southeastern Europe* (2009).

RIVAL BYZANTIUMS

Empire and Identity in Southeastern Europe

DIANA MISHKOVA

Centre for Advanced Study Sofia

CAMBRIDGE
UNIVERSITY PRESS

University Printing House, Cambridge CB2 8BS, United Kingdom

One Liberty Plaza, 20th Floor, New York, NY 10006, USA

477 Williamstown Road, Port Melbourne, VIC 3207, Australia

314–321, 3rd Floor, Plot 3, Splendor Forum, Jasola District Centre,
New Delhi – 110025, India

103 Penang Road, #05–06/07, Visioncrest Commercial, Singapore 238467

Cambridge University Press is part of the University of Cambridge.

It furthers the University's mission by disseminating knowledge in the pursuit of
education, learning, and research at the highest international levels of excellence.

www.cambridge.org
Information on this title: www.cambridge.org/9781108499903
DOI: 10.1017/9781108499903

© Diana Mishkova 2023

This publication is in copyright. Subject to statutory exception
and to the provisions of relevant collective licensing agreements,
no reproduction of any part may take place without the written
permission of Cambridge University Press.

First published 2023

A catalogue record for this publication is available from the British Library.

ISBN 978-1-108-49990-3 Hardback

Cambridge University Press has no responsibility for the persistence or accuracy of
URLs for external or third-party internet websites referred to in this publication
and does not guarantee that any content on such websites is, or will remain,
accurate or appropriate.

Contents

Acknowledgements		*page* vii
Note on the Text		viii
	Introduction	1
PART I ON THE ROAD TO THE GRAND NARRATIVE		9
1	Precursors: The Historiography of the Enlightenment	11
2	The Century of History: Byzantium in the Budding National-Historical Canons	35
3	In Search of the 'Scientific Method'	76
4	Between Byzantine Studies and Metahistory	123
5	Byzantium in Ottoman and Early Republican Turkish Historiography	170
PART II METAMORPHOSES OF BYZANTIUM AFTER WORLD		
	WAR II	197
6	From Helleno-Christian Civilisation to Roman Nation	199
7	Towards 'Slavo-Byzantina' and 'Pax Symeonica': Bulgarian Scripts	219
8	How Byzantine Is Serbia?	242
9	Post-Byzantine Empire or Romanian National State?	264

v

10	In the Fold of the 'Turkish-Islamic Synthesis'	286
	Epilogue and Conclusion	305
	References	320
	Index	350

Acknowledgements

I am indebted to Historisches Kolleg in Munich, the birth-city of modern Byzantine studies, for hosting me during a crucial phase of my research and providing me with precious time to work on the book. I have to thank Roumen Daskalov and the team of the Entangled Histories of the Balkans project, who encouraged me to press on with my investigation and develop an originally modest enterprise into a book. Tchavdar Marinov, Alex-Drace Francis, Ivan Elenkov, Konstantina Zanou, Ioannis Koubourlis, Ahmet Ersoy, Koray Durak and Ivan Biliarski helped me with my many queries. I am deeply grateful to the anonymous reviewers of the manuscript, who offered invaluable advice and insights and saved me from many mistakes and misconceptions. If there are any left, they are all mine. Acknowledgement is also owed to the New Critical Approaches to the Byzantine World Network and the Oxford Centre for Byzantine Research for inviting me to present parts of the book and receive valuable feedback and encouragement. The help Milena Varzonovtseva lent me with the References was indispensable. To the editorial staff at Cambridge University Press, the editor Michael Sharp in particular, I express my appreciation for their engaged management and cooperation.

Substantial parts of a chapter published in Roumen Daskalov and Alexander Vezenkov (eds.), *Entangled Histories of the Balkans*, vol. III: *Shared Pasts, Disputed Legacies* (Leiden: Brill, 2015) have been integrated into the book. My thanks are due to the editor of the Balkan Studies Library for permission to use this essay here.

Note on the Text

Several different systems to transliterate Cyrillic scripts have been used. For Serbian, the commonly accepted Latin transliteration is used. For Bulgarian and Russian, English-derived digraphs are used rather than characters with diacritics: ch for ч, sh for ш, zh for ж and ts for ц. The y stands for the й in Bulgarian and Russian but also for the ы in Russian Cyrillic – a small inconvenience triggered by the preference for a more practical 'English' transliteration. Accordingly, the ю and я are transliterated as yu and ya. The Russian soft sign (ь) is denoted with an apostrophe ('). In order to distinguish between the vowel a and the schwa (ə), the character ă is used for the latter (namely, for what is ъ in the Bulgarian Cyrillic). Well-known geographical names have retained their conventional spelling (such as Sofia instead of Sofiya).

Frontispiece: Detail from *Byzantium* by Svilen Blazhev (1988),
Bulgarian National Gallery

Introduction

In 1935 the Romanian historian Nicolae Iorga, who coined the celebrated formula *Byzance après Byzance* in order to capture the centuries-old 'survivals' of Byzantine culture and institutions in southeastern Europe, declared the outbreak of the Greek war of independence in 1821 as the endpoint of this legacy – of *l'immuable pérennité byzantine* that had outlived the collapse of the empire by more than four centuries.[1] In many respects, however, the emergence of the modern Balkan nations and sovereign states in the nineteenth century signalled not the endpoint but the birth of Byzantium as a subject of these nations' history. The interest in Byzantium and its legacy in this part of Europe emerged simultaneously and was closely linked with the interest in the medieval precursors of the Balkan nation-states – an interest itself bolstered by the projects of national awakening and modern state-building.[2] This convergence had several momentous consequences. Since the medieval history of the Balkan societies and states was largely shaped in and by their relations with Byzantium, the question about the empire's role and impact became, and remained, a central theme in their national-historical self-narratives and identity politics. Byzantium came to be implicated heavily in issues such as ethnogenesis and collective identity, historical 'rights', national patrimony, culture and 'mentality'. As such, it was exposed to political and ideological deployment. At the same time, Byzantium – and Byzantine studies generally – long remained subsidiary to or subsumed under these countries' national medieval histories. Since the nineteenth century, Byzantine history has constituted, methodologically if not always

---

[1] Iorga 2000 [1935]. As is known, the term 'Byzantine', used to describe a political phenomenon beginning in the fourth century, is both a retronym, being coined in the sixteenth century, and an exonym, naming an entity in a different way from how its members themselves did.

[2] While this author is fully aware of the conceptual distinction often made between southeastern Europe and the Balkans (see Mishkova 2019), for the purposes of this study and its geographical purview, the two terms are used interchangeably.

institutionally, an essential part of the Balkan national historiographies, and Byzantium and its legacy were, and still are, interpreted from discrete national points of view.

This book explores the national interpretations of the impact of the Byzantine empire and the Byzantine legacy in the historiographies of Greece, Bulgaria, Serbia, Romania and Turkey – countries which once belonged to the Byzantine political and cultural orbit and whose modern history, it is often held, bears, to a greater or lesser extent, the hallmark of these political and cultural entanglements. Dimitri Obolensky's famously couched idea of Byzantine Commonwealth – a community cutting across linguistic and ethnic boundaries and united by Byzantine traditions and Orthodoxy – easily comes to mind. In the perspective of Byzantium's 'afterlife' in the historiographies of southeastern Europe, however, it is this notion's ironic retraction that stands out. Variously appropriated and instrumentalised, and subject to often conflicting interpretations, Byzantine culture and legacy subverted rather than asserted the idea of a shared past.

The question of Byzantium's multifarious *survivances* – their continuity and metamorphoses – after the collapse of the Byzantine polity in 1453 is an old one for students of the empire and for those concerned with the national manifestations of these survivals.[3] The object of this survey is different, namely to show the ways in which the Byzantine impact and legacy were perceived, interpreted and constructed by the historiographies of the modern Balkan 'successor states'. For, as sociologist Johann Arnason notes, 'if it makes sense to speak of the path-dependency of nation-formation, in a cultural as well as a political sense, the post-Byzantine constellation is an exceptionally complex and interesting one: no other historical empire has had a similar variety of national claimants to or depositories of its legacy'.[4] The modern representations of Byzantium by the national claimants do not, however, constitute monolithic wholes reflecting some overarching consensual narratives about the past. Instead, we are faced with internal contestations, tensions and dialogue between different interpretations, which unfurl in transnational communication

---

[3] Nicolae Iorga (2000 [1935]) is considered the great initiator in this area. Obolensky 1982 is an important reference in discussions of the Byzantine Commonwealth's afterlife. Clucas 1988, Ševčenko 1991 and Yiannias 1991 are devoted primarily to the Byzantine heritage in Russia and Greece. Stamatopoulos 2009 examines late nineteenth- and early twentieth-century narratives of Byzantium by selecting a confined number of authors and ordering them in contrasting pairs representative of the 'canonical' and 'deviating' versions of these narratives. A recent collection devoted specifically to southeastern Europe is Delouis, Couderc and Guran 2013.

[4] Arnason 2000: 56–7.

Introduction 3

within regional and extra-regional academic currents amid the backdrop of and in conjunction with changing political, geopolitical and intellectual contexts. Therefore, while elaborating on the individual national cases, this study seeks to juxtapose and compare the narratives stemming from various modern cultural contexts.

Non-Balkan, Western and Russian historiographies of Byzantium are being factored into the analysis insofar as they have demonstrably influenced the construction or modification of the local narratives. Central to the discussion, and a main argument of the book, is the gravity of the interplay between Western conceptions of ancient Greece and Byzantium and the claims of scholars based in the region; the series of interactions – and, in the political sense, 'reactions' – between persons writing from outside and those working within (and speaking on behalf of) a given polity. Consequently, writings of both émigré or expat scholars and Western scholars, who lack any personal connection with the region but whose works effectively entered the bloodstream of political thinking and historiography there, are integral to our story. A recently proposed cultural semiotic reading of the meanings and functions of Byzantium in modern and post-modern European culture suggests the existence of two different semiotic spheres – a Byzantine one with its cultural centre in Constantinople and a Western one with its normative cultural centre in Paris. The negative meanings of Byzantium – itself a term that originated from within the Western semiosphere – are said to be characteristic of the Western and not of the Byzantine semiosphere; the same features that are valued negatively within the Western semiosphere are turned into their opposites when related to the Byzantine cultural centre.[5] Normative cultural orientations have no doubt been important in fathoming Byzantium as 'ours' or 'theirs' – the Balkan 'modernisers', for example, were as a rule extremely critical of everything Byzantine in their own semiosphere. But as this study will try to demonstrate, in order to be understood, the 'fundamentally different meanings, functions and values' attributed to the notion of Byzantium are in need of painstaking historicisation. Thereby a 'semantic situation' in both Western and Balkan historiographies will emerge, which is more complex and protean than divergence or appropriation between the two semiospheres might lead us to expect.

Several caveats ought to be made clear from the outset. The purpose of this book is not the examination of the Balkan traditions, or the 'Balkan' history, of Byzantine studies in each of the nations under investigation,

---

[5] Bodin 2016: 11–42.

which is an interesting and worthy but secondary task here. Nor can it serve as a comprehensive catalogue of those regional historians who dealt with Byzantine themes. While accounting for the gradual institutionalisation and the directions Byzantine studies took, the intention here is to explore the various projections or appropriations of Byzantium – the assessments of its role and effects by the national historiographies in the region – but also how Byzantium was deployed in the service of weaving, or contesting, the master historical narratives of these societies. It is, therefore, a study of the mirrored reflections of Byzantium, not the historical actuality. These reflections are also historical facts but they belong less to the history of the Byzantine empire than to that of modern historiography. The present book should rather be seen as an exploration of the *politics* of Byzantine studies – of the images, perceptions and understandings this field has cultivated during the last two and a half centuries – and a critical interrogation of 'Byzantium' as a historiographical construct with considerable ideological potential in shaping national history and national identity.

The elusiveness of the Byzantine phenomenon itself has made it unusually easy for scholars, intellectuals and politicians to 'pick and mix' what they wanted from it. Byzantium meant different things to different people inside and outside the imperial frontiers at the same time, and was marked by significant variety and mutability, its sphere of radiation far from congruent with its areas of direct politico-military control at any one moment. The will-o'-the-wisp quality peculiar to this 'variable-geometry empire', as one of this book's anonymous reviewers shrewdly observed, does not lend itself to tidy definitions and this lies behind the interminable debate over the proper signifiers for denoting the phenomenon of Byzantium. Taking a stance on which signifier is 'correct', and which is not, has not been among the pursuits of this author, who prefers to retain the status of a 'neutral observer' of the ongoing debate among specialists over the nature of Byzantium. Admittedly, the pliancy of the concept of 'Byzantium' to vastly different classifications and uses is to a great extent a reflection of Byzantium's mercurial qualities.

Reception studies, a burgeoning field of late, tends to foreground the substantial role of popular culture – particularly historical fiction, movies and popular magazines – and political discourses in the dissemination of historical imageries. Exploring the uses of Byzantium in Balkan literature and popular culture and of the perceptions they cultivate falls outside the remit of this study.[6] Up to a point, it is geared towards elucidating the way

---

[6] See on this Marciniak and Smythe 2016 and Auzépy 2003.

Introduction

the historiography on Byzantium was, and is, contributing to these perceptions – a question that has not been tackled. The discourses that made use of Byzantium permeated a number of other disciplines: literary studies, philology, theology, law, architecture, the visual arts, music. All of these subjects draw cognitive validity from history, which puts historiography in a 'strategic' position in the field. At the same time, the national schools of medieval and Byzantine studies were often suffused with meta-political messages, thus blurring the boundary between public (or political-ideological) and academic discourses.

The field thus charted is vast, encompassing five national historiographies across more than two and a half centuries of development. Although varying in degree, the presence of the 'Byzantine factor' in all national histories – either of the medieval period or in historical syntheses – and the frequent 'national references' in the specialised literature on Byzantium proper call for rigorous selection of the sources. No single study can claim to represent an exhaustive survey of the historiographic emplotments of Byzantium across such an ambit; the present one attempts instead to identify and discuss in some depth a representative sample of scholars, mostly historians, whose writings can help us capture the dynamics and connotations of Byzantium's 'presence' in the histories of the empire's heirs. Methodologically speaking, the least cogent choice this author had to make was to leave out scrutinising the way Byzantine art and architecture has been treated in art-historical literature. This was a difficult choice considering how important these interpretations are in academic discussions of Byzantium. However, the vastness of the literature on Byzantine art and architecture and exigencies of depth made it unavoidable. Partly mitigating the lacuna is the fact that, compared to other sub-fields, critical history of Byzantine art and architectural history, occasionally subsumed under 'heritage studies', has benefited most during the last years from closer engagement with ongoing theoretical debates, and in several Balkan countries there have been promising breakthroughs.[7]

To allow the major patterns to emerge, the chronological purview of the analysis is kept wide, emphasising transformative trends and main schools of thought. The historiographical 'eras' around which the book is organised – pre-Enlightenment and Enlightenment perspectives; the Romantic era; the late-nineteenth-century turn towards critical ('scientific') historiography and the institutionalisation of Byzantine studies; the interwar period; the post-World War II and post-1989 narrations – should not be

---

[7] Laurenţiu 2001; Popescu 2004; Yıldız 2011; Ćurčić 2013; Ignjatović 2016.

taken to imply neatly ordered entities and clearly separated cultural/ideological formations. For one thing, none of these divisions, not even the typically taxonomic like the Enlightenment or Romanticism, represent coherent bodies of thought. Moreover, there has been much overlapping and criss-crossing between epochs. The late-nineteenth-century Turkish narrative, for instance, signalled the appearance of Byzantium as a historical referent in a framework blending Enlightenment, Romantic and 'modernist' registers. The complexity of the evolution often contravenes common historical sensibility to transformative change, itself sometimes conceptualised as such at a much later date. Hence in historical evolution the line of demarcation between historical periods can never be but arbitrary. Such epochs in historiography serve to mark (often gradual) semantic and discursive shifts, or 'crises of representation', where old and new representations co-exist and where the rate of change across the different historiographic traditions may vary.

It is at the same time undisputable that certain sets of cultural/ideological formations came to prominence during particular historical epochs, reminiscent of 'paradigm shifts', typically in contestation with alternative formations and amid ideological struggles. Moreover, apart from diachronic conceptual transformation and cleavages, there are synchronic divergences across the given traditions. Obviously, the salience of Byzantium with respect to national symbolism and representation was not evenly distributed over time in the different countries. Whereas the Romantic era was decisive in devising the master narratives of Byzantium in the Greek and Bulgarian narratives, it was far less crucial for the Romanian and Serbian interpretations and least so for the Turkish, where 'critical' historiography made much greater contributions; the positivist turn at the beginning of the twentieth century was more important for the crystallisation of the Romanian historical canon than of the Greek, and so on. The incidence of competing narratives also varied from one national case to another: whereas the Greek and Turkish interwar historiographies failed to produce rival interpretations, this was not the case in the Bulgarian and especially the Romanian during the same period, or the Serbian in the preceding one. As expected, for all these historiographies the post-World War II period proved most fecund and variegated, whereas the higher degree of professionalisation of Byzantine research dampened (or at least posed as eschewing) overt ideologisation and politicisation. Hence in the analysis that follows different weight (and space) is assigned to the discrete periods in the respective national historiographic traditions.

Introduction 7

From such premises, adopting chronologically circumscribed chapters operates as a tool for bringing order to the change and difference of the responses given to the question under investigation. In doing so, the author has given preference to conveying the actual 'voices' of the protagonists and heeding the readers' 'feel' for the arguments put forward rather than to a chronologically exhaustive but necessarily succinct recording of the various interpretations. An attempt has thus been made to strike a middle ground between a broad overview, covering the formative phase, institutionalisation and thriving of historical and Byzantine studies, and an in-depth case study of the main actors in an effort to unravel the actual motivating forces and stakes of the debate within a broader transnational framework.

PART I

On the Road to the Grand Narrative

CHAPTER I

Precursors
The Historiography of the Enlightenment

The Eastern Roman empire, named 'Byzantine' a century after its demise, is a latecomer to European historiography. Following its fall to the Ottomans in 1453, its history evoked scant interest in the Latin West and among the humanists of the Renaissance. Émigré Byzantine intellectuals such as Manuel Chrysoloras, John Argyropoulos and Bessarion inaugurated the study of Greek philology in Italy, but what motivated their work and that of their pupils was an interest not in the history of the 'Greek empire' but in classical learning. 'Byzantium', George Ostrogorski observed about this period, 'was regarded as the store house in which the treasures of the classical world were to be found, while there was little interest in the schismatic Byzantine Empire itself.'[1]

The very idea of a 'Byzantine empire' as a cultural-political concept radically different from the Roman empire was slow to take root before the nineteenth century as power politics kept sustaining the terminological obscurity surrounding the notion of Byzantine. On the one hand, following the institution of the self-professed Holy Roman empire towards the end of the eighth century, the Latin West had sought to deny the Romanity of the Byzantines, branding their empire as 'Greek', 'Orthodox', 'Lower' or 'empire of Constantinople' and laying exclusive claim to the prestige, legacy and power of Rome. Byzantium in this sense functioned as an exonym of Western European coinage intended to convey its 'otherness' to Rome and, by extension, 'Europe'. At the same time, however, when Louis XIV laid bare his aspirations to the imperial dignity of the emperors of Constantinople, he did so not because he wanted to show himself as a Byzantine emperor but because he saw himself as the successor of the Roman emperors. In his *Considérations sur les causes de la grandeur des Romains et de leur décadence* (1734), Montesquieu also acknowledged, for strategic polemical reasons, the idea of a continuous Roman empire.[2]

[1] Ostrogorsky 1980: 2.
[2] On the abiding effects of the 'rhetorical violence of Latin propaganda' that painted the Byzantines as not really Romans but something else (typically Greeks and/or Orthodox), see Kaldellis 2019: 3–37.

II

Western interest, philological and historical, in the 'East Rome' and its heritage originated in the sixteenth century, initially in Italy. Its stimuli were primarily political (the threat from the expanding Ottoman state that served to arouse interest not only in the Ottoman Turks themselves but in the Eastern Roman imperial past as well), humanistic (the discovery of the Greek and Byzantine worlds) and religious (the attention to the Eastern Orthodox doctrine aroused by the denominational struggles between reformers and counter-reformers).[3] In Germany, it was an interest in German unity in the face of the Turkish danger and considerable stakes in oriental trade that inspired the powerful business-house of the Fuggers in Augsburg to finance, and its librarian Hieronymus Wolf to undertake, work on the edition and translation of Byzantine authors' *Corpus historiae byzantinae* in 1562 – an enterprise that Wolf's pupil, David Hoeschel, continued with philological skill and 'scrupulous dealing with historical criticism'.[4]

The flourishing of Byzantine studies and Byzantine history in seventeenth-century France, on the other hand, was directly connected with the development of French absolutist and imperial ideology and France's particularly strong diplomatic and economic relations with the Ottoman empire.[5] Hellenist and religious *érudits* were called upon to explain the history of Byzantium in such a way as to legitimise the rights of the king of France over the imperial title at the expense of the Ottoman sultans and Habsburg emperors. Closely linked with this political historical interest was the study of the Greek language in its various forms and historical evolution – a preoccupation 'tied in with the very immediate demands of the cultural politics of the period which produced it'.[6] The crowning achievement of the French school, financed by the royal court, was the corpus of the Byzantine historians, the so-called *Byzantine du Louvre* (or *Corpus Parisiense*), published in twenty-four volumes between 1645 and 1711. These bilingual editions, in Greek and Latin, were executed by learned Jesuits, Benedictines and Dominicans, notably Philippe Labbé, Pierre Poussines, Charles du Fresne du Cange, François Combefis, Jean Mabillon and Bernard de Montfaucon, who combined imperial visions

---

On Byzantium as an 'avatar' of the Roman Empire in seventeenth-century French imperial ideology, see Spieser 2016: 199–210.

[3] A standard reference for the historiography of Byzantine history in the sixteenth and seventeenth century is Pertusi 1967. Characteristically, this erudite work draws a distinction between the intellectual work done by scholars and the use made of it by the powerful – a dichotomy that is no longer acceptable from an epistemological point of view. See Reinsch 2010: 435–44.

[4] Reinsch 2016: 43–54.   [5] Bréhier 1901: 1–36; Auzépy and Grélois 2001.

[6] Jeffreys, Haldon and Cormack 2008: 7.

Precursors 13

with a new interest in the traditions of the Eastern Church in the spirit of the 'positive theology'. Labbé, remarkably, urged European scholars to search out and publish Byzantine texts, and stressed the importance of the Eastern empire, 'so astonishing in the number of events, so alluring in its diversity, so remarkable in the length of its duration'.[7] Du Cange, considered by some to be 'the real founder of Byzantine historical studies', produced several works on Byzantine history, among them *The History of the Empire of Constantinople under the French Emperors* (1657), which he dedicated to Louis XIV, and *Historia Byzantina* (1680), exhorting the young ruler to undertake a new conquest of Constantinople and regain the imperial throne earlier occupied by his ancestors.[8]

Until the eighteenth century, the historiography of Byzantium closely followed the theological, dynastic and annalistic traditions. Historical narratives of the empire, in the best case, remained focussed on the history of emperors, wars and intrigues. Significantly, until the eighteenth century, Byzantium was not considered a historical reality in itself but as the (degenerate) successor to the Roman empire. The greatest achievement of the humanists of the 'Age of Erudition' was the collection of and critical philological work on the Byzantine sources and the development of the auxiliary disciplines. The erudite studies on Byzantine history, which had begun in Italy and Germany and spread to France during the reigns of Louis XIII and Louis XIV, accumulated an impressive amount of material ready to be used for a monumental work: a history of the millennial Byzantine 'civilisation'. The rationalism and religious scepticism of the Age of Enlightenment transformed this potential into a history of the millennial 'decadence' of the empire. One had to wait until the late nineteenth century for the erudite research of the preceding three centuries to bear fruit and for the new science of Byzantine studies to acknowledge the value of the Eastern Roman world.[9]

In Russia, the seventeenth and early eighteenth centuries also saw a revived interest in the history of the Greek Orthodox world. But there, too, this interest was neither purely academic nor unequivocal. The attitude of Muscovite society to Byzantium and its legacy was marked by what Dimitri Obolensky defined as an 'ambiguous blend of attraction and repulsion', while Byzantine history was put to highly selective, didactic and tendentious use in support of power politics or ecclesiastical reform.[10]

---

[7] Vasiliev 1952: 4. [8] Spieser 2016: 200–4; Ostrogorsky 1980: 4. [9] Pertusi 1966: 3–25.
[10] Obolensky 1966: 62–3.

Before the late eighteenth century, engagement with Byzantium in the countries that were part of its heritage in the period of Ottoman control was far weaker and tallied with the long-standing tradition of ecclesiastical history and theological literature. In the seventeenth and eighteenth centuries, there was some interest among the Greek-speaking literati in editing and publishing Byzantine manuscripts. However, this interest was directed towards certain philological and religious aspects of Byzantine intellectual activity and did not entail a systematic engagement with, let alone serious exploration of, Byzantine history.[11] All this was to change starting with the later eighteenth century.

'By the Enlightenment, *Aufklärung*', R. G. Collingwood wrote, 'is meant that endeavour . . . to secularise every department of human life.'[12] Recent scholarship has added prodigiously to our understanding of the complex relationship between religion and the Enlightenment, yet it remains beyond doubt that, in the polemical drive towards secularisation, not only the medieval church and clergy but also the Middle Ages themselves were treated as meaningless. The historically minded representatives of this new intellectual movement drew up a historical picture in which the Roman Republic became the exemplary and binding norm of every state order; in comparison to this classic Roman community, everything that followed the Roman empire and its Eastern incarnation, Byzantium, appeared as a harmful and nefarious deviation – an accumulation of abuses and a triumph of barbarism and obscurantism. It was from such premises that Byzantium came to be evaluated, most resoundingly in the works of the French state theorist Charles de Montesquieu, the French philosopher and historian François Voltaire, the founder of Russian research in Germany August Ludwig von Schlözer and the British historian Edward Gibbon.[13]

For Voltaire, Byzantine history was nothing but 'a worthless collection of declamations and miracles' and 'a disgrace for the human mind'.[14] Montesquieu's *Reflections on the Causes of the Greatness and Fall of the Romans* and Gibbon's *History of the Decline and Fall of the Roman Empire* gave expression to the revulsion and rationalist hostility many Enlightenment thinkers felt for absolutism and the politics of the medieval church, both Eastern and Western. The Byzantine empire, Montesquieu contended, had so many organic defects in its social structure, religious life

[11] See in this respect Gazi 2000: 67–8, note 38.   [12] Collingwood 1974: 76.
[13] Guillou 1966: 27–39.
[14] Voltaire, *Le pyrrhonism de l'histoire*, ch. 15, quoted in Vasiliev 1952: 6.

Precursors

and methods of warfare that the only explanation he could find for the millennial survival of so corrupt a polity was some 'unusual outside causes'.[15] Beginning with the early seventh century, Gibbon avowed, Roman history turned into 'a tedious and uniform tale of weakness and misery. On the throne, in the camp, in the schools, we search, perhaps with fruitless diligence, the names and characters that deserve to be rescued from oblivion.'[16] To Gibbon, the business of the historian of the Eastern Roman empire appeared to be sad and infertile, a repetition of a boring, monotonous narrative of decay. In his eyes, 'the Greeks' of the Middle Ages were a degenerate people, bound by the bonds of low, oppressive superstition, their minds raving about metaphysical disputes, their belief in visions and miracles supplanting all principles of moral certainty – a veritable 'triumph of barbarism and religion'. Voltaire's '*Écrasez l'infâme!*' speaks from these invectives, which projected the dangerous opponent of the present back into a less dangerous past.[17]

For Enlightenment thought generally, neglectful of the study of medieval history as it was, Byzantium became the epitome of everything the Age of Reason disdained: despotism, religious fanaticism and irrationalism, political corruption, ignorance, and effeminateness (as attested by the presence of eunuchs and the influence of women in public life). This imaginary Byzantium of the philosophers was not supposed to be historical: 'it functioned as a screen on which they could safely project all that they feared and disliked about their own world and its pitfalls, a dystopian mirror for the early modern nation-state'.[18] This attitude survived the period of the French Revolution and persisted through the early part of the nineteenth century. From the position of his evolutionary theory of progress, Georg Wilhelm Friedrich Hegel considered Byzantium a historical aberration. In his *Lectures on the Philosophy of History*, he saw the 'general aspect' of Byzantine history as presenting

> a disgusting picture of imbecility; wretched, nay insane passions, stifle the growth of all that is noble in thoughts, deeds, and persons. Rebellion on the part of generals, depositions of the emperors by their means or through the intrigues of the courtiers, assassinations or poisoning of the emperors by their own wives and sons, women surrendering themselves to lusts and

---

[15] Voltaire, *Le pyrrhonism de l'histoire*, ch. 15, quoted in Vasiliev 1952: 7.

[16] Runciman 1976: 103–10. According to Runciman, it was chiefly because of Gibbon's widely read *History* that the word 'Byzantinism' came to mean tortuous intrigue and corruption (106). It should be noted, however, that Gibbon was not proficient in Greek, and his interpretation of the internal history of the Empire after Heraclius is superficial and abounds with factual errors.

[17] Irmscher 1976: 241–68.   [18] Kaldellis 2019: 14.

Precursors

abominations of all kinds – such are the scenes which history here brings before us; till at last about the middle of the fifteenth century (A.D. 1453) the rotten edifice of the Eastern Empire crumbled in pieces before the might of the vigorous Turks.

Byzantine history, Hegel summed up, 'exhibits to us a millennial series of uninterrupted crimes, weaknesses, basenesses and want of principle'.[19]

That this eighteenth-century conception could be maintained, so that despite its historical fragility it is still alive today in the consciousness of a broad Western public, is due to the fact that it accommodated many other tendencies which had little to do with the 'progressive spirit' of the Enlightenment. For the representatives of classical philology, for example, who were educated in the neoclassical and neohumanist spirit, Byzantium was of significance only insofar as it conveyed ancient ideas; its own achievement was only recognised inasmuch as it adapted itself to this tradition in form and content. The Romantics, on the other hand, looked exclusively at the Occidental empire, whose glorification left no room for the empire of Constantinople, let alone for its claims to priority and exclusivity. The Roman Catholic point of view, in turn, was able to recognise only schismatics in the Eastern Church. Finally, the historiographical tradition left behind by illustrious historians such as Leopold von Ranke and François Guizot underwired the Eurocentric perspective that recognised only the Romanesque-Germanic state system as historically significant, while denying the Greco-Slavic East any historically formative power.[20]

Finally, the contempt for Byzantium, merging nationalism with orientalism, was instrumental; it helped Western European scholars 'to place the origins of the European states in the Latin Middle Ages . . . and also to claim the heritage of ancient Greece civilisation through Rome and the Renaissance'.[21] Its reverse side was the profound concern with and pervasive admiration for Greek antiquity, where the 'West' believed its cultural origins were located – an ideological view underpinned by what Peter Gay has termed 'the rise of modern paganism' during the Enlightenment and which infused most of the Romantic and post-Romantic historical literature devoted to the cultural genealogy of 'Europe'.[22] True, in Germany the indefatigable Barthold Georg Niebuhr (1776–1831) kept the flame of Byzantine research burning by initiating the compilation of the fifty-volume *Corpus scriptorum historiae*

---

[19] Hegel 1857: 352.   [20] Irmscher 1976: 252–3.   [21] Agapitos 1992: 238.
[22] See, among others, Canat 1951, 1953, 1955; Jenkins 1980. On the reception of classical antiquity in the West since the eighteenth century in opposition to the East, see Bernal 1987.

byzantinae (1828–97) – usually referred to as the Bonn Corpus and hailed as the greatest editorial enterprise in the field of Byzantine secular literature in the nineteenth century – but elsewhere in Western Europe the study of Byzantium was all but abandoned for nearly a hundred years.

In eighteenth-century Russia, Byzantine history continued to be used as a weapon in the debate over specific policies in church and state rather than as a field of erudite research. In a vein reminiscent of Voltaire or Gibbon, Peter the Great blamed the bigotry of the Byzantine emperors, Byzantine monasticism, civil disobedience and treachery for the unenviable fate of the empire.[23] Since the 1770s, stimulated by Catherine the Great's expansionist policies (as epitomised by the Treaty of Kuchuk Kainarji of 1774 and her 'Greek Plan' of 1782 to crush the Ottoman empire and reinstate Byzantium under Russian protection), interest in Byzantine history and the collection and publication of sources had been increasing. Pioneering these studies were a number of German scholars – Theophilus Siegfried Bayer, Gerhard Friedrich Müller, August Ludwig von Schlözer, Johann Gotthilf Stritter, Johann-Philipp Krug and, somewhat later, Ernst Eduard Kunik – who settled in Russia in the latter half of the eighteenth century and became, in the words of F. Uspenskiy, 'the first heralds and transmitters [in Russia] of Byzantine studies properly speaking'. Until the 1870s, German academic traditions were decisive in shaping Russian historical scholarship generally and the (later illustrious) St Petersburg school of Byzantine studies in particular.[24]

Investigations during this period concerned only marginally Byzantium proper and its history. The German scholars, many of them elected members of the Imperial Russian Academy of Sciences (founded in 1725), emphasised the importance of Byzantium and Byzantine sources for understanding ancient Russian history and mainly treated questions that might elucidate this history. The first major outcome of this work was a four-volume collection of Byzantine sources (1770–5) edited by Johann Stritter and containing information about the ancient inhabitants of the Russian lands and their neighbours. Johann Philipp Krug's important work on Byzantine chronology and chronography also approached the study of Byzantine texts from the point of view of Russian history. Overall, until the second half of the nineteenth century one can barely speak of serious and systematic Byzantine studies in Russia.[25]

---

[23] Obolensky 1966: 63. [24] See Medvedev 2006: 9–32.
[25] Medvedev 2006: 11–13; Vasiliev 1927: 539–45.

Precursors

The late-Enlightenment period in the Balkans set the stage for what later became known as 'national awakenings' – a process undertaken by a handful of 'enlightened' clergymen and internationally connected intellectuals that centred on the creation of national historical narratives, national languages and national folklore. And if the search for the historical roots of these nations-in-the-making reached back to ancient times, their emergence as real 'subjects of history' in the then-prevalent Hegelian understanding of the term – that is, as political entities or centralised states – was firmly located in the Middle Ages. The Greeks were an exception to this rule, a fact that confronted the 'neo-Hellenic enlighteners' with specific challenges that would be ultimately solved by the full appropriation of Byzantium as a 'Greek state'.

Generally speaking, the particulars – geographic, social and political – of the process of medieval state-building, as well as certain methodological shifts in the writing of history, put Byzantium at different removes from the core of the respective national historical narratives. Because of its proximity to Constantinople, relatively early state formation and territorial expansion, medieval Bulgaria was more intensely and lastingly exposed to direct confrontation with and influences from Byzantium than were the Serbs and especially the Romanians and Turks. The historiography of the Enlightenment, on the other hand, paid little attention to questions of continuity per se. It was primarily concerned with issues of genealogy and the search for historical models of the modern organisation of society, hence with 'revivalism'.[26] These two groups of causes made Byzantium a constant, albeit variously valued, key reference in the Greek and Bulgarian historical canons already at their inception in the late eighteenth and early nineteenth centuries. For the Serbian, Romanian and Turkish historiographies, the empire emerged as a powerful factor during the late nineteenth century when the task of asserting ethnic continuity and historical mission amid growing competition over the 'legacy' of the empire began to loom large on the agenda of the 'national historians'.

A vital aspect of our theme, especially for the period of 'national awakenings', is the fact that the historical successor to the Byzantine empire was the Ottoman empire, which since the fifteenth century had ruled over the Balkan Christians and whose regime, during the age of nationalism, was experienced as increasingly oppressive. The Ecumenical Patriarchate itself – the intact powerful survivor of the Byzantine era – formed an integral part of the Ottoman governing system. This

---

[26] Liakos 2008: 204–6.

Precursors 19

determined in great measure the persisting negative attitude of the revolutionary and many moderate 'awakeners' towards Byzantium and its legacy, to which European Enlightenment thought contributed with arguments about the 'anti-European' and 'regressive' nature of both empires.

Present-day Greeks, as Alexis Politis observed, have great difficulty grasping that the sense of continuity of the Greek nation, as it is widely shared and taught at school, was the invention of the mid-nineteenth century. Most of the founders of modern Greece felt a cultural and political affinity with the ancient Greeks alone and considered the entire Byzantine period to be one of foreign, Roman rule and subjugation.[27] Domestic and foreign currents fused to give ancient history and culture a pervasive allure to the mind of the 'neo-Hellenic Enlightenment', which would only later and rather slowly be tempered, though never surpassed, by the romantic concept of a Greek Byzantium and the notion of historical continuity.

It is just as remarkable that ancient Greece's prominence in Greek historical awareness was itself only a few decades old. Migrant Byzantine humanists to Italy and their pupils, typically converts to Catholicism, endeavoured to cultivate Hellenic consciousness under the influence of the Renaissance – Hellenism as a cultural *topos* ('place'/'category') was, after all, an intellectual product of the Renaissance. However, the Hellenocentric narratives of the post-Byzantine thinkers operating in an Italo-Byzantine context barely had any impact in the Ottoman realm, where religiously determined, all-Balkan Christian identity nurtured by the administrative system of the *Millet-i-Rum* overrode linguistic and cultural differences.[28] Until the third quarter of the eighteenth century, all the historical works written or available in the Greek-speaking areas of the empire espoused a strictly Christian perspective on the past informed by Orthodox providentialism, and observed chronographic and ecclesiastical patterns of narration, replicating a Byzantine literary tradition and completely omitting ancient Hellenism.[29] Coming from the most socially (and politically) elevated Greek-speaking Christian stratum of Ottoman society, Phanariot literary culture and historiography is revealing in this sense: the world it was concerned with was not that of *ellinismos* but of Orthodoxy, with its centre in Constantinople, and it was this world that it sought to recreate and that the Christians sought to regain.[30] In the traditional historiography, tinted since the early eighteenth century by

---

[27] Politis 1998: 1.   [28] Kaldellis 2014: 227–33; Zelepos 2002: 43–4.   [29] Politis 1998: 4–5.
[30] Mango 1973: 49–55. The Phanariots were members of the wealthy Greek families of the Phanar, the Greek quarter of Istanbul, who served as administrators in the civil bureaucracy of the Ottoman empire and dominated the administration of the Patriarchate of Constantinople.

20   Precursors

the ecclesiastical humanism of the church, Byzantium constituted the immediate and obvious historical past of the Ottoman empire and its Christian subjects.

From around the 1770s, things began to change, as can be seen in the writings of the Phanariot Dimitrios Katartzis (c.1730–1800), an exponent of enlightened despotism and an enthusiast of the *Encyclopédie* and the French *philosophes*. Katartzis is said to be the first to systematically use the term *ethnos* in the singular and to make a clear distinction between the (genealogy of the) Greek-speaking Romans, *Romaioi*, and the other Christian subject peoples of the Ottomans. Among the illustrious ancestors of the *Romaioi*, he counted Pericles and Themistocles as well as (the Byzantine emperors and military leaders) Theodosius, Belisarius, Narses, the Boulgaroktonos ('Bulgar-Slayer', the nickname of Emperor Basil II) and Tsimiskes.[31] Significantly, the descent thus purported did not translate into national (self-)identification: Katartzis posited the existence not of a 'Hellenic' but of a 'Roman' nation – and insisted that the correct phrase to describe his own identity is *Romiós Christianós* – since religion for him was a much more important criterion of identity than language.[32] Genealogy (or origin) and identity thus went separate ways. The Greek-speaking clergymen and historians living in Wallachia, Dimitrie (Daniel) Phillipides (1750–1832) and Grigorios Konstantas (1753–1844), as well as Rigas Velestinlis (1757–98) – the long-hailed harbinger of revolution and democracy in the Balkans – present interesting hybrid cases fusing ecumenist and nationalist visions. The first two contemplated an empire of 'enlightened despotism', freed from the Ottomans by Russian intervention in the Balkans. But they also spoke favourably of Alexander the Great and introduced the key notion that latter-day 'national historians' would use to bring about a re-evaluation of Byzantium in the Greeks' historical consciousness – namely, that what took place in Byzantium was the 'Hellenisation' of the Romans. 'Those Romans who emigrated to Constantinople abandoned the Roman language and mores and Hellenised themselves.'[33] The celebrated manifestos of Rigas Velestinlis, *Great Map of Greece* and *Constitution*, published in 1797, present a similar hybrid case superimposing different worldviews. Their phraseology is of unmistakable Western aspiration: Rigas spoke of a 'Hellenic Republic'

---

[31] Tabaki 2007: 90–1; Politis 1998: 7.

[32] Koubourlis 2005: 59–60. As Koubourlis adds, 'from this point of view, what separates "us" from the ancient "Hellene"' is more essential than what links "us" to them' (60). See also Kitromilides 1989: 153–4 and Kostantaras 2015: 173–7, emphasising the hybrid nature of Katartzis's thought.

[33] Philippides and Constantas 1791: 121, cited in Koubourlis 2005: 65.

Precursors

whose constitution would be modelled on the French constitutions of 1793 and 1795, and of the 'People descended from the ancient Hellenes', not of *Romaioi*. But this republic was to include 'Rumeli, Asia Minor, the Mediterranean islands, [and] Vlakhobogdania'—in other words, the space of the one-time Byzantine empire—in a unitary, not federal, state and its official language was to be Greek. Byzantine religious ecumenism was replaced by the universalism of human and citizenship rights—'a somewhat dechristianised Byzantine democracy'.[34] Byzantinism and the 'new ideas' thus sat side by side without apparent tension.

The peaceful coexistence of the Hellenes and the Byzantines did not last long, however, and from the early 1790s, with the Enlightenment antimedievalist indictments and the national ideas resonating ever more strongly, the 'decline' of Byzantium proceeded alongside the 'rise' of the ancient Greeks. For about half a century, the ideal of national purity eclipsed that of historical continuity. Following an anonymous translation of Montesquieu's *Reflections*, Adamantios Korais (1748–1833), a major figure in the Greek Enlightenment, issued in 1798 – the year Napoleon landed in Egypt – a furious denunciation of the lawlessness, greed, bloodiness and theological dependency of the 'Grecoroman kings'. 'The despots transplanted from ancient Rome [the Byzantine emperors]', he wrote a few years later, 'after frittering away, by an administration that was as stupid as it was tyrannical, all the resources of society, hindering the influence of the best climate, defiling and shattering their throne by the most frightful crimes, ended up delivering you to even more stupid and more ferocious tyrants.'[35] What Korais actually did was to transform the Byzantine state into 'a medieval version of the Ottoman empire'.[36]

The 'orientalising' of the Byzantines reached its peak during the Greek war of independence (1821–30), when Korais castigated the disastrous Byzantine emperors for adopting the trappings of the Persian and Parthian courts and establishing a court of truly Asiatic luxury. The 'church of the monks' was for him a resort for idlers and the patriarchs of Constantinople cynical manipulators just like his contemporary Phanariots. Indeed, Byzantine emperors, patriarchs and clergy, Ottoman sultans and Phanariots were lumped together in a single parasitic group that sapped the material and mental resources of the Greek nation. The

---

[34] Velestinlis 1797, cited in Clogg 1976: 149; Mango 1973: 57; Tabaki 2007: 91–2. For a somewhat different interpretation of the evidence, see Myrogiannis 2012: 131–66.
[35] Quoted in Zakythinos 1966: 92. Korais, a philologist by vocation, spent most of his life in Paris, which augmented his impact on the intellectual life of his home country.
[36] Agapitos 1992: 238.

Turks, however, were credited with having saved the Greeks from both the Byzantine nobles and the papal yoke.[37] All this, on the other hand, fit well not only with the heroic neoclassicism disseminated by the Greek war of independence but also with its social undertones and the democratic and anti-clerical leanings of many Greek intellectuals at the time. For the only true but very powerful remnant of Byzantium in the life of the Greeks (and the other Balkan populations) at that time was the Constantinople-based Orthodox Church, which formed an integral part of the power elite of the Ottoman state. The multi-ethnic character of the empire (hence the 'impure' language of Byzantine literature) was another feature distasteful to the father of Greek liberal nationalism.[38] The anti-clericalism and nationalism of the rationalist enlighteners thus logically led them to deplore Byzantium and its legacy.

In the end, Korais's writings rendered the Byzantines oppressors of the Greeks, as were the Macedonian kings before them, because they had 'relegated the Greek nation to barbarism'. By imitating the barbarian Orient rather than the classical Hellenes, the Greco-Roman emperors paved the way for Byzantium's ultimate surrender to a wholly oriental conqueror. The name *Romaioi* (or *Romioi*), which the modern Greeks commonly used to designate themselves, was a shameful testimony to their centuries-long enslavement by the (Eastern) Romans, so it had to be eliminated and replaced by *Graikoi* – a name that was, according to Korais, older even than 'Hellenes' and one by which the Greeks were known in Europe. Significantly, it was Gibbon whom Korais amply cited to verify his polemic against the Byzantine oppressors.[39]

Korais set the tone for a series of writings where Byzantium was presented as the antithesis of ancient Hellas – an embodiment of corruption, debauchery and decadence, of foreign domination and tyranny by Roman emperors, church hierarchs and wealthy notables. In a speech on the Acropolis in 1841, Iakovos Rizos Neroulos (1778–1849), president of the Athens Archaeological Society and a government minister, portrayed Byzantine history as 'a very long and almost uniform series of foolish and shameful violations of the Roman empire transplanted to Byzantium. It is the ignominious exemplar of the extreme wretchedness and debasement of the Greeks.'[40] Most of the Greek intelligentsia in the first half of the nineteenth century were committed to divulging the ancient roots of the modern Greeks and the links

---

[37] Mackridge 1998: 50. [38] Mackridge 1998: 52.
[39] Fassoulakis 1993: 169–73. The suggestion to use *Graikoi* rather than *Romaioi* or *Ellenes* was first made by Evgenios Voulgaris in 1768 for the same reasons.
[40] Cited in Gazi 2000: 68.

Precursors

between modern and ancient Greece, almost completely obviating the Byzantine and Ottoman past. Official historiography squarely confronted popular 'myth-memories' of the Byzantine past bequeathed by a long-standing religious tradition.[41] Parallel to these intellectual efforts, place names were changed from medieval to (often allegedly) ancient ones, medieval monuments and Byzantine churches were destroyed and 'the language question' emerged, to remain unresolved for the next century and a half. Ancient history thus directly moulded Greece's modern identity.

As we have seen, however, the immense symbolic value of Hellas and the myth of an eternal Greece were not of the Greeks' making: they were Western cultural constructions, inculcating the image of ancient Greece as the original and indigenous 'Ur-Europa' imbued with the key values of modernity, and which were communicated to the Ottoman realm by 'Hellenised' diaspora intellectuals. While the other European nations had to create their own national symbols, stories and monuments, the Greeks on the contrary received their national identity from western Europe as a ready-to-use package.[42] The indigenous reception of philhellenism had momentous consequences for the emerging Greek state and identity. European philhellenic thought had led the Greeks to believe that they were different from the other ethnic groups with whom they had been living for centuries, in that their nation had a universally accepted civilised status which set them apart not only from the Ottoman 'barbarians' but also from the other Christian communities in the Balkans. Cultural Hellenisation of these other nations meant, in this sense, their taking the side of progress, rationality and truth.[43] On the other hand, the philhellenic Europe's essentialist interpretation of its cultural origin in ancient Hellas and disdain for the Byzantine empire meant that Greece's self-identification involved, more dramatically than in other cases, a choice between the 'West' and the 'non-West', 'Europe' and 'Asia', progress and decadence. Much as the aura of grandeur surrounding Greekness was imported from abroad, so was the horror of being 'oriental'. Next to the effort to dissociate the new state from its Ottoman past, the reception of the Western model of cultural history, juxtaposing a glamorised ancient Greece with the East, determined modern Greece's wholesale initial self-identification with classical antiquity and the West. 'By accepting Western

---

[41] Hatzopoulos 2013: 219–29.   [42] Mackridge 2009: 63.

[43] Tsoukalas 1999: 7–14. In his famous 1844 speech on the 'Great Idea of Hellenism', Ioannis Kolettis spoke not only of liberating 'our still oppressed brothers' but also of the necessity for the Greeks to 'civilise [again] the East' on the one-time example of Alexander the Great – a popular formula of contemporary colonialism (Koubourlis 2005: 28).

culture', Markos Renieris wrote in 1842, 'Greece does not renounce its national spirit but rather fulfils it.'[44] There was thus a striking convergence of the exigencies of the Greek national emancipation, state-building and legitimation – in brief, Greek nationalism—the indigenisation of Western philhellenism as a national ideology (a process that some had described as 'self-colonisation', but which carried the glamour of exceptionalism that was instrumental in securing national statehood for Greece against all political odds) and the intellectual dispositions and political values of the late Enlightenment.[45] These different threads were woven together in a historical narrative featuring a resurrected 'progressive' Greece after twenty centuries of slavery and darkness and infused with strong anti-Byzantine sentiments.

Ever since the Enlightenment, interpretations of the relations with Byzantium have stood at the heart of the Bulgarian historical narrative. This is not hard to explain, since for seven centuries the medieval Bulgarian *ethnos*, statehood and culture were being formed in constant close interaction and frequent political confrontation with the Byzantine empire.

The Bulgarian state emerged at the end of the seventh century as a result of the Bulgars, a relatively small but well-organised nomadic tribe of Turkic background hailing from the Eurasian steppes, who subjugated the Slav inhabitants of the eastern Balkans. This was the first durable barbarian and essentially monarchical polity set up on the lands of the Byzantine empire. Already before their Christianisation, the Bulgarians managed to expand their territory, taking over large areas of formerly Byzantine possessions.[46] In 864, after a lost war with the empire, Prince Boris I (852–89) was compelled to adopt Christianity from Constantinople rather than Rome – a decision that paid off with the setting up of an autocephalous Bulgarian Church and later patriarchate but that also opened the way for the penetration of Byzantine temporal and ecclesiastical influence. Under Boris's son, Simeon (893–927), the spread of Byzantine culture continued through the introduction of church services in the Slavic language (Old Church Slavonic) and the proliferation of Slavic versions of Byzantine-derived writings, which crowned the work of

---

[44] Agapitos 1992: 236.

[45] On European philhellenism as a form of 'Orientalism', see Gourgouris 1996: 140; as 'self-colonisation' carried out by a diaspora cultural elite, see Calotychos 2003: 38–53; as 'crypto-colonialism', Tziovas 2014: 2–3.

[46] In a relatively short time the numerically preponderant Slavic population in the new state assimilated their 'state-creative' conquerors demographically and culturally but kept the latter's ethnic name and that of their state.

the Byzantine missionaries Constantine (Cyril) and Methodius and their disciples, and were championed by the (increasingly byzantinised) Bulgarian court. The Christianised South Slavs (Bulgarians and Serbs) thus gained an important instrument for establishing permanent states and sustaining individual identities. At the same time, Simeon engaged in a protracted struggle with Byzantium for hegemony over southeastern Europe and, by claiming the title of *basileus kai autokrator* of the Bulgarians and the Romans, made plain his intention to take over the empire.

The Byzantine *reconquista* of the late tenth and early eleventh centuries led to the conquest of the Bulgarian state, turning it into a province under the direct military and administrative control of Constantinople for almost two centuries. In 1185 an uprising against the weakened Byzantium led to the formation of the Second Bulgarian Kingdom (1185–1396). However, waning Byzantine political control did not mean fading political and cultural influence: feeding on the conditions created during the long Byzantine rule, this influence continued to expand almost until the very end of the Bulgarian state (1396) under the onslaught of the Ottoman Turks.

Predictably, therefore, medieval Bulgarian culture and much of the modern Bulgarian identity – religion, literary heritage, state and historical traditions, art – bears imprints of the civilisational entanglement with Byzantium. In both politics and culture, the empire was an overwhelming presence and a powerful standard-bearer for the medieval Bulgarian state. Indeed, Byzantium has shaped the Bulgarians' historical canon and self-perception as much as it has shaped those of the Greeks. 'Our close proximity to Byzantium', wrote an eminent Bulgarian historian, 'charted the directions of our entire medieval life; its influence on us determined, as regards both state and culture, our historical destiny.'[47] But the interpretations and valuations of this key presence by the Bulgarian and the Greek historiographies are very different.

The national movement of the Bulgarians, it should be remembered, was directed not only against the Ottomans as political masters but also against the Patriarchate of Constantinople and the high clergy, who were (linguistically) either Greek or Hellenised. To the Ecumenical Patriarchate's position as an integral part of the Ottoman system of administration – the common ground not only for the Balkan enlighteners' but also some lower clerics' critical attitude to it – was added, in the age

---

[47] Mutafchiev 1987: 24.

of nationalism, its imputed 'anti-Bulgarian', 'Greek' character. The Bulgarian national 'Revival' began largely as a reaction against 'Hellenism' and evolved into a struggle against the 'Greek' Church and cultural assimilation. The notion of the 'double yoke' – political (Turkish) and spiritual (Greek) – became a common trope in the crusade for national mobilisation.

The early modern Bulgarian historical narrative of the second half of the eighteenth and the beginning of the nineteenth centuries, still largely anchored in traditional (providentialist) visions, was similar in its treatment of Byzantium to that of the contemporary Greek enlighteners but for very different reasons. For monk Paisiy Hilendarski (1722–73), later hailed as the first Bulgarian national 'awakener', the Bulgarians' chief enemy during their historical peak in the Middle Ages was the 'Greeks' that is, the Byzantines. His primary aim was to discredit Greek insinuations that the Bulgarians had always been an amorphous ethnic mass subjugated to the Greeks, to demonstrate that they had had their own state, church and high culture and to show that the military might of Byzantium and the brilliance of its culture were fraudulent. In his *Slavobulgarian History* (1762), Paisiy presented the 'Greek emperors' as deceitful and ruthless; they had often been overpowered by the Bulgarian tsars and forced to pay a tribute. Their domination over the Bulgarians in the eleventh and twelfth centuries, won by deceit rather than valour, was branded a 'Greek yoke'. Paisiy also blamed them for the Ottoman conquest, as they called on the Turks to fight the Bulgarians.[48]

Paisiy made no effort to discriminate between the Byzantines and the contemporary Greeks and referred to the 'Eastern Greek empire', 'Greek emperors' and 'Greek land' when writing about Byzantium. That was a convenient conflation. Paisiy and his followers reproduced the medieval Slavic and Latin convention of using 'Greek' as a synonym for Romans (*Romei*, i.e. 'Byzantines') but they gave it a national meaning that it originally lacked. This re-signification was instrumental in mobilising the Bulgarians' resentment towards the contemporary Greeks by pointing to the age-old confrontation between the two nations.

> Why was King Simeon Labas illustrious? Because he waged a severe and unremitting war against the Greek kings and always beat them. Four times he went to Constantinople with an army and seized and burned many areas. During his reign for thirty-five years Bulgarians and Greeks had no peace.

---

[48] Hilendarski 1972: 43–4.

Precursors 27

> From that time much enmity and condemnation remained between Greeks and Bulgarians – and [it continues] until this day.[49]

The anxieties of the present provided the view of the past: the cultural (and political) role of the 'Greek Church' was identified with that of Byzantium, and the ongoing nationalist strife with the Greeks was seen as the legacy or the extension of the confrontation between the medieval Bulgarian state and the Eastern Roman empire.

In hindsight, it can be argued that Paisiy's rather simplistic and crude representation supplied the matrix for the subsequent historical accounts. In its fundamentals, especially in portraying Byzantium as the eternal nemesis of the Bulgarians, it proved remarkably stable. The next, Romantic period in Bulgarian history would add new aspects without changing it.

In many ways, the Serbs' relations with Byzantium were no less crucial to their medieval history. But in addition to the relatively late foundation of a Serbian state, hence political confrontation with the empire, there was one more important difference. Byzantium was not the only gravitational centre for the Serbs; much more intensely and palpably than medieval Bulgaria, the Serbs experienced the rival political and cultural impact of Rome.

Between their settlement in the western provinces of the Balkans (in parts of today's Bosnia-Herzegovina, Dalmatia, Montenegro and western Serbia) in the first half of the seventh century and the Byzantine subjugation of the Bulgarian Kingdom in the eleventh century, the Serbian tribes' contact zone with Byzantium was reduced to the Adriatic coast. For about three centuries the empire had practically no direct control over the interior of the Balkan peninsula, while the Bulgarian Kingdom (which included the lands of present-day Serbia) barred land access to the western provinces. As a result, the Christianisation of the Serbs came about only gradually, over more than a century, and was carried out primarily by Byzantine missions but also by the Dalmatian bishoprics administered by Rome. The 'Byzantine' traits that the Serbs had taken on since the late ninth century, most notably the spread of Orthodox Christianity and the Slavic church service, were largely mediated by the Bulgarians. After the defeat of the First Bulgarian Kingdom in 1018, Byzantium regained its effective control on the peninsula, whereby the Serbs acquired a long frontier with Byzantium for the first time and much of the territory

---

[49] Hilendarski 1972: 234–5.

inhabited by Serbs came under the jurisdiction of the 'Greek' archbishops of Ohrid appointed directly by the emperor of Constantinople. In political terms, until the second half of the twelfth century, local Serbian military leaders, *župans*, had made several attempts to establish more consolidated polities but the results proved ephemeral. Of these 'proto-states', only two endured for somewhat longer periods – Serbia (later also called Raška) in the interior and Zeta (Montenegro) on the Adriatic seacoast. Both felt the political impact of Constantinople, yet the grand *župan* of Zeta received his royal title from Rome (1077). The second half of the twelfth century saw the rise of the Nemanjić dynasty, canonised in Serbian historiography as the quintessentially 'national' dynasty of the Middle Ages, under which the Serbian medieval state reached its political pinnacle. Serbian medieval state-building, similar to that of the Bulgarians, took place in a context of alternating alliances and wars with Byzantium, although most of the time Serbia was in a vassal relationship with Constantinople. But the Latin south (centred on Dubrovnik) and west posed a greater threat to the Serbian centralisation and the Orthodox ecclesiastical structure that the Nemanjić sought to foster.

From around the mid-twelfth century, taking advantage of the major conflict between Byzantium and Hungary, the Nemanjić dynasty extended its power over a large territory in the western Balkans, including Raška and Zeta (but not Bosnia). As in Bulgaria a few centuries earlier, the new ruling dynasty embarked on a continuous effort to attain as much independence and legitimacy as it could wrest from Constantinople and Rome.[50] In this it went down a well-worn path: following the Crusaders' capture of Constantinople in 1204, the Patriarch (then residing in the Empire of Nicaea) endorsed the founding of an autocephalous Serbian Church (1219), while the first king of Serbia – Stefan the First-Crowned (*Prvovenčani*) – received his title from Rome (1217). Medieval Serbia reached the height of its political power and territorial expansion under Tsar Stefan Dušan (1331–55), whose empire incorporated large tracts of formerly Byzantine lands (Epirus, Thessaly, Macedonia, Albania). Dušan claimed that the Njemanić dynasty originated with Constantine the Great, proclaimed himself emperor of the Serbs and the Greeks (*car Srba i Grka*) while elevating the Serbian Church to the rank of a patriarchate, strove to imitate the Byzantine emperor in every respect and opened the doors of his court wide to Byzantine influence. At the hands of his heirs and

---

[50] Throughout the twelfth century, despite its attempts to get rid of Byzantium's tutelage, Serbia remained a vassal state to the empire, whose rulers were treated by the emperor as his administrators.

Precursors 29

contenders, this loosely knit and heterogeneous empire quickly disintegrated into a number of short-lived states.[51]

Within this framework, charted mainly by political events and institutional evolution, various interpretations of the actual place of Byzantium in the Serbian history and culture emerged, often in conjunction with a corresponding treatment of the role of the 'West'. For the Serbian enlighteners, this was not yet a central issue: in addition to the paucity of information for the period until the thirteenth century, this first generation of national awakeners was busy attesting to and emphasising above all the strength and achievements of Stefan Dušan's empire. The major adversary in this story was Byzantium; Rome, the 'Latins' and the Muslims followed suit. Yet, unlike the Bulgarians, it was long believed that the Serbs in the Middle Ages 'were at different times allies, vassals, rivals and opponents of the Byzantines, but never direct subjects of the emperors of Constantinople'.[52] And since in the formation of the modern Serbian identity the confrontation with the Greeks played a far lesser role, Byzantium never acquired the explicitly negative features and harmful role it was assigned in Bulgarian historiography. The overriding theme in the Serbian historical narrative during not only the Enlightenment but also the Romantic period was different: the capacity of the Serbs' rising and fresh forces to take over the decaying Eastern Roman empire and found on its ruins their own Serbian (or Greco-Serbian) empire. In this scenario, the Serbs were endowed with the potential to lead a new 'Serbian Byzantium' that would fuse Byzantine imperial and historical traditions with Slavic vitality and energy.

Jovan Rajić (1726–1801), considered the 'founder of Serbian historiography', wrote the *History of the Various Slavic Peoples, Particularly the Bulgarians, the Croats and the Serbs* (1794–5). This 2,000-page work followed the medieval religious historiographical tradition and was influenced by, among others, Caesar Baronius's *Annales Ecclesiastici* and Mavro Orbini's *Il regno de gli Slavi*. Using Byzantine sources but in Latin translations, Rajić's *History* chronicles the political relations between Byzantium and the South Slavs, treated as a particular entity. Next to the importance of Byzantine sources for Serbian history, the latter's close connection with Byzantium was thus acknowledged from the dawn of Serbian historiography. However, before the second half of the nineteenth

---

[51] Ćorović 1989: 97–211, 251–62.
[52] Jireček 1922. Later historians would disprove this statement (see Ćirković 2004: 21–2).

30 Precursors

century, the nature and effect of these relations, and the empire's influence in general, failed to attract the interest of the Serbian historians.

The Latin origin of the Romanians was as central to their modern historical consciousness as the Hellenic extraction was to the Greeks. And, like the Greeks, the Romanians thus developed a claim to a privileged position in the community of civilised peoples and to partake in the groundwork of European civilisation.

The Romanians discovered their Latin origins over a century before the modern Greeks discovered their Hellenic roots. Since the seventeenth century, the question about the formation of the Romanian people had 'become a constant, and even obsessive, preoccupation of Romanian historiography'.[53] Its mythological point of reference was Rome, which fused the two major components of the European tradition – the imperial and the Christian – and lent the Romanian lands nobility and prestige. The story behind it was simple: at the beginning of the second century AD, Emperor Trajan had conquered ancient Dacia and his armies had colonised it, annihilating or else completely assimilating the indigenous Dacian population. Byzantium within this framework was seen as an extension and perpetuation of the Roman model – a powerful yet derivative symbol overshadowed by Rome.

The humanist writers of seventeenth-century Romanian principalities Moldavia and Wallachia, Grigore Ureche (c.1590/5–1647), Miron Costin (1633–91), Nicolae Costin (c.1660–1712), Radu Popescu (c.1658–1729), Constantin Cantacuzene (c.1640–1716) and 'the most brilliant of all humanists', the Moldavian prince Dimitrie Cantemir (1673–1723), are considered to be 'the real founders of national Romanian historiography'.[54] They were the first to emphasise the greatness of the early Romanians and to engage in the process with Byzantine sources on Romanian history and the Romanian-Byzantine relations. The attitude to Byzantium that transpires from their writings is one of attachment to the memory of the empire and its civilisation. They remained faithful to the view of Byzantium as the lawful continuation of the Roman empire, the guardian of the Orthodox faith and the possessor of political legitimacy. In the same breath, they would stress the formative connection of Romanian history with that of Byzantium in order to assert the 'nobility' of the Romanians and the legitimacy of their political autonomy. Cantemir, later acclaimed as the first Romanian byzantinist and *intellectuel byzantinisant*, created the myth of the Byzantine ancestry of the Romanian states

[53] Boia 2001b: 31–2. [54] Tanaşoca 2002: 50.

Precursors   31

and dynasties and of their primordial attachment to the Orthodox faith. 'In the spirit of the Romanian humanists of the seventeenth and the eighteenth centuries', Romanian medievalist Nicolae-Şerban Tanaşoca writes, 'the idea about Orthodox solidarity and the nostalgia for the Byzantine empire goes along with a very strong feeling of national identity that acquires an important Byzantine dimension.'[55]

The Latinist orientation of Romanian historiography broke radically with this humanist tradition. Its heyday, like that of the Hellenic orientation of Greek historiography, was during the Enlightenment era and was epitomised by what was known as the Transylvanian (or Latinist) School (*Şcoala ardeleană*) – an intellectual and political movement whose purely Romanian project dominated Romanian history writing from the late eighteenth century through the 1860s. The three great historians of the Transylvanian School, the Uniate (Catholic of the Eastern Rite) clergymen Samuil Micu (1745–1806), Petru Maior (1761–1821) and Gheorghe Şincai (1754–1816), took up the task of demonstrating the Latin purity of the Romanian race. Much like the neo-Hellenic enlighteners around the same time, their aspiration was to rehabilitate Romanian culture and Romanian ethnicity as ancient, native, established and respectable. In Dacia and the area south of the Danube, the Romanians were *the* Romans of the one-time empire of Trajan. Samuil Micu began the history of his people (1800) with the foundation of Rome, and many after him also presented it as a continuation of Roman history.[56] The dominance of the Latinists in the historiographical canon-building not only in Transylvania but also in Wallachia and Moldavia until the last quarter of the nineteenth century set the framework for the interpretation of Byzantine history during this period.

Despite some nuances, Micu, Şincai and Maior shared essentially the same ideas about the identity of Byzantium, its civilisation and its relations with the Romanians. These ideas were informed by Enlightenment nationalism and a determination to substantiate the Latin origins and continuity of the Romanians. Gheorghe Şincai's *Chronicle of the Romans and of Other Peoples* (1807–9) and Petru Maior's *Early History of the Romans in Dacia* (1812) articulated clearly the new image of Byzantium emerging through these lenses, which would dominate Romanian thought in the subsequent decades. For Şincai, a 'Byzantine empire' properly speaking never existed: neither the transfer of the capital from Rome to Constantinople nor the division of the empire into western and eastern parts nor even the fall of the

[55] Tanaşoca 2013: 269–71; Tanaşoca 2002: 54.   [56] Boia 2001a: 85–9.

32   Precursors

Western empire had marked the beginning of Byzantium and its proper history. The event that, according to Şincai and Micu, marked a decisive break in the history of the Roman empire was the seventh-century invasions of the Bulgarians and the formation of their state. The latter had separated the Latin-speakers (the Romanians) from the body of the eastern part of the empire and made the Greeks its only masters. From that moment on, Şincai wrote, the empire based on Constantinople became a 'Greek state' – 'Romaic', not Roman:

> After the conquest of the Dacias [*sic*] and Lower Moesia by the Bulgarians, many authors stopped calling the emperors in Constantinople 'Romans' [*ai romanilor*] and began calling them 'Romaics' [*ai romaichilor*], as the present-day Greeks call themselves, because without the help of the Romanians, the Greeks would not have succeeded in inheriting the glory and grandeur of our ancestors . . . . The Greeks . . . without any justification had given and are giving to themselves the name Romans only because they later managed to capture the Roman empire of the East and to destroy it.[57]

The transformation of the Roman empire into the 'Byzantine empire' in the seventh century, therefore, meant Greek usurpation of the name 'Roman' and of the role of custodians of the empire – usurpation that provoked the angry reactions of the Romanian national historians. The Greeks, Şincai held, had dubbed Latins the peoples of the left bank of the Danube and those of the West in order to pose as Romans, whose subjects, instead of blood descendants, they actually were, unlike the Romanians and the Italians, from whom they stole the empire by deceit.[58] The name and identity the Romanian Latinists bestowed on Byzantium was that of an 'Eastern empire' or simply 'the East', 'kingdom of the Greeks or the Romaic' or 'the Greeks'. Following a different route, the Romanian enlighteners thus came to a view identical to that of their Bulgarian counterparts which underscored the allogeneic, culturally and ethnically Greek character of Byzantium.

Like their Bulgarian compeers, the Transylvanian enlighteners held in low regard the 'Greek Church' and post-Byzantine and contemporary Greek culture, and they saw the Phanariots as remnants of Byzantium. The national underpinnings of this anti-Greek attitude were similar: resistance against both the contemporary Phanariot regime in Wallachia and Moldavia and the budding Greek nationalism.[59] The narrative method was also similar – projecting on a distant past controversies unfolding in the present, occasionally through absurd fabrications: 'It is not surprising that Saints Cyril and Methodius refused to submit to Patriarch Photius,

---

[57] Tanaşoca 2003: 189–91.   [58] Tanaşoca 2013: 272.   [59] Tanaşoca 2003: 198.

Precursors

since he was a Greek, while they, as genuine Romanians, descendants of the colonists of Trajan . . . who were associated with the Bulgarians, could not bear to have the Greeks as their masters.'[60] Against this backdrop the fall of Byzantium was portrayed as a just punishment for the Greeks, who had sinned by usurping the Eastern Roman empire at the expense of its legitimate heirs – the Romanians. The rupture with the erstwhile humanist tradition was complete.

The Latinist historiographic school deserves our attention for yet another reason directly linked with Byzantine history: the important role it attributed to the Romance-language-speaking population south of the Danube. This focus was largely forced upon them by the paucity of sources referring to the area north of the river (the territory of the future principalities of Wallachia and Moldavia) between the withdrawal of Roman rule in 271 and the foundation of the Romanian states in the fourteenth century. During this 'dark millennium', the focus of Romanian history shifted to the territory of the 'New Rome' and, after the seventh century, to that of the Bulgarian Kingdom. The national Romanian historians held that Romanians and Bulgarians enjoyed a political symbiosis in the Middle Ages: both the First Bulgarian Kingdom (seventh to tenth centuries), which incorporated territories to the north of the Danube, and the Second one (twelfth to fourteenth centuries) were said to be 'Romanian-Bulgarian kingdoms'. For Micu, the Romans who fell under the influence of the Bulgarian state and Slav civilisation were transformed into 'Vlachs' – a name given to them by the Greeks, who wanted to preserve for themselves the name Romans as a symbol of political legitimacy, denying it to the Romanians and Italians. Şincai, Micu and Maior discovered a multitude of 'crypto-Romanians' hiding in the Byzantine sources 'under the name of Bulgars, Coumans, and Pechenegs', as well as Scythians. The situation with the term 'Vlachs' was completely different, though. As Petre Maior put it, 'the name of the Vlachs never meant anything else but Romanians, that is Romans, Latins, Italians'.[61] They were widely dispersed under these various names across the whole Balkan peninsula, from Thessaly and Pindus to ancient Dacia and beyond. Their political force, Micu argued, was displayed by the numerous Vlach uprisings against the Byzantines, the most consequential being those of the eleventh and twelfth centuries which led to the creation first of a number of autonomous 'Dacias' and then of the (second) 'Vlacho-Bulgarian

---

[60] Şincai as cited in Tanaşoca 2003: 211.
[61] Boia 2001a: 114–15; Tanaşoca 2002: 59–65; Tanaşoca 2003: 166–85, 204.

34   Precursors

Kingdom' – the actual *translatio imperii*. Once again, the Transylvanian historians could assert that the Romanians, not the Greeks, were the bearers of the authentic imperial tradition.

It should now be obvious that the negative interpretation of Byzantium that the Romanian enlighteners shared with their Western counterparts had different grounds and pursued different goals. It was not driven by a philosophical critique of oriental despotism, religious fanaticism and corrupted mores; it was driven by Latin self-identification and the aspiration to reclaim the history of the Vlachs as an integral part of the Romanian nation. Rather than a debauched continuation of the Roman empire, justified by natural right, Byzantium was the result of a felony, a theft from the Romanians, the rightful heirs of the Roman glory.[62]

---

[62] See in this sense Rados 2005: 372–3.

CHAPTER 2

The Century of History
Byzantium in the Budding National-Historical Canons

The development of historicism since the eighteenth century entailed the discovery of both the 'historicity' of the past as a continuous, ever-changing process of creation and the nation as the central and a priori agent of history – currents that nineteenth-century Romanticism brought together and endowed with perfected means of expression. The best-known and most notorious outgrowths of the rise in historical consciousness, Isaiah Berlin observed, were the ideologies of nationalism and power politics, whereby the great monistic conception of the universe under the sway of natural law was superseded by a concept of the nation, 'conscious of its unique individuality and its overriding claims, and answerable only to itself'.[1] Against this backdrop, the rationalist hostility to Byzantium characteristic of the Enlightenment was replaced by the prurient moralising hostility of writers of the Victorian age such as William Lecky, who wrote in 1869:

> Of that Byzantine empire, the universal verdict of history is that it constitutes, without a single exception, the most thoroughly base and despicable form civilisation has yet assumed . . . . There has been no other enduring civilisation so absolutely destitute of all the forms and elements of greatness, and none to which the epithet *mean* may be so emphatically applied . . . . The Byzantine Empire was pre-eminently the age of treachery. Its vices were the vices of men who had ceased to be brave without learning to be virtuous . . . . The history of the empire is a monotonous story of the intrigues of priests, eunuchs and women, of poisonings, of conspiracies, of uniform ingratitude, of perpetual fratricides.[2]

For Jacob Burckhardt, a leading cultural historian of the Italian Renaissance, byzantinism was a 'spirit compounded of Church and politics' that 'had

---

[1] Berlin 1972: ix–xii.
[2] Lecky 1896: 13–14. See also Jeffreys 2008: 7–8.

35

36 The Century of History

developed analogously to Islam'.[3] Burckhardt described the spirit of Byzantine civilisation in the following way:

> At its summit was despotism, infinitely strengthened by the union of churchly and secular dominion; in the place of morality it imposed orthodoxy; in the place of unbridled and demoralised expression of the natural instincts, hypocrisy and pretence; in the face of despotism there was developed greed masquerading as poverty, and deep cunning; in religious art and literature there was an incredible stubbornness in the constant repetition of obsolete motives.[4]

Forceful moralising invectives of this kind impacted much of the incipient Balkan historiographies, in the post-Ottoman successor states and the Ottoman empire itself, at a time when they were trying to conform to Western standards of social virtue and modern scholarship. Concurrently, though, the nineteenth century saw the crystallisation of another narrative, representing Byzantium 'as a beacon of classical civilisation shining in the barbarous gloom of the Middle Ages'. On this view, the Byzantine 'deposit of ancient culture' was vital to the Western rediscovery that came to fruition in the Renaissance. Its by-product – Byzantium's portrayal 'as a bridge uniting ancient Greece to modern Greece' – was to provide a lasting connection of Western classicism with the mainstream of Greek nationalism.[5] This one-sided rehabilitation of Byzantium, reminiscent of the one that took place in the seventeenth century, was carried out on the assumption that it had served as the mediator and conduit for the classical tradition to the 'West', its 'true' heir, not on its recognition as a new, composite Christian civilisation.

The aftermath of the Napoleonic wars, however, witnessed a reaction – most notable in Germany and northern and east-central Europe – against the unifying cult of classical tradition cultivated by French and Italian thought, one that stimulated a pan-European search for alternative, distinct archaic sources of identity in the past and legitimacy in the present. 'For much of Europe, this search for alternative pasts led to the Middle Ages, a poorly defined period from roughly the fifth to the fifteenth century that saw the dissolution of the Roman Empire, the emergence of "new" peoples and polities, vernacular literatures, architectural and artistic traditions, and new forms of urban life and associations.'[6] The 'Neo-Byzantine style', an architectural revival movement that emerged in western Europe in the 1840s and spread towards eastern and southeastern Europe in the last

---

[3] Burckhardt 1943: 202. [4] Burckhardt 1949: 345; Angelov 2003: 10.
[5] Mango 1984: 48. See also Arnason 2000: 53. [6] Geary and Klaniczay 2013: 2.

The Century of History

quarter of the nineteenth century, was another manifestation of Romantic historicism.

The 'Age of Romanticism' did not generate a synthetic work, a Romantic *chef d'oeuvre*, on the Byzantine empire comparable with Gibbon's *History*. Its impact on the development of modern historiography, however, was decisive in that its protagonists embarked on appropriating the Middle Ages as the period of the genesis of modern nations, nationalising history and turning the nation and the national genius into the main engines of historical evolution. While these new currents underlay the inception of the national histories of the Greeks, Bulgarians, Romanians, Serbs and, with some delay, Turks, they also stimulated the study of Byzantium and the reassessment of its historical role.

The engagement of the western European Romantic tradition with these double-edged developments in the Balkans is best seen in the case of Greek historiography. The Greek war of independence (1821–30) led to an eruption of philhellenic sentiments and a corresponding historiographic strain that animated modern Greece's connection with ancient Greece but also aroused interest in the 'Greek Middle Ages' and the 'medieval Greek empire' (*Imperium graecum, Imperium graecorum*). In 1824–5 Claude Fauriel published in Paris *Chants populaires de la Grèce moderne* (immediately translated into German by Wilhelm Müller as *Neugriechische Volkslieder* (Leipzig, 1825)). Five years later James Emerson's *The History of Modern Greece from Its Conquest by the Romans B.C. 146 to the Present Time* (London, 1830) came out. The decisive turning point in this respect was the appearance of Jakob Philipp Fallmerayer's *Geschichte der Halbinsel Morea während des Mittelalters*, to be discussed later. This work held that the Greeks of the Byzantine period were linguistically assimilated Slavs and Albanians who had no connection with the ancient Hellenes.

Remarkably, the effort to refute this claim marked perhaps the closest convergence of the Romantic western European and Greek historiographic schools. In 1832 Johann Wilhelm Zinkeisen (1803–63) engaged with a substantial rebuttal of Fallmerayer's thesis and started (but did not finish) writing 'a complete history of Greece'.[7] He chided the historians of Greece before him that 'instead of joining [Byzantine history] with the history of Ancient Greece, [they] rather searched for the most striking contrasts between the two; they thereby lost, quite inevitably, the opportunity for

---

[7] Zinkeisen 1832. In Germany this history was followed in the 1860s by Karl Hopf's synthesis of medieval Greece, *Geschichte Griechenlands vom Beginn des Mittelalters bis auf unsere Zeit* (Leipzig, 1867–8), which tackled in detail the question of the Slavs in Greece, defying Fallmerayer's theory.

38 The Century of History

an appreciation of the Byzantine imperial era in purely historical terms'.[8] Zinkeisen's thesis of the continuity of Greek history drew on his Hegelian understanding of the *Geist* of a nation, meaning 'the power by which a people emerges by itself as a distinct entity and ... develops to a higher degree its inherent qualities which in turn enable it to sustain its uniqueness ... it is the natural consequence of the descent and original destiny [of the people]'.[9] As Ioannis Koubourlis observes, these premises 'explain why Zinkeisen was destined to become the most cherished point of reference for Greek national historians, even after the turn of the twentieth century'.[10]

The Scottish historian and philhellenist George Finlay (1799–1875), who considered himself to be a historian of the 'Greek nation' rather than of the Roman empire (or Greece), also stressed the continuity of its history and distinctiveness. He opened the preface to his seven-volume *History of Greece from Its Conquest by the Romans to the Present Time B.C. 146 to A. D. 1864* (1844–61) with the statement that 'two thousand years of suffering have not obliterated the national character, nor extinguished the national ambition'. He then went on to stress:

> Neither the Roman Caesars, nor the Byzantine emperors, any more than the Frank princes and the Turkish sultans, were able to interrupt the continual transmission of a political inheritance by each generation of the Greek race to its successors . . .. They have maintained possession of their country, their language and their social organisation . . .. A combination of causes enabled [the Greeks] to preserve their national institutions even after the annihilation of their political existence. . . . These local institutions ultimately modified the Roman administration itself, long before the Roman empire ceased to exist; and even though the Greeks were compelled to adopt the civil law and judicial forms of Rome, its political authority in the East was guided by the feelings of the Greeks, and moulded according to Greek customs.[11]

Finlay thus gave an answer to the most crucial question faced by any aspiring author of a truly national history of the Greeks – that of the Hellenisation of the Eastern empire. Next to their racial and cultural continuity, the ability of the Greeks to 'absorb' their conquerors and incorporate them into their national body was affirmed – to the extent that under the 'Byzantine emperors' (from the accession of Leo the Isaurian in 716 to the conquest of Constantinople by the Crusaders in 1204) they became identified with the imperial administration.[12]

---

[8] Zinkeisen 1832: 7; Koubourlis 2009: 56.   [9] Koubourlis 2009: 57.   [10] Koubourlis 2009: 57.
[11] Finlay 1877: xxii.   [12] Finlay 1877: xv–xvii; Koubourlis 2009: 58.

The Century of History 39

Finlay has been praised for having been the first to turn his attention to the study of the internal history of the Byzantine state. Yet, as Alexander Vasiliev observed, 'he studied Byzantine history only as a preparation for writing a history of modern Greece'.[13] From such positions Finlay embarked on redeeming the history of Byzantium by pointing out, 'The views of Byzantine history unfolded in the following pages are frequently in direct opposition to these great authorities [Voltaire and Gibbon]' and indicating that 'the splendid achievements of the [Greek] emperors, and the great merits of the judicial and ecclesiastical establishments will be contrasted with their faults'. He associated the transition from the Roman to the Byzantine empire with its territorial shrinkage, which had ensured 'the prevalence of Greek civilisation and the identification of the nationality of the people and the policy of the emperors with the Greek church'.[14]

Thus the discourse about the perseverance and vitality of the 'national character', 'national ambition', 'national existence' and 'national institutions' of the Greeks across centuries, withstanding political calamities and cultural ruptures, and the portrayal of Byzantium as a Greek empire were already forged by Western historians before they came to dominate Greek national-Romantic historiography. 'Philhellene writers not only paved the way for the writing of a "genuine Greek national history" but essentially, and through different paths, actually founded the very premise of the historical continuity of the Greek nation from ancient to modern times'; the proper Greek contribution thereof was elaborating on the Greeks' 'timeless ability to "hellenise" the people they would come into contact with (either by conquering them or by being conquered by them)'.[15]

To a great extent, Russian Romantic thought was as important for the Balkan Slavs' national awakening and for the discovery of their medieval roots as Western philhellenism was for the Greeks. It should be stressed, however, that this current itself owed much to western European Romanticism and to German idealist philosophy. Nowhere was this more evident than in the heated debate between Westernisers and Slavophiles in the 1830s and 1840s, in which Byzantium was evoked by both parties and with different connotations but typically as the opposite of western Europe. While Pyotr Chaadaev, a radical Westerniser philosopher, argued in 1829 that the sterility of Russian culture was due to 'miserable Byzantium, the object of profound contempt', another leader of the movement and a professional historian, Timofei Granovsky, maintained in 1850,

---

[13] Vasiliev 1952: 15–16.   [14] Finlay 1877: 8–9.   [15] Koubourlis 2013b.

We received from Constantinople the best part of our national inheritance, that is our religious beliefs and the beginnings of civilisation. The Eastern Empire introduced young Russia into the family of Christian nations. But besides these connections, we are bound up with the fate of the Byzantine Empire by the mere fact that we are Slavs. This side of the question has not been, and could not be, fully appreciated by foreign scholars.[16]

The Slavophiles' views were just as value-laden and ambiguous. Some of them contrasted the contemplative culture of the Byzantine world with Western legalism and rationalism. Others, even if not denying its spiritual achievements, stressed the Roman character of the empire's law and state, hence its underlying paganism, formalism and institutionalism. 'Rome's juridical chains', Aleksey Khomyakov wrote, 'clasped and choked the life of Byzantium.'[17]

The political underpinnings of the growing Russian interest in Byzantium were signalled by the Treaty of Kuchuk Kainarji (1774), with which Russia assumed the protector role of Ottoman Christians, and Catherine II's 'Greek Plan' (1782), envisaging the regeneration of the Byzantine empire with its capital in Constantinople and under a Russian prince as an emperor. Panslavism, the political offspring of Slavophilism, which grew after the Crimean War (1853–6), made plain the connection between byzantinism and the 'Eastern Question' concerning the successors to the Ottoman empire. Whereas Fyodor Dostoyevskiy insisted that 'Constantinople must become Russian' on the grounds that Russia served 'as a leader of Orthodoxy, as its protectress and guardian', Nikolay Danilevskiy argued that Russia's historical mission was to restore the Byzantine empire in the form of a federation consisting of the Slavs, the Greeks, the Romanians and the Magyars, under the political leadership of Russia and with Constantinople as a free city of the union.[18] Of note in these Panslav pronouncements is that they aimed at recreating Byzantium as an empire characterised by Slavic rather than Greek culture and as one based on the union between Russia and the Balkan Slavs. In this vision Orthodoxy, imperialism and ethnic particularism formed one whole.

Reinforcing the political aspect of the debate was another one, which concerned Russian identity and Russia's 'unique' civilisation in relation to Byzantium and Europe. The philosopher and diplomat Konstantin

---

[16] Vasiliev 1952: 32–3; Obolensky 1966: 63–4. Granovsky believed that only Russian and Slavic scholars could reach the proper solution to the main problems of Byzantine history.
[17] Obolensky 1966: 64.   [18] Dostoevsky 1995: 74–6; Danilevsky 1871: 388.

The Century of History

Leont'ev (1831–91) offered an ultra-conservative and highly idiosyncratic reading of what he called 'byzantism' (in opposition to the Western derogatory notion of 'byzantinism'), which he saw as comprising two major components: political autocracy and Orthodox ascetics. The survival of Russia and the Slavs according to Leont'ev hinged on neither the idyllic-utopian image of 'Slavdom' as a social ideal nor the Panslavic project of summoning all Slavic nations around Russia, but on byzantism – the key factor and the formative idea of Russian and Slavic history. 'Byzantism', he argued, 'organised us, the system of Byzantine ideas created our greatness . . . . If we should betray this byzantism, *even in our secret thoughts*, we will ruin Russia.'[19] He pleaded for a Greco-Slavic Orthodox union ('Great Eastern Union'), with its cultural centre in Constantinople, which had to be in the personal possession of the Russian tsar. This union would be the political expression of a new 'Slavo-Asiatic civilisation' – fully original and distinct from that of 'Romano-Germanic Europe'.[20]

Above and beyond the differences between Slavophiles, Panslavists and philosophers of 'reactionary Romanticism' like Leont'ev, a common thread in the Russian discussions was Byzantium's 'anti-Western' quality as a positive alternative to Western culture. 'Byzantium gave us all our strength. Under its banner we shall withstand the onslaught of the entire Europe if indeed it dares impose on us the rot and filth of its prescriptions for an earthly paradise', Leont'ev wrote.[21] These thinkers' attitude was driven by national-ism in that all of them associated the Byzantine legacy with the cultural and political identity of Russia. However, the pro-Byzantine nationalist mood did not go unchallenged. The attack, remarkably enough, came from respect-able theologians and religious philosophers. Vladimir Solov'ev (1853–1900) argued that Byzantium had betrayed Christ's legacy to humankind, that it was a 'pseudo-Christian empire' that had succumbed to paganism, schismat-ics and 'Caesaropapism' and that it was therefore deservedly 'judged and condemned by history'.[22] Seeking to imitate Byzantium, philosopher and literary critic Vasiliy Rozanov (1856–1919) concurred, meant betraying Russia's 'deeply original and unique aspects': 'Sophisticated and depraved Byzantium that mixed abstract disputes of theological and philosophical nature with orgies, with the noise and debauchery of the circus, can hardly be seriously regarded as an antecedent and prototype for Muscovy.'[23] So, if Russian Slavophilism was essential for the discovery of the Balkan Slavs for European scholarship, its impact in shaping their historiographical views of

---

[19] Leont'ev 2005: 331.   [20] Grosul 1996: 265–73.   [21] Ivanov 2016: 61–2.
[22] Soloviev 1922 [1889]; Solov'ev 1896: 283–325.   [23] Ivanov 2016: 62.

42   The Century of History

Byzantium was controversial, ranging from admiration to critical reception to complete repudiation.

'Our Medieval Kingdom'

The Romantic ideological matrix in Greek historiography, whose high point was between the 1830s and 1860s, 'marked the transition from one mental structure of historical imagination to another: from the schema of revival to one of continuity'.[24] This entailed, first and foremost, filling the gap between antiquity and modern times – in other words, a complete metamorphosis of attitude towards the 'Greek Middle Ages' and Byzantium. It meant not only a radical restructuring of the Greeks' historical self-narration but perhaps the most striking development to have taken place in Greek national ideology in the nineteenth century.[25] In the face of the political and social realities in the first decades after the Greek state was set up, the myth of the resurrected Hellas appeared too weak to sustain a national ideology for at least three reasons: it opened a huge time gap between the ideal past and the present, it was incompatible with the Orthodox Christian identity of the 'living' Greeks and it could not satisfy the ideological and foreign policy needs of the young state. The emergence of national Greek history was inherently bound up with the integration of the histories of the ancient Macedonians and Byzantines in a single 'general history of the Hellenic nation', since it 'produces not only a homogeneous historical (national) time – without "falls" or temporal gaps – but also a national space by establishing the geographical limits of the ideal Greek state'.[26] Such integration is, therefore, an essential aspect of the nationalisation of Greek history.

Behind the shift of historical references, one can discern the changing political-ideological needs and national objectives originating in the Greek present: whereas the classicist orientation of the enlighteners was closely linked with the ideal of national dignity and liberty, the byzantinist orientation of the national-Romantic school of historiography pursued national integration – in other words, territorial expansion. The 'Romantic nationalists' were young, highly trained and sophisticated intellectuals and professionals, 'heterochthons' (born outside the Greek state), who had arrived in independent Greece in the early 1830s.[27] For them, the Byzantine monarchy was a better symbol for unity and statehood than

---

[24] Liakos 2008: 208.   [25] Mackridge 1998: 49.   [26] Koubourlis 2005: 21.
[27] Petmezas 2009: 123–35.

the ancient city-state and democracy. If they wanted to appropriate Byzantium, it was not because they venerated everything it represented or felt particular affection for its civilisation: 'It was rather because the Byzantine past, like the Macedonian and the Hellenistic past, was useful for the Greek nationalists of the second half of the nineteenth century as a "past of a conqueror".'[28]

In 1837, in a direct address to King Otho, Athens University's first dean and professor of history, Konstantinos Schinas, noted: 'Hellas, your Highness, was never an autonomous and indivisible state, but was first small in size and fought with adjoining states, and then a small province of three successive large monarchies, of which only with that of Byzantium did it have so much as language and faith in common.'[29] Seven years later, Prime Minister Ioannis Kolettis's speech in the Greek National Assembly (14 January 1844) completely obliterated this view, disassociating Hellenism with a fixed polity. His speech is generally considered to mark the birth of Greece's 'Great Idea' (*Megali Idea*) and set the frame of the ideological discourse of Greek nationalism. Induced by the rift between 'inside' and 'outside' Greeks – those living within the frontiers of the state and those left outside it – the Great Idea became the ideological platform for the Greek state's efforts to absorb 'any land associated with Greek history or the Greek race', as Kolettis worded it.[30]

Kolettis's nationalist manifesto remained silent on Byzantium: in the political and intellectual climate of the time, evoking it would have been counterproductive. Yet both the ideal of the united nation, bringing together the Greeks from inside and outside the kingdom, and the vision of Greece's cultural and political hegemony in the Near East – *i kath'imas Anatoli* ('our East') in the evocative Greek diction – led the national ideologue in this direction. In 1833 he argued: 'The capital of the Kingdom of Greece must be Constantinople. It is the city where the foundations of the throne of our old emperors are located and the seat of our religion, the city upon which we should all turn our eyes . . . we should not desire any other capital than Constantinople.'[31] Kolettis's desiderata were only one step away from the realisation that Greece's claim to rule the East from Constantinople entailed the need to demonstrate that the Greeks had already done this in the past.

The immediate push to reorientate Greek historiography towards Byzantium came, however, from a different quarter. In the 1830s the

---

[28] Koubourlis 2013a: 261.   [29] Cited in Christodoulou 2010: 451.   [30] Augustinos 1977: 14.
[31] Cited in Christodoulou 2010: 450.

44   The Century of History

already mentioned Jakob Philipp Fallmerayer (1790–1861), an Austrian liberal and historian of the Empire of Trebizond and of Frankish Peloponnese, published his *Geschichte der Halbinsel Morea während des Mittelalters* (vols. I–II, 1830–6). In this work he argued that the massive Slavic invasions of the Byzantine empire between the sixth and ninth centuries led to total racial assimilation of the Greek population of the Peloponnese. Modern Greeks, according to this theory, were descendants of Slavs and Albanians. 'Not one drop of Hellenic blood flows in the veins of the modern Greeks', Fallmerayer averred – a shocking revelation for the newly minted Greek nationalism, which not only deprived the Greeks of their illustrious forebears and the Hellenic purity of their race but took away their European credentials as well.[32] Considering the heavy reliance of the Greeks at that time on European support for their newly acquired independence, there could hardly have been a more inappropriate moment to say that the Greeks were really all Slavs. It is at the same time noteworthy that Fallmerayer's attitude to Byzantium and its ideological legacy was extremely critical: he denounced both the autocratic emperors of Byzantium and the 'reborn' Byzantine autocracy in Russia. In fact, his intention was not to hurt the national feelings of the Greeks but to warn against the danger of a resurrected Greco-Slavic 'Byzantine' empire on the Bosporus subservient to Russia and to undercut philhellenic propaganda on behalf of the Greek cause.[33]

What is of interest here is that it was through the patriotic endeavour to prove Fallmerayer 'wrong' that the medieval roots of Greece were discovered and the national Greek historical narrative emerged. Long after this task was accomplished – not without substantial aid from western European scholarship – the Greek historians continued to battle with Fallmerayer.[34] For them it was a battle for recognition of the 'historical rights of Hellenism', which would allow the modern Greeks to reap the benefits of their descent from the ancient Greeks and perform the leading role in the geopolitical reshufflings related to the Eastern Question. In this effort, which was both scientific and diplomatic, the interpretation of the Byzantine past became crucial. The 'national historian' Konstantinos Paparrigopoulos made all these connections crystal clear when writing, in 1852, that to admit that 'those calling themselves today Hellenes are

---

[32] On Fallmerayer's theory and the Greek reactions, see Veloudis 1970: 43–90 and more extensively Veloudis 1982.
[33] Fallmerayer 1990 [1861].   [34] Herzfeld 1982.

'Our Medieval Kingdom' 45

nothing other than Slavs, Albanians, Bulgarians and Vlachs' is to admit that

> the position of the Greek nation in the East is reduced to that of the Serbs and the Montenegrins, and that this nation cannot claim more important rights than those of the nations and races that live among or alongside them. It is obvious, therefore, that the question is not purely scientific, but also political . . .. The true and national history of Hellenism in the Middle Ages is not indifferent to its fate in this century.[35]

Therefore, both the exigencies of forging a coherent – continuous and encompassing – national history and those of legitimating Greek political ambitions by 'historical right' coalesced to impel Greek intellectuals to develop a new historiographical model capable of filling what Konstantinos Dimaras called 'the void of Byzantium'. This was an operation that proceeded in stages during the second half of the nineteenth and the beginning of the twentieth centuries and that brought about radical changes in the Greek national identity. It posited three successive eras spanning almost 3,000 years of uninterrupted historical evolution – ancient, Byzantine and modern – with the Byzantine era as the key to the crystallisation of a unified Greek nation, and was the work of at least three generations of scholars, mostly historians. Paramount among them are Konstantinos Paparrigopoulos (1815–91) and his amateur colleague (and literary scholar) Spyridon Zambelios (1815–81) – 'the two founders of the Greek romantic historiography, namely the two main theoreticians of Neohellenic nationalism',[36] and Spyridon Lambros (1851–1919) – the mouthpiece of 'critical historiography' in Greece at the turn of the nineteenth and twentieth centuries.

The 1840s and 1850s was the period during which this shift in the Greek historical consciousness took place, and it was marked by the parallel existence of contradictory interpretations of the Byzantine past. In 1845, when Th. Manousis and C. Asopios, professors at Athens University, announced the Greek edition of the *Corpus scriptorum historiae byzantinae* (inaugurated by B. G. Niebuhr in 1828), they made the then patently unconventional statement that it was during the Middle Ages that the constitutive elements of the modern Greek nation – its language, religion, private law, mores and customs – took shape. They added that 'medieval Greek history' was closer to the Greeks 'not only in terms of time, but also [in terms of] interests'.[37] There were two conspicuous propositions thus

---

[35] Cited in Koubourlis 2005: 285. [36] Dimaras 1993: 464. [37] Koulouri 1991: 316.

46 The Century of History

being made: that the roots of the 'neo-Hellenic' nation lay not in ancient times but in the Middle Ages – the period from the founding of Constantinople until its fall to the Ottomans – and that this realisation had a direct bearing on the political (that is, national) interests of the contemporary Greeks. Significantly, this medieval Greek era was not (as yet) identified with Byzantium. Even in 1850 one could read in a Greek history textbook that '[Greece], crawling under the despotism of the empires of Rome, Byzantium and Turkey, did not exist as a nation', and that it was reduced to a province in these empires (which was actually the case).[38] The evolution in both Zambelios's and Paparrigopoulos's own views is indicative of the timing and characteristics of the paradigm shift in the Greek historical canon.

Spyridon Zambelios is the person commonly credited with devising the tripartite schema ancient-medieval-modern and including 'Byzantine Hellenism' in it. However, in the first of his two major works, *Folk Songs of Greece* (1852), he makes an emphatic distinction between the Romanism of the 'monarchy of Constantinople', the *basileus* and the court on the one hand, and Hellenism, incarnated in the *demos* and the church, on the other. To him they presented 'two different political histories, one which refers directly to the Roman empire, exclusively relating its fortunes, and, as such, remains completely foreign or at least external to the *ethnos*; and the other ... refers exclusively to Hellenism, noting the terms of its existence and the levels of its development'.[39] In Zambelios's early interpretation, the Byzantine state preserved the familiar repulsive features that the Enlightenment tradition had endowed it with. What changed was that he did not discard the medieval period on this basis as one of total decay but posited the existence and sought to reveal the culture of the oppressed people as the actual bearer of Hellenism and 'acculturator' of the Eastern Roman empire.

Engagement with Hegelianism and the French Romantic-historical school, itself strongly influenced by German historicism, had a great deal to do with Zambelios's approach to all this. His theory about the Hellenisation of the Byzantine empire and the importance he attributed to the Middle Ages in the general explanatory scheme of Greek national history are steeped in these intellectual traditions. Zambelios's perspective was emphatically teleological: taking 1821, the year of the outbreak of the Greek War of Independence, as the master key to Greek history, he interpreted all preceding eras as an inevitable movement towards the

---

[38] Koulouri 1991: 313.   [39] Cited in Christodoulou 2013: 245.

'Our Medieval Kingdom' 47

formation of a Greek national state. What hitherto was presented as a series of national disasters and conquests – by Romans, Franks and Ottomans – Zambelios turned into necessary steps towards an independent Greece. (Indeed, Zambelios believed that had Gibbon and Montesquieu witnessed 1821, they would have written very different histories of the Eastern Roman empire.) In this continuous chain Byzantium was the missing but, for him, crucial link between antiquity and modernity, as well as the actual source of the modern Greek nation.[40]

In a review of *Folk Songs of Greece*, Paparrigopoulos praised Zambelios for having 'understood what very few had understood' by postulating the endurance of Hellenism in the Middle Ages. However, he criticised him for considering 'the monarchy in Byzantium to be a foreign element, and the only national elements to be the people and the Church'.[41] Five years later (1857), in his second major work, tellingly titled *Byzantine Studies*, Zambelios came up with a considerably altered scheme 'with a view to a more Greek interpretation', as he phrased it. The Byzantine monarchy (and not just 'medieval Hellenism') was rehabilitated and associated with the intellectual heritage of ancient times, and an organic unity was established between people (and language), religion and state:

> The Byzantine Middle Age appears once more in its true colours as a system resting firmly on three dominant elements, the ancient Greek, the Christian and the Roman. . . . Instead of the fatalism that hastens the decline and fall of Rome, the operative force in the Byzantine state is the law of Greek intellectual and spiritual revival. This law prevails, to a greater or lesser degree, according to the extent to which each of the three traditions holds its proper place; the ancient Greek tradition uppermost, the Christian tradition in the middle and the Roman lowest.[42]

In 1852 Zambelios forged the term 'Helleno-Christian' (*ellinochristianikos*) to capture this symbiosis, thus uniting two notions that were hitherto (especially during the Byzantine period itself) mutually exclusive. The central idea of 'Helleno-Christianity' came to bridge paganism and Eastern Christianity, democratic Hellas and imperial Byzantium, and Hellenism and Romanism, but also – in ideological terms – the two separated political worlds of 'Modern Hellenism': that of the 'autochthones' (the inhabitants of the Greek Kingdom) and the 'heterochthones' (the Christian subjects of the sultan).[43] The term denoted an entity resulting from the fusion between classical Hellenism and

---

[40] Koubourlis 2009: 60–1; Koubourlis 2005: 313–14.
[41] Koubourlis 2005: 284–92; Christodoulou 2010: 454. [42] Cited in Zakythinos 1976: 197.
[43] Koubourlis 2005: 107.

48   The Century of History

Orthodox Christianity – an entity with the immense power to absorb foreign influences and Hellenise other people. 'Christianity becomes the new fatherland for Greece, and Greece the capital of Christianity', Zambelios avowed.[44] In 1857 Zambelios firmly implanted the roots of modern Greece in medieval Greece, and the tripartite scheme of ancient-medieval-modern Hellenism – the backbone of modern Greek historiography ever since – came into place:

> The springs of modern Greece ... break the surface in the time of Constantine and Theodosius; they seek a more direct and unimpeded channel from the time of Leo the Thracian (457–474) to that of Leo the Isaurian (717–741), and they become an irresistible current in the days of Basil the Macedonian (867–886) and his successors, and from that time onwards they flow straight forward to the revival or our own time.[45]

The political implications of these historical speculations transpire compellingly from what D. A. Zakythinos called the mid-nineteenth-century 'daring vision of the universal Greek empire of the East'. According to Zambelios, this vision foreshadowed 'the fourth age of Greece', that is, its future:

> If ever a New Greece is fated to arise from the ruins of Ancient Greece and Byzantium, two principles will be fused in the nation that will return to life – first, that of the old Greek tradition, bearing also the imprint of the earlier medieval period, and secondly, the principle of the later medieval doctrine of the Nation according to which all the various peoples which made up the Byzantine Orthodox world, when the later Middle Ages began in the ninth century at the time of Basil the Macedonian, will amalgamate to form a single political unit having the same religion.

Within this 'great confederation of equal peoples', he went on, 'the complete fusion of racial elements' may be arrived at.[46] Zambelios never produced a major historical synthesis that would organically insert Byzantium into the flow of Greek history. That task was left to the Athens University professor of history Konstantinos Paparrigopoulos, the creator of the Greek grand narrative. Paparrigopoulos elaborated at length on and fleshed out Zambelios's tripartite framework, buttressed the national role of the 'Greek empire residing in Constantinople' and placed that empire back into European history on the premise of the continuity and unity of Hellenism. His early writings from the mid-1840s, significantly enough, were still imbued with the negative late-Enlightenment attitude to Byzantium prevailing at that time. In his first book, *On the Settlement of Certain Slavic Tribes in the*

---

[44] Matalas 2002: 150.   [45] Cited in Zakythinos 1976: 197.   [46] Zakythinos 1976: 200.

Peloponnese (1843), he described the Byzantine period as the 'darkest and most ignorant era', a 'barbaric epoch', and spoke reverently of Gibbon's 'marvellous writings'.[47] At that time he was convinced that Byzantium was not an integral part of Greek history. 'Medieval Greek history', he wrote, 'differs very essentially from Byzantine history. It is therefore this medieval Greek history that we must teach in detail, not the Byzantine.'[48]

Paparrigopoulos's first book was sparked by the compulsion to refute Fallmerayer. The anti-Slavic frenzy provoked by the Fallmerayer affair coincided, moreover, with the upsurge of Bulgarian nationalism and the expansion of the anti-Patriarchalist movement – new phenomena that threatened the realisation of the Great Idea and exacerbated the question of the position of the Slavs vis-à-vis the Greek nation. Bringing evidence of 'the continuity of the Greek nation across history' to supplement its spatial fulfilment through the conquest of Constantinople was a critical undertaking in the direction of securing Greece's political aims. A notable aspect of Paparrigopoulos's argument is that, without openly opposing the racial dimension of what constitutes the nation (*ethnos*), he did not try to refute the idea of the racial mixture resulting from the settlement of the Slavs. Reversing Fallmerayer's thesis, however, he argued that the Slavs 'were tamed by the Hellenic race and, having adopted its religion and language, they mixed with it'.[49] This signalled a change of tactic: since Greek intellectuals could not produce racial nationalism, they had to seek recourse in a nationalism that emphasised 'cultural continuity'. In an 1846 article, the future 'national historian' made this strategic choice graphically clear:

> The question is not therefore to prove that the modern Hellenic nation descends in a direct line from Pericles and Philopoimen; the battle, as you can see, would have been not only impossible but also futile. What we will, what we have to prove historically is that from the mixture that had been produced and is still being produced between different tribes does not result, as it has been asserted, a brutal, inert and stupid mass, but a nation that contains in itself the elements of a great political existence and, more particularly, that the spirit of Hellenism perpetually animates this new outgrowth of the succession of centuries.[50]

Important here is a sense not of linear, direct or biological continuity but a cultural and spiritual one, and, more crucially, the ability of the spirit of

---

[47] Koubourlis 2009: 54.　[48] Koubourlis 2005: 96.

[49] Koubourlis 2005: 94; Veloudis 1982: 33, 39, 74.

[50] 'Introduction to the History of the Regeneration of the Greek People' (1846), cited in Koubourlis 2005: 95. See also Sigalas 2001: 21.

50   The Century of History

Hellenism to absorb weaker and inferior cultures, such as the Slavs. This Hegelian idea became the cornerstone upon which the grand narrative of Greek perenniality came to rest.

Paparrigopoulos's five-volume *History of the Greek Nation from the Most Ancient Times until the Present* (published between 1860 and 1874) brought these threads together – intellectual and political, domestic and foreign – in an all-encompassing synthesis. It lay at the core of the Greek historical canon and is considered to be 'the most important intellectual achievement of nineteenth-century Greece', which managed to 'bring Byzantium and Kolettis's conception of the Great Idea together as components of the political culture of "romantic Hellenism"'.[51] As in the case with the erstwhile Helladocentric discourse, the said culture was not just a domestic Greek product. Paparrigopoulos himself acknowledged his debt to several historians who had attempted to write comprehensive histories of the Greek nation from antiquity to the present: the aforementioned James Emerson, Johann Zinkeisen and George Finlay. For Zambelios as well, Johann Gustav Droysen (1808–84), and German historicism more generally, was another major source of inspiration. As a student of the Hellenistic world, Droysen supplied Paparrigopoulos with numerous arguments in favour of the imperial ideal and the eastward expansion of the Hellenic civilisation and, most crucially, with the key concept of the Greek national school of history: Hellenism, denoting in Droysen's (and in his student Otto Abel's) usage a 'Hellenic genius', a *Geist*, with a distinct historical trajectory.[52] As Yannis Hamilakis notes, Droysen offered to the Greek national historians and the Greek nation as a whole the terminological and philosophical justification for several revisionist projects: 'the idealisation of an imperial and expansionist political model; the rehabilitation of Byzantium and of the Middle Ages in general; and the adoption of Hegelian concepts of spiritual (rather than racial) continuity'.[53]

Around the topos of Hellenism, continuously unfolding in time and acquiring a distinct meaning in each period, Paparrigopoulos constructed the monumental 'unity' of Greek history. The latter appeared as a teleological succession of Hellenisms – First (Ancient/Classical) Hellenism, Macedonian Hellenism, Christian Hellenism, Medieval Hellenism (the Byzantine empire) and Modern Hellenism (said to have begun in the thirteenth century). Each marked a specific mission and

---

[51] Kitromilides 1998: 28. For a summary of his views, see Paparrigopoulos 1878.
[52] Droysen 1833; Droysen 1836–43; Koubourlis 2009: 60.   [53] Hamilakis 2007: 117.

a specific contribution of the Greek nation to world history without, however, losing its innate identity. As Antonis Liakos formulated it, 'Paparrigopoulos used the theological concept of the Holy Trinity (the same essence in multiple expressions) as a metaphor for Hellenism: the uniqueness of the perennial nation amidst a multiplicity of temporary Hellenisms.'[54]

Among these various Hellenisms, the Byzantine was vital for salvaging the Greek identity: 'to the Byzantine state we owe the conservation of our language, our religion and more generally of our nationality'; 'that kingdom saved us from the Slavs, Bulgars, Arabs, Franks', Paparrigopoulos asserted.[55] He pinpointed the outright dangers ensuing from the neglect of this part of Greek history: as long as '[the Greeks] talk of [their] medieval fathers in the same way as [they] do about foreigners and recognise as [their] true ancestors only a few like Leonidas and Themistocles', they abdicate their 'will to govern the East' and of being 'the sovereigns of a very vast country', limiting their historical rights to a tiny state – 'and this at a time when the Serbs and the Bulgarians . . . are assiduously pressing their historical claims'.[56] Paparrigopoulos thus made clear that his interest in the Middle Ages and Byzantium was guided as much by preoccupation with the idea of national continuity as by the necessity to lend historical and intellectual legitimacy to Greek irredentism – a commitment the Greek state duly rewarded.[57]

Consequently, for Paparrigopoulos, Byzantine history became *identical* with national Greek history:

> The Greek nation, after its subjugation to the Romans, not only did not lose its language and its traditions, but perpetuated itself by spreading this language and these traditions throughout the whole East. Thus the eastern part of the Roman empire was for a long time entirely Greek; and after the fall of the western part of the Roman empire . . . it became a separate kingdom in the East; that kingdom became necessarily Greek.[58]

The cultural, rather than racial, conception of the Greek *ethnos* was needed not only for the incorporation of a medieval multi-ethnic and multi-lingual empire into the Greek past; it was just as vital for the nationalisation, through the 'Greek language and traditions', of its middle bond.

---

[54] Liakos 2008: 211.   [55] Kitromilides 1998: 28; Christodoulou 2010: 458.
[56] Paparrigopoulos 1963: III, xxii.
[57] The Greek state supported large purchases, successive reprints and new editions of the *History* and promoted its distribution (as it did Paparrigopoulos's schoolbooks), funded its translation into French and offered its author several important positions at state institutions.
[58] Cited in Argyropoulos 2001: 43.

52   The Century of History

With a good deal of intimacy, Paparrigopoulos called Byzantium 'our medieval kingdom' and 'our monarchy'. He called its rulers 'our emperors' and 'our medieval forefathers'. In this identification there was barely a place for non-Greeks, if not as 'races' then certainly as creative elements, because, as Cyril Mango has noted, 'the essence of Byzantium is seen to reside in its Greekness and its value as an object of study in the survival of that same Greekness, often threatened and obscured, yet always able to reassert itself'.[59] For Paparrigopoulos, Byzantium was even more than that, for in it, 'polytheism has been replaced by the unity of Christianity; the variety of dialects by the unity of language; the different tribes by the unity of the nation. Fortified in this three-dimensional panoply, the Greek people is struggling to recover its political unity'.[60]

What Paparrigopoulos came up with, therefore, was not simply a Romantic elegy or a lament for Byzantium. His *History* was, in the sympathetic words of Paschalis Kitromilides, 'a Greek epic': it conveyed an appreciation of 'the great empire's most admirable achievement: the unification of the Greek nation ... the realisation in the bosom of the Christian empire of that most noble and most elusive of social ideals, national unity, solidarity and cohesion. That greatest of Byzantium's accomplishments'.[61] Rather than a shameful incarnation of foreign domination and decay, as the enlighteners had it, Byzantium was now presented as an age of liberty and unity for the Greek nation. The remarkable outcome of his tour de force was to canonise Byzantium in Greek political thought as 'the *telos* to which the Greek state and Greek destinies were expected to strive to approximate' and to establish the image of the Byzantine empire (before 1204) as 'an ideal territorial and geographical model which was felt in Greek political culture to be a pointer to the future destiny and mission of Greece'.[62] Paparrigopoulos thus consecrated the Byzantine empire as the model and forerunner of the modern Greek state, providing a standard for unity and expansion.

The institutionalisation of Paparrigopoulos's scheme did not pass without resistance. The historian Theodoros Manousis (1793–1858) refuted the thesis that Byzantine history was part of the national history of Greece, while the professor of Roman law Pavlos Kalligas (1814–96) questioned the criteria (language and religion) Paparrigopoulos had used to prove the Hellenism of the Byzantines as well as the connection between Byzantines and modern Greeks. Two other historians, Georges Theophilos and

---

[59] Mango 1981: 48.   [60] Kitromilides 1979: 13.   [61] Kitromilides 1998: 30.
[62] Kitromilides 1998: 31.

'Our Medieval Kingdom' 53

Ioannis Kokkonis, provided evidence of the Christian but not uniquely Greek character of Byzantium.[63] Most substantive was the critique by Dionyssios Therianos (1834–97), a Greek scholar living in Trieste, whose detached location may have contributed to the sobriety of his views about the perennial nature of Hellenism. Following Manousis's theses, Therianos considered the expression 'Byzantine Hellenism' to be unconvincing, as it mixed two historically different phenomena. For him, the history of the Byzantine empire and that of the Greek nation were totally distinct, even if he acknowledged the changes that Christianity brought to the Greeks, and argued that the diffusion of Hellenic culture was one of the Byzantine emperors' lesser preoccupations.[64] However, Paparrigopoulos's supporters far outnumbered his critics, and the debate had no lasting consequences other than the efforts to provide further 'evidence' for his imposing construction.

The dissemination of this new version of Greek history, particularly via education, was a lengthier process. Paparrigopoulos's 1852 history textbook set the stage for the gradual 'assimilation' of Byzantium, but until 1880 this did not entail re-evaluation of Byzantium's role in and contribution to national and global history. That came about only after 1882, when Paparrigopoulos's scheme was officially adopted by the new school curriculum and Byzantium began to be appreciated for preserving the 'Greek nationality', safeguarding and transmitting ancient civilisation to its 'barbarous neighbours' and becoming 'a guide and teacher of Renaissance Europe'.[65] Yet even in 1893 the state commission for textbook evaluation found it necessary to press for eliminating the convention of presenting the Byzantine state 'as an abode of criminals or the insane'. It is also significant that until World War I, national history education assigned to Byzantium the role of 'a bridge via which the spirit of [the modern Greeks'] immortal ancestors is transmitted – through the preservation of language – or ... a hoop linking the history of the descendants to that of the ancestors', rather than of a creator of proper heritage.[66] The latter portrayal would only gradually take shape in the following decades.

On a different level, the incorporation of Byzantium into the national narrative can be seen as emancipating Greek history from a view about the nature of the Greeks that had been imposed on them by European classicism. It rendered an indigenous Hellenism, different in its intellectual and ideological forms from Western Hellenism, and an indigenous Hellenic

[63] Argyropoulos 2001: 44–5. [64] Argyropoulos 2001: 46.
[65] Koulouri 1991: 339–40, 349–50, 359–61. [66] Koulouri 1991: 365–6.

narrative conjuring up 'a classical antiquity that was more at home in the Orthodox Christian east than in the Catholic and Protestant west'.[67] But it was also an attempt to redefine Greece's contribution to Western civilisation. The appropriation of Byzantium was thus at once an act of resistance to the Western canon of history and of the desire to participate in it. Entire historical eras – Macedonian, Hellenistic, Byzantine – located outside the Western cultural canon and originally suppressed by the Greeks were now re-valorised as distinct cultural features and as contributions to universal civilisation.[68]

To recapitulate: between the 1850s and 1880s the Hellenisation of Byzantium (concurrently with that of the Macedonian and Hellenistic periods), mainly via language and the 'transcending' assimilative powers of the Greek race, was completed, and by the 1880s the Greek historical grand narrative postulating the continuity of Greek history was firmly in place. For the next century this scheme would remain intact as an official version of Greek history. Individual scholars and academic schools would contribute some bricks to the tripartite edifice of the canon without modifying the overall construction and Byzantium's central place in it. Indeed, much of the subsequent scholarship was undertaken with the purpose of reinforcing this edifice and broadening its 'popular-Romantic' base with the help of other disciplines – ethnography, philology, archaeology.

The forging of the Greek national narrative illustrates, eloquently, the embroilment of political and intellectual currents. The choice of Byzantium or classical Greece as historical references was a dilemma originating not in historiography but in politics and ideology. The new national tasks required – and received – new histories. The doctrine of national unity and continuity is a classic case of an ideological construct, in the Mannheimian sense, in that it veiled profound or even irreconcilable structural contradictions and cultural antinomies between classical Greece, medieval Christian Byzantium and the Greek nation-state.[69] 'Paparrigopoulos's unified tripartite schema of national history', Despina Christodoulou notes, 'was overwhelmingly successful on one level: it is how Greeks understand their past today.'[70] But in another sense it met with failure: the Asia Minor Disaster in 1922 forever buried the Greeks' vision of a restored 'Greek empire centred on Constantinople'.

[67] Hamilakis 2007: 123. [68] Liakos 2008: 207–9. [69] Kitromilides 1989: 167–8.
[70] Christodoulou 2010: 459.

In the Mirror of the 'Greek' Byzantium

During the first half of the nineteenth century, medieval Bulgarian history attracted an increasing number of writers. The growing engagement with the medieval past and the Byzantine empire sprang from pressing questions of the Bulgarians' present and future that involved the definition of their identity, the outlining of their political borders and the delimitation of their past. As elsewhere in the region (and beyond), these were questions formulated in the context of the national history that was then under intensive construction.

The mounting interest in the medieval past brought few changes in the general conception of Byzantium set by Paisiy and disseminated through transcripts of his *History*. Unlike the Greek case, there was a neat continuity between the Enlightenment and Romantic interpretations, the main difference being the amplification of anti-Greek associations. Suggestive of the actual interaction involved is that most of this historical literature was produced by students of Greek schools (the first Bulgarian-language schools opened only in the 1820s) and some of it was even written in Greek. While advocating the knowledge of Greek as a 'noble and quite useful' language, Christaki Pavlovich (1804–48) reproduced almost literally Paisiy's narrative: he held 'Greek' perfidy and guile responsible for past Bulgarian military defeats and attributed the Bulgarian state's fall to the Ottomans to 'Greek treachery'.[71]

Ivan Seliminski (1799–1866) was a prominent intellectual and political thinker of the first half of the nineteenth century, a graduate of the Greek gymnasium in Kydonia (Asia Minor) and participant in the Greek war of independence. His historical analyses (written in Greek) illustrate the close engagement with contemporary Greek writings, in reference to which the Bulgarian historical narrative began to be fleshed out. Seliminski (like many authors before and after him) considered the Slavs to be the autochthonous population in a territory stretching from Illyria and Moravia to Galicia and Russia, whose 'political organisation' dated back to 1000 BC. He affiliated the Bulgarians with these 'hundred and twenty million Slavs' bound together by 'common nationality, similar language and religion' – a clear replica of (and counterforce to) the 'Hellenised East'.[72] Following this line of argument, Seliminski claimed that the Bulgarians' assaults on Byzantium and occupation of Byzantine lands were not barbarian invasions but acts of 'liberation of their enslaved brothers' and punishment for

---

[71] Danova 2003a: 102–3, 107.   [72] *Biblioteka 'D-r Iv. Seliminski'* 1905: 99.

56 The Century of History

the Byzantine greed for expansion.[73] Seliminski questioned whether the greatness of classical antiquity could be attributed to the Greeks. According to him, the ancient Greeks had pirated the achievements of the neighbouring 'barbarian' peoples – Indians, Phoenicians, Egyptians, Thracians and Scythians – whose pupils they were. Therefore, 'Greece is not a teacher of the West, but only a bridge, via which civilisation moved from East to West, from Asia to Europe'. Likewise, the Byzantine empire was 'Roman, not Greek', since it was inhabited by many peoples with equal rights and its emperors were not Greek. Orthodox Christianity too was the shared patrimony of all who professed it, and its dissemination owed little to the Ecumenical Patriarchate.[74] These views were evidently informed by the contemporary Greek interpretations but were shaped in reaction to them and adjusted to serve a specific subversive claim. Notably, Seliminski was also the first Bulgarian writer to subscribe fully to, and even improve on, Fallmerayer's theory by stating that 'there is no pure Greek nation ... but a rabble of Egyptians, Assyrians, Arabs, Italians, Slavs ... proved by archaeology and history'.[75] In the following decades, as we will shortly see, the thesis about Byzantium's non-Greek character would be superseded by the opposite one – with an equally national agenda in mind.

Since the 1840s, when Bulgarian resistance to the ecclesiastical control of the Ecumenical Patriarchate began to intensify, condemnations of not only the Greek priesthood but everything Greek increased palpably. The Bulgarian projections of the confrontation with the Patriarchate back to the Byzantine past were a direct response to a thesis already incorporated in the Greek national narrative: that Orthodox Christianity and the Orthodox Church – the most tangible Byzantine legacy – played a crucial role in preserving Greek identity under the Ottomans and preparing for the advent of Greek independence. That the Greek national historians extolled the 'national clergy' for safeguarding the Greek identity of its flock during the dark centuries of the 'Ottoman yoke' was barely original – all national historiographies developed almost identical narratives in this sense. But they also insisted that the history of the Ecumenical Patriarchate, under whose jurisdiction all Ottoman Orthodox Christians were placed, was inseparably entwined with the national and political history of the Greeks.[76] The growing affinities, from the 1850s onwards, between the Greek state's expansionist scheming and the efforts of the

---

[73] Kochev 1979: 158–61.
[74] *Biblioteka 'D-r Iv. Seliminski'* 1904: 96; *Biblioteka 'D-r Iv. Seliminski'* 1907: 16–17; Kochev 1979: 284–8.
[75] Konstantinova 2010: 174.   [76] Koulouri 1991: 394–5.

In the Mirror of the 'Greek' Byzantium

Patriarchate of Constantinople to curtail the nationalist aspirations among its flock, especially in Macedonia, added to the identification between the 'Greek' Church and Greek irredentism, past and present, in the minds of the Bulgarian patriots.

This explains in large measure why in nineteenth-century Bulgaria Orthodox Christianity was not perceived as a Byzantine 'gift' – as an element of a shared great civilisation and a link to the symbolic capital of East Rome.[77] Next to the central place assigned to religion in the emerging national consciousness, the appropriation of the Byzantine Orthodox tradition by the Greeks left little room for the Bulgarians' identification with it. The reaction was a replay, in a practical sense, of the Greek precedent and, in an ideological sense, of the one established by the medieval Bulgarian state: a 'national' church as a token of sovereignty and a religion bolstering national, not ecumenical, identity. In the 1840s one of the leading Bulgarian intellectuals, Konstantin Fotinov (c.1785–1858), coined the expression 'Bulgarian religion' (*bolgarskoe veroizpovedanie*) – a formula closely paralleling the contemporary Greek notion of 'Helleno-Christianity'.[78] There was a similar logic to the idea of the 'Slavicisation' of Constantin (Cyril) and Methodius, the Byzantine emissaries sent by the Byzantine emperor to Moravia to spread Christianity, and who forged to this end an alphabet, the Glagolitic (later replaced by Cyrillic), which enabled preaching Byzantine Christianity to the Slavs in their own idiom and the creation of a Slavic vernacular literature. Since the benefits of their inspired labours were only experienced by their pupils, who found refuge in the already Christianised Bulgarian state (885), the budding Bulgarian national ideology endeavoured to appropriate not only the nationality of the two brothers but also their achievements – in the words of a prominent national revivalist, Petko Slaveykov, they both 'originated from the Bulgarian people' and performed an apostolic mission on its behalf.[79] Byzantium's two major cultural legacies to the Bulgarians – the religion and the Slavonic script – were thus fully alienated from it and assigned to the national patrimony. The logic of nationality, where religion and language played the key role, largely predetermined this outcome.

The political radicalisation of the Bulgarian intelligentsia on the eve of and especially after the Crimean War stabilised the image of Byzantium as a hostile foreign power. Now some new elements appeared. Byzantium was no longer merely the political rival and oppressor of the Bulgarians. Byzantium and its cultural influence were now held responsible for

---

[77] Lilova 2013: 325–7.   [78] Danova 1994: 317.   [79] Lilova 2013: 326.

58   The Century of History

corrupting the Bulgarian national character and causing deep cleavages in
Bulgarian society. Georgi Rakovski (1821–67), another graduate of Greek
schools, a historian, writer and revolutionary, was the first to forcefully
formulate this thesis. According to him, the Christianisation of the
Bulgarians in the second half of the ninth century and the intermarriages
between the Bulgarian and the Byzantine courts led to de-nationalisation
and social disruption. Since then, along with the Greek mitres and titles,
'contagious luxury and debauchery crept into Bulgaria'. The Bulgarian
nation gradually began to deteriorate and intrigues and discord came to
reign; only the villagers preserved 'the almost primeval innocent nature of
the old life'.[80] Lyuben Karavelov (1835–79), a national-liberal writer and
influential journalist, vehemently denied that the Greeks had any right to
deem themselves heirs of the ancient Hellenes and often made analogies
between Byzantium and the Ottoman empire in terms of 'the opulence of
the court ... the anarchy, despotism, corruption and hubris [of the
sultans]'. The Bulgarians and Serbs had led heroic 'liberating' wars against
'the Byzantine plague, which was infecting everything around it'. Like
Rakovski, Karavelov did not consider the Bulgarian medieval tsars to have
espoused Bulgarian identity and stated that only their pre-Christian predecessors and the 'simple ploughmen' had the right to claim it. 'Anyone
would be disgusted', he wrote, 'by the Byzantine habits and customs that
were implanted in our semi-Byzantine tsars.'[81]

Another major step in this direction was made by Hristo Botev (1848–
76), a poet, essayist and radical democrat. For Botev, Bulgarian medieval
history in general, and especially the time of Tsar Simeon when the First
Bulgarian Kingdom (681–1018) reached its political and cultural pinnacle,
was 'our abominable bygone history'. Neither it nor the medieval
Bulgarian tsars embodied Bulgarian identity:

> Take a look at the history of the Bulgarian kingdom from Boris [the
> ruler who adopted Christianity from Byzantium as the official reli-
> gion in 864] until its fall under the Turks [1396], and you will see
> that the whole historical-political past of our nation was almost
> entirely purely Byzantine, that it was inhabited solely by tsars, boyars
> and clerics, while the people itself was always separated by its deep
> public morality from the debauchery of its government, debauchery
> that, along with Christianity, slipped into the higher strata of the
> population.[82]

[80] Danova 2003b: 69–70.
[81] Karavelov 1967, vol. 7: 227, 321, 474–6; vol. 8, 528–9; Danova 2003: 72–6.   [82] Botev 1958: 139.

In the Mirror of the 'Greek' Byzantium 59

With Christianisation, the alienation of the Bulgarian elite from the commoners reached its zenith, since the Bulgarian people

> was forced to become infected by the sickness of the then rotten and lecherous Byzantium. The constant fight for survival, the [establishment of] family relations of the Bulgarian tsars with the Byzantine emperors and the adoption of the then-Orthodox-idiotic culture of Byzantium, on the one hand, gave our people no time to develop its national character and create a firm foundation for its future and, on the other hand, detached a part of it and turned it into a Bulgarian aristocracy [that became] notorious for its profligacy and lecherousness .... At the time of Simeon, that is, the time of Bulgaria's golden age, Bulgaria reached not only the peak of its glory and might, but also the apex of its deadly disease.[83]

The thesis about the split between the elite and the people as a result of the former's 'byzantinisation' came to occupy a key place in the emerging historical narrative and was propagated by not only the radical (republican and laicist) but also the moderate wing of the national movement. Like Botev, Petko Slaveykov (1827–95), an emblematic figure of the Bulgarian cultural revival, believed that from Tsar Simeon and the Bulgarian 'Golden Age' onwards, the distance between the democratically organised Slavic communities and the increasingly Hellenised and alienated elite was growing to reach 'that ugly anomaly that we see towards the end of our state life': the tsars and nobles, who 'had relinquished the people's life', perished under the yataghans of the Ottomans.[84] This sweeping historical scenario pursued two quite obvious contemporary objectives. On the one hand, it was intended to allude to the ruinous effect that the modern Bulgarian elite's 'Hellenisation' had on the community. On the other hand, it implied that the Slavs, not the Greeks, were the harbingers of the ideas of equality and democracy and as such were destined to lead humanity towards modernity.[85]

But there was also a third, supposedly less obvious, contemporary reference Botev had in mind when denouncing Byzantium – the effects of the western European influence on the Bulgarian 'self'. 'Just as by adopting Byzantine culture we displayed ourselves as monkeys and came to be enslaved by Asiatic barbarians', he warned, 'so by blindly emulating Europe we will reach the state of being enslaved by ourselves.' The Bulgarians first needed to free themselves from 'the new Byzantium' – the

---

[83] Botev 1958: 139. [84] Lilova 2003: 251–2.

[85] Lilova 2003: 253. Both these themes became commonplace in the Bulgarian political press in the 1870s.

60   The Century of History

Ottoman empire – and 'only then borrow from Europe that which we need'.[86] This striking analogy between Byzantine spiritual domination and that of the 'West', as we will see, would enjoy wide circulation and receive metahistorical clout in the radicalised anti-liberal environment of the inter-war period.

The interpretations discussed so far were not those of professional historians, but they had a decisive impact on both the historical conscious-ness of the contemporary Bulgarians and the historical narrative under construction. Romantic historiography, as epitomised by the first gener-ation of trained Bulgarian historians, adopted and elaborated on most of these themes, drawing on the up-to-date historiographical approaches, mainly in Russia, where this generation had received its education. Spiridon Palaouzov (1818–72), the first professional Bulgarian historian trained in the Romantic tradition in Russia and Germany, expounded the thesis of the disastrous influence of Byzantium and its 'ideology' – 'byzantinism' (a term he was the first to use in Bulgarian history-writing) – not only on the medieval Bulgarian state but also on the South Slavs generally. Their connections with Byzantium

> as a focal point of diverse and unusual elements of citizenship . . . operated to the detriment of their nationality and independent development . . . . Are there still gentlemen who . . . believe that decrepit byzantinism could contain in its bosom the seeds of its future revival? Did the millennial empire . . . ever try to cultivate in itself at least a fraction of those principles on which the edifice of modern civilisation grew? Byzantium, set up by a special commandment of God . . . remained immovable, and this immo-bility it transmitted completely to Turkish Istanbul, the centre of the Ottoman empire, which has preserved intact the character of medieval byzantinism.[87]

In his book *The Romanian Principalities of Wallachia and Moldavia* (1858), Palaouzov made almost explicit the connection between the Byzantine empire, the economic ruin and political venality of the Romanian states under the Phanariots – the conduits of byzantinism – and 'the economic and spiritual enslavement' of the Bulgarians imposed by the new Phanariots in his own day.[88] At the same time, as an acquaintance of Jakob Fallmerayer from the time of his university studies in Munich in 1842–3, Palaouzov translated some of Fallmerayer's writings and lent full support to his 'Slavic theory'.

---

[86] Botev 1958: 141.   [87] Kolarov and Gyuzelev 1972: 56.   [88] Palaouzov 1977: 408–28.

In the Mirror of the 'Greek' Byzantium

The history textbooks reiterated the basic elements of this anti-byzantinist discourse: the presentation of Byzantium as inhabited by 'Greeks'; the harmful impact of byzantinism on the Bulgarian political and spiritual elite, ultimately leading to subjugation by the Turks; the characterisation of the Byzantine domination of the eleventh and twelfth centuries as a 'Byzantine yoke'; and the treatment of the peasant folks as the only guardians of the 'purity' of the national traditions and mores.[89]

All in all, by the second half of the nineteenth century, the openly hostile image of 'byzantinism' was firmly in place. This was a process whereby Bulgarian and Greek narratives mutually, albeit not symmetrically, constituted and reinforced each other. The Bulgarian late-Enlightenment and Romantic narrative traced the origins of the contemporary Greek-Bulgarian struggle for dominance in the Balkans back to the Byzantine era. In time, the historiographical myth that Byzantine history was exclusively Greek history was adopted by many Bulgarian scholars in confirmation of their attitude to Byzantium as a Greek power hostile to their nascent nation-state. Petko Slaveykov went so far as to praise the Ottomans for 'breaking the neck of proud Byzantium and putting an end, in political life at least, to the Greeks' aspiration to destroy the Bulgarians'.[90] Eventually, the Greeks' imperious appropriation of the empire's cultural legacy and their insistence on the medieval roots of the Great Idea reinforced the Bulgarian writers' rejection of all things Byzantine which Enlightenment thought had spurred.

It is therefore no exaggeration to state that the Bulgarian national historical narrative, with its strong grounding in the medieval era, was largely forged against the backdrop of and in response to the Greeks' Hellenisation of Byzantium. The Bulgarian historians sought to thwart the contemporary Greek national-political claims derived from the Byzantine legacy less by contesting the Eastern empire's Greek character than by downplaying its historical role and prestige – a ploy that drew heavily on western European Enlightenment imagery – and by contriving a rival medieval imperial model: that of the Bulgarian Kingdom. The identification of the Byzantines with the Greeks (and occasionally also the Turks) facilitated the transfer of unpleasant qualities from one group to the other. But it also prevented the nineteenth-century Bulgarians from capitalising on the benefits they had reaped from having been part of the Byzantine ecumene. In the words of a latter-day Bulgarian medievalist, 'This lack of objectivity became the main reason for never treating

[89] Danova 2003: 122–3. [90] Slaveykov 1980: 176.

62   The Century of History

Byzantium, its history and civilisation as a truly scientific subject and recognising all that which the Slavs owe to it in their secular development.'[91] Bulgaria, the most heavily byzantinised Balkan country, ended up as the fiercest detractor of Byzantium.

The only feeble attempt at appropriating the Byzantine legacy was prompted by the 'findings' of Fallmerayer. It is hardly surprising that the Bulgarian national elite did not miss the opportunity to indicate that 'Byzantium owed its mightiness to people with Greek names but Slavic blood'.[92] Emperors, patriarchs and military leaders (most conspicuously Constantine the Great, Justinian and Belisarius) were bestowed a Slavic provenance. This zero-sum scenario, however, suffered an intrinsic defect: apart from the fact that Byzantium was never, at the time or later, accepted as an unequivocal civilisational model, the crucial question that its 'Slavic character' raised was how to explain the continuous wars that the Bulgarian Kingdom waged against it – epic wars that, as already noted, served not only to assert the existence of a submerged repository of military might and national energy but also to mobilise the Bulgarians against the socially more powerful and culturally self-confident modern Greeks. (An additional 'defect' was the apparent assimilability of the Slavs, who had 'rejuvenated' the Greek ethnos at the cost of losing their Slavic identity.[93]) The 'Grecisation' of the Byzantine empire in the Bulgarian historical writings since Paisiy had firm nationalist logic and rationale. The Slavic 'genes' of some eminent Byzantines and the abundance of Slavic blood in the veins of the Byzantine commoners would often be emphasised, but the overall 'Greek' complexion of the Byzantine state and culture would not be questioned. With the exception of the interwar historian Petăr Mutafchiev, until after World War II the Bulgarian historians, unlike their Romanian and Serbian counterparts, were not so interested in proving that Byzantium was as much 'theirs' as it was to the Greeks. Instead, they sought to transpose the 'defects' of the empire, as contrived by the 'Europeans', onto the modern Greeks. For the Bulgarian historical narrative, Byzantium's ethnic and cultural 'strangeness' was instrumental: it made it possible simultaneously to present the medieval confrontation with the empire as nationally propelled and to justify the contemporary resistance against the 'de-nationalising' policies of the Greek state and the Patriarchate of Constantinople. Its political implications were also palpable as Lyuben Karavelov's projects for a Balkan federation indicate: his plans made no place for the Greeks 'until they give up their folly dreams and

[91] Dujčev 1966: 73–4.   [92] Lilova 2003: 222.   [93] Lilova 2003: 222–3.

In the Mirror of the 'Greek' Byzantium   63

their rusty Byzantine empire'.[94] Here we can see the curious linkage of the same (false) argument – that of the Greek identity of the Byzantine empire – with two warring national causes and the instrumentalisation of the same thesis by two conflicting national narratives.

The reverse impact of the Bulgarian perceptions on the Greek historical narrative was less the result of scholarly interpretations than of political realities. Before the mid-nineteenth century, the Bulgarians were still perceived as posing no threat to the 'irresistible force' of Hellenism, so Greek historical literature barely touched upon them. They were either mentioned briefly under the category of the (tame and hard-working, yet undercivilised) 'Slavs' or treated with indifference.[95] In the early 1850s Zambelios and Paparrigopoulos remained mute on the history of conflicts between Byzantium and the medieval Bulgarian states and preferred to discuss the assimilative power of 'Byzantine Hellenism' and the common struggles of Greeks and Bulgarians against the Latin West. The Bulgarians and Romanians were seen as the 'adopted children' of the 'Hellenic nation' in both its historical past and political present.[96] (The Serbs already had a state since 1830, so they were left out of the picture.) The Greek scholarly world and public began to 'discover' the Bulgarians as a rival during the late 1850s, in the wake of the Crimean War and in the midst of the new phase of the Eastern Question and the growth of the Bulgarian movement for ecclesiastical independence. Paparrigopoulos's *History* marshalled this new attitude by converting the once-submissive Bulgarians into national enemies of the Hellenic nation, who had provoked incessant conflicts and wars against the medieval bastion of Hellenism. In fact, his re-evaluation of Byzantium was not without connection to the Bulgarians' increasingly assertive nationalist claims.[97] Following the ecclesiastical schism (1872) and the annexation of Eastern Rumelia by the Bulgarian Principality (1885), the Bulgarians definitively replaced the Turks as the prime adversaries of the Greeks. In 1877 the first Greek history of medieval Bulgaria, written by N. Kokkonis, set the stage for a new historiographical era with a long future. The book described Bulgarian medieval history as an endless series of murders and acts of pillaging and destruction and the Bulgarians as lacking 'national spirit' – an insult that was particularly hurtful to their budding national awareness. Henceforth the contention that the Bulgarians suffered a deficit of nationality feeling and that their nationalism was defective would become a recurrent theme in Greek historiography.[98] Efforts to disprove it would propel much

---

[94] Karavelov 1967, vol. VIII: 321.   [95] Hering 1980: 47–66; Livanios 2003: 71–5.
[96] Koubourlis 2010: 137–41, 144.   [97] Koubourlis 2010: 142–3.   [98] Livanios 2003: 76–8.

64 The Century of History

of the 'scientific' Bulgarian historiography, starting in the latter half of the nineteenth century and gaining momentum after the liberation of the country in 1878.

Heading for a Serbo-Byzantine Empire

The Greek-Serbian relations in the nineteenth century presented a contrasting picture. The Serbs' political emancipation, contemporaneous with the Greek, was not perceived as harming Greece's interests, and Serbian irredentism did not clash with Greek irredentism; if anything, Belgrade's anti-Bulgarian position on the 'Macedonian question' drew the two countries closer to each other. Antonios Spiliotopoulos, the author of the first Greek history of Serbia (1912), noted that 'there is nothing that divides the two nations' and that their accord 'has never, until today, been seriously harmed by the medieval raids of Stefan Dušan against Byzantium or any other historical misdeed'.[99] Consequently, Greek and Serbian historiographies never experienced a major confrontation on the battlefield of the medieval past comparable to the Greek-Bulgarian one, even though Dušan had posed no less of a threat to the 'Greek empire' and showed no slighter ambition to hold its reins than some Bulgarian tsars did. The difference bespeaks once more the considerable weight of political expediencies in the portrayals of Byzantium.

The central theme of Romantic (and post-Romantic) Serbian historiography was the rise, expansion and glorious feats of the Serbian state under the Nemanjić dynasty (1159–1367), culminating in the 'Greco-Serbian' empire of Stefan Dušan (1346–55). In this story Byzantium was assigned the role of the chief yet declining adversary, with a prestigious and alluring but aging culture which, in stark contrast with the youthful vitality and creativity of the Serbs, lacked the verve, energy and vision to carry its civilisational mission any further. The personification of this strain of history-writing was Pantelija Srećković (1834–1903), whose two-volume *History of the Serbian People* (1884, 1888) – recognised in its day as the standard historical work – provides an archetype of the genre and an extensive list of interpretative motifs that would reappear in different rhetorical guises in subsequent historical accounts.

Added to the internal reasons for the failure of the Serbian local dynasts (*župani*) to create a 'unified state' was, according to Srećković, the Byzantine empire's policy of promoting 'state multiplicity' under the

---

[99] Livanios 2003: 79. See also Gounaris 2005: 205.

Heading for a Serbo-Byzantine Empire

župans and 'help[ing] all the contenders and opponents to national unification'. This political fragmentation continued until the mid-twelfth century and the rise of the Nemanjić dynasty that 'united Serbia' – a trope literally replicating that of 'united Bulgaria' under Simeon and Ivan Asen II.[100] Projecting the nineteenth-century national ideal into the medieval past, Srećković interpreted the subjugation of the Adriatic bishoprics by Stefan Nemanja (1166–96) in 1177 as 'a victory of the independent national development, a triumph among the Serbian tribes of the Slavonic faith and script, and a victory of the national consciousness over the influence of both Rome and Constantinople'. The newly established Serbian state and church made all Serbian tribes realise that 'they were members of a single organism, a single nation'.[101]

Srećković described late-twelfth-century Byzantium as a decaying state, where brutal and bloody dynastic rivalries, stupidity and horrors reigned. This not only played into the hands of Stefan Nemanja, who succeeded to expand the Serbian state to the south and east, but also warranted the characterisation of his wars as 'liberating many Serbs from the Greek yoke'. Furthermore, Srećković continually painted Byzantium as a place of growing political and moral degeneration, civil anarchy and economic weakness – the very opposite of the vibrant, irresistible and auspicious Serbian state.[102] From day one, Serbian history, in Srećković's telling, led inevitably to Dušan's empire.

Dušan had been captivated by the idea of 'found[ing] in the place of the Byzantine Empire a new Serbian empire' – an idea that, after Serbian military victories, 'developed naturally in the mass of Slavic people'.[103] Srećković's predecessor, historian Grigorije Geršić (1777–1835), had already developed the view that the Serbian succession to Byzantium was neither primarily the result of the empire's decline nor an extravagant royal fancy, but the consequence of the organic development of the Serbs into a 'state-endowed and historically and politically advanced nation which in its time stood fully on a par with the Germanic and Romanic cultural nations'.[104] Dušan, Srećković tells us, had more right than anyone else to sit on the throne of 'Orthodox Byzantium' because he had fought against both the Latins and the Muslims and 'was the protector and patron of Orthodoxy in the East'. Byzantium had little power and vigour left, but it

> lured him as the centre of the Orthodox learning and culture, with its forms of imperial power and with that gleam and importance that the Byzantine

---

[100] Srećković 1888: 4–8. [101] Srećković 1888: 31. [102] Srećković 1888: 36–42.
[103] Srećković 1888: 344, 360–1. [104] Cited in Ignjatović 2016: 520.

66   The Century of History

emperors had had since its founder Constantine the Great ... Dušan's newly created empire sought to become a second or popular Slavic Byzantine empire similar to the empire of Constantine the Great, with Orthodox ideals and aspirations whose representative until then was the Byzantine empire.

In his pursuit 'to become the chief of the Serbs and the Greeks', Dušan saw himself as a 'defender of the Orthodox Greek-Slavic world, countering the aspirations of the western world' – a determination that, according to Srećković, reflected Dušan's 'independent political action'.[105]

Srećković was evidently wavering between seeing Dušan as an alternative to the Byzantine emperor and as a contender for the Byzantine throne – that is, between the idea of a vibrant Serbian empire to be erected on the ruins of a decaying Byzantium and the aspiration for Serbian participation in the running of the Eastern Roman empire and repossession of its imperial dignity. Other historians of his generation, like Milan Ubavkić, unequivocally asserted Dušan's firm decision, ensuing from his 'robust consciousness of nationality', 'to destroy the Byzantine empire and create in its place in the Balkan peninsula a huge Serbian empire, steered by a Serbian hand' yet exerting strong attraction for 'educated and rich Greece'.[106] For none of these historians, however, was there any doubt that by pursuing the Byzantine throne, Dušan was performing a nationally constructive, 'patriotic' mission; those who supported him demonstrated 'national patriotism', while his imperial title and the independent Serbian Church evoked 'the pride and joy of all contemporary [Serbian] patriots and the people'. In this totally nationalised medieval context, it is not surprising that Srećković saw the Orthodox creed as the 'Serbian faith' and credited the Serbian clergy for having 'defended the interests of the land and the empire' and cultivated Serbian consciousness among the people.[107] Like in the other Balkan states, this nationalisation (or secularisation) of religion was a crucial instrument in the construction of the modern Serbs' collective identity. As another contemporary historian, the author of a book evocatively titled *The Nemanjić and the Obrenović Dynasties or a Comparison of Two Bright Periods in Our History*, put it, since the founding of the independent Serbian church, 'the faith of the Serbs became the popular faith, and faith and nationality merged in the same term'.[108]

---

[105] Ignjatović 2016: 674–5, 483–4.   [106] Ubavkić 1886: 145, 150–1.
[107] Ubavkić 1886: 61, 669, 675, 677, 881.
[108] Vrbavac 1900: 10. The Obrenović dynasty was one of the two reigning dynasties in nineteenth-century Serbia.

Heading for a Serbo-Byzantine Empire

While acknowledging the great prestige and magnetism of Byzantine state tradition and culture, the Serbian historians, in remarkable similarity to the Bulgarian historians, bemoaned their disruptive effect on the traditional social order in Serbian society, purportedly based on organic solidarity and social harmony. The original statement to this effect belonged to Vladimir Jovanović (1833–1922), a philosopher-politician and chief ideologist of Serbian Romantic liberalism, who set out to prove the Serbs' age-old and inborn affinity for the values and institutions of (Western) modernity. To this end, he contrived a historical narrative demonstrating the existence of an authentically Serbian liberal-democratic tradition, embodied in 'grassroots democratic forms', that became suffocated by Byzantine autocracy and opulence. In the manner of his Bulgarian peers, Jovanović held that initially the great *župans* used their power in accordance with the 'general will of the nation'; however, after their conversion to Christianity they yielded to the 'Byzantine System', which divided the Serbs into social classes and corroded their fundamentally democratic spirit. The plague called 'Byzantine supremacy' was also found responsible for the fall of the Serbian empire and its being 'reduced to a small despotic state'. In Jovanović's reading, therefore, medieval Serbia had all the resources to develop into a 'liberal Christian state' had the Byzantines not grafted their monarchic system onto Serbian institutions by manipulating its political elite.[109]

The emerging historical master narrative followed the same trail. The byzantinisation of Serbian state life, especially after the proclamation of the empire, Srećković claimed, was the result above all of the vanity, snobbery and selfishness of the Serbian nobility. 'Wafted by the breath of byzantinism', they began to lead an opulent and sumptuous life; the egotism and lust for power that they had copied from the Greek aristocracy 'prevailed over patriotism', while Dušan's autocratic rule, 'modelled after the Byzantine', destroyed the last remnants of local self-government.[110]

> When Serbia began to act as the Byzantine empire, the customary Serbian national life lost its meaning, life in accordance with the Greek ceremonies had begun to the detriment of the Serbian national life . . .. In general, we can say that as long as our kings were living the life of the people, their state was growing and advancing. With the adoption of foreign customs there began an anti-national life [that] ended with the collapse of the [Serbian] empire.

Even so, the state idea that had created this empire lived on and 'prepared [the Serbs] for fighting for their survival and the restoration of their

---

[109] Jovanović 1870: 11–12, 22. See also Gietzen 2018: 101–8.   [110] Srećković 1888: 811–16, 952.

68   The Century of History

empire'.[111] Srećković did not venture to surmise what would have happened with the Serbian state idea and popular traditions had Dušan ascended the Byzantine throne. However, he did project that, in such a case, by his own era there would have been not four different Slavic states but only one, which would have dominated the whole peninsula.[112]

In the end, what modern Serbia inherited from the Middle Ages was not just the medieval Serbian empire but the 'Serbian-Greek' (or 'Serbo-Byzantine') empire – one that had conquered most of the territory and appropriated the imperial dignity of Byzantium but which had exceeded it in political vigour, creativity and social arrangement. In subsequent Serbian historical surveys it would feature as a stable trope, conveying both the Serbs' cultural animation and their state-building credentials. Once more, the porousness between historical discourse and the nation-state's political agenda is readily demonstrated. The first formal political programme of modern Serbia, which drew the map of its future expansion in the Balkans (*Načertanije*, 1844), reads:

> The roots and foundations of the Serbian state are firmly embedded in the Serbian empire of the thirteenth and fourteenth century and in the rich and glorious Serbian history. Our history testified that the Serbian emperors had plundered the Greek imperial heritage . . .. Furthermore, they almost demolished the fallen Byzantium in order to rejuvenate the Eastern Roman empire and to lay the foundations of a new, Serbian-Slavic empire. This venture, however, was disrupted by the Turkish invasion . . .. It is only now that the foundations of the Serbian empire are about to rise from the rubble of its historical base . . .. This state [which would replace European Turkey] could not be any other than Serbia, for, even in the Middle Ages, she would have been the successor of the Byzantine empire if the Turks had not destroyed it. In this case, moreover, Serbia would do no more than revive the ancient empire of her ancestors. Europe could see nothing more in our action than the resurrection of the old Serbian State, founded on historic rights and the law of nations.[113]

Evidently, the multi-ethnic character of neither enervated Byzantium nor its bracing would-be Serbian successor presented any obstacle to the modern reconstitution of this medieval empire into a Serbian nation-state, so 'historic rights' and 'the law of nations' could sit comfortably next to each other. Rounding up the political history of medieval Serbia

---

[111] Srećković 1888: 689, 799, 816–17.   [112] Srećković 1888: 801.   [113] Cited in Stavrianos 1944: 52.

Heading for a Serbo-Byzantine Empire

some fifty years later, Ubavkić, too, cursively subsumed empire within nation-state in his political vision:

> Serbia, which [at the time of the mighty Tsar Dušan] spread from the Adriatic Sea to the Danube, from [rivers] Drava and Iskar to Cetinje . . . is a pivot, around which all Serbs, all Serbian lands should be united, so as to become, once again, a *great, glorious and powerful empire* . . .. The task of present-day Serbia is to unite and create a *Great Serbia*, whose boundaries will stretch to wherever there is a single Serbian cottage.[114]

With the benefit of hindsight, one can discern here the roots of the themes around which the Serbian historiography would evolve all the way to World War II: the paramountcy of the national principle in the ideology, politics and culture of medieval Serbia enshrined in the idea of 'national unification' of all 'Serbian lands' in a single independent state; the moral and martial superiority of the Serbs among the Balkan contenders for the Byzantine heritage; and, in consequence, the idea of *translatio imperii* from Byzantium to Serbia.[115] These three themes would constitute what Aleksandar Ignjatović calls a 'Serbo-Byzantine discourse', an epistemological-ideological structure, fusing the myths of national authenticity and imperial legacy, which formed 'the core of the national imagination about the national self, history, culture, past and future'.[116] But whereas conflation of imperial and national visions is a common characteristic of all three historiographic traditions discussed thus far, distinctive of the Bulgarian and Serbian narratives is another ambiguity, which the 'historians as nation-builders' failed to address. In both countries the 'people', the common peasant 'folk', were said to be the bearers of the national authenticity, the source of all social and moral virtues and a sturdy counterforce to byzantinism and the 'byzantinised' local elites. Such a populist rendition of the national ideology, largely foreshadowed by the agrarian (egalitarian, anti-elitist) nature of these societies, rested uneasily with the imperial (monarchical and hierarchical) imaginations cultivated by the historical grand narrative. Remarkably, the post-Romantic generations would not eliminate the inconsistency: they would continue to devolve responsibility for all kinds of social cleavages and misfortunes on those national leaders and groups who, by following the Byzantine 'ways', had jeopardised the chances of erecting a truly 'national empire' epitomising the nation's sacrosanct traditions, integrity and solidarity.

---

[114] Ubavkić 1886: 181 (original emphases).
[115] On these themes in Serbian historiography, see Ignjatović 2016: 343–662.
[116] Ignjatović 2016: 110–22, passim.

70   The Century of History

The 'West in the East'

The Transylvanian Latinist school set the tone for the anti-Byzantine current that would dominate, for the better part of the nineteenth century, Romanian historiography and culture 'on behalf of the national idea and Latin solidarity'.[117] On the level of national ideology, the main target of the young independent Romanian state was the 'Ottoman-Phanariot' heritage. Romanian irredentism and hopes for political unification, on the other hand, coveted parts of the Habsburg and Russian empires rather than territories to the south of the Danube. None of these priorities entailed close association with Byzantium and its political or cultural legacy. But there was another, perhaps deeper reason for the empire's relative absence from the purview of the Romanian national historians.

Although they belonged to the Byzantine cultural sphere, Byzantium never exercised direct control over the Romanian lands, except on Dobrudzha (a historical region lying on the left and right banks of the Danube river), the mouth of the Danube river and, during brief periods, a larger area on its left bank. The strategic objective of the empire to the north was and remained the consolidation of the Danube Limes against assaults by peoples of the Eurasian steppe. For the better part of the Middle Ages Byzantine influence on the Romanians was not direct but mediated by the Slavs. Literature in Old (Church) Slavonic spread from Bulgaria and Serbia to Wallachia and Moldavia as early as the tenth century. From the establishment of the two principalities in the fourteenth century until the mid-seventeenth century, Old Slavonic was the language of the chancellery and of the liturgy, and continued to be used by the lesser clergy until the eighteenth century. While conversion to Christianity was a long-drawn-out process, marked by oscillation between Rome and Constantinople, the growing incorporation of the Romanian lands into the Orthodox sphere of influence came about concurrently with the adoption of the Slavonic liturgy mainly under the influence of the First Bulgarian Kingdom. Following the emergence of the first more unified and centralised political institutions and the establishment of the metropolitan seats in Wallachia and Moldavia in the fourteenth century, as Obolensky observes, 'the church and culture of Constantinople became dominant in those lands and the Romanians made their belated entry into the Byzantine Commonwealth of nations'. Byzantinism in the Romanian principalities took the form of a 'composite "Graeco-Slav" culture' through which

[117] Tanaşoca 2003: 213.

The 'West in the East'

Byzantine religious scriptures, theological writings and legal texts were transmitted.[118] This in itself presented a problem to the Romanian historians, grappling with the issue of cultural authenticity and continuity, but it was left for the next, positivist generation to face up to it. For the nineteenth-century national Romantics, this problem was overshadowed by a more immediate task: coping with the 'post-Byzantine' legacy of the Phanariots.

Similar to the Bulgarian case, the 'Greeks' became an issue in the Romanian context of the late eighteenth and early nineteenth centuries, when a Romanian national consciousness was crystallising, by virtue of the significant Greek (Phanariot) cultural and political influence. Although they were part of the Ottoman empire, until 1716 the two Danubian Principalities, Wallachia and Moldavia, were ruled by native princes. Thereafter the Sublime Porte handed over the governing of the principalities to the Greek-speaking and culturally post-Byzantine 'administrative nobility' of the Phanariots. For almost a century the Greek language and Phanariot political culture were dominant in the principalities; this era was also associated with political instability and economic decline. On the other hand, it was largely through (some of) the Phanariots that the subversive ideas of the Enlightenment reached, and spread throughout, the principalities. As in Bulgaria, all this deeply embroiled the construction of Romanian national identity and history with an assessment of the role of the 'Greeks', a process whereby the prevailing cultural-political orientation of the present gave shape to the interpretation of the past.

The cultural and political upper class in nineteenth-century Romania, both conservative and liberal, looked towards 'the West'. The theory of the Romanians' Latin purity, avidly promoted by the Transylvanian school, matched this orientation. As Lucian Boia recaps, 'Through the Romans, the Romanians could present themselves to the West as the equals of anybody, and the phenomenon of acculturation no longer meant borrowing, but rather a return to the source, to a ground of civilisation shared with the civilisation of the West.'[119] Such disposition and the corresponding 'Westernisation' of Romanian history implied, according to the contemporary civilisational coordinates, a distancing from the 'lethargic East' and its cultural symbols. 'The break with the East took the form of a massive devaluing and inculpation of peoples and cultures which had hitherto offered the Romanians more models than motives of lamentation. The first victims were the Greeks.'[120] Both the nationalist drive for emancipation from Greek cultural dominance and

---

[118] Obolensky 1971: 141, 207–8, 257–9, 341; Joudiou 1998. [119] Boia 2001a: 87.
[120] Boia 2001a: 158.

72   The Century of History

regeneration of society by renouncing the Ottoman-Phanariot past and the drive towards modernisation and 'Europeanisation' pointed in the direction already charted by the Latinist school: refutation of the post-Byzantine and, by implication, Byzantine world. For the Romanian Romantic historians, as for the Bulgarian, the Ottomans were the heirs of the empire of the East. Hence their anti-Ottoman ideology largely predetermined their attitude to Byzantium and its survivals.

In the Romantic conception of history of the 1848 generation and the one that followed, emphasis was laid on the unique position of the Romanian medieval states in southeastern Europe due to their resistance which, by checking the Ottoman threat, was claimed to have saved not only their own existence as autonomous states but also the rest of Europe. Byzantium and its relations with the Romanians were not of interest to those who dominated the humanities and culture in the principalities until at least the 1880s. Nicolae Bălcescu's (1819–52) main work, *The Romanians under Prince Michael the Brave* (1849), focussed on the relations with the Magyars, the Ottomans and the Poles, not the Byzantines, and did not relate the trajectory of the Romanian nation in any way to that of Byzantium. Mihail Kogălniceanu's (1817–91) magisterial *History of Wallachia, of Moldavia and of the Transdanubian Vlachs* (1837) and Bogdan Hasdeu's (1838–1907) *Critical History of the Romanians* (1873 and 1875) dealt with the fundamental problems for Romanian historiography at the time, such as the origins, continuity, ethno-historical space and strength of the Romanians in the Middle Ages (after the fourteenth century), mentioning only in passing the Romanians' contacts with Byzantium. All of them and most of their fellow historians were extremely critical of the post-Byzantine Greek influence, both sociopolitical and cultural. Their virulent and even obsessive anti-Greek attitude focussed primarily on the 'Phanariot eighteenth century', typically portrayed as the darkest period in Romanian history, but was often extended to 'Grecism' in general.[121] At the same time, only rarely would these anti-Phanariot and anti-Greek feelings be explicitly associated with Byzantium or the Byzantine-Romanian relations. In his essay 'Romîni şi fanarioţii' ('The Romanians and the Phanariots'), Bălcescu contented himself with counterpoising the debauched 'Greeks of Tsarigrad [Constantinople] and Roumelia' with the 'healthy Hellenic nation of today that we love and respect'.[122] Those who made the connection less tacitly barely went beyond reiterating the clichés bequeathed by the Western Enlightenment, such as

[121] Ionescu-Nişcov 1974: 152–4.   [122] Zane 1940: 118–23.

The 'West in the East'   73

Mihail Anagnosti, who lamented the transfer to the Phanariot courts of the 'ill-famed debris of the old Byzantine court, including the intrigues of servants and the perfidious criminal politics', or Gheorghe Săulescu, who explained the degeneration of the Eastern Romans through their contact with the harmful ideas of the 'Greeks'.[123] More often than not, historians explained the rapacious behaviour and detrimental impact of the Phanariots by citing their position as Ottoman functionaries rather than referring to the Byzantine legacy, even if their psychological portraits were often cast in the stereotypical aura of the Byzantines, as in the historical plays of Vasile Alecsandri or the journalistic articles of Bogdan Hasdeu.

It is perhaps telling that the person who made Byzantium an integral part of the anti-Phanariot discourse came from (Habsburg) Transylvania. In an article published in 1871, fifty years after the end of the Phanariot regime, the historian and journalist George Bariț (1812–93) argued that the Byzantine nobles, who had saved their lives from the Turkish yataghan by immigrating to the principalities, were none other than the forefathers of the Phanariots. He thus connected the 'character' and fate of the Ottoman-Greek administrators with that of the one-time Byzantine aristocracy, secular and ecclesiastical. This superimposed Byzantine stratum, Bariț asserted with frequent references to Gibbon, was 'bastard, broken, corrupt' and its 'nefarious' and 'shameful' deeds were innumerable. The political conceptions of the princes from Phanar were also of Byzantine origin: for them, the principalities were only a means towards restoration of the Byzantine empire and expulsion of the Turks 'as far as the Euphrates'. Like the Magyars with respect to Transylvania, moreover, the Phanariots considered the principalities to be provinces of the Byzantine empire conquered hundreds of years before the Turks.[124]

Bariț's liberal-Romantic outlook and the political grievances of the Transylvanian Romanians within Dualist Hungary may help us under-stand the national-didactic pursuits of such genealogical and comparative constructions. They drew on both Western Enlightenment thought and the tradition of the Latinist school of contrasting Romans and Greeks to stress the Romanians' ethnic vitality and imperial legacy. It was these characteristics that made the Transylvanian anti-Greek and anti-Byzantine discourse so similar to the Bulgarian discourse.

In the Romanian principalities, engagement with Byzantium and post-byzantinism remained marginal. Interestingly, it was also marginal for the

---

[123] Anagnosti 1837: 18; cited in Rados 2005: 136, 139.
[124] Bariț 1871, 4/6: 61–4; 4/7: 73–6; 4/8: 89–92. See Rados 2005: 165–9.

74   The Century of History

few Greek scholars, like the historian G. G. Papadopol, the only one who bothered to delve into Greek-Romanian relations in historical perspective – a fact that underscores the inconspicuousness of both these relations prior to 1453 and the 'Byzantine origins' of the Phanariot issue. The growing preoccupation with 'Balkan Romanity', however – an issue that was not new but was becoming increasingly topical and politicised with the exacerbation of the 'Macedonian question' in the last quarter of the nineteenth century – was bringing the Romanian historical narrative closer to Byzantium. Following in the footsteps of their Transylvanian predecessors, leading authorities such as Bogdan Hasdeu (*Critical History of the Romanians*), Alexandru Xenopol (*History of the Romanians in Dacia Traiana*) and Constantin Erbiceanu 'discovered' the great many Vlachs inhabiting the lands south of the Danube and their even greater role in opposing the Byzantines and founding the Second Bulgarian Kingdom. In doing so, they made use of Byzantine sources only to verify the unbroken continuity of Eastern Romanity south and north of the Danube.

Connections with French Romantic thought and reliance on French political support had much to do with this mental orientation. 'In our West we have our own Byzantiums', wrote Edgar Quinet in 1856, in allusion to the Western legacy of autocratic and arbitrary rule, and he urged the Romanians to look for the sources of civilisation in their proper national tradition, not in the superficial mores of modernity or in an uprooted cosmopolitanism.[125] The appeal was well heeded by the intellectual vanguard of the newly independent state: while in 'spirit' and 'race' the Romanians were said to be the bearers of 'the West' in 'the East', in terms of cultural identity they were the inheritors of a distinctive civilisation. The Byzantine elements there, especially in material culture, became construed as testaments to an authentic Romanian medieval tradition. The legacy of Byzantium in later nineteenth-century Romania was effectively nationalised, cutting it off from both its historical source and its self-proclaimed custodians, the Greek Phanariots.[126]

The formative phase in the national historiographical canons in southeastern Europe thus already signalled the markedly different ways in which the individual historiographic traditions would accommodate the 'Byzantine factor' in the national master narratives. The Greek historiography devoured the empire and its cultural heritage wholesale, turning it

---

[125] Leanca 2013: 290–3.
[126] Leanca 2013: 292–3. On the repossession of Byzantine art and architecture as part of the Romanian cultural patrimony, see Laurenţiu 2001 and Popescu 2004.

The 'West in the East'

into an integral part of national continuity and assimilating the canonical (and teleological) European division of history into classical, medieval and modern periods. For the Bulgarians, Byzantium, which they equated with contemporary Greeks, featured as the main adversary in confrontation with whom the Bulgarian national state and identity were crystallised and sustained. The Serbian historians foregrounded the significance of the medieval empire of Stefan Dušan as an actual heir and improved version of the Eastern Roman empire. Romania, the latecomer on the medieval political scene, reconfirmed its claims to represent the Latin West in the (post-)Byzantine East. Interaction with Western perceptions of Byzantium played an important part in much of this, whereas Western classicism and Romanticism were decisive for the discovery of the Greek continuity via Byzantium. In the process, borrowed conceptions and interpretations were re-configured to serve specific national needs. The Latinist school in Romania adopted the Western Enlightenment notion of Byzantium in order to advance the Romanians' claim of being the only rightful heirs to the Roman imperial tradition and to divest 'Greek' Byzantium of such a role, while the Greeks' appropriation of Byzantium came to serve as both an act of emancipation from the Western canon of history and an attempt at its subversion.

CHAPTER 3

In Search of the 'Scientific Method'

The second half of the nineteenth century witnessed a gradual re-valuation of Byzantium and its history, confronting the stereotypes bequeathed by the age-old antagonism between Catholicism and Orthodoxy and embellished by Enlightenment scholarship. The Eastern Roman empire was being gradually re-discovered not only as a saviour and transmitter of the classical tradition but also as representing a unique historical phenomenon. In the 1870s, English medieval historian and liberal activist Edward Freeman (1823–92) pleaded for the recovery of 'some of the most wonderful pages in the history of the world' – the story of 'that mighty Empire which for so many ages cherished the flame of civilisation and literature when it was well-nigh extinct throughout Western Europe . . . till the nations of the West were once more prepared to receive the gift and despise the giver'.[1]

This shift involved the institutionalisation of Byzantine studies as a separate field, comprising a number of sub-fields – history, philology and literature, art history, architecture, law – first in Germany and France and then in Russia and England. The most significant step in this direction was made by Karl Krumbacher (1856–1909), who founded in Munich in the late 1890s a Chair in Medieval and Modern Greek Philology as an autonomous institution focussed on Byzantine studies, and the specialised *Byzantinische Zeitschrift*. In the preface to the first issue of the journal, Krumbacher announced the platform of liberating *Byzantinistik* from its status of an auxiliary servant to other disciplines: 'The independent importance of this discipline', he wrote, 'cannot be emphasised enough; for it is difficult for most to free themselves from the deeply rooted error that all Byzantine deserves attention only to the extent that it has enlightening relations with classical antiquity or any other discipline'. Krumbacher called for 'a new way of looking at Byzantine matters' ('die neue Betrachtungsweise byzantinischer Dinge'), namely in terms of the

---

[1] Freeman 1879: 231–2. Compare Stephenson 2007: 119–56.

In Search of the 'Scientific Method'

historical method that would seek to understand the 'grand, finely structured, richly fateful biography of this Byzantine era that lies before us'.[2] The French Alfred Rambaud (1842–1905), the Russian Vasiliy G. Vasil'veskiy (1838–99) and the English John B. Bury (1861–1927) were each able to establish Byzantine studies in their own countries as an independent branch of learning.

The progress in the study of Byzantine civilisation and the growing recognition of its influence on world culture underwrote the development of the new academic field – Byzantine history and literature in particular. Charles Diehl (1859–1944), head of the first Chair of Byzantine Studies at the Sorbonne, wrote an outline of Byzantine history up to the fall of the empire, averring that

> For almost a thousand years, the Byzantine Empire was the seat of a civilisation that outshone all others ... the centre of outstanding development both in thought and art. Because of the marked superiority of its civilisation, it was to exert a deep and lasting influence on East and West, thereby leaving its mark on history and doing great service to the world.[3]

Krumbacher embarked on a general outline of Byzantine literature and John Bury inaugurated systematic research in Byzantine administrative history, which was later continued by Ernst Stein and Franz Dölger. Gustave Schlumberger, Louis Bréhier, Henri Monnier, Carl Neumann, Karl Eduard Zachariae von Lingenthal and others developed a whole set of auxiliary historical sciences and sub-disciplines vital to the field – numismatics, sigillography, iconography, Byzantine law/legal history, art history.[4] Archaeology partook in this upsurge. British and French explorers were the first to record and investigate Byzantine monuments in Anatolia and Constantinople. In the late nineteenth and early twentieth centuries, art historians and archaeologists such as Charles Texier, Aguste Choisy, Gertrude L. Bell, Joseph Strzygowski, Charles Diehl, Sir William Ramsay and Guillaume de Jerphanion produced some of the most comprehensive works on Byzantine monuments on the basis of systematic and comparative studies of Byzantine remains in the Ottoman empire.[5] By the beginning of the twentieth century, byzantinology was well on the way to constituting an autonomous field within the historical discipline that continued to grow rapidly in the decade preceding World War I.

[2] Agapitos 2015: 14–16.   [3] Diehl 1957: 228.
[4] Tinnefeld 2011: 27–38; Diehl 1905: 21–37, 38–106; Ostrogorsky 1980: 6–9.
[5] Yıldız 2011: 64; Üre 2014: 60–1.

78   In Search of the 'Scientific Method'

But if 'recent research and wider conception of history' had restored Byzantium 'to its place as the true centre of Culture during the Dark Ages', as the prominent historian of the Habsburg empire and the Balkans Robert W. Seton-Watson held in 1917, this did not necessarily entail a corresponding change in its perception as essentially the opposite of Western dynamism and potential for development, especially among non-byzantinists.[6] Freeman, a high-profile champion of Greek and South-Slavic nationalism, called it a 'not altogether attractive spectacle of a thoroughly un-progressive state' and contrasted its 'conservative and not creative existence' with the youthful nations of the West. Tellingly, he found fault with the empire for 'not being kindled into life by any strictly national spirit' and with the Byzantine emperors for never having become national sovereigns. 'The centralised despotism of Constantinople', he concluded, 'was positively the best government in the world [at that time], where civilisation was most flourishing. But essentially conservative and unprogressive, it had not the same hope for the future which dwelled in the vigorous barbarism of the Western nations.'[7] Ferdinand Schevill (1868–1954), author of the only synthetic historical overview of what he called 'Balkania' undertaken by an American academic during that period, held that Byzantium barely produced anything truly original and that its civilisation 'cannot remotely rank with the great civilisations ... which quicken our spirit and excite our admiration'.[8]

Students of Byzantium rushed to disprove such judgements. John Bury, who authored three much-read volumes on the history of the 'Later Roman Empire', took issue with the philosophers and writers of the eighteenth century for having entirely ignored one of the most important and essential factors in the development of western European civilisation, namely the influence of the later Roman empire and New Rome.[9] In a similar vein, Charles Diehl, who earned the fame of a brilliant populariser of this burgeoning field, went to great lengths to demonstrate 'Byzantium's contribution to the world' in terms of the 'intelligence, subtlety, and lively curiosity of the Byzantine mind' and 'intellectual superiority', literary achievement and 'splendours of art'; as 'the great educator and initiator' of the Slavic and the Arab East; and as the teacher of the West through art and intellectual influence.[10]

Such differences of interpretation were to an extent due to differences of perspective and agenda: a Western-centric, typically liberal vantage point

---

[6] Seton-Watson 1917: 3.   [7] Freeman 1879: 235–8, 275.   [8] Schevill 1922: 123.
[9] Vasiliev 1952: 22–3.   [10] Diehl 1957: 227–88.

was characteristic of scholars seeking the historical foundations of, as well as impediments to, the Balkans' modern development. They used to stress the progressive quality, indeed inevitable accession, of the national state as inscribed in the Western pedigree, which pre-empted their judgement on moribund empires and aligned them with the local scholars who read the history of the region from a strictly ethnocentric perspective.[11] The academically more robust byzantinists looked at the region from the imperial centre – Constantinople – which made them less susceptible to a normative, anachronistic or ex post reading of the empire through the lens of the 'Western pattern' of development. Representatives of the younger generation of byzantinists, like Norman Baynes (1877–1961), wrote with great empathy about the 'thought-world of East Rome' and called on their colleagues 'to look upon the world as a Byzantine saw it'.[12]

The two perspectives were not necessarily discordant, as the interpretation of Hellenism amply demonstrates. Crucial was the role played by ostensibly apolitical institutions like the French *École française d'Athènes* (1846) and *Association pour l'encouragement des études grecques* (1867), the British Society for the Promotion of Hellenic Studies (1879) and British School of Athens (1886), and even the widely international Munich-based Chair for Byzantine Studies titled *Seminar für mittel- und neugriechische Philologie* (1898) in cultivating exclusively pro-Greek versions of scholarly Hellenism, geared towards 'illustrating the history of the Greek race in the ancient, Byzantine and Neo-Hellenic periods' at the expense of 'unclassical' neighbours.[13] The rise of Western interest in the Byzantine past itself was strongly pegged on the political interest in modern Greece and its medieval history. Professed byzantinists like Krumbacher baldly applied the concept of national literature to the Byzantine textual production, writing that 'Byzantine literature is the most important expression of the intellectual life of the Greek nation and of the Roman state from the end of Antiquity up to the threshold of the Modern Age. It is on this fact primarily that its evaluation must be based'. He also stressed the importance of Byzantine folk poetry and folk language for understanding the 'medieval Greek national spirit', itself the source from which the spirit of the modern Greek nation sprang.[14] John Bury, certainly the most erudite of the British byzantinists at that time, was less unequivocal. He held the

---

[11] See, for example, Forbes, Toynbee, Mitrany and Hogarth 1915: 49–50; Schevill 1922: 303–4.
[12] Cameron 2016: 169–70.   [13] See, *pars pro toto*, Newton 1880: 1–6.
[14] Agapitos 2015: 19, 29–30. Significantly, in the second half of the nineteenth century most Greek intellectuals did not yet see things in this way. Krumbacher was also deeply involved in the Greek 'language question', to be discussed later, on the side of the 'demoticists'.

utterly unconventional view that 'No "Byzantine empire" ever began to exist; the Roman Empire did not come to an end until 1453'; 'such expressions as Byzantine, Greek, or Romaic empire are highly objectionable, because they tend to obscure an important fact and perpetrate a serious error'. He nonetheless believed that 'the civilisation of the later Roman Empire was the continuation of that of Ancient Greece' and by 1919 opined that Greece had the best claim to Constantinople.[15] All in all, the convergence between the domestic, nationally informed perspective of the byzantinists brought up within the nationalised Hellenic tradition and the 'Western' point of view, tapping into the Graecophile discourse of Byzantium, is more palpable and lasting than is usually acknowledged.

Between the 1870s and 1917, Byzantine studies in Russia thrived: its high scholarly quality, Dimitri Obolensky avows, was 'probably unrivalled by any other branch of historical studies in Russia'.[16] Unlike in western Europe, Russian Byzantine studies grew out of preoccupation with national history and Slavic studies rather than classical Greece and Rome, and were imbricated into the affirmation of Russian religious, national and imperial identity. In large part the exponential growth of scholarly interest in Byzantine antiquity was inherent in the very logic of the historical development of Russia, namely its foreign policy 'pull towards Constantinople' and the view inherited from medieval times about the Russian empire as the natural heir to Byzantium. As Russian expansion approached the lands of the eastern Mediterranean once dominated by Byzantium, this self-understanding was boosted by military and economic considerations, outlining Russia's 'most essential geopolitical interests there'. It has been argued, however, that this process resembled only superficially colonial interest, such as the French in the North African Christian antiquity (that similarly trailed the French armies) in that 'the rapid development of Byzantine studies was a function of Russia's striving to examine and understand its own past' and 'liberate kin peoples from an alien yoke'.[17]

Vasiliy G. Vasil'evskiy (1838–99), a student of the famous German classical historian Theodor Mommsen, is considered to be the real founder of modern Byzantine historical research in Russia, whose sagacious and broad-ranging occupation with Byzantine history went way beyond the Russian-Byzantine relations. In 1894 he founded the periodical *Vizantiyskiy vremennik*, which became the other esteemed forum of international

[15] Cameron 2016: 172.
[16] Obolensky 1966: 69. On the 'Golden Age' of Russian byzantinistics, see Vasiliev 1927: 539–42; Medvedev 2006: 107–37.
[17] Belyaev 2000: 189–90, 276.

In Search of the 'Scientific Method' 81

Byzantine studies next to *Byzantinische Zeitschrift*. Among his contemporaries were several first-class byzantinists. Vladimir Lamanskiy (1833–1914), who was renowned for his studies on the relations between Byzantium and the South Slavs, held that the 'Greco-Slavic world' was a cultural unit which should be studied as a separate and independent historical entity. Nikodim Kondakov (1844–1925) inaugurated work on and established an international school in Byzantine archaeology and art, the significance of which he saw in the adaptation and elaboration of all elements of the history of art between the sixth and twelfth centuries. Fyodor Uspenskiy (1845–1928), the most productive and versatile, if less fastidious, in this group, was the author of a massive three-volume *History of the Byzantine Empire* (1913–48).[18] An indication of the great impetus given to Russian Byzantine research was the establishment in 1915 of yet another periodical, *Vizantiyskoe obozrenie*, which, however, was halted in 1917.

Besides Byzantine–Slavic relations, both Vasil'evskiy and Uspenskiy paid special attention to the study of the social-economic aspects of Byzantine history, the landowning and tax regime in particular, which continued to be a favourite subject of research for their numerous followers. Both upheld vigorously the view that the Slavs' occupation of the Balkan Peninsula profoundly altered the social, economic and legal structure of the empire's European provinces. The 'byzantinisation' of the Roman empire, Uspenskiy maintained, manifested itself in three phenomena, which underwrote the essentially Hellenistic nature of the Roman and Byzantine empires: the replacement of the Latin tongue by the Greek, 'or properly speaking, Byzantine language', the struggle of nationalities for political supremacy and the new development of art and literature under the influence of oriental culture.[19] Uspenskiy was also concerned with situating Byzantium in world history, emphasising its role as a 'bastion of civilisation' with respect to Europe and its 'educative role' with respect to its Western and Slavic neighbours.[20] He used to stress the organic links between Russia, the Balkan Slavs and the Byzantine empire, which served to underline the antiquity of Russian presence on both sides of the Black Sea. For him, 'byzantinism' was a 'historical principle [that] directs the development of many states [in southern and eastern Europe] even in our own times, and expresses itself in a particular set of beliefs and political institutions, and, one might say, in special forms of class organisation and land relations'.[21]

Uspenskiy was straightforward in linking distant history and contemporary issues and fusing academic and political reasoning on the field of

[18] Vasiliev 1927: 539–41. [19] Vasiliev 1952: 37. [20] Üre 2014: 79. [21] Vasiliev 1952: 36–7.

82   In Search of the 'Scientific Method'

critical historiography. For him, the Eastern Question was a civilisational encounter between the East and the West that had begun with the Crusades and predestined Russia's role in solving it:

> We should be greatly mistaken were we to insist that it is within our power to avoid taking an active part in the settlement of matters connected with the Byzantine heritage. Although it usually depends upon the heir to accept or refuse the heritage left to him, still Russia's part in the Eastern question was bequeathed by history and cannot be changed voluntarily unless some unforeseen shock will give us the faculty to forget and stamp out the memory of the things which made us live, strive, and suffer.[22]

In fulfilling this vocation Uspenskiy initiated the Russian Archaeological Institute in Constantinople (1894–1914) – the first foreign archaeological institute in the Ottoman empire and the first set up outside Russia. A typical imperial orientalist enterprise placed under the patronage of the Russian ambassador to the High Porte, it was intended to act as a centre for Byzantine and Slavic studies focussed on the collection (and often relocation to Russian archives and museums) of ancient monuments, especially medieval manuscripts and icons, and on the study (and archaeology) of Byzantine history, theology, art and ancient Slavic history. Its 'soft power' pursuits were ambitious: by taking the lead in areas where Western scholarship was less developed – the history of Orthodoxy and the Slavs – Russia aspired to become on a par with 'Europe' as an enlightened and civilising great power and serve as a role model in science for the Balkan Slavs.[23] In essence, the academic study of Slavic antiquities and Eastern Christianity served several strategic purposes: it coincided with Russian political interests in the region and was deemed necessary both 'for the formation and proper guidance of Russian political and national consciousness', as A. Vasiliev phrased it, and for raising Russia's cultural and international scientific respectability, intrinsic to its great-power status. 'Russian scholarship could perform a great service to Russia's political influence in the East', read the proposal for the establishment of the archaeological institute in Constantinople. 'Before it is too late, before others have taken over lands in the East that belong to Russia, it is necessary that we take advantage of this slow but faithful weapon, which the Romano-German world has always resorted to in its fight with the Slavs.'[24]

---

[22] Vasiliev 1952: 36.   [23] Üre 2014: 125–69; Belyaev 2000: 211.

[24] Cited in Belyaev 2000: 190. On the expeditions and archaeological excavation carried out by the Russian Institute in Palestine, Syria, Lebanon, Egypt, Asia Minor, Constantinople and the Balkans, see Belyaev 2000: 203–12, 275–9.

Characteristic of the field of Byzantine studies in both western Europe and Russia during this period was the pre-eminence of those sub-fields that were primarily concerned with the processing and analysis of source material – 'skills rooted in the positivism of the nineteenth-century notion of "scientificity" which have dominated and moulded European and North American historiographical thinking'.[25] The emphasis on developing skills for 'critical text analysis' was one of the two major influences for which the critical historiographical schools in the Balkan countries were indebted to Western and Russian scholarship. The proven scientific value of such methods allowed byzantinists at large to view the way they generated knowledge of the past as being essentially neutral. This complacent self-perception was manifestly deceptive, as all too often – and this was the second major impact – extra-regional Byzantine research was coloured by political leanings, either in the direction of Helleno- or Slavophilia, or by being steeped into imperialist visions. If Western *Byzantinistik* was instrumental in congealing the idea of Hellenism's millennial continuity, its Russian counterpart successfully inculcated to its Balkan Slavic acolytes the understanding of Byzantine scholarship as indispensable for cultivating their nations' counter-Byzantine identity.

By the early twentieth century, the rigorous methodological conventions of professional historiography were well established in the four newly founded Balkan successor-states – Greece, Bulgaria, Serbia and Romania. This, however, did not necessarily entail a radical shift in historiographical discourse, where method was only one, and usually not the decisive, element. The turn of the nineteenth century was a period of progress and modernisation but also of an intense nationalist and irredentist fervour, culminating in the two Balkan wars (1912–13). There was a visible shift away from the frantic national mythology of the Romantic Age, and direct knowledge of the sources and specialised research featured high on the list of professional credentials. Even so, history remained pliantly responsive to the exigencies of the day and the national ideology in particular – indeed, many historians believed this link was indispensable and beneficial. As Nicolae Iorga memorably put it in his inaugural speech to the Romanian Academy in 1911, 'The historian is an old man with the experience of his nation'; his duty is to be 'a tireless recaller of national tradition, a witness to the unity of the folk over and above political and class barriers, a preacher of racial solidarity and discoverer of ideas towards which he himself should advance, giving an example to the youth who

[25] Jeffreys et al. 2008: 9.

84 In Search of the 'Scientific Method'

come after us'.[26] The positivist, scientific standards of research and 'truth' itself, from this point of view, came to buttress the fulfilment of the historian's moral duty to his nation, with all the decisive judgements of the past this duty entailed.

The introduction of the critical method in the national historiographies coincided with the emergence of the first cohort of professional Balkan medievalists and byzantinists in these countries. Departments or seminars for Byzantine studies were set up at Belgrade University (1906), Bucharest University (1907), Athens University (Chair of Byzantine Archaeology and Art, 1911) and Sofia University (1921, as part of a Chair in East European History). Romantic and dilettante scholarship began to be supplanted by 'scientific' historical scholarship, which often reiterated the underlying tenets of Romantic historiography while bringing in some new themes, perspectives and, most importantly, a claim to rigorousness.

Hellenes or *Romaioi*?

In Greece, as elsewhere in the Balkans, the last quarter of the nineteenth and the first two decades of the twentieth centuries marked the heyday of irredentist nationalism. Buoyed by the arguments of the most prominent Greek scholars, the Greek political class now openly associated the Great Idea with the resurrection of the Byzantine empire in the form of a great Greek state. The then paramount Greek medievalist (and member of the nationalist *Ethnike Etairia*, founded in 1894) Spyridon Lambros (1851–1919) stated in 1886 that 'historical Greece also contains Epirus, Thrace, Macedonia and Asia Minor. Any place that has been inhabited by Greeks, any place that has received the influence of Greek civilisation, is Greece'.[27] Nikolaos Politis (1852–1921), the founding father of Greek folklore studies (*laografia*), believed that 'to reoccupy Constantinople and again turn Saint Sophia into an Orthodox church – this is the apex of the Great Idea'.[28] Consequently, the centre of gravity in historical production moved from Hellenism to byzantinism. Or, as the historian Dimitrios Vikelas put it, 'the centre of Hellenism has been displaced. It has moved from Athens to Constantinople'[29] – 'the dream and hope of all Greeks', as Ioannis Kolettis called 'The City' back in 1844. For all these and many other intellectuals, scholarly vocation and scientific method were strongly interwoven with commitment to a political idea. Pavlos Karolidis (1849–1930), an eminent historian and orientalist and K. Paparrigopoulos's successor as the Chair of

---

[26] Cited in Boia 2001a: 64.   [27] Gazi 2000: 119–20.   [28] Politis 1928: 153.   [29] Vikelas 1885: 24.

Greek History at the University of Athens, pointed to the momentous political implications of scholarly byzantinism when stating that before and after the revolution of 1821 the Great Idea 'had as its guidelines for national and political unity Byzantine Hellenism and Byzantine traditions'; modern Hellenism looked upon Byzantium as its 'religious and at the same time national centre'.[30] As Richard Clogg has stated, 'the *Megali Idea* was not merely the dominant ideology of the nascent Greek state, it was in effect the *only* ideology'.[31]

By the outbreak of World War I, the continuous history of the Greeks, with the organic 'middle bond' of Byzantium, had been definitively consolidated. An increasing number of Greek scholars began to look for the origins of Greek institutions, customs and mentality in the Byzantine past. But as A. Liakos observes, a lengthy period of time passed between the acceptance of Byzantium as a part of the national narrative and the actual interest of historians in Byzantium and their use of it in national symbolism and representation. Byzantium was not rehabilitated in school textbooks until the end of the nineteenth century and, at the beginning of the twentieth, classicist aesthetic ideology was still determining the characteristics of the national ideology.[32] The Byzantine Museum was not established until 1914 and the Society for Byzantine Studies not until 1918; the first professors of Byzantine art and Byzantine history were only appointed at the University of Athens in 1912 and 1924, respectively. It was only after World War I that the Greek Archaeological Society began to turn its attention to Byzantine monuments. The first decrees classifying Byzantine churches and fortresses in Greece as archaeological monuments were issued in 1921, which led to the foundation, in 1935, of the Archive of the Byzantine Monuments in Greece.[33] Appropriation took place not only in stages but also in different fields: the theory of the unity of Greek history was transferred from the field of political history to the field of language and folklore.

The language question (*glossiko zitima*) – a major intellectual debate in modern Greece between purists, advocating an archaic, 'purified' form of Greek (*katharévoussa*), and demoticists, arguing for the literary codification of the vernacular – involved not just language but two different interpretations of the past.[34] The former insisted on Hellenism as a timeless national

---

[30] Augustinos 1977: 27.   [31] Clogg 1988: 254.   [32] Liakos 2008: 210, 224.
[33] Karamanolakis 2006: 320–4.
[34] On the Greek-language controversy, see Hering 1987: 125–94 and Mackridge 2009: 159–240. For an insightful discussion of the normative function of language in Greek nation-making, see Liakos 2008: 220–9.

86 In Search of the 'Scientific Method'

essence, capturing the connection to the glorious classical past, and on classical Greek as the authentic form of expression. The latter espoused the notion of *Romiosyne*, which recognised the demotic (vernacular) language as integral to the great chain of the Greek language – the epitome of the core values of Hellenism 'from Athenian philosophers to the illiterate captains of the Greek Revolution'.[35] In each of the two cases the written language aimed to express a different relationship between the modern Greeks and their ancient forebears. 'Whereas the proponents of *katharévousa* favoured the revival of ancient features after a period of hibernation, demotic demonstrated, for its supporters, the unbroken continuity of the Greek language and Greek culture since antiquity.'[36] Demoticism proposed the term *Romiosyne* instead of Hellenism in an attempt to mediate modern Greek identity to the classical past and adopt 'a more diffused, popular, and immediate feeling for identity, that of *Romaioi*, the self-nomination of Greeks during the Byzantine and Ottoman centuries'.[37] The broader implications of this issue were not lost on contemporaries: as Ioannis Psycharis (1854–1929), the most influential figure in the demoticist movement before World War I, phrased it, 'the language question is a political question . . . [it] comprises everything – country, religion, the whole national heritage . . . . Language and fatherland are one'.[38]

Against this background, it should not surprise that the long-standing language controversy did not impinge on the hegemonic version of Greek continuity and the official perception of the national past. Demoticism was basically aiming at the transformation of the discourse of national identity through literature and linguistic change and not through historical writing; for the demoticists, historiography was not a privileged terrain. 'The ancient Greek and the modern Greek are two moments of the same history', Psycharis argued, but 'the Greek written by the [purists] is not ancient Greek, it is the scholastic Greek, the exact historical equivalent of the Latin of the Middle Ages.'[39] The aim was thus to dissociate the practical question of language from the historical arguments to allow national literature to emerge. Two decades later, in 1915, Dimitris Glinos (1882–1943), one of the leaders of demoticism in the twentieth century, tried to (re-)fuse these two aspects of identity in the vein of the demoticist agenda by making a poignant distinction between 'the historical discipline', which he attributed to the purists' sterile way of mimicking Hellenism, and

---

[35] Liakos 2008: 227.   [36] Mackridge 2009: 185.   [37] Liakos 2008: 214.
[38] Cited in Augustinos 1977: 33.   [39] Psichari 1897: 222.

Hellenes or Romaioi? 87

'historicism' as espoused by the demoticists; that is, 'the conscious effort to retain the values of the past as absolute values for the present, or to transubstantiate them into seeds of a new life'.[40]

It was in this intellectual milieu that, since the latter part of the nineteenth century, new scholarly approaches, boosted by the institutionalisation of linguistics and ethnography as national sciences, came to dominate research on the Byzantine period. Now popular culture and memory, rather than (political) history, steered the study of Byzantium and the nationalisation of the Byzantine past. The new discipline of *laographia* (Politis's translation of the German term *Volkskunde*) was intended to provide evidence of Byzantium's contribution to both the transmission of Greek popular culture from ancient to modern times and the formation of a distinctive Greek *ethnie* via Christianity and the Hellenisation of the empire. To unearth the 'national epic' of the ancient and the Byzantine periods – in other words, to demonstrate that the legacies of ancient Greek myth and Byzantine history were encapsulated in modern Greek folksongs, folk tales, customs and beliefs – was the task that, down to at least the 1960s, supplied the rationale for this academic branch of study. As for the language issue, although the *katharévoussa* remained in official usage for decades to come, by the interwar period demotic had completely taken over literature. This made possible the incorporation of a rich literary tradition excluded until then from the literary canon, which foregrounded the unity of national culture above and beyond the discontinuities of political history and the inconsistencies of ethnic ('racial') history.

The prominence of cultural history, already noticeable in Paparrigopoulos's intention to outdo assertions about the racial impurity of the Greeks, was accentuated by the necessity to integrate the periods after the disintegration of the Byzantine empire in 1204 – the Frankish occupation (1204–61), the Venetian occupation (which in certain areas lasted until 1797) and the period of Ottoman rule – into the national narrative. Without the central backbone of political history, Greek historiography fell back on cultural history. Research became orientated towards the vernacular texts of the last centuries of the Byzantine empire, with special emphasis on literature and culture in Crete during the five centuries of Venetian rule. Byzantine scholars' contribution to the Italian humanism of the fourteenth and fifteenth centuries morphed into the myth that the Greeks were the cause of the revival of civilisation in modern Europe.[41] As Prime Minister Ioannis Kolettis

---

[40] Liakos 2008: 227–8. [41] Liakos 2008: 209, 212.

88 In Search of the 'Scientific Method'

memorably put it already in 1844, 'Greece is destined to enlighten the West with its decline and the East with its resurrection. The former task was fulfilled by our ancestors; the latter falls to us.'[42] By the turn of the century this powerful myth had become part and parcel of the Greek national myth.

Many of these tendencies and themes converged in the historical work of Dimitrios Vikelas (1835–1908). In Vikelas Byzantine Hellenism found one of its most passionate purveyors, not only in Greece but also abroad.[43] He made plain his admiration for Paparrigopoulos's monumental structure and committed himself to boosting the edifying aspects of Byzantine 'Helleno-Christian' civilisation, whose existence, he argued, 'guaranteed the preservation of the most precious interests of real civilisation'. Vikelas attributed a specific mission to Byzantium in that it had preserved civilisation at a time of barbarian onslaught on 'the rest of the world' and bequeathed it to the European Renaissance. The empire's main task 'was not to create but to save; and that mission she fulfilled for the benefit of the Europe of the future'. Far from being the decaying organism described by Montesquieu and Gibbon, its endurance demonstrated organisational power and vitality. The modern world owed it lasting gratitude, first, for continuing and handing down to posterity 'the civilisation of the ancients, modified by the Christian Religion' and, second, for saving Christian Europe from 'a slavery where the religion of the Koran would have been propagated by the sword'. Thanks to Byzantium, 'a martyr in the cause of the human race', and its centuries-long battle against the Muslims, western Europe had the time to develop its strength.[44] Sadly, however, 'the fall of Constantinople [under the Ottomans] was in great part the work of that very Europe which owed and owes her so much'. For Vikelas, 'the most deplorable epoch in the history of the Byzantine Empire . . . was that in which it was exposed to the influence of the Crusaders, and thus brought into contact with Western Europe'. He was ultimately grateful for the failure of the Western Crusaders to take permanent possession of Constantinople, for otherwise 'the consequences might have been even more fatal to the free development of the purely Hellenic genius than has been the Ottoman sword': the Greeks 'would have lost the traditions and memories of their own

---

[42] Dimaras 1982: 406.
[43] Vikelas's major works were translated into French, German and English (see, e.g., Bikelas 1890 and La Grèce byzantine 1893). He also published regularly in widely read scholarly journals like *La Nouvelle Revue*, *Scottish Review* and *Revue des deux mondes*.
[44] Bikelas 1890: 3–4, 27–34.

Hellenes or Romaioi?

ancient glories' and their faith and would have become a 'hybrid mixture of Eastern and Western races'.[45]

Significantly, Vikelas declared that his fellow countrymen had given Fallmerayer's theory a great deal more attention than it deserved and invested too much patriotic zeal in refuting 'the whimsical fancy in question, and denounc[ing] its author, upon every possible occasion'. Even supposing, for the sake of argument, that Fallmerayer was right in asserting that Hellas was flooded by Slav immigration, Vikelas maintained, it would have been no disgrace to the Hellenes to receive an infusion of foreign blood. On the contrary, such mixtures provided many great nations in modern history with the union of qualities that had raised them high. Moreover, regardless of whether the Slavs spread across Greece or not, they had since been completely absorbed. 'The entirely and exclusively Hellenic character of all the features, physical and intellectual, presented by the present inhabitants of the country, is a most striking fact, almost unique in history, a glorious mark of our race, and a wondrous proof of the intensity of our national vitality.' Far from violating historical continuity, therefore, the fact that even the Byzantine emperors lacked racial ties to Pericles or Philopoimen underscored the power 'of the solidarity which Byzantinism had effected with Hellenism', for it was the transmission not of the pure Hellenic stock but of 'the spirit of Hellenism' that really mattered.[46] Judging from the continued frantic reactions on behalf of Greek racial continuity and against Fallmerayer's thesis, this argument seems not to have gained much traction at the time. But it definitely spelled out the actual problem the Bulgarian argument faced when trying to exploit the thesis to its own ends – namely, the historical reality of the Slavs' complete assimilation in the territories later constituting the Kingdom of Greece, a reality that reverberated painfully with the cultural assimilation of many well-off Bulgarians in the Greek nationality in more recent times.

Nor did Spyridon Lambros – the aforementioned leading pre-war representative of the 'scientific study' of Greek history and briefly prime minister of Greece during World War I – challenge the romanticist narrative as contrived by Zambelios and Paparrigopoulos. But drawing on the theoretical and methodological principles of German historicism and the French positivist school, he transformed the Romantic historical discourse into a coherent taxonomic system. Claiming meticulous and critical use of sources, Lambros asserted the organic link between the different periods of

---

[45] Bikelas 1890: 12, 18–19, 34, 39–40. [46] Bikelas 1890: 22–3, 61.

90 In Search of the 'Scientific Method'

Greek history, among which Byzantium loomed large: 'Christian Greece, which, under the banner of the cross, fought for freedom is more important than ancient Greece. The Roman domination, the Byzantine kingdom and Christianity unified the differences and assuaged the passions.'[47] Underwriting Paparrigopoulos's assumption that 'the desire for national unity ... has its roots in our medieval history', Lambros saw the Byzantine era as crucial for the national formation and self-definition of the Greeks. He was therefore frustrated by the Byzantines' own deficit of historical consciousness, complaining that 'analysing the Byzantines' national feelings in their historiography and the rest of their literature, we come across major inconsistencies. Although as linguists, orators, and scholars they were perfect Greeks, as far as their historical consciousness is concerned they were simply Christians and members of the Roman civitas'.[48] But although they described themselves as Roman and Christian, the Byzantines' actual identity was Greek – an abstruse argument enjoying wide currency in byzantinist literature to this day. Lambros exerted himself to bring out this suppressed 'reality', while seeking to put his work, and Byzantine studies generally, on a solid scientific basis in terms of collecting and analysing primary sources – 'a scientific work', he wrote, 'that I am glad to describe as a purely Greek one'.[49]

A major focus of Lambros's research was the history of the Peloponnese – the core province of the new nation-state and the 'research base' of Fallmerayer's theory. However, Lambros's interest was spurred by ambitions greater than a mere rebuttal of Fallmerayer. He aimed to demonstrate that, following the capture of Constantinople by the Fourth Crusade in 1204, the Peloponnese became the centre of activity of the last Byzantine dynasty, the Paleologues, thus making a case for the continuation of the empire, along with Greek ethnic dominance, in the area. The core of the future nation-state was thus highlighted as the legitimate successor of Byzantium after its disintegration.[50] In this way Lambros set the frame for a key argument, widely shared by later generations of historians, that the Greek 'national idea' had emerged at the time of the Paleologue dynasty and was focussed on the future national centre of the Greeks.

---

[47] Lambros 1902: 64.   [48] Gazi 2000: 93.

[49] Gazi 2000: 94. Lambros spared no effort in collecting manuscripts and other sources, introduced a course on palaeography at the University of Athens and set up a specialised journal in Byzantine and post-Byzantine studies, *Neos Hellenomnemon*, which became one of the most influential Greek historical periodicals.

[50] Gazi 2000: 97–8.

Lambros saw his efforts at securing scientific status and quality for Greek byzantinism as an important national task. He also intended to establish a respectable place for Greek scholarship in 'historical science abroad' which, as Paparrigopoulos had bitterly noted in 1879, 'had not yet admitted the historical unity of the Greek nation'.[51] Lambros made explicit his intention to shift the centre of the writing of national history from outside to inside the nation when stating, 'Western scholars have undertaken the systematic illumination of a past which is the past of the Greek nation itself. For this reason, it is our obligation, for reasons not only scientific but also national, to construct this building to which so far we have made only small contributions.'[52] This appeal and the byzantinist school that Lambros left behind did not go unheeded inside and outside Greece. His prodigious activity has been closely associated with the inception of professional Byzantine studies in Greece and acclaimed for having 'given substance to what had hitherto been isolated, groping, crumbled-into-dust research efforts'.[53]

Around the turn of the nineteenth century, Byzantine studies in Greece, which until then had focussed mostly on history, linguistics and ethnography, began to infiltrate other disciplines such as philosophy, literature, art history and theological and political thought (as shown in the works of scholars such as Athanasios Papadopoulos-Kerameus, Konstantinos Sathas and Ioannis Sakellion). Alongside his main work on editing Byzantine sources, which earned him the fame of co-founder of Byzantine and post-Byzantine studies in Greece next to Lambros, Konstantinos Sathas (1842–1914) initiated a 'Medieval Library' that presented various Byzantine authors to a broader public. The aforementioned D. Vikelas founded the Society for Dissemination of Useful Books in order to publicise the works of scholars delving into Byzantine topics.[54] Significantly, between the Greek military debacle in 1897 and the Young Turk revolution of 1908, experienced by the Greeks as a period of national humiliation, was a time when the 'memory' of Byzantium spilled far beyond the world of scholarship into a much broader intellectual and performative field. Byzantine themes and admiration for what Constantin Cavafy called 'our glorious byzantinism' entered poetry (Kostis Palamas and Cavafy) and historical novels (by, among others, Alexandros Papadiamantis and Penelope Delta). In the traumatic post-1897 years, this broader interest in Byzantium was connected to the rise of a new kind of nationalism – neo-Romantic and

---

[51] Paparrigopoulo 1879: 7.   [52] Gazi 1998: 119–20.   [53] Laurent and Dalleggio 1949: 91.
[54] Rados 2005: 50–1.

92   In Search of the 'Scientific Method'

anti-rationalist – that rejected the supremacy of classical Greece and the emulation of the West.[55]

Byzantinism versus Authenticity: The Procrustean Bed of Bulgarian Historicism

As in Greece, the positivist paradigm shift in Bulgarian historiography did not lead to amending the key notions pervading Romantic history-writing. Marin Drinov (1838–1906) is considered the first representative of the 'critical-historical method', who had overcome the Romantic phase in Bulgarian historiography and imposed an 'impartial and critical attitude toward the [historical] sources'.[56] From such positions he fully subscribed to both Fallmerayer's 'compelling evidence' confirmed by 'the unbiased science' and the idea of the deleterious effects of byzantinism on medieval Bulgaria. The main conduit of the latter was the Greek high clergy, with its wasteful life and penchant for intrigues – a reflection of the era, in which Drinov was writing and which saw the peak of the Greek-Bulgarian ecclesiastical conflict, rather than of his 'unbiased method'.[57] He stuck to the dominant thesis about medieval Bulgaria's relentless fight with Byzantium for the preservation of its political and cultural independence. Several Bulgarian tsars – Simeon, Samuil, Asen and Ivan Asen II – tenaciously strove to capture the capital of the empire, 'which they wanted to turn into a Slavic capital'. The Bulgarians were the first among the Slavs to confront and begin absorbing Byzantine civilisation. Unlike most of his predecessors, however, Drinov insisted that the medieval Bulgarians 'assimilated but did not blindly obey' this civilisation. In contrast to other 'new-European nations' which, by adopting Christianity, surrendered their conscience to Rome or Byzantium, the Bulgarians 'immediately endeavoured to establish their own national Church as entirely independent from both Rome and Byzantium'. They also acquired a 'national alphabet that, as far back as the tenth century, tried to catch up with Byzantine literature, the richest and, so to say, the most fashionable at that time'.[58]

The Balkan Slavs, who were 'forcibly bound to the Greek church and the Byzantine political and social life', another eminent representative of the turn-of-the-century Bulgarian historiography seconded,

> did not undergo major intellectual changes. Byzantinism impacted mainly the literature, the state order and lustre, but it failed to penetrate the mass of

---

[55] Augustinos 1977.   [56] Nikov 1920–1: 300–1; Dujčev 1966: 77.   [57] Drinov 1909: 42–4.
[58] Drinov 1915: 24–6.

Byzantinism versus Authenticity

the population, who continued to observe the patriarchal customs of fraternal, congenial arrangements that characterised the ancient Slavs. The bleak and dreary Byzantine literature, with its scholastic orientation and lifelessness, found response only among the clerics and the scribers, at the same time as the Byzantine state order, by eliminating the democratic Slavic arrangements, raised to the top an unrestrained autocrat surrounded by the glory and sheen of the Byzantine emperors.[59]

Detrimental byzantinism was thus largely restricted to the clerics and the court, whose economic and cultural oppression, Drinov argued, caused Bogomilism to emerge in Bulgaria. In the following decades this thesis would extend byzantinism's adulterating impact to the social, political and cultural sphere and, at the same time, present Bogomilism as the genuine (democratic, progressive, rational) national religion, the precursor of the western European Reformation. This interpretation, tellingly, mirrors the Greek one about iconoclasm in eighth-century Byzantium: Paparrigopoulos considered the iconoclasts to be progressive and rational, defying religious fanaticism and promoting reforms and secular education; despite their defeat, their legacy lived on and strongly influenced the character of the Byzantine empire. Dimitrios Vikelas went one step further: for him, iconoclasm was a reformist movement that not only exercised a strong influence on Byzantine society and history but was also a point of departure for the Reformation in the West.[60] The Bulgarian and Greek historical narratives thus also clashed on the issue of 'parenthood' of the European ecclesiastical reform.

Vasil N. Zlatarski (1866–1935) was the most prominent Bulgarian medievalist and the personification of the 'critical (scientific) school' in historiography at the beginning of the twentieth century. His contribution to the foundation of the Bulgarian historical canon, crowned by his three-volume *History of the Bulgarian State in the Middle Ages* (1918–40), was comparable to that of Paparrigopoulos's *History* to the Greek national narrative. Against the backdrop of Zlatarski's systematic training (he was a student of the Russian Slavicist V. I. Lamanskiy and the byzantinist V. G. Vasil'evskiy) and critical method, it is striking to see how much he had inherited from the national-Romantic construal of Byzantium, which had taken shape between Paisiy and Drinov.

In his introductory lecture to the Bulgarian history course at the University of Sofia in 1895, devoted to 'The Main Periods in Bulgarian History', Zlatarski prefigured some of the main theses – or, more properly, ideologically

---

[59] Ivanov 1898: 102.   [60] Gazi 2000: 92; Argyropoulos 2001: 53.

94   In Search of the 'Scientific Method'

informed positions – that would form the bedrock of his *History*. He drew attention to the 'striking similarity' in the history of the First (861–1018) and Second (1185–1396) Bulgarian Kingdoms, most notably the spectacular rise and tragic fall of both. He began the search for the underlying reasons for this peculiar phenomenon by noting the 'global-historical importance' of the lands that the Bulgarians came to occupy – Thrace and Moesia, where 'the centuries-old antagonism between Hellenism and Romanism, between East and West [had begun], an antagonism that continues until today'. The settlement of the Slavs in these lands was tolerated at first by Byzantium because the empire aimed 'to use them as a shield against new barbarian invasions and attacks ... hoping that they would bow down before byzantin-ism and would merge with the [other] peoples of the empire'. However, these hopes were not fulfilled – the Bulgarians managed 'to create their own national foundations ... [the] beginnings of an independent culture and to differentiate themselves politically'. The Slavs who came under Bulgarian rule were dubbed 'Bulgarian Slavs' (or Slavs of the 'Bulgarian group'), while the incipient Bulgarian state was devolved the providential role of the Slavs' liberator from Byzantium – rescuing them from 'denationalisation' ('Hellenisation') – and unifier of the 'Bulgarian Slavs'. Accordingly, all wars waged against Byzantium before the reign of Simeon were described as wars for the 'liberation' and 'unification' of the Slavs.[61]

Against this nationally consolidating and politically robust state, Byzantium's military power was helpless, so it resorted to another weapon – Christianisation. However, the Bulgarians' conversion to Christianity was not, according to Zlatarski, the fruit of Byzantium's missionary activity, even less a foreign import, as his predecessors believed, but a conscious and carefully considered act aimed at accomplishing a threefold programme of national consolidation: 'political and cultural unification of the Balkan Slavs under the sceptre of the Bulgarian master', 'strengthening of central power' against the nobility and 'jolting the ethnic dualism [between Bulgars and Slavs] in favour of the Slav element'.[62] The main result of the adoption of Christianity from Byzantium (rather than Rome) was the 'establishment of a national church, through which the Bulgarian nation-ality was preserved' and the 'opening of a wide road to our people for a unique (*samobitno*) cultural-educational development on a national basis'. Likewise, the creators of the Slavic alphabet – the other 'milestone

---

[61] Zlatarski 1971: I/1, passim.
[62] Zlatarski 1971: I/2, 56–65. To this day, these three domestic motives, plus the one about the international legitimisation of the Bulgarian state, constitute the schoolbook explanation for the Bulgarians' Christianisation. See also Zlatarski 1895: 4–11.

Byzantinism versus Authenticity

in the imminent struggles of the Bulgarians for spiritual freedom' – acted not as Byzantine missionaries but as 'Slav apostles' and partook in the creation of a 'new cultural-historical type, the Slavobulgarian, which became a model for all Slavic- and non-Slavic Eastern European countries that were under the cultural influence of the Eastern Church'.[63] Thus the firm medieval foundation of the Bulgarian 'national spirit' that the contemporary Greek historians found wanting was forcefully asserted, and the universalistic cultural pretences of the 'Greeks' were dispelled.

In a salient agreement with the revolutionary Romantics of the previous period, Zlatarski considered the reign of Tsar Simeon – when the First Bulgarian Kingdom reached the peak of its territorial expansion and political strength – to be a betrayal of the 'national spirit' and the 'political and social life of the Slavo-Bulgarians'. It concerned Simeon's absolute autocracy and bureaucratisation, 'fully adopted in [their] Byzantine form', the glittering pomp and the privileges of the boyar estate, 'now dressed in the form of the Byzantine aristocracy with all its rights and prerogatives', and the clergy who 'adopted the Byzantine church hierarchy with all its privileges . . . and vices'. All this, according to Zlatarksi, caused deep social disruption and cultural estrangement that severed the political and spiritual elite from the people.[64] Since Byzantium proved unable to defeat the Bulgarian state, it set out to conquer it from the inside by infiltrating the Bulgarian court and government. After Simeon's death (927), this became 'the main task of Byzantine policy towards Bulgaria and remained so until the final demise of the empire'. The reign of Tsar Peter (927–69) ushered in a period of intensive penetration of byzantinism throughout the state machinery and a deepening of the split between the nation and its leaders. This rift led to the emergence and fast spread of the heretical teachings of Bogomilism – an expression of 'the popular protests . . . against the moral decay and indiscriminate imitation of everything non-Bulgarian, which the alien Byzantine influence harmful to the state had brought in'. The decadence at the top and the subversion at the bottom ultimately caused the country to fall under Byzantine domination in the eleventh century, 'when the full routine of the decaying empire came to reign'.[65] Zlatarski's reading of the significance of the long resistance of the 'Western Bulgarian Kingdom' under Samuil to Byzantine military pressure is meaningful:

> The main importance of Tsar Samuil in our history lies not only in the fact that he defended the independence of Bulgaria [for forty-five more years],

[63] Zlatarski 1971: I/2, 159–65.   [64] Zlatarski 1971: 520–5.
[65] Zlatarski 1971: 532–7, 600–2; Zlatarski 1895: 13.

96 In Search of the 'Scientific Method'

but also in the fact that ... he succeeded, through his many years of stubborn struggle with Basil II, to educate and raise his people in the spirit of freedom by opposing the destructive foreign influence, and to inspire in them a strong hatred for the cruel and ruthless conqueror of Bulgaria – Byzantium, and to everything Byzantine – a merit to which the preservation of the nationality of the Bulgarian people during the onerous Byzantine domination undoubtedly owes a great deal.[66]

Zlatarski went on at length about the Bulgarians' suffering and exploitation during the Byzantine domination of the former Bulgarian lands (1018–1185), especially with Byzantium's relentless pursuit of what he called a '[policy of] Romeisation', carried out, according to him, since the late eleventh century mainly by the Church of Constantinople. This Romeisation, however, failed to strike deep roots, and 'the Byzantine government and the Constantinople Church failed to achieve their ultimate goal – to denationalise the Bulgarian people through [their] cultural influence'.[67] The Second Bulgarian Kingdom (1185–1396), Zlatarski argued, displayed the same pattern as the first: as long as Byzantium was weakened by the Crusades, Bulgaria grew in prosperity and strength; once the empire was re-established and its influence in the Bulgarian court resumed, the Bulgarians headed down the road to their destruction: 'The Byzantines, by transferring to the Bulgarians their laws and literature, mores and vices, dragged their followers and disciples along with them in the common grave – under the Turkish yoke.'[68]

For Zlatarski, therefore, the political ascendancy, prosperity and cultural flourishing of the Bulgarian state were possible only during periods free of Byzantine influence. Conversely, Bulgaria's decline and ultimate demise became inevitable once its doors were open to the rotting power of byzantinism. All this is a remarkably faithful reiteration of the 'prescientific' Romantic interpretation of Bulgarian medieval history, as is Zlatarski's other main thesis: that the Byzantine influence infected only the court and the boyars, while 'the people always stayed away from it; [the people] were always hostile to it and upheld their [national] ideal'.[69] Bulgarian history thus ensued from the confrontation between 'two diametrically opposite currents': an internal, pushing towards ethnic differentiation, unification and development of national culture; and an external,

---

[66] Zlatarski 1971: I/2, 702–3.
[67] 'Romeisation', Zlatarski argued, was pursued mainly through the substitution of Church Slavonic with Greek and through the 'persecution of Bulgarian books'. See Zlatarski 1972: II, 252–366, 399–409.
[68] Zlatarski 1895: 12–14.   [69] Zlatarski 1895: 14.

with 'the constant pressure of foreign influence' always aimed against and aspiring to destroy the first current. Combined with the special position of Bulgaria in the eternal antagonism between 'East and West', these two currents defined the permanent features of Bulgarian history, which were also observable in Bulgaria's present.[70]

The interpretation of Bulgarian history and Byzantium's role in it, which Zlatarski elaborated on with the techniques of professional history, remained remarkably stable all the way from the 1890s through the wartime years to the radically altered political and intellectual context after World War I. But it also reveals a deep ambivalence, almost a schism, between two largely incompatible images of the Bulgarian medieval past – the political and cultural prominence of the First and Second Bulgarian Kingdoms and their imputed 'anti-national', 'Byzantine' character. The Bulgarian case perhaps best exemplifies the inherent and insurmountable problems of building a national narrative out of imperial material. The proposed 'compromise' – pitting the 'national' popular masses and the 'byzantinised' elite against each other – only aggravated the problem. There was still a long way to go before the claims to the symbolic capital of Byzantium – seen not as Greek but as Slavo-Byzantine – would attempt to redeem the Bulgarian historical imagery from its Procrustean bed.

Meanwhile, gestures in this direction were not altogether missing, yet, significantly, they did not come from historians. In an extensive review of D. Vikelas's *Historical Essays*, Ivan Shishmanov (1862–1928), an eminent Bulgarian literary scholar and ethnographer, outlined a perspective towards Byzantium and its impact consistent with that of the Greek author (and the budding Byzantine studies in western Europe and Russia) but still unpopular with the Bulgarian historians. Shishmanov applauded the fact that attitudes towards the Byzantine empire had shifted from regarding it as 'a political monster' and 'cultural swamp' (an attitude that he, too, attributed to the 'witty dialectics of Montesquieu and the subjective criticism of Gibbon') to being informed by 'a soberer look at the history of Byzantium and its importance to medieval culture'. 'The most recent historical critique', he wrote, 'arrives at results that are not far from a complete rehabilitation of the state that, until recently, bore the contemptuous name "*Empire de la décadence*".' This change of attitude was, according to him, 'a good sign of a sound, unbiased critique [and] well-founded objectivity'. It was beginning to implant the idea that 'Byzantium is far better than its reputation' and form 'a broad recognition for the benefits that Byzantium

---

[70] Zlatarski 1895: 14–15. See also Zlatarski 1920: 30–56.

98   In Search of the 'Scientific Method'

undoubtedly offered to Europe in its darkest times'. As far as the Slavs were concerned, Shishmanov saw Byzantium as their 'teacher and civiliser'. Interestingly, next to such forums of this new, enlightened attitude like *Byzantinische Zeitschrift* and *Vizantiyskiy vremennik*, Shishmanov named as 'the most sober Greek scientific historians' Paparrigopoulos, Sathas, Zambelios, Lambros, Skarlatos and Byzantios.[71] Yurdan Ivanov (1872–1947), a student of Shishmanov and an authority on Byzantine and Bulgarian medieval literature, also used to stress the beneficial 'strong and multidimensional impact of the Byzantine culture' and the 'advanced Byzantine empire' on the historical life of the Bulgarians.[72]

At the same time, in an essay discussing the 'tragedy' of the Balkans having skipped that 'great cultural-historical process', the Renaissance, Shishmanov attributed responsibility to more than just the Ottomans. Byzantium, he claimed, also had a share in this, since it

> failed to elevate humanity in Eastern Europe to new spiritual, artistic, moral and social heights, as this took place in Italy during the Renaissance and [the Age of] Humanism. Its merit lies elsewhere: in contrast to Rome, it converted to Christianity and civilised specifically the barbarian tribes by using their native dialects, which was later of great importance for the development of their national literatures.[73]

In Byzantium and the Balkans, Shishmanov surmised, even before they fell to the Ottomans, there failed to develop the large-scale and deep socioeconomic changes that had conditioned and prepared the Western Renaissance – above all, the transition from subsistence to capitalist economy and the emergence of a 'conscious citizenship'. The 'weak socioeconomic development' was what made these areas too 'immature to embrace the innovative ideas of the Renaissance', a fact most clearly demonstrated by 'Byzantium, which really has certain merits for the genesis of the Italian Renaissance, [but] failed to release itself for a long time, even after the fall of Constantinople, from the medieval scholastics. For the influence of one culture over another always involves some similarity in social psychology and in the social order'.[74] Shishmanov thus moved the beginnings of the Balkan 'socioeconomic backwardness' back to the pre-Ottoman, Byzantine past – a thesis that would come to the attention of (mostly economic) historians only during the last quarter of the twentieth century.

---

[71] Shishmanov 1894–5: 4–5, 210–12.   [72] Ivanov 1982: I, 157–82.   [73] Shishmanov 1965: 76–7.
[74] Shishmanov 1965: 78.

'Evolution towards Byzantium'

The new generation of Serbian historians, who came of age professionally at the turn of the century, lived at a time of intense national-political ferment. Serbia had emerged victorious from the Customs war with Austria-Hungary (1906–8), which added to the assertiveness and nerve of Serbian nationalism. In 1905 the Croats and Serbs of the empire concluded a coalition that made a future South Slav union look less unlikely. In Bosnia and Herzegovina, which was administered since 1878 and annexed in 1908 by the Habsburg monarchy, agitation was rising, not without considerable help from the Serbian state. The 'military propaganda' in Ottoman Macedonia and the adjacent areas (also called 'Southern' or 'Old Serbia') was in full swing. As could be expected, few Serbian historians could, or wanted to, remain detached from the contemporary 'needs and interests' of their nation in such critical times. The way they interpreted these interests and the 'lessons' they drew from the medieval past were not always congruent, but they were all motivated by the ambition to buttress with the instruments of modern science the role that Serbia was supposed to play in the impending transformations in the Balkans.

At the end of the nineteenth century, the Romantic approach to history, and Srećković in particular, encountered severe criticism from the critical school of Serbian historiography. Its founder, Ilarion Ruvarac (1832–1905), and the Austro-Hungarian Czech historian Konstantin Jireček (1854–1918), whose two-volume *Geschichte der Serben* (1911, already translated into Serbian in 1912) became the cornerstone of critical Serbian medieval historiography, challenged the romantic glorification of the medieval past and pleaded for an objective knowledge and critical use of historical sources. Among their illustrious followers were Stojan Novaković, Ljubomir Kovačević, Jovan Radonić and Stanoje Stanojević, who, more insistently and explicitly than their predecessors, identified Serbian history as inseparable from that of Byzantium. In 1890 a group of historians at the Great School, the predecessor of Belgrade University (instituted in 1905), proposed the creation of a new chair with the unusual title 'History of the Middle Ages, with a View to the History of Byzantium'. The idea did not materialise because of a lack of resources but was suggestive of, as the supporting argumentation went, 'the various permanent and close connections of the Serbian lands with Byzantium'.[75] A Seminar for Byzantine

---

[75] Maksimović 1988: 655–6; Pirivatrić 2010: 483.

100 In Search of the 'Scientific Method'

Studies was set up in 1906, which until after World War I focussed primarily on Greek language and palaeography. It was generally recognised that, as one of Serbia's first trained byzantinists Božidar Prokić put it, the Serbs 'are absolutely unable to understand their medieval national history, their cultural and political institutions in the old Serbian state without comprehensive knowledge of the Byzantine state .... To get to know Byzantine history means to get to know our own life and past.'[76]

A foremost Serbian medievalist at that time and into the interwar period, Stanoje Stanojević (1874–1937), who had worked with F. Uspenskiy at the Russian Archaeological Institute in Istanbul and K. Krumbacher in Munich, had the ambitious idea of writing a ten-volume history of *Byzantium and the Serbs*. The first nine volumes were to survey political relations from the settlement of the Slavs until the fall of Constantinople in 1453, while the last one was to be devoted to 'the overall cultural impact of Byzantium on the Serbian people'. Only the first two volumes ultimately came out (in 1903 and 1906), but they comprised some key historiographic theses that would steer the field in the decades to come. In his general introduction, Stanojević spelled out with clarity and force the importance of the Serbs' historical relationship with Byzantium:

> The entire state organisation of the Byzantine Empire and its whole culture, material as well as intellectual, with all their results, had exerted a strong influence on the Serbian people right from the moment of its arrival in its new homeland. ... Undoubtedly, the Byzantine empire impacted more strongly than all other factors both its political and cultural history. ... The entire political and cultural life of the Serbs until the arrival of the Turks is so intertwined with Byzantine history and imbued with Byzantine influences that [one can say that] Byzantine-Serbian relations during the first ten centuries of Serbian history constitute the core of the history of the Serbian people.[77]

A combination of political resistance (continuous 'struggle for freedom and independence, struggle for emancipation from Byzantium', as Stanojević put it) and cultural emulation (partaking in the 'grand civilisational power of Byzantium') was as characteristic of the Serbian narrative as it was of the Bulgarian. The protean notion of 'Serbo-Byzantine' legacy, which the Romantic historiography had already forged, sought to strike a balance between sharing in the Byzantine heritage and asserting national authenticity. The Serbian Middle Age, Stanojević argued, was the period when the Serbian nation 'moved more and more into the History of

[76] Prokić 1906: 56.   [77] Stanojević 1903: i, iii.

'Evolution towards Byzantium'

Europe and the History of Mankind'. And even if the Serbs' connections with 'the West' also grew during this period,

> the political relations with Byzantium, the struggle against its dominance and the internal disputes in the individual Serbian states around the cultural and political relations with Byzantium continued to absorb the main forces of the Serbian People. ... The organisation of the state, church, army and administration, religion, literature, education and many elements of material culture the Serbian people had borrowed from Byzantium – either completely or by grafting them onto their national institutions, onto their distinctive national features.[78]

The botanical metaphor of 'grafting', as Stanojević's writings indicate, suggested the opposite of cultural mimicry: a creative and original symbiosis – a superior 'Serbo-Byzantine style', distinguishing the Serbian existence politically as well as artistically. Moreover, by 'Byzantine culture' Stanojević meant the combination of several disparate elements: the material culture of the Thraco-Illyrian tribes, Celtic culture, Hellenic culture imbued with Eastern elements, and Roman culture. It was this 'aggregate' of outstanding ancient legacies that impacted the Serbs so massively.[79] Stanojević saw the Byzantine state as a controversial permutation of creative and destructive factors that constantly fought for predominance, hence its continuous fluctuation 'between strength and malaise, vigour and decay'. But despite the great ordeals and crises it had experienced during its long history, the empire had always managed to withstand them and recover its forces. The reason, according to Stanojević, was that 'it was constantly resuscitated by the fresh blood of the various tribes that settled on its territory'. From them it drew not only its strength and tenacity but also its 'unusual capacity for recuperation, revival and rejuvenation'.[80]

Not all Serbian historians were prepared to subsume Serbian history primarily within the Byzantine sphere of radiation, though. Like Stanojević, Jovan Radonić (1873–1956), another major representative of the critical historiographical school, was eager to highlight the growing self-determination, expansion and strengthening of the Serbian state within the Byzantine cultural sphere, the setting up and later independence of the Serbian Church (whereby 'already at that time the Serbian nationality began to identify with Orthodoxy'), and Serbia's rise to 'the chief power in the Balkan peninsula' in the late thirteenth and early fourteenth

---

[78] Stanojević 1903: I, iii–iv.　　[79] Stanojević 1903: I, ii–iii; Stanojević 1906: II, 110, 119.
[80] Stanojević, 1903: I, 112; II, 128.

centuries, which brought about rapid penetration of the Byzantine 'culture and fine and sophisticated way of life'.[81] He, too, pointed out that although Byzantium, then the main cultural centre in eastern Europe, exerted a powerful influence on the spiritual and material culture of the 'young and fresh Slavic peoples', the Serbian spirit was not content with simply imitating the Byzantine style and demonstrated a 'striving for independent creativity in literature, legislation and architecture'.[82] Stefan Dušan 'came forward as a successor to the Byzantine emperors' aiming at the conquest of the remaining part of Byzantium. Radonić admitted that Dušan arranged his court 'fully in a Byzantine fashion' and that the incorporation of numerous Greek populations impelled him to adopt new legislation that took into account the different (from the Serbian) structure of Byzantine society. But for all that, he chose to compare medieval Serbia not with Byzantium but with the medieval states in 'western Europe'. This was also the case when he discussed the rigorously centralised political structure of Dušan's empire or Serbia's social strata in the thirteenth and fourteenth centuries. In contrast to Novaković, as we will shortly see, he juxtaposed the rule of the Nemanjić dynasty against Byzantine absolutism, stressing the role played in state affairs by 'the court dignitaries and the state assembly'.[83] In the realm of culture – the area conventionally considered to have been most strongly influenced by Byzantium – Radonić preferred to emphasise the intermediary location of Serbia between the two great cultural centres, Rome and Byzantium. Byzantine influence on Serbian architecture and religious paintings was 'crucial', yet Romanic influence was also present. Most importantly, since the latter half of the fourteenth century, growing emancipation from Byzantine patterns and aspiration for a proper Serbian creativity in literature and material culture were becoming increasingly visible.[84]

Radonić, therefore, appeared reluctant to either demonise Byzantium or repossess its symbolic cultural status for Serbia. He was keen instead to assert Serbia's pivotal place between 'the East and the West', having benefited from the culture of each yet ultimately moving towards its own original culture and patrimony.

It is not hard to detect, in both Stanojević and Radonić, as indeed in Serbian historiography generally from the turn of the twentieth century through the interwar period, a tension between the idea of cultural

---

[81] Radonić 1912: 6–8, 10–12.   [82] Radonić 1912: 11–12.
[83] Radonić 1912: 14–18, 21. Radonić also discussed the trade relations only with the 'West'.
[84] Radonić 1912: 19–21.

'Evolution towards Byzantium'

diffusion, intimating a hierarchy between radiating cultural centres (Constantinople or Rome) and emulative 'peripheral' cultures, on the one hand, and the thrust to assert the creative potential of the 'receiver', on the other. Aleksandar Ignjatović's observation about the pervasive presence of the theory of diffusion in pre-World War II Serbian history-writing can be extended to all Balkan historiographies.[85] The diffusionist paradigm, particularly in its German rendition during the first half of the twentieth century, provided the perspective from which the Byzantine 'influence' on the Balkan cultures and their civilisational 'transition' were explained. Up to a point, it meant 'upgrading' of these societies in that it ensured their inclusion in a cultural zone of 'higher order', marked by three prestigious legacies: Hellenic culture, Roman statecraft and Christian faith. Simultaneously, however, it underwrote these societies' inferior position in relation to the Byzantine centre. Notwithstanding certain differences in timing, intensity or interpretation, the thesis about the 'byzantinisation' of Balkan societies was characteristic of all Balkan historiographies save the Turkish. What distinguishes the Serbian case is the early effort at conjuring up a counterbalancing thesis – one insisting on the creative understanding and refinement, not blind emulation, of the Byzantine cultural-political model, whereby the continuity of empire meant not simply conquering Byzantium but the transfer and rejuvenation of its civilisation through a vibrant national culture. Similar interpretations, each with its own set of 'national creativity' elements, would make their way into the Bulgarian and Romanian historiographies after World War II, when the notion of acculturation into the local culture would overshadow that of diffusion.

The most unorthodox perspective on our subject matter around the turn of the century came from Stojan Novaković (1842–1915). From the 1880s to the first decade of the 1900s he was, next to Ruvarac, the greatest authority in the study of the Serbian past. His dissenting premise, one that strongly impacted his interpretation of the role of Byzantium in Serbian history, concerned above all the national consciousness and its relation to state-building in the Middle Ages.

Without confronting the Romantics directly, Novaković sought to expose the irrelevance of projecting modern notions about nation and state into the past. Srećković, for example, had argued that the Serbian kings had launched wars not to invade and conquer but to 'liberate and unify the Serbian lands ... [into] a single organic state', and that the

---

[85] Ignjatović 2016: 425–31.

104 In Search of the 'Scientific Method'

Serbian 'state organisation derived from purely national principles'.[86] Novaković, however, challenged the very idea that the congruence of ethnic and state boundaries was at all relevant for the medieval Balkans and hence that 'national unification' had anything to do with state interests.

The Eastern Roman empire, he argued, was built on the monarchic, imperialist and centralist basis of Roman law. (Novaković rarely called the empire 'Byzantine' and insisted on the preservation of the 'old Roman order' throughout its duration.) The major defect of this system was that it soon turned into a personal and despotic rule, where the only source of power was the emperor. That same principle of state was adopted 'as dogma' by all those who aspired to the Byzantine throne, whereby 'autocracy seized and became entrenched in the whole Balkan peninsula'. For Novaković this autocratic principle was responsible, first, for the inability of either the Greeks or the Slavs to assimilate and unify the various ethnicities (such as the Vlachs or Albanians) into bigger national entities, in contrast to the developments in the other parts of the former Roman empire, and second, for the failure of feudalism to develop and strike roots in these areas.[87] The local nobilities drew their strength not from their status, as in the West, but from the riches and the lands they could capture. Under such conditions, it was only natural that all Balkan monarchs should pursue the imperialist idea, striving to gain control of the whole peninsula, without much heed for the mutual exclusion of their designs – a fact that opened the door to outside invaders.[88]

Nationality had little role to play in this situation: it served only to distinguish the origins of a king, emperor or state, but the people were fully subdued and 'did not count for anything'. A conquered land always followed its new master, and the nationality to which this master belonged was also the nationality of the populations inhabiting his lands. Thus the Bulgarian Kingdom kept its ethnic name despite the complete assimilation of the Bulgarians into the Slav mass, and in Dušan's empire the Greek dignitaries had no problem agreeing to obey their new Serbian sovereign as long as their privileges remained intact.[89] 'We should never disregard', Novaković wrote, 'the state of subdued passivity in which the sense of nationality existed at that time. The main characteristic feature of the Middle Ages was the noble, aristocratic supremacy or organisation.'

[86] Srećković 1888: II, 810–11.
[87] Here Novaković echoes the then-prevailing views in Byzantine studies in Europe about the 'lack of feudalism' in Byzantium, views that were later challenged from Marxist and non-Marxist positions.
[88] Novaković 1966: 87–91.   [89] Novaković 1966: 92–5.

'Evolution towards Byzantium'

What mattered was the state, while nationality 'was a historical factor deprived of any moral initiative'. Novaković's final conclusions run against the grain of the historiographical canon: first, 'the sense of nationality among the masses during the Middle Ages was missing completely'; second, this sense was embodied only by 'the high classes, the rulers, the nobles (aristocracy) and the clergy'; third, and as a result, the state borders between the Bulgarians and the Serbs, who showed almost no national differences at that time, 'had always indicated the borders between their nationalities as well'. Therefore, Novaković inferred, if history was to serve as *magistra vitae*,

> we should instantly accept as a first teaching, a final rule for all modern tasks [that] the Middle Ages must be left aside; we must seek [to define] our position on the basis of the contemporary state of affairs, regardless of what had been in the past; we must rely on a real and living power . . . .. The unsavoury past should remain history: the life of the people must be rearranged freely and, without second thoughts, be directed to where the fundamentals of modern criticism lead.[90]

What Novaković actually pleaded for, much like other contemporaries in the Balkans such as Ivan Shishmanov in Bulgaria or the *Junimea* circle in Romania, was not divorce between historiography and nationalism but shifting the battlefield of competing national programmes from 'medieval-historical' to 'ethnographic' and 'linguistic rights', themselves not deficient in, albeit more recent, history. Moreover, when stressing the irrelevance of the South Slavs' medieval past to their present, Novaković was primarily concerned with the divisions between Serbs and Croats. While admitting that 'Serbdom and Orthodoxy formed an indivisible whole', he bemoaned the fact that, at least from the tenth century, the two rival religious propagandas, the Byzantine and the Roman, had split 'the same people with the same language into two distinct cultures and two distinct literatures'. Since then, the Serb people and the Croat people had been at loggerheads fighting a life-or-death combat, 'one for the love of Byzantium, the other for the love of Rome, while at the same time Byzantium and Rome never ceased to treat both with contempt'.[91] (Interestingly, Novaković considered the Bulgarians to have been far more fortunate in this respect: since from the very beginning they had come under the exclusive influence of the Byzantine culture, it was natural that all their rulers should look towards the Eastern Roman throne; 'the

[90] Novaković 1966: 96–7.   [91] Novaković 1966: 69–70.

106   In Search of the 'Scientific Method'

rivalry between Constantinople and the Bulgarian state concerned not civilisation but only politics'.[92])

Furthermore, Novaković directly challenged two myths underpinning the Serbian national narrative – the myth of the ethnic and communal feeling of the Slavic multitude that flooded the Balkans from the sixth century and the myth of the Serbian kings' perennial drive to unify all the Serbs in a single and unitary Serbian state as the rationale for their continued confrontation with Byzantium. The Slavic tribes that invaded the lands of the Byzantine empire, he argued, were fully missing both an 'ethnic sentiment' and a 'sense of community'. This plundering and pillaging mass 'bereft of any form or organisation' were *not Slavs but Slavic tribes and brotherhoods*, who lived in a blissful state of anarchy and were strongly attached to their 'particularistic tribal life'. This portrayal fitted poorly with the erstwhile idyllic picture of social harmony and solidarity inherent to the 'pre-byzantinised' Serbian society. Nor was there, Novaković maintained, any attempt at political or national consolidation, or 'trace of any kind of political ideas that would have suited such a numerous people'. Had the Byzantine statesmen showed a little more skill and diligence, they would have found it easy to vanquish and organise these Slavic settlers as they wished. As it happened, they 'tried with all the means of their civilisation to subdue the barbarians', and their effort did not miss the mark: lacking unity, the Slavs readily adapted to the Roman administrative system and adopted the Byzantine civilisation, a fact that 'exerted a strong impact on the development of this ethnic mass' and on 'the very formation of its nationality'.[93] The idea of the state was introduced among the Slavs of Byzantium by the 'Turanian Bulgars', who supplied them with the 'adhesive' they were lacking and a common orientation – first towards building a powerful state and then towards 'conquering the entire Eastern Roman empire'. In this, 'the Bulgar chiefs did not think in the least of the South Slavs, of their convergence or national idea. They thought about how to get their hands on power in Constantinople, such as it was, with all its elements and entire organisation'. Without openly stating it, here Novaković challenged one of Zlatarski's main theses: the Christianisation of the Bulgarian Slavs and the adoption of Byzantine learning in a Slavic form, he argued, had nothing to do with nation-building; they were adopted in order to sanction the Bulgarian tsars'

---

[92] Novaković 1966: 104.
[93] Novaković 1966: 128–31 (original emphases). Novaković used to stress the role in this respect of the adoption of 'Byzantine Christianity' above all as a 'life-world' moulding every aspect of individual and social life, hence nationality was closely identified with the Orthodox faith (1966: 139–40).

'Evolution towards Byzantium'

exercise of power and conquest of Constantinople. At stake was into whose hands, Bulgarian or Greek, the entire government of the empire would fall, and nothing else.[94]

Remarkably, Novaković considered not the direct emulation of Byzantium but the 'example and political concepts of the Bulgarians and their tsars Simeon and Samuil' to have been decisive not only in building the Serbian state but also in shaping its relations with Constantinople. Ever since its inception, he repeatedly stressed, Serbia had followed in Bulgaria's footsteps in pursuing a fully independent power that would strengthen and expand the state and thus 'satisfy the selfish whims of medieval proprietors [i.e. the Serbian rulers]'. And since the Magyars, Germans and Venetians were barring the Serbs' advancement to the northwest, the only option for expansion was to the southeast, towards the centre of the Byzantine empire and Macedonia. Despite the belief of many Serbs to the contrary, Novaković pointed out, none of their leaders at that time were at all concerned about the 'sense of nationality' or were moved by the vision of uniting all the Serbs in a single 'national state'. What they cared about was the seizure of power and the existing titles (for new ones were not allowed); the imperial title came with the capture of the bigger part of the empire.[95] In a way, Novaković, similar to Zlatarski, thus implied the existence of a gap between the Serbian people and the Serbian elite that had been caused by the elite's byzantinisation. But for him that gap was not caused by cultural alienation (as it was for Zlatarski) – indeed, in his analysis Orthodoxy stood out as the only binding social glue in the Serbian society of that time. For him a gap had emerged from the non-democratic and non-national principles of the statehood emanating from Byzantium and imitated by its rivals.

These were the ideas that, according to Novaković, connected the Serbs with Byzantium and 'grew from the complete adoption of the Byzantine civilisation and the Byzantine religious ideas'. The resulting picture, although not fully dark, was fairly gloomy:

> Thus the Eastern Roman empire had come to resemble a fenced battle-ground in which the competitors fought each other for the supreme power. As soon as they came out of the borders of second-order small states, as soon as they, so to speak, expanded a bit, the Balkan Slavs succumbed to the infection of Greek megalomania. In the Eastern Roman empire itself, that infection raged continuously . . . . To the observer this centuries-old Eastern Roman empire presents an odd sight: with its weaknesses and its internal

[94] Novaković 1966: 132–3.   [95] Novaković 1966: 117–18, 120–1, 133.

108   In Search of the 'Scientific Method'

unrest it constantly inspired in its generals and rebel vassals the idea to destroy or seize it. In this odd empire everyone without distinction, Greek or Slav, thought only about how to become its master, but no one ever thought to abandon the Byzantine religion or faith. The great achievement of [Stefan] Nemanja is that he definitively elevated the Serbs into the ranks of the known competitors for the throne in Constantinople and placed them among the acolytes of Byzantium, thus detaching them once and for all from the West and from Latinism.[96]

The byzantinisation of Serbia during the reign of the Nemanjić dynasty, Novaković asserted, went hand in hand with the rise of its 'imperialist idea'. The model of the Bulgarian Kingdom of Simeon and Samuil ('whose traces were everywhere') enthralled Stefan Dušan and became the source of his own 'megalomania'. The outcome was similar: lacking practical political ideas to serve the genuine national interests, both empires died with their creators. And since 'all Serbian state creations were purely personal, without strong internal organisation [and] a feeling of unity', soon after Dušan's death the 'particularistic and individualistic atavism' of the Serbian lords predominated: 'The idea of a great empire or a great state was not alive either in the people or among the nobles of that time. This idea was purely Dušan's. Political arbitrariness and disrespect for law and order were the other side of this 'personal rule', which also made any political success transitory. Here Novaković not only demonstrated his customary imperviousness to Slavic sentimentality but also proposed a radical revision of the teleological romantic story about the 'preordained' rise of Dušan's empire to the height of power and about the Serbs' potential to succeed Byzantium had the Turks not invaded. Both his critical-historical method and modernist and elitist nation-building project in the vein of the Serbian Progressives led him to a conclusion that must have startled a great many among his contemporaries:

For the needs of our age we have nothing to learn or resurrect from what the Middle Ages left us; the principles of our times have nothing in common with the principles of that time. There is nothing to be particularly recorded or highlighted of these sorrowful times; by the deeds or examples of that time one should pass with eyes closed . . .. Today we should look at this past only in order to understand the mistakes made or the examples we must avoid.[97]

Despite Novaković's wide scholarly (and political) reputation, however, most 'critical' Serbian historians were not swayed from their patriotic mission

---

[96] Novaković 1966: 119–21.   [97] Novaković 1966: 69, 133–7.

to bring the medieval (imperial) past to bear on the construction of modern Serbia or project contemporary desiderata onto that past. The authors of a major historical compilation, Ljubomir Kovačević and Ljubomir Jovanović, for example, explained the protracted process of converting the South Slavs to Christianity by their 'strong sense of national singularity (*zasebnost*) with respect to Byzantium and warm affection full of pride for everything that separated and distinguished them from Byzantium'. Christianisation, they argued, would have led to the complete suppression of the 'popular Slav resistance against the Byzantine influence' had not the Slavic script and liturgy been introduced; this, however, came about by chance, thanks to the expulsion of Methodius's followers from Moravia, not on a decision by Constantinople.[98] Rather than imitating the imperialist demeanour of the Byzantine emperors, Stanojević agreed, the Serbian rulers, together with the people, worked 'consciously, systematically and hard' to strengthen Serbia politically, economically and culturally in order to prepare it for the time 'when the destiny of the Balkan peninsula would be decided'.[99] The overall teleological scheme of nineteenth-century historiography was also left intact: nothing could stop the 'young state' from displaying its full potential and rising to prime contender for the Byzantine legacy.

Later critics, on the other hand, would berate Novaković for having over-exaggerated the Byzantine influence and disregarded other Western 'civilising' influences.[100] In point of fact, all Serbian historians discussed so far saw Serbia's medieval history as an 'evolution towards Byzantium', in Novaković's wording, which peaked with Stefan Dušan's empire. But while the national-Romantic canon viewed Dušan's ambitions as both morally justified and politically feasible, the critical historiographic school was more sceptical. In the words of S. Stanojević, Dušan 'had neither the strength nor the talent to carry out the consolidation of the heterogeneous elements' that came to constitute his empire; his plan was 'impressive from a political but not from a national point of view'.[101]

'Eastern Romanity' in the Byzantine Orbit

In Romania, too, the turn of the twentieth century was marked by the co-existence of contesting versions of the national narrative, which sought to assess the effects of the Byzantine influence on the Romanians before and

---

[98] Kovačević and Jovanović 1893: I, 186–7.
[99] Stanojević 1908: especially 95, 101, 106, 112–13, 116, 123, 163.   [100] Maksimović 1995.
[101] Maksimović 1995: 187.

110   In Search of the 'Scientific Method'

after 1453. Outside the 'historians' guild', a new generation of liberally minded Western-looking scholars delving into Romanian history, national psychology and sociology, such as Pompiliu Eliade, Dumitru Drăghicescu and Eugen Lovinescu, radically denounced Byzantium, the Orthodox Church and the Byzantine civilisation as the source of all the historical woes of the Balkan nations and of the vices, bad penchants and repulsive habits of the Romanians. 'One can find the remote causes of today's decay of the Ottoman Empire', the sociologist Drăghicescu wrote in 1907,

> in Byzantium itself, and its end will not come from elsewhere. The chronic disease that has condemned this patient to remain perpetually nailed to its bed is none other but the intoxication by the moral decay of ancient Byzantium . . . . The modern Greek influence infused in the public mind [of the Romanians], especially in the cities, something of this perfidious spirit of intrigue of Byzantium, of its envious and corrupt crookedness, its lack of dignity and flattery, coupled with its famous sickly pride.[102]

The actual arena, where different readings of Byzantium's role confronted each other, was that of the increasingly professionalised Romanian history-writing. The towering figure there at the end of the nineteenth century was Alexandru D. Xenopol (1847–1920), who argued for history being a true science following clearly defined laws and logic, through which the reasons for the historical processes could be clearly defined. His great work of synthesis, which is credited as being the first of this genre, the multi-volume *The History of the Romanians in Dacia Trajana* (1888–93), covered the entire history of the 'Romanian people' from 513 BC, the first mention of the Getae by Herodotus, to 1859, the year of the union between Wallachia and Moldavia. The second volume, entitled *The Barbarian Invasions (270–1270)*, dealt with relations with the Slavs, the Magyars and other 'newcomers', embroiled with theories about Romanians' migrations and continuity. Its main objective was to assert the 'Transylvanian' origin of the Romanians and rebuff the Austrian scholar Robert Roesler's 'immigrationist theory' positing their late migration from the Balkans towards the lands north of the Danube. As in the case of Fallmerayer in Greece, this outside challenge stirred up a series of historical rebuttals, which propelled the crystallisation of the Romanian historical canon.

Xenopol dubbed the whole period between 900 and 1650, which he defined as the medieval period of Romanian history, the 'Era of

---

[102] Cited in Tanaşoca 2013: 278.

'Slavonism'. Throughout this whole era Byzantium is mentioned only in passing, and its direct impact appears negligible compared to that of Bulgarian political tradition and culture. The political institutions in the emerging Romanian principalities, Xenopol explained, had their roots in and were modelled after the Bulgarian (and partly the Hungarian); the legal system was 'Romano-Bulgarian'; and the Romanian Church 'remained steadfast in [its] Slavic form of worship', while the Patriarchate of Constantinople's attempts to establish its supremacy are qualified as 'tendencies of usurpation' and as impinging on the principalities' sovereignty. Rather than abating, 'Slavic Orthodoxy' was strengthened after the Turkish conquest of the Balkans, since many Bulgarian and Serbian prelates found refuge in the principalities. Slavic language and culture (*slavonismul*) thus remained dominant until at least the midseventeenth century, when it was replaced by the *grecismul* of the Phanariots and, in Xenopol's own day, by French influence.[103]

From the perspective of our topic, this is perhaps the most interesting aspect of Xenopol's *History*: the almost complete overshadowing of Byzantine legacy by that of the Slavs. Xenopol deviated from what would soon become the conventional interpretation, which regarded the Bulgarian political and cultural presence to the north of the Danube as little more than a channel for the massive penetration of Byzantine influence among the Romanians before and after the creation of the principalities. Ioan Bogdan (1864–1919), who, like Xenopol, emphasised the 'overwhelming impact' of the Slavs on Romanian culture, insisted on the positive aspects of Byzantine influence that had reached the Romanians through the Bulgarians during the latter's domination north of the Danube between the seventh and tenth centuries. While the Romanians, he wrote, 'were departing more and more from Roman culture and becoming savage', the Bulgarians, 'who came like barbarians over us, took from their Byzantine neighbours, under the protective wings of an organised and powerful state, a civilisation which was then advanced, that of Byzantium, which was none other than the continuation, in a Greek form with oriental influences, of the old Roman civilisation'.[104] The historian Demostene Russo went much further by stating, 'When one says Slavism one means Byzantinism, because Slavism was nothing but the body moved by the Byzantine soul.'[105] For his part, Xenopol referred solely to 'Slavonism', not to '(Slavo-) Byzantinism', and – remarkably – his evaluation of the impact of this Slavic dominance on Romanian culture

---

[103] Xenopol 1925: 146–205.   [104] Bogdan 1895: 15.   [105] Russo 1939: 11.

112   In Search of the 'Scientific Method'

was not unlike that of the contemporary Bulgarian historians about the effect of Byzantine dominance on Bulgarian culture.

The Slavic language and the cultural forms related to it, according to Xenopol, were 'foreign to the nature and [way of] thinking of the Romanian people'. As such, they presented, over a full eight centuries, an obstacle to Romanians' intellectual creativity and advancement. The Slavic language could not be compared with Latin in the West, since it was 'a language of a barbarian people' and was later responsible for the 'undivided dominance of the religious ideas on the spirit and consciousness [of the Romanians]'. Indeed, cultural Slavonism was one of the main causes for the historical retardation of the Romanians compared to the Latin peoples of western Europe. On the other hand, he averred, the Slavisation of Romanian language and culture concerned the 'high strata of society' only – the court, nobility and church – not the ordinary people. Xenopol saw in this the beginning of a lasting and destructive tendency: 'Thus we encounter, as early as this era, that dualism with respect to culture which will not leave us in any of the periods of our history: a high class usually alienated from the mentality of the people, thus tearing apart its moral unity' – first adopting Slavic culture, then Greek and finally French (the latter being the only one corresponding to the 'Latin mentality' of the Romanian people). In the 1650s, according to Xenopol, the modern period of Romanian history began, 'which was characterised by the predominance of Greek influence (*grecismul*), first in culture and soon after in the whole political and social life of the high strata [of society]'.[106] For him, Grecism was much more dangerous than Slavonism, which was 'a form of thought, uncoated with political goals to dominate and oppress', whereas Grecism used political power to strengthen its domination and 'suppress Romanian culture'.[107]

The parallels with Zlatarski's rendition of the impact of Byzantine cultural influence on the Bulgarians are remarkable, pointing to the overriding national viewpoint and common understanding of national authenticity among the 'critical' historians. But even if Xenopol shared the Romantic negativism towards the Greeks, he was not interested in projecting their 'harmful' impact back on Byzantium (whose direct influence on the Romanians he never considered to be significant anyway). Xenopol had no serious interest in Byzantine-Romanian relations and preferred to measure the Greek factor in the context of the Ottoman system of administration and the modern history of the Romanians, not

---

[106] Xenopol 1925: III, 205–6; VI, 178–9; VII, 7; VIII, 171–2.   [107] Xenopol 1925: VIII, 237; IX, 6.

'Eastern Romanity' in the Byzantine Orbit

as a revived remnant of a distant past. Xenopol's prominent work, like that of his predecessors, was far from integrating Byzantium into the Romanian narrative and even further from the byzantinist discourse that his students and successors were soon to develop. He was perhaps the most outstanding representative of that cohort of Romanian historians who, ever since the Enlightenment, saw the (Slavo)-Byzantine influence on Romania as the major cause of its inferior position vis-à-vis the Latin West and as having disrupted its 'organic' development as a Latin country. This construal did not end with Xenopol; after him, however, it had to co-exist with and confront a range of contesting construals.

The dawn of the twentieth century saw the beginning of a radical re-evaluation of the place of Byzantium in Romanian culture and history. Byzantine studies were introduced as an academic discipline in 1907, when a Chair of Byzantine Philology was founded in the Faculty of Literature at the University of Bucharest led by Constantin Litzica, who had specialised in Byzantine literature under Karl Krumbacher. In 1913 it was renamed the 'Chair of History of Byzantine-Romanian Civilisation', despite the protests of the abovementioned Ioan Bogdan, the then-dean of the Faculty of Literature, who professed that 'such a civilisation had never existed'.[108] Behind this institutional thrust was the conviction, formulated already by C. Erbiceanu, C. Litzica and G. Murnu, that research in the national language, literature and history was impossible without knowledge of Byzantium and the Byzantine sources.

It should be noted that the interest in Romanian-Byzantine themes evolved concurrently with a 'regionalist turn' in Romania's political agenda. The early twentieth century was the period of a very active Balkan policy, when Romania aspired to the role of principal regional power and arbiter of the Balkans and when it was establishing itself as the protector of the Aromanians (as the Balkan Vlachs came to be increasingly named), who inhabited some parts of the peninsula. An imperial vision of the Romanian past tallied with these new horizons. The ultimate triumph, just around that time, of the Daco-Roman synthesis as the accepted formula of the Romanians' ethnogenesis indicated the need for a wider perspective on Romania's history, bringing together indigenist and universalist elements.

The first strong impetus in this direction came from a Greek. In 1915, Litzica's successor at the Chair of Byzantine Philology was Demostene Russo (1869–1938). Russo, a student and follower of Spyridon Lambros,

---

[108] Rados 2005: 320.

114   In Search of the 'Scientific Method'

was a native of Ottoman Eastern Thrace who moved to Romania in 1894. He was among the first to venture into rehabilitating the historical role of Byzantium generally and for Romanian history in particular. In his book *Hellenism in Romania* (1912) and his inaugural university lecture of 1915, suggestively entitled 'Byzantium Rehabilitated', Russo set out to elucidate the historical justification for such rehabilitation and chart the 'desiderata of Romanian byzantinology'.[109] With arguments reminiscent of those of Dimitrios Vikelas and Ivan Shishmanov, he attributed the long-standing negative attitude towards the Eastern Roman empire to the fact that, until a few decades earlier, knowledge about it had been drawn 'from the surveys of the Western Catholics – the mortal enemies of the Orthodox East – and from the epigrams of Montesquieu, Voltaire and Gibbon'. More than anyone else, Gibbon had contributed to the slandering and denigration of Byzantium because of his inability to overcome his prejudices against Christianity and acknowledge the political importance of theological problems. Gibbon's fundamental error, according to Russo, was that in the millennial history of the Byzantine empire he saw nothing but continuous decay. 'In what kind of decline is an empire', Russo asked rhetorically, 'which produces the most significant civilisation of the Middle Ages, which Christianises and civilises a large part of Asia and Europe?' Equally responsible for the denigration of Byzantium were classical philologists and art historians, who 'were disgusted' when failing to discover the pure Attic forms in Byzantine literature and art.[110]

Like Vikelas, Russo launched his rehabilitation campaign by pointing out that the defects attributed to the empire were not at all limited to Byzantium. More crucially, because of the accumulation of sources and the upsurge of Byzantine studies – notably in Germany, Greece and Russia – scholars 'have reached a completely different opinion of byzantinism' and 'a different appreciation of Byzantine culture and history'. The empire was no longer compared to Hellas but was 'studied in itself as a creation of the environment in which it was produced'. It began to be valued not as a continuation of Hellas and Rome but as a 'freestanding unity' whose culture had its 'moments of decline, but also brilliant periods of rebirth and glory'. The millennial survival of the empire against incessant barbarian assaults testified, according to Russo, to its 'extraordinary vitality, civic virtues and superior organisation'. And if it ultimately succumbed to the Turks, 'the blame largely belonged to Western Europe, whose Fourth Crusade had delivered it a blow from which it never recovered'.

---

[109] Russo 1939: I, 3–15; II, 487–541.   [110] Russo 1939: I, 3–5.

'Eastern Romanity' in the Byzantine Orbit

Commenting on the shift of attitude, Russo noted that byzantinophobia was being replaced by byzantinolatry – a trend to which he himself was an accomplice. He foregrounded the 'inestimable services' that Byzantium rendered to humanity, and Europe in particular, by resisting and weakening for a century the aggressive Turks; otherwise, Turkish armies would have reached London unimpeded and 'imposed on the whole of Europe the Koran instead of the Gospel'. The empire had also Christianised and civilised the peoples with whom it came into contact and had kept the first reliable testimonies about their past. Finally, thanks to Byzantium, 'the masterpieces of Hellas were transmitted to Western Europe'.[111]

It is easy to notice the close alignment of Russo's views with those of Vikelas and Shishmanov and, as elsewhere in the region, the inspiration they drew from the upsurge and new status of Byzantine studies in Europe. But they are also of interest to us because they come from a Greek scholar specialising in Byzantine-Romanian relations and are thus indicative of the contemporary Greek interpretation of these relations. Greek-Romanian connections, claimed Russo, had begun long before the fall of Constantinople in 1453: 'for many centuries the Danubian Principalities were under Greek influence and have received from Byzantium plenty of cultural borrowings' related to language, customs, faith and institutions. These borrowings took place, on the one hand, via direct contact of the Romanians with the empire (though Russo did not specify when and where these direct contacts took place), then the Greek immigrants to the principalities after 1453, and continued 'to a more pronounced degree' during the Phanariot era. Most crucially, the influence of Byzantine culture reached the Romanian space in the garb of Slavism, which, Russo argued, contrary to Xenopol, was merely a form of Byzantine culture. 'Even at the time when the Slavic influence was omnipotent in the Principalities, it should not be forgotten that it was the Byzantine influence that reigned'; 'in reality Byzantinism held sway, initially under Slavic etiquette'.[112]

Thus instead of minimising the weight of Byzantine culture during the (late) Phanariot domination in favour of that of the Enlightenment – a strategy adopted by most Romanian 'revisionist' historians – Russo recalibrated its value and status. Instead of emphasising Byzantium's intermediary function between ancient and modern Hellenism, as most of his compatriots were doing at the time, he advocated the 'freestanding' eminence of Byzantine culture which, although inherently Greek in character, deserved to be appreciated and studied in its own right. There is

[111] Russo 1939: I, 6–10.   [112] Russo 1939: I, 10–11.

116 In Search of the 'Scientific Method'

much to commend about Russo's de-stigmatisation of Byzantium and insistence on the collection and critical edition of 'Greek' sources as an indispensable resource for the understanding of Romanian history. At the same time, his radical devaluation of the Slavic cultural and political heritage as merely nominal, without engaging with the opposing arguments of Ioan Bogdan or Alexandru Xenopol, suggests a political rather than a 'positivist' stance, which more accurately reflected the imperial vistas of the Greek state than the actual state of historiography in Romania.

The reassessment of the 'Byzantine factor' in Romanian history was closely linked with the increase of literature in a number of related academic fields. Research in medieval philology, theology and church history, law, art history, the Romance-speaking population south of the Danube, numismatics, and even national psychology considerably broadened the sphere in which Romanian and Byzantine studies interacted.[113] Before World War I, Nicolae Iorga (1871–1940), the most influential Romanian historian in the first four decades of the twentieth century, became the emblem of the new view of Byzantium in association with Romania's new regional role. Iorga's enormous oeuvre had a lasting impact not only on Romanian historiography but on the Romanian political culture too. His insistence on the agrarian essence of an idealised Romanian past was reflected in both his writing and political career as a member of parliament, president of the national assembly, minister and prime minister until 1940, when he was assassinated by a commando of the Fascist Iron Guard.

Significantly, Iorga disagreed with many of Russo's assertions, although he himself was the main champion of incorporating the Byzantine legacy into the Romanian historical canon. He accepted neither the thesis of the centuries-long Greek influence on the principalities ('significant and valuable' as it had been) nor that of the nominal Slavic influence as actually Byzantine 'only because at the basis of the South Slav culture was the Byzantine model'. All in all, Iorga (and his associate Vasile Pârvan) accused Russo of having infused 'Greek nationalist spirit' and 'pan-Hellenic propaganda' into his interpretations of Byzantine history and Greek-Romanian relations, as well as of a 'lack of knowledge about Romanian history'.[114] Given Iorga's own construals and claims to trailblazing, one can understand his annoyance at the fact that a 'foreigner' should have taken up these, for him, crucial issues and given them a nationalist slant contradicting his own.

---

[113] For an overview, see Rados 2005: 349–59.   [114] Iorga 1940.

'Eastern Romanity' in the Byzantine Orbit 117

To understand Iorga's take on Romania's relation to Byzantium, we have to bear in mind his complex and seemingly contradictory profile as a scholar. On the one hand, he was the model and standard-bearer of Romanian nationalism, who had authoritatively elaborated on the autochthonism, continuity, national specificity and unity of the Romanians. On the other hand, he championed Romanian civilisation's European belonging, which prevented him from relapsing into cultural autarchy and isolationism and stimulated him to stress the 'reciprocal dependence of civilisations' resting on 'most ancient common bases'.[115] One might argue that it was his virulent nationalism, seeking to create an honourable place for the Romanians in European history and civilisation, that led him to look for a 'broader integrative space', to stress interdependencies and cultural exchanges and to try to associate the Romanians with the big 'universalisms' – Latin identity, Byzantium and East–West transmissions. It led him to inscribe the history of the medieval Romanian states in a cultural geography that was much bigger and much more prestigious in terms of symbolic connections and transfers.[116] Such scholarly projections, at the same time, mirrored Iorga's concerns as a political figure, where the national and the supranational co-existed in an apparently uncontroversial way. 'The new state of affairs in the Balkans' following the two Balkan wars of 1912–13, he argued, had brought home a new realisation of the commonalities between the peoples of southeastern Europe. In this process the Romanians had to redefine their regional role 'in accordance with the historical development of the Romanians and with a tradition that no one can seriously think to deny [them]'.[117]

In weaving his Romanian-Byzantine narrative Iorga pursued, often together or in parallel, several mutually reinforcing strategies. One was to disprove that the South Slavs had a right to consider themselves adequate counterparts of or rightful heirs to the Byzantine tradition and culture. Another was encapsulated in the notion of *Romanité orientale* as a historical unity bringing under a single national category the Romance-speaking population, which was scattered throughout the Balkan peninsula and politically circumscribed by the Byzantine, Bulgarian and Serbian medieval states, and the Romanians north of the Danube. The third, and key, strategy concerned the Byzantine survivals in the post-Byzantine era and was captured by Iorga's acclaimed (often for reasons only superficially related to its original meaning) formula, 'Byzantium after Byzantium'. It

---

[115] Boia 2001a: 65.   [116] Leanca 2013: 286.
[117] Iorga 1912; 1913b: 5. On Iorga's notion of Southeastern Europe and Romania's pivotal place in it see Mishkova 2019: 56–9.

118 In Search of the 'Scientific Method'

should be noted that, in his case, the division between pre-war and interwar periods is to a large extent arbitrary, as many of the themes he would elaborate on at length in the 1920s and 1930s, in a rather changed geopolitical context, were already present in different programmatic texts at the beginning of the century. Therefore, in what follows, both the separate examination of the aforementioned strategies and the chronological split between discrete periods is undertaken solely for analytical purposes and for the sake of chronological consistency.

Iorga was the first regional historian to highlight the significance of the shared history and culture of southeastern Europe for the understanding of national histories. A major component of this common legacy, next to the Daco-Thracian-Illyrian substratum and the 'Roman order', was the 'neo-Roman' one – the Byzantine tradition. On many occasions since the 1910s Iorga would insist that this tradition and the Orthodox Christianity played a considerable role in the 'particular [culture] common to all southeastern Europe', in the essential unity and civilisational 'synthesis' between all those peoples. At the same time, however, he made it clear that this fact did not mean that all the peoples in question had contributed to (the perpetuation of) this common culture or that they were entitled to an equal share of its heritage. After the Slavic language gained the upper hand over Greek, Iorga stated at the International Congress of Historical Studies (London, 1913), the Bulgarians and later the Serbs had failed to produce a single great poet, chronicler or religious literature comparable to those of the Byzantines: 'these converts and imitators', as Iorga portrayed them, were completely lacking an original high culture.[118] Nor had they contributed to the salvation of the Byzantine legacy: 'The Bulgarians and the Serbs are not successors but imitators of Byzantium of Constantinople, since their states coexisted with the original Empire, and their downfall is contemporaneous with that of this Empire.'[119] The Romanians, on the other hand, had an 'undeniable tradition' of Byzantine succession. In a book on the modern history of the Balkan peoples, published in the wake of the Balkan wars, Iorga wrote,

> There was a time when it appeared that the entire Byzantine Balkan legacy would be inherited by the Romanian princes who, as the only ones who remained standing among the Christians, showed that they wanted to preserve it and that they were capable of sacrificing themselves for it.[120]

In the 1930s he would elaborate further on this thesis and devote a special study to it.

---

[118] Iorga 1921: 12.   [119] Iorga 1924a: 40.   [120] Iorga 1913b: 8.

It should be noted that Byzantium for Iorga provided the form, the exterior enfolding a living yet foreign content – the nations inhabiting the Balkan lands. His aim, therefore, was 'to elucidate the relations which existed between this great *theoretical reality of the Empire* and the *national realities*'.[121] Considering the late appearance of the Romanians in the historical records, this task was neither easy nor unproblematic. It took Iorga's highly speculative bravura, visionary flair and opaque and ornate style to accomplish it with such a resounding effect.

Two thematic focusses were of paramount importance in building the Romanians' connection to Byzantine history. Like the Transylvanian and the Romantic historians before him, Iorga made much of the Romance-language-speaking populations (the Vlachs) south of the Danube, whom he saw as an integral part of the Romanian ethnos. These large populations (larger than the Bulgarians and the Serbs, as he rarely missed hinting) played a major role in the history of both Byzantium and the Bulgarian state. The Romanians, he said, could be considered 'latecomers' on the Balkan political scene only concerning the creation of a 'state in proper national, independent forms', because 'long before 1300 ... they were taking part, under the names of their barbarian masters Pechenegs, Cumans and Tartars, in the wars for the possession of Constantinople'. The Byzantine emperors and Bulgarian tsars recruited their armies from among these 'brave and enduring' descendants of the 'Thraco-Romans', who had preserved 'the memory of their special condition, which was in no way inferior to that of the *homines romani* in the West under the old [Roman] Empire and after its fall'.[122] The other related theme concerned what Iorga called 'popular Romanias' (*Romanii populare*), that is, the purportedly autonomous organisation of the indigenous Romanised population north and south of the Danube, which preserved the tradition of Roman civilisation and attitude of superiority in regard to the invaders over this entire contact area and from which the Romanian states in old Dacia and the Vlach autonomies in the Balkans arose and expanded. The 'popular Romanias' owed their perseverance first to the 'great tolerance of Byzantium' for the local autonomy of the diverse Byzantine populations and, second, to the democratic foundations and principles of government which they shared with the Latin West.[123]

---

[121] Iorga 1922b: 31 (original emphases). This is how Iorga titled one of his studies, *Formes byzantines et réalités balkaniques* (1922a).

[122] Iorga 1921: 13–14. See also Jorga 1907.   [123] Iorga 1939b: I, 220–1, 286.

120   In Search of the 'Scientific Method'

Both themes converged in Iorga's notion of southeast European 'Romania' – the vast space of a continuous eastern Romanity, whose centres were the Adriatic littoral and the two banks of the Danube river, and whose enclaves were spread all over the Balkan peninsula in between. There Latinism 'continued to live according to the ancient traditions'. It continued to nourish the 'creative power of the Roman element', from which the originality and all the transformations of the Middle Ages derived, as well as the idea of the restitution of the 'single' Roman empire. As such, it partook in what he called 'the true unity of the history of the Middle Ages'. By upholding the 'spirit of the West' in the East, this Romania constituted an important 'element of integration' of the East and the West.[124] In this perspective, the Romanians appeared as bearers of the same imperial tradition as the Byzantines. They were neither rivals nor imitators of the Roman imperial idea (as the Bulgarians and Serbs were) – they were its embodiment and carriers, along with the Byzantines. With such Roman inheritance, a later critic would observe, 'a whole Romanian imperial phase was inscribed in the history of the world' and the Romanians could envision themselves as being destined, in more favourable conditions, to remake the Latin empire of the East.[125]

In the same stroke, by claiming that the Vlachs participated at the highest level in the structure of the First and especially the Second Bulgarian Kingdoms, Iorga practically 'smuggled' the Romanians into Byzantium via Bulgarian history and opened up another channel of communication and 'interpenetration' of Romanian and Byzantine culture. To a large extent, Iorga's narrative about the Romanian past, prior to the creation of the Romanian medieval states in the fourteenth century – that is, in the period when documentary sources are almost silent concerning the Romanians – fed off the Bulgarian narrative.[126] The aforementioned distinction between 'Byzantine forms' and 'national realities' was important in this strategy. Byzantium provided the 'forms' ('theoretical reality') for its various peoples, which the medieval Bulgarian and Serbian states had failed to fill with national reality: their forms were 'borrowed' from Byzantium and, as such, alienated the people and doomed these states to 'a great tragedy' – the ruinous ambition to conquer Constantinople. The 'definitive forms' of the Romanian state as they had emerged in the fourteenth century, on the other hand, rested on a completely different basis: that of 'the popular conception of an Empire with no seat in either

[124] Iorga 1939b: I, 178–80, 193; Berza 1972: 141–4.   [125] Boia 2001a: 178.
[126] A good example is Iorga 1922a.

the Ancient Rome or the New Rome, but whose ideal seat was in the very consciousness of [the Romanian] nation'. Thus, while the Slavs were completely exhausting their race in pursuit of the impossible possession of Byzantium,

> the Romanian patriarchal organism conserved in popular, naive, rural garments the traditions of the [Roman] Empire, anticipating in the Carpathians the principles that would steer the modern era across Europe . . .. It was at the same time an indelible memory of the imperial dignity and a modern creation coming from the midst of the popular masses . . .. The new state was conceived based on an original idea, rooted solely in the local tradition. The ruler reigned over 'the entire Wallachian land' and, for the first time in the East, a national idea emerged similar to the Western territorial one, on which the modern states are founded . . .. Thus, at the dawn of modernity, Wallachians came out with the idea of the modern state.[127]

In Iorga's metahistorical narrative about 'Romania before Romania', therefore, the imperial and the national, the ancient and the modern harmoniously permeated each other. The negative Bulgarian (and to a lesser extent Serbian) references had a vital function here. In fact, one would think that Iorga had stolen Zlatarski's interpretation concerning the destructive effects of Byzantium on Bulgaria and reformulated it to serve his own ends. On the one hand, he belittled what Zlatarski (and many after him) considered the Bulgarians' greatest cultural achievements – the adoption of the Slavonic script and Christianity – while attributing their military feats and imperial growth to the Vlachs. On the other hand, the byzantinisation of medieval Bulgaria, which Zlatarski bemoaned, served as the bad example against which the Daco-Roman purity and authenticity of the Romanians could be celebrated, along with their deep awareness of being heirs to the Roman tradition. The blind emulation of Byzantium by the Bulgarians and Serbs had foreshadowed their demise. By contrast, Romania's consciousness of nationality and imperial legacy made it capable not only of creatively continuing the imperial tradition of Byzantium but also of becoming a herald of the modern age, being both more ancient and more modern than Byzantium, at once an empire and a nation-state.

Apart from Russo and Iorga, Romanian historiography's discovery of Byzantium came late. Until after World War I, scholars in the field focussed on philological issues and those related to the history of Romanian medieval literature. This bias was largely embedded in what

---

[127] Iorga 1922b: 40–4; 1984: 61.

was perceived as *the* crucial need: to write the history of the Romanians. As the first Romanian university professor in Byzantine studies, C. Litzica, put it, 'for us, Byzantine studies are important for the light they can throw on Romanian history'.[128]

The critical post-Romantic turn in all four national historiographies discussed thus far led away from a purely emotional view of the nation's history and imposed discipline on Romantic nationalism. Yet historical Romanticism proved easier to denounce than to eliminate and the Romantic strain continued, with few notable exceptions, to nourish attitudes and interpretations. The scientific paradigm was readily adopted to legitimise particular readings of the national cause, precisely because scientific terminology tends to conceal ideology and make it opaque. Buttressed by it, nationalism became firmly entrenched as an intellectually respectable mentality among the literate classes, and preoccupation with constructing national identity came to be seen as the core vocation and moral duty of the professional historian. The resultant politicisation of medieval history goes a long way towards explaining the gap between the acceptance of Byzantium as an indispensable part of the national narrative and the actual interest of historians in Byzantium. The positivist historiographic phase thus came to be characterised by different ways of conceptualising and instrumentalising the Byzantine history and legacy not just across national narratives but also within discrete historiographies, on behalf of sometimes diametrically opposed political values and competing political projects.

[128] Rados 2005: 360.

CHAPTER 4

Between Byzantine Studies and Metahistory

After World War I, medieval history retained its central place in historical writing. In all these countries, including Turkey (which will be discussed separately), the most prominent and prolific national historians, particularly those who embarked upon producing national syntheses, were trained as medievalists. At the same time, this period saw the further professionalisation and institutionalisation of Byzantine studies in the region and abroad. It should be noted that almost the entire first generation and many in the second generation of Balkan byzantologists received their specialised education with Karl Krumbacher or August Heisenberg, Krumbacher's student and successor at the head of the *Seminar für Mittel- und Neugriechische Philologie* in Munich, and many of them contributed regularly to the respectable *Byzantinische Zeitschrift*.[1] The French tradition in the field was less formative, with the partial exception of Romania. Other important forums for international exchange and professionalisation included the international congresses of Byzantine studies that took place in Bucharest (1924), Belgrade (1927), Athens (1930) and Sofia (1934) (a congress in Istanbul was convened only in 1955). In the mid-1920s there appeared several new professional journals: *Byzantion: Revue Internationale des Etudes Byzantines* (Brussels), *Studi bizantini e neoellenici* (Rome), *Byzantinoslavica* (Prague) and *Annuaire de la Société des Études Byzantines* (Athens). The continuing work on the collection and publication of Byzantine sources and the increasing number of studies dedicated to Byzantine history properly speaking were now accompanied by cumulative specialisation in the sub-fields of the history of law, institutions, art and architecture, alongside the traditional preponderance of philology and literature. In the process, the amount and diversity of Byzantine studies

---

[1] From Serbia this cohort included S. Stanoejević, V. Ćorović, J. Radonić, N. Radojčić and D. Anastasijević; from Greece, Dimitrios Vikelas, Spyridon Lambros and Georgios Hatzidakis; from Romania, C. Litzica, G. Marnu, N. G. Dossios and N. Bănescu; and from Bulgaria, P. Mutafchiev and P. Nikov.

123

rose but at the cost of their increasing compartmentalisation. This situation goes some way towards explaining the relatively weak impact of this expert empirical knowledge on (the perpetuation of) the mainstream historical discourses that had taken shape until then.

Until the mid-1930s, the regional political and intellectual context operated in the same direction. Henri Grégoire, a Belgian historian and co-editor-in-chief of *Byzantion*, communicated the political and national relevance of Byzantine studies for the Balkan countries in such (somewhat exaggerated) terms: 'From a historical perspective the Balkan Wars and the World War were only the long struggle for the Byzantine succession. The Balkan states, which emerged strengthened from the struggle, were all the more ardent in claiming their share of the glorious legacy . . .. The rebirth of the Southeastern European states thus prepared a brilliant revival of Byzantium.'[2] In each individual national case, the post-World War I peace arrangements solved major old problems and engendered new ones, which, throughout the 1920s and early 1930s, continued to foment intraregional tensions and historical disputes. If anything, the general anti-liberal intellectual climate and integrationist national projects stiffened the erstwhile nationalist orientation of scholarship, which proved capable of accommodating various ideological positions. It was only in the face of the growing hegemonial pressure on the region after 1933 that new regionalist projects began to emerge, which brought with them non-nationalist frameworks of history. Significantly, both the nationalist and the non-nationalist historical schemes drew arguments from particular readings of the 'Byzantine legacy'.

'The Culture of Our Fathers'

The 'Asia Minor catastrophe', or simply the 'Catastrophe', is the expression Greeks use to describe the crushing of the Great Idea following the rout of the Greek army from Asia Minor under the onslaught of the nationalist forces of Mustafa Kemal in 1922 and the exodus to Greece of more than a million destitute Greeks fleeing this area. The dreams of a reconstituted Byzantium, which had united most Greeks for almost eighty years, were over. A whole chapter of Greek history, filled with optimism and expansionist dreams, was closed. Did this entail a re-definition of the nation and a shift in the conceptualisation of Greek history?

---

[2] Cited in Nystazopoulou-Pélékidou 2008: 17–18.

'The Culture of Our Fathers'   125

The answer to this question cannot be subsumed within the whole range of intellectual sub-cultures and disciplinary traditions as the reactions could differ considerably across as well as within discrete fields. For the influential group of modernist writers known as the 'Generation of the 1930s', the direct link to the classical past was once again at the top of the agenda, interrogating the compatibility between the perennial Hellenic psyche, or what they called *hellenikotita* – 'Greekness' or Hellenicity conceived as an immutable *Weltanschauung* ('worldview') since archaic times – and Greek modernity, while the Byzantine legacy dropped out of literary sight until after World War II.[3] A member of this group, the novelist Giorgos Theotokas (1906–66), famously urged his countrymen to forsake Balkan and Byzantine paradigms and focus instead on Greece's place in western Europe. He pinned his hopes on the free spirit of the young generation to throw off the lethargy and pettiness of Greece's eastern heritage; in other words, to cleanse Hellenism of its Byzantine (and Balkan) traditions and conform to a new, 'Eurocentric Great Idea'.[4]

Things looked different in historiography, where the conflict between Hellenism and Romanism appeared to have terminated with Zambelios's impressive 'Helleno-Christian' construction, Paparrigopoulos's nationalisation of the Byzantine empire and Lambros's 'scientific' translation. Far from corroding the political and ideological underpinnings of this vein of historiography, the ignominious collapse of the 'Great Idea' amplified Greece's Balkan sensitivities and concerns about the security of its territorial acquisitions, especially in Macedonia. Paparrigopoulos's heirs remained doggedly attached to his magisterial plot, making only marginal methodological and organisational changes. The foremost venues of this mainstream were Nicos Veis's *Byzantinisch-Neugriechische Jahrbücher* (published since 1920) and K. Amantos and S. Kougeas's *Hellinika* (since 1928), along with the Archive of the Byzantine Monuments in Greece at the Academy of Athens.

The story of the institutionalisation of Byzantine studies in Greece tells us a great deal about the way Byzantium and its place in Greek history came to be approached during this period. Between 1911 and 1931 at the University of Athens, three Chairs were established that focussed on the empire – of Byzantine Archaeology and Art (1911), of Byzantine History (1924) and of Public and Private Life in Byzantium (1931). Chairs related to Byzantine studies existed also at the Faculties of Law and Theology.[5] At the

---

[3] Beaton 2012; Liakos 2008: 216.   [4] Colotychos 2003: 159–66.
[5] Karamanolakis 2006: 317–20, 369–70; Christophilopoulou 1994: 983–91.

126 Between Byzantine Studies and Metahistory

same time, the first Chair in Modern History was established only in 1937. Until then, modern Greek history was largely regarded as a continuation of Byzantine studies, and the Ottoman period was described as one of post-Byzantine continuity.[6] The interest of the state in strengthening this new field of education, research and national representation had already led to the founding, in the 1910s, of the Museum of Byzantium in Athens and the Society of Byzantine Studies. A series of state decrees were issued in the interwar period sanctioning the status of the Byzantine churches and fortresses as archaeological monuments and supporting their restoration and the excavations of Byzantine monuments. Meanwhile, the Greek government invested in the establishment of a Chair at King's College London, in part 'to refute the calumnies that had been uttered against the medieval Greek Empire by Edward Gibbon'.[7] Thus, in the 1920s and 1930s, Byzantium, though still far from superseding the glow of classical Greece, moved to the forefront of state-sponsored cultural heritage, scholarly research and public attention, thus boosting its status as a legitimate 'Hellenic' field.

The focus of this wide network of institutions, as their subjects indicate, was the study and display of Byzantine culture. A visible shift in representation took place. During the 'long nineteenth century' Byzantium was valued above all for having preserved and transmitted ancient Greek culture and Christian faith to the modern Greeks. The Greek historians' prime preoccupation at that time, as Dimitrios Vikelas's work exemplified, was to demonstrate the survival of the ancient legacy through Byzantium, while remaining sceptical about the empire's own cultural achievements. After World War I, the connection between Byzantium and modern Greece, which S. Lambros was among the first to emphasise, became far more important for the Greek historians, counterbalancing the erstwhile fixation on the transmission from ancient times to the Middle Ages. The nature of Byzantine culture changed accordingly. Rather than just being a custodian and conduit of the ancient heritage, Byzantium itself became a generator and source of heritage, rendering to world culture 'services comparable to those of ancient Greece', as an eminent contemporary historian put it.[8] All this went hand in hand with the assertion of Greece's 'sovereignty' over this cultural patrimony. Only those elements that attested to the Hellenic character of the empire were worthy of investigation and display. Phaedon Koukoules (1881–1956), founder of the Society of Byzantine Studies and a head of the Chair of Public and

---

[6] Liakos 2004: 357.   [7] Mango 1965: 29; Clogg 1986.   [8] Amantos 1969: 176.

Private Life in Byzantium, in fact took little heed of the 'public life' in the empire, which was closely associated with the institutions of the Roman empire. Instead he devoted himself to the study of 'private life', which, according to him, embodied the continuation of the ancient Greek world and could serve as scientific proof of the millennial continuity of the Greek nation.[9] A number of sister disciplines – art history, archaeology, philology and folklore – highlighted the eminently 'Hellenic' identity of the Byzantine empire and linked its significant cultural achievements to modern Greece. In essence, this meant refocussing attention from the intellectual elites to the 'common' people, in whose language, artefacts and 'spirit' the Greek cultural 'authenticity' was found to reside.

The field's expansion was underpinned by political anxieties. After World War I, Greece was busy attending to its 'legitimate' rights on the newly acquired territories, particularly Macedonia, to which its neighbours also laid historical and ethnographical claims. With the centres of ancient Greece lying further to the south, it was through Byzantium that scholars hoped to confirm the Hellenic character of these lands. The younger generation of Greek historians ardently took up the task of highlighting the Greek nature of the Byzantine monuments and of putting it in a scholarly context. In his 1913 memorandum recommending the founding of the first museum of Byzantine art in Thessaloniki, only a few months after these lands were conquered by Greece, Adamantios Adamantiou (1875–1937), a student of Lambros and the first head of the Chair of Byzantine Archaeology and Art, pointed out that a museum centred on Macedonia would be 'a shrine to the art and history of medieval Greece' and that the Byzantine monuments gathered in it would 'bear the imprint of the thought and soul of medieval Greece, passed on throughout the centuries, as an eternal flame of the artistic and historical tradition emanating from a singular and unmediated national life'.[10] Adamantiou considered Byzantine studies to be a 'terrain of political antagonism with the Russians and the peoples of the Balkans' and lamented the fact that first the Romanians and then the Serbs had organised international congresses of Byzantine studies, thus boosting their claims to the Byzantine legacy, while the Greek delegation had not been convincing in demonstrating the Greekness of Byzantium and had failed to leave a 'dignified impression of the Hellenes'.[11] His pleas with the Greek government were heard, and the third congress was convened in Athens in 1930.

---

[9] Koukoules 1948–57; Karamanolakis 2006: 321–2, 325. [10] Cited in Karamanolakis 2006: 322.
[11] Kioussopoulou 2013: 405, 409.

128   Between Byzantine Studies and Metahistory

Within the system of Byzantine culture, art now came to occupy a key place, attesting to the gradual appropriation of the different areas of Byzantine legacy. Adamantiou's successor at the head of the Byzantine Museum in Athens, the archaeologist Georgios Sotirios, stated in 1924 that as 'art [is] the highest expression of the culture of a country, it is understandable that the Museum of Byzantium, which holds Christian objects of Greek art, represents the culture of our fathers in the same way as the Archaeological Museum represents the culture of our grandfathers'.[12] What the previous historians of Byzantine art, like Georgios Lambakis, a founder of the Christian Archaeological Society (1884), considered to be an essentially Christian Orthodox artistic tradition, the new generation of Greek historians reformulated into a continuation of ancient Hellenic art and an intrinsic part of Greece's national contribution to world culture.

Meanwhile, the structuring of the historical field continued to unfold against the backdrop of the confrontation on the language question. The institutionalisation of the scientific study of the Greek language under the purists' mastermind, Georgios Hatzidakis (1848–1941), the most important linguist of modern Greece, was seriously implicated in the politics of *katharevousa* by linking the findings of historical linguistics to a particular (conservative) political cause.[13] The late institutionalisation of Byzantine history as a separate sub-discipline (1924) was due mainly to resistance on the part of the champions of the *katharevoussa*, who identified the preoccupation with Byzantium with the demoticist agenda and insisted that Byzantine history should be part of the general university course on Greek history.[14] The composite discipline of Medieval and Modern Greek Philology, on the other hand, was intended to underscore the link between Byzantium and modern Greece and the importance of *laographic* heritage, especially the 'popular literary tradition', as the transmitter of this national tradition. Its main purveyor, Nicos Veis (1883?–1958), an ardent demoticist and editor of *Byzantinisch-Neugriechische Jahrbücher*, has been credited for cementing the link between Byzantine, or what he also called the 'middle', and modern Greek philology through the ages of Ottoman domination.[15]

Language and ethnography lay at the core of the historical method of Konstantinos Amantos (1874–1960), a student of Lambros, Krumbacher and Diehl, professor of Byzantine history, and member (in 1944, president) of the Academy of Athens. His major work, the two-volume *History of the Byzantine State* (1939 and 1947), made little contribution to the field of

[12] Karamanolakis 2006: 338.   [13] Mackridge 2009: 271–7.
[14] Nystazopoulou-Pelekidou 1994: 169.   [15] Karamanolakis 2006: 225–6.

Byzantine studies. But it won him the recognition of his contemporaries for going one step further than his predecessors in underwriting the image of Byzantium as a proto-national Greek state and raising it a few rungs higher on the ladder of world culture. Already in 1923 Amantos made his premises clear when stating that 'two thousand years before the Slavs came to its northern borders, the Greek nation was living in Greek lands, and after their settlement the Greek state of Byzantium existed for another thousand years'.[16] The underlying theme in his *History* was, as usual, the continuity of the Greek nation, whose unity in space and time persisted from one century to the next because of its ineradicable civilising power. The transference of the capital of the Roman empire to Constantinople took place, Amantos tells us, 'by degrees to deliver its eastern half to the Greeks'. Originally it was Greek in culture and language (whose spoken forms 'might be termed Modern Greek since it . . . had acquired almost all its modern characteristics'), and from the seventh century, with the loss of Egypt and Syria, it became 'Greek from the racial point of view'.[17]

With Amantos, however, the stress was not on continuity per se but on its application. One was the assertion of the European character of Byzantium with arguments already compellingly spelled out by Vikelas. The empire's greatest accomplishment, he reiterated Vikelas, was the long-standing resistance it put up against various Asiatic, especially Muslim, invaders, thus 'rendering supreme service to Europe, to which it afforded time to take shape and develop'. Together with 'rescu[ing] the works of the ancient Greek genius and preserv[ing] them for the perpetual use of mankind', the 'defence against Asiatics' made the Byzantine empire an integral part of European civilisation. The incessant wars, however, had prevented the 'transformation of the monarchic constitution into a democratic one' and made it essential to uphold military rule, which was often arbitrary, causing frequent dissentions and rebellions. But if the latter never led to more radical political or social upheavals, it was thanks to the philanthropic activity of Greek Christianity, whose multitude of charitable foundations and monasteries 'sufficed to meet all the needs of the community and relieved the social distress which was caused by the injustices of military rule'.[18] Amantos thus transfigured the notion of the stagnant religious character of the empire still prevalent in much of the Western writings – the strongly castigated monasticism in particular – into an essential condition for its social cohesion and political endurance to the benefit of Europe.

---

[16] Amantos 1923: 327, cited in Livanios 2003: 81.   [17] Amantos 1969: 174–6.
[18] Amantos 1969: 177–8.

130   Between Byzantine Studies and Metahistory

Amantos made no secret of the fact that the weight he gave the questions of oral tradition and language was directly linked to the ongoing dispute with Bulgaria over the 'ethnographic identity' of Macedonia and the Greek Communist Party's support for Macedonia's secession based on the right of self-determination. In both his work as a historian and public pronouncements, he set out to prove, with historical, ethnographic and 'popular' linguistic materials, the Greek character of Macedonia and thwart 'all those conspiring against Hellenism in the recently acquired territories' that were once part of Byzantium. All things considered, K. Dimaras was probably right when he stated in his speech at Amantos's funeral that 'there has barely been another Greek who had served the national interests in a more scientific way'.[19]

This is not to say that dissenting voices were altogether missing. Ioannis Kordatos (1891–1961), the founder of Greek Marxist historiography, issued the first serious challenge to the conventional scheme of Greek history. Starting from a crude Marxist analysis of modern Greek nationalism, in several writings since the 1930s he disputed the continuity of the Hellenic nation. Kordatos argued that the founders of modern Greek historiography, K. Paparrigopoulos and his followers, used false arguments to support their claim that the modern Greek nation was directly descended from the ancient Hellenes and that the Byzantine empire was Greek. In his *History of Later Greece* he wrote:

> If Metropolitan Greece (Hellada) had lost the glory of ancient Hellenic culture and become a land which, from an economic and social standpoint, had declined, with only the marble tablets left to remind us of an ancient culture, then how can we talk of a medieval Greek state and claim that the Byzantine state was the Greek nation? . . .. The name Hellene became a synonym for an evil person, an anti-Christian, and was despised, which is why the name Graeco was accepted, though it also was considered to be something humble . . .. It was only after 1054, when the Schism between Catholic and Orthodox took place in the Church, that the term Graecos acquired a religious meaning and was used to signify something that was not Roman . . .. ('His mother was a Christian, his father was a Hellene' – Cypriot proverb) . . .. Until the fourteenth century the terms Hellene and Hellenic were not encountered in the state language. These names came into use later on.[20]

Kordatos was the first to use the term *ethnotita* (ethnic group) to describe the Grecophone communities of medieval times as qualitatively distinct

---

[19] Karamanolakis 2006: 332–4.   [20] Kordatos 1957: 20.

'The Culture of Our Fathers'

from the modern Greek nation. He held that the nation was a historical phenomenon that originated in the late Middle Ages, when feudalism began to recede and the bourgeois class was rising. Catalysed by long-term social and economic changes, the Greek national consciousness began to emerge among the inhabitants of the great commercial and economic centres of Byzantium no earlier than the fourteenth century.[21] He thus questioned the idea of a three-thousand-year-long continuity in Greek history, which posited the ancients and the Byzantines as modern Greeks' precursors, and deliberately concentrated on the study of Greece rather than the Greeks.

Kordatos's dissenting voice was a lonely one in the interwar Greek historiography (even if it did not fade without reaction, as K. Amantos took it upon himself to strongly denounce Kordatos's subversive views).[22] During the dictatorship of General Ioannis Metaxas (1936–41), nonetheless, it acquired a wider public resonance. Capitalising on the presumptions of the by then firmly anchored canon of Greek history, the Metaxas regime embarked on propagating the ideological formula of the 'Third Hellenic Civilisation': a utopian construction that was meant to combine the best elements of the two previous Greek civilisations, the classical (in terms of art and science) and the Byzantine (in terms of Christian religion and a centralised state). The premises of the construction were unabashedly racist, with the Greek language providing the strongest proof of the nation's *fyletiki synecheia* (racial continuity), 'the natural development of one and the same race through time', and propelled by the idea of national rebirth.[23] The most radical rejection of this historical constructionism – indeed, of the whole ideological basis of the foundation of the modern Greek state – came from the political left. Echoing Kordatos, the communist leader Nikos Zahariadis wrote in 1939, 'The "Great Idea" proclaimed, against all historical and scientific data, that modern Greece is a descendant, inheritor and successor of an Ancient Greece of slave-owners, and of the Byzantine Empire of the Asiatic despotism. And that its historical mission, which has been given to her "from above", is to recreate the "Hellenic Empire" that never existed.'[24] As Yannis Hamilakis has noted, though, such complete rejections of the deployment of antiquity and Byzantium were uncommon even among the Greek left. After the fall of the Metaxas regime, the majority of it found no answer to the accusations levelled by the conservative right that its ideology was anti-Greek

---

[21] Katsiamboura 2005: 73.   [22] On the Kordatos–Amantos debate, see Livanios 2003: 80–1.
[23] Gounaridis 1994: 150–7; Carabott 2003: 30.   [24] Hamilakis 2007: 191.

132   Between Byzantine Studies and Metahistory

other than to accommodate its resistance to the national narrative and discourse and endorse, openly or subtly, the foundational myth of origins and the notions of cultural supremacy and continuity.[25]

On the whole, between the two world wars, inquiries into the history of Byzantine art, daily life, folklore, philology and archaeology brought to light new aspects of the 'Byzantine period of Greek history'. These new directions of research reflected the need for a new understanding of Byzantine culture, impelled by the difficulty of adapting an ethno-nationalist concept of Hellenism to Byzantine realities and the continuing nationalist strife over 'post-imperial' territories among the Balkan contenders. Under such conditions, neither the rise of Byzantine studies nor the association of these studies with progressive demoticism and the subversive intervention of Marxist historians brought about any visible change in the tripartite scheme of Greek history bequeathed by the nineteenth-century historians. The inner balance had shifted somewhat away from the obsession with the connection between Hellas and Byzantium towards that between Byzantium and neo-Hellenism, but the overall construction and its underlying 'Greek ideology' remained intact. As Amantos brazenly formulated it: 'It was only because this Byzantine Empire was based upon the Greeks of Europe and Asia Minor that it was able to confer supreme benefits on European civilisation and on a multitude of nations, services comparable with those of ancient Greece.'[26] The emergence of byzantinology as an autonomous field of research in the other Balkan states during this period tried to defy precisely this notion of the Greekness of Byzantium and of the Greeks as its exclusive inheritors and privileged custodians.

The Evil Demiurge of Bulgarian History

The post-war period was a traumatic one for the Bulgarians, who regarded themselves as the great losers of the geopolitical order established after the Second Balkan War and World War I. The distress was all the stronger as the 'national disaster' had struck at a moment of growing self-confidence for Bulgarian nationalism both at home and abroad, in the coveted 'Bulgarian lands', especially in Macedonia. Combined with the post-war social and political crisis, this feeling spurred a painstaking search for the roots of the disaster and a remedy for the social and political disruption. While most of the new intellectual 'offers' to this end originated outside

[25] Hamilakis 2007: 192–5.   [26] Amantos 1969: 178.

The Evil Demiurge of Bulgarian History

history-writing, typically in the burgeoning field of 'national character-ology', Bulgarian historians were anything but impassive observers of the contemporary state of the nation.

In Bulgaria, the tortuous emancipation of Byzantine studies from the grip of national history proceeded even more slowly than in Serbia or Romania during the same period. The past tendency of engaging with Byzantine history almost exclusively for the sake of illuminating certain aspects of national history continued to predominate. Byzantine studies were not institutionalised as an autonomous part of education and research.[27] 'The inherent, intimate relationship of medieval Bulgaria with Byzantium', as V. Zlatarski defined it in his opening speech to the Fourth International Congress of Byzantine Studies, which took place in Sofia in 1934, seemed to have impeded rather than stimulated the independent development of Byzantine studies in the country.

All these trends converged in the works of Petăr Mutafchiev (1883–1943), the most important Bulgarian historian and byzantinist of the first half of the twentieth century, who had studied with August Heisenberg in Munich. Mutafchiev's starting point was the recognition that despite Byzantium's huge impact on the 'historical fate' of Bulgaria and the need, for this reason, to know its history, 'hardly any perceptions elsewhere about Byzantium and its culture are as untrue as they are in our country'. He found the source of these misconceptions in the national Revival period, when the fight against Greek cultural assimilation, on the one hand, and the Greek appropriation of the Byzantine empire 'far exceeding the limits of the objective truth', on the other, engendered a correspondingly overinflated Bulgarian self-image and a distorted image of Byzantium. Remarkably, the reason why Mutafchiev sought to 'rectify' these misconceptions was by no means less intentional: by presenting the empire, the main and often only adversary of medieval Bulgaria, as a 'feeble organism', the Bulgarians were denying their own 'qualities of a healthy, strong people, capable of development'. Therefore, 'in order not only for the historical truth to be restored but also to rehabilitate ourselves in our own eyes as a people whose past is not devoid of values, the conceptions about Byzantium accumulated in our country should be corrected'.[28]

---

[27] Byzantine history was taught in the frame of the Chair in East European history set up in 1921 at the Faculty of History and Philology of Sofia University (*Actes* 1935: 22).

[28] Mutafchiev 1987: 24–5. This book, synthesising Mutafchiev's previous publications and ideas, was written in the late 1920s and the 1930s. However, because of his ostracism by the communist regime, it was published only in 1987.

134   Between Byzantine Studies and Metahistory

Mutafchiev's rehabilitation of Byzantium, conducted with insight and erudition, encompassed almost every aspect of its millennial existence: political arrangement and *raison d'état*, cultural and religious preeminence, and economic, financial and military power. Despite its enormous wealth, he argued, Byzantium never became a plutocracy (unlike Venice). Nor was its political power used for the accumulation of private wealth or the promotion of 'crude mercantilism'. Despite his absolute power, the emperor, who was 'a temporary conductor of the providential mission' and whose duty was to look after the interests of the state community, never became a despot. In no other medieval or even early modern society were the popular masses as free to openly challenge or even insult their ruler when he performed badly; no other medieval state had recognised equality before the law and meritocracy, rather than hereditary privilege, in recruiting its higher classes. Indeed, in contrast to Novaković and a long line of post-Enlightenment intellectuals, Western and Balkan, Mutafchiev maintained, 'In its deep essence the Byzantine monarchy remained democratic; its supreme task was the preservation of the Eastern Roman community.' In many respects it 'was centuries ahead of the medieval western European societies': while in the West feudalism flourished and the right of force reigned, 'Byzantium was aware that it could rest as a state only on the economically independent rural population'. Hence it was the first and only state that, already in the tenth century, had adopted a law for the protection of the small rural property against the encroachment of rich landowners, as well as the first to practise public charity.[29] Like Vikelas, Russo and Shishmanov before him, Mutafchiev denied that the much-castigated 'Byzantine' mores and conducts were specifically Byzantine and evoked the history of the Italian Renaissance states, the papacy and the Catholic Church, and even present-day 'so-called civilised nations' as analogous examples. Moreover, alongside the vicious and corrupted Byzantium, he argued, there was another one consisting of 'daring thought and internal discipline, of iron will and indomitable energy, of puritanism and selfless performance of [its] duty'. The empire owed its might and millennial survival to these moral forces and to its military power, supported by peasant-soldiers defending their own lands.[30] To this Mutafchiev added its unmatched cultural and economic prosperity, as well as knowledge and the 'complex science' of statesmanship.

While all this was meant, as he himself indicated, to highlight the kind of adversary the Bulgarians had to confront and co-exist with, Mutafchiev

---

[29] Mutafchiev 1987: 29–32.   [30] Mutafchiev 1987: 33–8.

The Evil Demiurge of Bulgarian History

135

also took pains 'to dispel the widely held delusion that Byzantium had *always* been a Greek empire'. Until the last two or three centuries of its existence, it had been an 'empire of the Romans', where the self-designation '*Romaioi* indicated a state, not a national belonging'. Similarly to Iorga and Novaković, Mutafchiev maintained that 'in the Byzantines' worldview the question about race and origins was irrelevant'. What mattered was Roman citizenship and submission to the law – embodied by the emperor – and to Orthodox Christianity. And if, after the sixth century, Greek took the place of Latin as the official language, it was not due to the Greeks constituting a majority or holding a dominant position in the political life of the Eastern empire. It was instead the fact that, since the time of Alexander the Great, Greek had become 'the main binding link between the component parts of Eastern Roman society'. By virtue of 'this external but at the same time visible to everybody feature', since the seventh century the Eastern empire 'appeared to its close and distant neighbours as a Greek state, and its population as Greeks' – a perception further reinforced by the fact that in the thirteenth century, when its territories shrank to the Balkan littoral, Byzantium also became ethnically Greek.[31] Mutafchiev's conclusion, consequently, did not derive from Fallmerayer but aimed to open the access of the Balkan and near-Eastern 'non-Greeks' to the symbolic capital of the empire and its legacy:

> If, therefore, claims to the Byzantine heritage can be raised today and if the arguments of history can be at all relevant where the distinct and awakened nationality with its imperative wants and needs has already risen – this heritage belongs not so much to the present-day Greeks, whose ancestors were a small minority, as to the various other peoples who then inhabited it and who still live in its former lands. For if the merit of the said Greek or Grecised minority to the Eastern empire lay in the fact that it had given it the official language, the peoples alien to Grecism cemented it with their blood and propped it up with their swords and with the creative genius of their best sons.[32]

In all these respects Mutafchiev's reading of the constitution of Byzantium signals a clear break with the national-Romantic tradition in Bulgarian historiography. It was informed as much by his erudition as by contemporary developments in Byzantine studies. At the same time, his evaluation, as a national historian, of the empire's impact on the 'historical

---

[31] Mutafchiev 1987: 26–8. For Mutafchiev's detailed rebuttal of the modern Greeks' appropriation of Byzantium, see Mutafchiev 1922: 3, 58–63; 4, 84–9.
[32] Mutafchiev 1987: 4, 87.

136   Between Byzantine Studies and Metahistory

life of the Bulgarians' rendered a very different picture, one that maintained a substantial continuity with the revolutionary Romanticism of Rakovski and Botev and the post-Romantic 'critical historicism' of Drinov and Zlatarski. Mutafchiev took one big step further in this direction in that he transformed the 'Byzantine factor' into the evil demiurge of all Bulgarian history. In an essay entitled 'Towards the Philosophy of Bulgarian History' and subtitled 'Byzantinism in Medieval Bulgaria', he sought to answer a question similar to the one Zlatarski had raised more than thirty years earlier when seeking the reasons for the meteoric rise and abrupt fall of the First and Second Bulgarian Kingdoms. Mutafchiev formulated the question in more dramatic, metahistorical terms, seeking to explain what he defined as 'the strange absence of continuity, consistency and gradualism in the political and spiritual life of the Bulgarians', which was marked by 'abrupt turns of might and weakness, contradictions, extremes and crises, impetuous and unexpected rises and rapid falls'. The root cause for this 'abnormal' dynamism of Bulgarian history was, according to Mutafchiev, 'the influence of byzantinism on medieval Bulgaria'.[33]

Because of their proximity to Byzantium, or what Mutafchiev dubbed 'geographic fate', the 'self-preservation' of the Bulgarians and that of their state doomed them to constant conflict with the empire. In this conflict 'the Bulgarian political and spiritual leaders were forced to borrow *deliberately* from [Byzantium] everything to which, according to their understanding, it owed its superiority'. The growing political rivalry thus led to growing political and cultural imitation. This process pushed the country onto an unnatural path of development, eliminating the possibility of creating anything healthy and durable. The inorganic nature of this path manifested itself in both the mental and the social condition of the people.

For Mutafchiev, as for most of the historians before him starting with Rakovski, the conversion to Christianity in the mid-ninth century signalled the triumph of byzantinism:

> The adoption of Byzantine Orthodoxy was inevitably accompanied by the spontaneous flooding of the entire Bulgarian land with Byzantine culture, and mainly with those of its features that could be more easily assimilated by a people that had just left paganism …. Precisely this rather unilateral cultural influence had fatal consequences for the Bulgarian people.[34]

Byzantine theological thought, Mutafchiev maintained, 'failed to fertilise the popular spirit for true creativity'. It brought confusion in the 'people's

---

[33] Mutafchiev 1931: 27–36.   [34] Mutafchiev 1987: 189.

The Evil Demiurge of Bulgarian History   137

consciousness, cut[ting it] off from the faith of the ancestors'. While the conversion to Christianity accomplished the great mission of creating the ideological conditions for the complete merger of Bulgars and Slavs, 'the byzantinism that burst in along with it led to exactly the opposite results: in place of the old ethnic dualism, it created a new division – a spiritual one'. The 'vibrant and ever-active' Byzantine cultural model undercut national authenticity and provoked the hardy resistance of the 'popular mass that kept its attachment to the past'.[35] Along with this cultural and political dualism, there occurred a disruption of the nation's social coherence as a result of what Mutafchiev called 'the law of imitation': the 'unconscious and spontaneous infatuation with the Byzantine models' affected only the highest, ruling strata of Bulgarian society. Having 'breached the continuity in the state and the spiritual tradition', byzantinism caused the 'crumbling of the internal structure of the once-homogenous Bulgarian society, its cohesion [and] material base'. The nation saw in its spiritually alienated leaders 'representatives and vehicles of a hostile destructive force'. Thus, in its striving to catch up with and become equal with Byzantium, 'the medieval Bulgarian state committed treason against itself', each upsurge of high culture foreshadowing alienation of the elite from the nation, and each rise containing the seeds of a future fast decay.[36]

Under such conditions, the 'instinct for national self-preservation and authenticity' (*samobitnost*) found expression above all in the heresy of Bogomilism, which was not a simple religious sect but an embodiment of a 'particular socio-political outlook'. As Orthodox Christianity was 'at once the ideology and the weapon of byzantinism', Bogomilism came to represent the ultimate 'repudiation of all expressions of this byzantinism in the political and social life of medieval Bulgaria and to stand in overt opposition against the byzantinised Bulgarian state'. Unlike most of his predecessors and contemporaries, Mutafchiev saw no creative or constructive ideal underlying the Bogomils' 'socio-political outlook'. He characterised it as a 'veritable religion of despair' able to subvert and destroy but not to create – a 'social philosophy of total negation'.[37] Having emerged in opposition to byzantinism, the Bogomils' resistance, as Mutafchiev saw it, proved incapable of spawning a viable alternative to the 'decay' of the Bulgarian society, which was sapped by Byzantium's

---

[35] Mutafchiev 1931: 31–3.   [36] Mutafchiev 1931: 32–4.
[37] Mutafchiev 1934: 97–112. See also Mutafchiev 1992: 216, where the author contested the widely shared thesis that Bogomilism was an 'ideology of national authenticity'.

138 Between Byzantine Studies and Metahistory

gravitational pull. The barrenness of byzantinism, it turns out, plagued even its opponents.

It is through this prism that Mutafchiev assessed the 'Golden Age' of Tsar Simeon – the fulcrum of the national-historical canon. While admitting that the time of Simeon 'was in every respect the most brilliant era in all of Bulgarian history', his assessment was far gloomier than such an admission should have entailed. Even if the literature produced in Bulgaria during that time had become the venerable heritage of the whole Orthodox Slavic world, Mutafchiev argued in his unfinished 'History of the Bulgarian People', for the Bulgarian nation the best part of this literary repository produced no benefits. With its abstract and 'cosmopolitan-Christian character', it was 'a spiritual product of byzantinism, which was distinguished precisely by its anti-national tendencies'. The transfer of this literature to Bulgaria stifled the elite's interest in the 'national reality' and 'drained the living streams carried by folklore'. Thus Old Bulgarian literature, captivated by foreign models and values, too, was alienated from 'Bulgarian reality', while the 'national consciousness was denied the food without which it could not serve as a bulwark of Bulgarian statehood'.[38] The political consequences of the spectacular rise of Simeon's empire were no less hazardous. The Bulgarian king's ambition for cultural development and creativity 'independent of Byzantium' was overshadowed by his aspiration 'to raise Bulgaria in every respect to the level of Byzantium . . . to eliminate the cultural border separating them'. In this he greatly overestimated the forces of his people by entrusting them with the mission of replacing Byzantium and, consequently, taking over its state and cultural heritage – 'a task that at that time was outside the reach of any European nation'. Had Simeon fulfilled his dream, Mutafchiev maintained, 'it would have led to the disappearance of our national individuality', as he would have then become a 'Roman emperor' and been 'doomed to forget that he was tsar of the Bulgarians'. The Bulgarians were therefore lucky that Simeon's desire to sit on the throne of the Byzantine *basileus* was never realised.[39] (To Mutafchiev's exasperation, Iorga, as we have seen, made the same argument in order to foreground the 'advantages' of the 'nationally embedded' Romanian rulers.) Finally, the failure of the Bulgarian state to establish permanent rule over the lands 'that ethnically belonged to us' and 'become a political organisation of the entire (*tselokupniya*) Bulgarian nation' was yet another tragic consequence of the fatal proximity to and involvement with the Byzantine empire.[40]

[38] Mutafchiev 1992: 194–5.   [39] Mutafchiev 1992: 195–6.
[40] Mutafchiev 1987: 103–38, especially 137.

The Evil Demiurge of Bulgarian History

To sum up, Mutafchiev extolled the cultural and political grandeur of Byzantium and, in the same breath, bemoaned its ruinous impact on the Bulgarians as 'a foreign culture' whose spread 'had left behind only depravity or ruins'. Byzantium thus appeared as the primordial Other to the Bulgarians, who had set the pattern and mapped the chequered trajectory of their later development. Following a long-standing historiographic tradition, Mutafchiev projected the cultural and political dilemmas of Bulgaria's modern development, especially those emanating from its 'inorganic' Westernisation, onto the country's medieval past. But while building on the interpretations of Rakovski, Botev, Drinov and Zlatarski about the denationalising and socially disruptive impact of Byzantium, he weaved them into a 'philosophy of Bulgarian history', which allowed him to connect the nation's past and present more explicitly and forcefully in a single metahistorical narrative marked by cyclical repetitions. On various occasions Mutafchiev spoke of the 'amazing recurrences' pervading Bulgarian history and drew analogies between the fate of the first two (medieval) kingdoms and that of the third (modern) one.[41] In this narrative the role of Byzantium in Bulgaria's Middle Ages prefigured that of the contemporary West in the country's modern history, in that it had engendered a tragic split in the nation's social body and 'psyche' and launched a long-term historical process of inorganic imitation and denationalisation. Byzantium, in this sense, appeared to the Bulgarians to be the original 'West'.

Interestingly, as a positive contrast to Bulgaria's 'unnatural' dynamism, Mutafchiev pointed to medieval Serbia, which he saw as an example of delayed, slow and 'glamourless' yet gradual and sound 'progressive development'. His explanation, again, rested with the relatively weak role of the 'Byzantine factor' in Serbian history. Because of Serbia's geographical location, the Byzantine influence there was never as direct and strong as it was on the Bulgarians, and its political rivalry with Byzantium was never as 'inevitable and acute'. The Serbs' 'normal development' was disrupted only under Tsar Dušan, hence the fast disintegration of his empire after his death; yet even Dušan's Serbia 'was not as thoroughly permeated and as deeply corroded by byzantinism as was the case with Bulgaria under Simeon, Petăr and Ivan Asen II'.[42]

Later academic literature, especially after World War II, would revise and mitigate Mutafchiev's portrayal of Byzantium as the evil mastermind of Bulgarian history. However, his 'historical-philosophical' interpretation would continue to exert a strong diffuse influence both on the popular

---

[41] Mutafchiev 1987: 139, 149–51; 1940: 513–30.
[42] Mutafchiev 1931: 36; see also Mutafchiev 1987: 152–4.

perception of the empire as the archenemy and cultural Other of the Bulgarians – a perception standardised in the teaching of history – and on a wide range of academic and quasi-academic literature debating the Bulgarian *Sonderweg* or national character. At the same time, the master narrative of Bulgarian history proved relatively resistant to Mutafchiev's historiosophic scenario. Though intended to urge the Bulgarians to 'turn to themselves' and rediscover their 'organic' potential, this scenario was too bleak to serve the purposes of patriotic education and mobilisation. In their national-historical syntheses, interwar historians such as Nikola Stanev (1862–1949), one of the most prolific popularisers of history during that period, were much closer to the affirmative post-Romantic reading of Zlatarski than to the metahistorical gloominess of Mutafchiev. In his *Medieval Bulgaria*, Stanev was preoccupied with reiterating the major *topoi* of Bulgarian pride: the 'unified and independent Slavo-Bulgarian state' (which had saved the Balkan Slavs from 'Byzantine influence and Romanisation [and] directed them toward authentic life'); its remarkable rise; the state- and nation-building effects of Christianisation and the adoption of the Cyrillic literary code (whereby 'the people emerged unified, nationally uniform, as purely Slavic in language, faith and spiritual culture'); and Simeon's dedication, yielding to the 'yearnings of his people for full independence', to the 'complete liberation of the Slavs from Byzantine domination' and to 'erecting the edifice of the *third civilisation* [after the Greek and the Roman/Byzantine]'. Without directly confronting Mutafchiev's interpretation, Stanev stressed that there was no evidence that Simeon's wars were 'anti-popular'. Following in the steps of the nineteenth-century tradition, he attributed both the downfall of the First Bulgarian Kingdom and the defeat of the Second to the 'imitation of the Byzantine social and economic arrangement' and 'the Byzantine character of the state power' alienated from its 'national population'.[43]

Petăr Nikov (1884–1938), a high-profile historian and byzantinist, as well as chairman of the Bulgarian Historical Association, was much more emphatic in praising Simeon, *pace* Zlatarski and Mutafchiev, as the greatest among the Bulgarian tsars. Instead of effecting denationalisation, Simeon's conquest of Constantinople, according to Nikov, would have led to Slavicisation of the empire. No otiose conquests or vain ambitions but a 'profound state idea' moved him: 'to eliminate forever the dangerous competition of the Byzantine empire by taking hold of Constantinople and making the Balkan peninsula Slavic and Bulgarian. This great idea

---

[43] Stanev 1934.

The Evil Demiurge of Bulgarian History 141

deserved every sacrifice, and Simeon did not hesitate to make it without mercy'.[44] Nikov emphasised the 'magic power', the 'unusual and irresistible vitality' of the 'Bulgarian idea' and the 'glamourous and attractive image of the former Bulgarian state with all its substance' during the time of the 'Byzantine yoke' (the eleventh and twelfth centuries), while steering clear of any allusion to the corroding effect of byzantinism on this 'state-creative Bulgarian idea'. Nikov disproved the thesis (espoused by Zlatarski) that the Byzantine domination after the fall of the First Kingdom had been accompanied by an 'intensive Hellenising policy in our lands with the specific purpose to Grecisise [*pogărchi*] our people'. He pointed out both the irrelevance of the modern understanding of the 'national principle' at that time and the fact that the Byzantine empire 'had not been a national Greek state, but had a widely international character'. 'In this state the Bulgarian element was preserved and could develop.'[45] For Nikov, the Second Bulgarian Kingdom presented a bleak reminiscence of previous grandeur, yet he did not blame 'byzantinism' for it.[46]

Similarly, in his analyses of the social classes and conditions in medieval Bulgaria Stefan Bobchev (1853–1940), a historian of law, barely made any reference to the impact of the Byzantine model.[47] The borrowing of Byzantine law, however extensive, was largely 'Bulgarised' to fit the local legal concepts so that both the system of Bulgarian rule and the conventional law among the popular classes were subsumed within the customary law, which always remained 'an ardent defender of its originality and particularity'; it 'fought with energy and perseverance against foreign influence, especially Byzantine, and refused either to bend under this influence or to borrow anything serious from the Byzantine codes and laws'.[48] Rather than reckless infatuation or the 'inorganic' importation Mutafchiev was so concerned about, Bobchev saw everywhere the continuity and strong presence of the Slavic traditions, concepts, self-government and customary law, which 'battled against the Byzantine influence'.

Here, although in a more even-handed form, was a classical nationalist narrative in a progressive mould. Medieval Bulgaria, Bobchev intimated in the vein of Drinov, did adopt the outward trappings of power and the ornaments of Byzantine civilisation, but beneath these lurked the genuine and unspoiled Slavic social and political organisation. For Stanev, Nikov and Bobchev, substantiating the robustness of the medieval Bulgarian

---

[44] Cited in Daskalov 2018: 186.   [45] Nikov 1937: 5–14.   [46] Lyubenova 1987: 255–6.
[47] Bobčev 1929: 621–33; 1930: 99, 110.
[48] Bobčev 1934: 34–6, 44. Bobčev 1925, discussing the 'transfer' and 'Bulgarization' of the Byzantine law, remained a standard reference for scholars in the field in the following decades.

142   Between Byzantine Studies and Metahistory

society and its potential to survive and progress was what the traumatised nation was in need of, not pointing pedagogically at its corrosion – and therefore intrinsic frailty – under the impact of byzantinism.

This assertive national narrative received reinforcement from an unexpected quarter. In 1930, Steven Runciman (1903–2000), presumably the first, and only, student of John Bury, published *A History of the First Bulgarian Empire*. While steering clear of references to 'Bulgarian Slavs', a liberating or unifying mission of the Bulgarian rulers and the Bulgarians' anti-Byzantine predilections, Runciman's book betrayed a strong influence from Zlatarski. Written in a gripping storytelling style, it barely added anything unknown, while the tone of the 'Epilogue', a balance sheet of sorts, was emphatically benign. Even if 'Bulgarian history must always be read with Constantinople in sight, [since] it was Byzantium, the Empire, that decided its destiny', Runciman winded up his story,

> Bulgaria [need not] stand ashamed [of it]. It is a tribute rather to the greatness of her rulers that they could, as no other invaders had been able to do, build up a nation at the very gates of the mightiest empire of Christendom [with] the highest civilisation of its hemisphere . . . . The Bulgars had brought order to the Slavs and had lifted them out of chaos, setting an example for the whole Slav world to follow. The Serbian tribes could profit by it; and, moreover, had not Bulgaria lain between, they might never so have freed themselves from the influence of Constantinople, to form a proud nation . . . . But the great gift of Bulgaria to Europe lay in her readiness to take over the legacy of Cyril and Methodius . . . and thus put all the Balkan peninsula and all the Russias into [its] debt . . . . Though clouds pass at times over the face of Bulgaria, she may well be content with her history. The First Empire has left her memories rich in glory.[49]

As in the Greek case, the foreign contribution to the construction of the Bulgarian national grand narrative was not insignificant.

To round off the range of interpretations, Bogdan Filov (1883–1945), an eminent archaeologist, art historian and politician, deployed the arguments about the discontinuity between Hellas and Byzantium for the purpose of explaining the division between eastern and western Europe.[50] Filov agreed with the majority of Balkan byzantinists that in terms of ethnic composition, political representation, military participation and state structure, the empire's 'Hellenic' character was highly problematic. Regarding culture, it was the strongly orientalised Hellenistic culture rather than classical Hellenism that impacted

---

[49] Runciman 1930: especially 259–61.   [50] Filov 1927: 2/1, 32–41; 2/2, 125–35.

Byzantium. Byzantine culture, Filov stressed, was 'principally a Christian-Oriental culture', with the Greek and Roman elements (or what he called 'pagan-European' culture) playing a secondary role. The 'spirit of byzantinism', he wrote, presaging the arguments of some British byzantinists after World War II to be discussed later, could be better understood if we looked not for what connected it with antiquity and Hellas but for what distinguished it from them. 'Because the value of byzantinism as a cultural and political factor lies much more in what it succeeded in newly creating than in that which it could have preserved from the past.' According to Filov, while modern western and central Europe was raised in the traditions of the ancient culture, present-day eastern (or Orthodox) Europe was the child primarily of Byzantium.

> Byzantium and Hellas are not therefore two stages in the development of the same historical process; they are two opposite poles, two different worlds, two contrasts. Byzantium and Hellas are the scions of two different civilisations; they are the embodiment of the eternal conflict between East and West – a conflict that emerged at the dawn of European history and that, in one form or another, continues to this day. This explains the differences between present-day western and eastern Europe.

The 'dualism' in contemporary European culture would disappear and its unification would be accomplished, concluded Filov, 'only when in the all-European civilisation enter all lasting values that humankind had created so far during its entire existence'.[51]

An Improved Edition of Byzantium

Between 1910 and 1920, Serbia succeeded in fulfilling the major part of its national aspirations by including in its boundaries all territories that could be claimed as Serbian, and more. For a brief while, the essentially gratified Serbian nationalism changed destination. In the new, 'Yugoslav' phase of Serbian historiography in the 1920s, interest in the medieval past drifted away from the Byzantinocentric view of Serbian history and culture that prevailed in the previous period, even if the proper field of Byzantine studies made certain advances.[52] At the centre of attention were themes and (re)interpretations underscoring the community between the three

---

[51] Filov 1927: 2/2, 130, 133, 135.
[52] The erudite but specialised work of the first trained Serbian byzantinists, Dragutin Anastasijević (1877–1950) and Filaret Granić (1883–1948), remained accessible to a narrow circle of specialists, while only two doctoral dissertations in Byzantine studies were defended at Belgrade University during the whole interwar period (Maksimović 1988: 661–3).

144 Between Byzantine Studies and Metahistory

constitutive nationalities of the state. Rather than emphasising the Serbian medieval state's oscillation between the Byzantine and the Latin cultural-political spheres and its expanding 'byzantinisation', the Serbian historians of the 1920s and early 1930s preferred to present it as the site of 'reconciliation' and unison of these apparently contradictory orientations.

That said, in the Kingdom of the Serbs, Croats and Slovenes, where the confrontation between Serbian and Croatian nationalists swiftly came to a head, the questions about the definition of the Serbian national identity and the legitimation of the Serbian supremacy in the tripartite state remained high on the agenda. The growing disillusionment with the Yugoslav idea in the 1930s marked a return to a narrower national focus but no tangibly revived interest in Byzantine themes. The most significant Serbian historians of the interwar period, Stanoje Stanojević, Vladimir Ćorović, Jovan Radonić and Nikola Radojčić, although trained as byzantinists, either turned away from Serbian-Byzantine themes towards other medieval topics (Radojčić, Stanojević), switched to more specialised studies (Radonić) or approached the Byzantine presence in Serbian history from a strictly political viewpoint (Ćorović). In the general surveys of national history, discussions of the 'Byzantine factor' were largely restricted to the short-lived but historiographically and politically overexploited topic of Stefan Dušan's empire, conceived as the 'congenital' heir to Byzantium. The persistent focus on the Serbian, or 'Serbian-Byzantine', empire in the context of interwar Yugoslavia should not surprise because the combination of 'multinational' composition and Serbian leadership lent itself to divergent interpretations, which could serve the cause of Serbian nationalism and, alternatively or in parallel, that of integral Yugoslavism. As for research on Byzantium proper, it largely fell upon a non-local, immigrant community of byzantinists.

A strategy of pushing cultural differences between the constituent nations in new Yugoslavia to the background while at the same time foregrounding Serbian state craftsmanship is apparent in the work of Vladimir Ćorović (1885–1941), the most prolific and revered Serbian historian of that time, who wrote his *History of Yugoslavia* (1933) in the spirit of Yugoslavism and in defence of 'Yugoslavdom'. He tried to weave the medieval history of the three recognised nationalities that came to constitute interwar Yugoslavia (also encompassing the 'Macedonian Slavs' and 'Serbo-Croatian' Bosnia) into a narrative of a single people with different cultural-political trajectories. Against this ambitious canvas, Ćorović seemed uninterested in assessing the relative importance of the Byzantine 'model' for the Serbs, despite his minute survey of Serbian-Byzantine

An Improved Edition of Byzantium

political relations. That was also the case in his other synthetic study, *History of the Serbs*, written on the eve of World War II and published posthumously. In his coverage of the 'seminal' achievements of medieval Serbia – the emergence of the 'state idea', the organisation of the church, the creation of religious architecture and art – Byzantine influence was barely mentioned. True, Ćorović tells us (as others did before him) that the state formation among the Serbs came as a reaction to an outside pressure and threat; that on the 'Serbian lands' (Zeta and Raška) 'eastern and western influences intersected'; and that after the tenth century the Serbs' 'not only political but also religious-civilisational' orientation towards Constantinople and Byzantium definitely prevailed and were dominant during the next 'several centuries'. However, his narrative does not indicate that either of these was directly effectuated by Byzantium or that 'importation' of Byzantine models had much to do with the Serbian state and culture.

Thus Ćorović maintained that the Serbs' political and cultural reorientation towards Byzantium came about with the 'mediation of their kinsmen from Macedonia'.[53] If by the mid-twelfth century Raška 'was in the main a purely Orthodox domain', this was the result of the activity of the 'Slavic Macedonian element'.[54] The influence of the Byzantine model on the formation of the Serbian state and the institutionalisation of its autocephalous Orthodox Church remained unaddressed. The Serbian 'state idea' and notion of civilisation, first developed under Prince Stefan Nemanja, appeared as sheer Serbian creations testifying to 'the state growth and high cultural aspirations of medieval Serbia'. Similarly, the autocephalous Serbian Church set up by Stefan's son, Sava, in 1219 with the sanction of the Constantinople Patriarchate had a 'purely national character': 'Sava made the Orthodox faith the state religion of Serbia and tied it closely with the interests of the state and the people'; Sava's church was and remained 'popular and national', 'actively, lively and directly concerned with the overall progress of the people', and this was its 'greatest significance'. Therefore, Ćorović concluded, 'The Serbian state idea was created physically by Nemanja and intellectually by Sava.'[55] As in the Bulgarian storyline, 'Slavic Orthodoxy' is said to have been intended to achieve 'the full homogeneity of the Serbian state'. The important difference is that the Bulgarian historians' assessments of the national role of the clergy were

[53] A big tract of this former Ottoman province, which was part of both the First and Second Bulgarian Kingdoms and was unsuccessfully coveted by the modern Bulgarian state, became part of post-war Yugoslavia.
[54] Ćorović 1933: 58–9, 102–3; 1989: 72–3.   [55] Ćorović 1933: 121, 129–30.

146   Between Byzantine Studies and Metahistory

often ambivalent, seeing it as susceptible to 'byzantinisation', that is, cultural de-nationalisation and social estrangement from the people. In Serbian historiography, by contrast, the Serbian clergy invariably featured as *the* prime 'patriotic element', a firm repository of the Serbian state idea and love of freedom.[56] Typical of this narrative was the complete harmony between church and state on the road to accomplishing the 'Serbian state idea'.

All things considered, until the proclamation of Stefan Dušan's empire in the mid-fourteenth century, Byzantium appears in Ćorović's *History* as a formidable adversary to the Serbs, but not as their civilisational model. It was only after overtaking Southern Macedonia and entering deep into properly Greek areas that the Serbs are said to have been exposed to the influence of Greek culture: 'It appears that the byzantinisation of the Serbs started in the fourteenth century and first affected the court and higher society.'[57] Serbia's belated 'byzantinisation' by Ćorović can be read as an attempt to underscore the state-building and creative genius of the Serbs (and the South Slavs generally). In the same stroke he downplayed the importance for the Yugoslav nations of their imperial legacies – Roman, Byzantine, Ottoman and Habsburg – which continued to divide rather than unite them.

Ćorović lacked both romantic élan and the inclination to operate with the collective agency of 'the Serbian people'. However, Novaković's central critical theses – about the imitative imperialism of the Serbian state class, hence the insignificance of the principle of nationality, and the irrelevance of the historical precedent for the present – were not adopted by either Stanojević or Ćorović. They stressed instead the exigencies of the 'Serbian national and state life', or what Stanojević saw as the 'ethnic and state offensive of the Serbian nation', which had been under 'systematic preparation' since the days of Stefan Nemanja. Stanojević pointed out that in the strategic direction of Serbia's expansion – the Vardar River valley and Macedonia – it met with the resistance of both Byzantium, the traditional possessor of this area, and Bulgaria, which claimed it by state right. Against these historical and state rights, he argued,

> Serbia opposed the natural right [*životno pravo*] for its state interests and national power. At Velbužd [where the Serbs defeated the Bulgarians in a 1330 battle] a fight was waged between Byzantine-Bulgarian state-legalistic theories and Serbian national and state life. With its enduring forces, Serbia swept to victory, and the question of supremacy in the Vardar valley and Macedonia was definitively solved in favour of the Serbian people.[58]

---

[56] Ćorović 1933: 331.   [57] Ćorović 1989: 158.   [58] Stanojević 1922: 6, 7; 1931: 1–2.

An Improved Edition of Byzantium

Ćorović borrowed wholesale this remarkable declaration of the Serbs' right to *Lebensraum* in Macedonia:

> Whole new areas were included in the Serbian state which until then had never belonged to it and became, if they had not already been, our national possession in an ethnic sense as well . . . . The battle of Velbuzhd was one of the most absolute Serbian victories in the Middle Ages . . . Bulgaria was reduced to its natural borders from the Danube to the Rila Mountains and Maritsa River and never again dared to go beyond them at the expense of the Serbs to the west . . . Serbian domination in northern Macedonia was thus fully secured by this victory, while in the south the field was prepared for Dušan's further work.[59]

For both Stanojević and Ćorović, the Bulgarian medieval claims to Macedonia were more important than the traditional opposition to Byzantium precisely because of their 'relevance' for the contemporary Serbian-Bulgarian controversies over this region. Nothing remained of the ethnic filiation between the medieval Serbs and Bulgarians and of the inconsequence of the historical right on which Novaković had repeatedly insisted.

Most of these themes came together in a professed 'synthesis of Serbian history' authored by Nikola Radojčić (1882–1964), a student of prominent teachers such as the Swiss byzantinist Heinrich Gelzer, the Czech Slavicist and historian of medieval Serbia Konstantin Jireček and Karl Krumbacher. The book reads like a synopsis of the major conventions of Serbian historiography from mid-nineteenth to mid-twentieth century. Serbia's thrust towards replacing Byzantium in southeastern Europe, Radojčić tells us, was a protracted but uninterrupted process of internal, material and spiritual maturation, which began with the first Njemanićs and where the introduction of Byzantine institutions and the exertion to catch up with Byzantine culture proceeded synchronously. The ensuing territorial expansion of the state, therefore, was the result not simply of the Serbian rulers' talents and Byzantium's weakness but of the 'efforts of entire generations driven . . . by the vital needs of the Serbian people'. In this way, Radojčić wrote, Serbia cultivated its 'ability to replace Byzantium, the first power on the Balkan peninsula, and thus realise the dream of a succession of warrior nations, who see in the amalgamation (*utapanje*) of their country in an empire a higher political organisation, the fulfilment of the high idea of the Roman empire as the peak of political development'.[60] At the height of its power, he argued, citing Nicolae Iorga, a national state seeks 'to break the

[59] Ćorović 1933: 165, 171–2; 1989: 144.   [60] Radojčić 1942: 115–16.

148   Between Byzantine Studies and Metahistory

national borders and embrace much broader boundaries'; more importantly, 'next to conquering Byzantium by arms [the Serbian rulers] laboured
shrewdly and tirelessly, through their legislative work, to qualify for the
high and honourary goal of replacing Byzantium'. The fruits of this wilful
work were reaped and multiplied by Stefan Dušan, who stood at the helm
of 'the only people in the Balkan peninsula who could adopt the high idea
of empire and defend it against the increasingly violent attacks of the
Ottomans'.[61]

Since it constituted the apex of Serbian medieval power and, accordingly, a key turning point in the national historiography, Dušan's empire
encapsulated the different interpretations of the nature and long-term
consequences of the Serbian interaction with Byzantium. Although he
cut short the work he had begun at the beginning of the century on
Byzantium and the Serbs and moved to other themes, Stanoje Stanojević
wrote a study dedicated to *Car Dušan* (1922). Dušan, he held, had no
preconceived plan to create a Serbian-Byzantine empire, but 'the easy
successes, vanity and state interests impalpably dragged him ever
further'.[62] Dušan's solution to the 'hard question of how the Serbian
kingdom could take the place of Byzantium', namely the creation of
a 'Serbian-Byzantine state', was the result of his awareness that military
victory was not enough. His idea of such a state meant that 'in the
territories once ruled by Byzantium, Byzantine culture and Byzantine
state arrangement would [continue to] dominate' but that 'all military,
administrative and ecclesiastical executives and dignitaries would be taken
from the areas that constituted the core of the original Serbian state'. The
choice of Skopje for the site of his coronation as 'Emperor of the Serbs and
the Greeks' was another demonstration of his intention 'that in the new
empire the Serbian element would be the bearer of the entire state life'.[63]
This 'great plan and heavy task' ultimately failed because of the great
differences between the northern ('Serbian') and southern ('Greek') provinces of the Serbian-Byzantine state, which 'were the consequence of
different races, a different past and culture and different cultural
influences'.[64]

For his part, Vladimir Ćorović assumed that Dušan had come naturally
to the idea 'to replace the enfeebled and worn-out Byzantium with the
fresh empire of his own people'. Having conquered most of the Balkans,
Dušan believed that the imperial title belonged to him by right and that the

---

[61] Radojčić 1942: 116.   [62] Stanojević 1922: 12–13, 24.   [63] Stanojević 1922: 13–18.
[64] Stanojević 1922: 23–5.

An Improved Edition of Byzantium

state he had created was not a competitor to but 'almost a master of the Eastern Roman Empire'.[65] While Ćorović agreed that the Serbian-Byzantine empire was a 'hybrid creation', he still considered it a 'national project in the true sense of the word, having made the Serbs the main pivot of the state'. Dušan had invested considerable effort into trying to make a unified whole out of the disparate parts of his empire, his Legal Code being the best proof. However, during this period the Serbian upper classes came under the strong impact of the incorporated Greek population, of its culture and customs, while the royal court, the church architecture and art replicated the 'Greek forms'. Up to that point, Serbia, despite being an Orthodox state, had felt 'the strong influence of the West'. However, from the time of Dušan, because of the establishment of direct connections to the 'Greeks' and the deeper penetration into Byzantine areas, 'Serbia was increasingly acquiring a Balkan-Byzantine character'. Like Stanojević, Ćorović found that the biggest problem was not that Dušan's policy was becoming 'too imperialistic'. The main problem was that his state was 'lacking sufficient skills, traditions and time to introduce the Serbian spirit into the new lands', that is, 'to assimilate, nurture and really adopt them'.[66]

Both Stanojević and Ćorović thus blamed Dušan for the same thing the Bulgarian historians blamed Simeon, namely for seeking to create not a big national state but 'another' Byzantine empire, and for thus succumbing to, rather than assimilating, the 'Greek forms'. This failure, however, led neither of them to question the Serbs' inherent talents of an imperial master-nation ripe to replace the 'Greek', their propensity for empire-building and the 'national idea' behind Dušan's project. Nikola Radojčić hammered in the same message via a different route. Dušan's sense of mission, he avowed, was not conquest but 'enforcing the reign of justice in his lands', a task that, according to the assumption of the time, was best achievable in an imperial state format. He therefore waged wars in order to 'give the domestic mission of his empire the deserved outer form'. Dušan's predecessors 'had already closed the doors of the Serbian state to western feudalism with its utter degradation and utterly unjust social arrangement'. In contrast, in his Legal Code 'the great ruler developed in a sacred form the idea of justice and rule of law as the greatest tasks of each state, particularly an empire. With his honest efforts Dušan thought he acquired the indisputable right to inherit Byzantium'. Unlike Emperor John VI Cantacuzenus, who was simply obsessed with an imperial ambition, the Serbian ruler 'already disposed of a state with imperial boundaries, which

[65] Ćorović 1933: 179–80; 1989: 167.   [66] Ćorović 1933: 173–4, 179–82, 193; 1989: 167–70.

150   Between Byzantine Studies and Metahistory

he wanted to empower to fulfil the high purposes of his legislative and educational work'.[67] Ćorović's balance sheet, too, pointed to the superiority of the Serbs over the Byzantines (and the Bulgarians). From the fourteenth century, he maintained, 'the Morava was a purely Serbian river and the Serbian ethnic boundary extended to the Timok River; to the south, Macedonia acquired a Serbian character'. Unsurprisingly, these historical borders overlapped perfectly with Yugoslavia's post-war political geography to the east and south. The Serbs are also said to have been the only ones who resisted and fought the advancing Turks instead of 'bowing down' like the Greeks and the Bulgarians. 'Serbian corpses, numbering in the thousands, filled the defence trenches of Europe to safeguard it from Turkish invasion.'[68]

The complete disappearance from this narrative of Byzantium as a factor in Balkan politics, starting with Dušan's imperial coronation, is indeed striking: somehow Serbia appears as having taken its place, first as a prime military and moral force on the Balkan peninsula and then as a major barrier against the Turkish advance. Ćorović and Radojčić, in fact, quite unambiguously suggested that the role of defenders of Christianity, imperial dignity and freedom fell to the Serbs. Interwar Serbian historiography thus succeeded in highlighting simultaneously the multi-ethnic character of the medieval Serbian empire (an enhancement of the adopted Byzantine heritage and a paragon for post-war Yugoslavia), the state-building genius of the Serbs (to be counted in distributing political power between the national groups in the Yugoslav state) and the imperative for any state to assimilate ethnic and cultural differences if it is to survive (the task of the nation that can prove historically its potential to fulfil it).

It should not surprise that such a protean yet not inconsistent understanding of the relations between Serbia and Byzantium lent itself to alternative ideological uses. The well-known philosopher and foremost 'national psychologist' in interwar Yugoslavia, Vladimir Dvorniković (1888–1956), came up with an interpretation whose metahistorical characteristics were comparable to Mutafchiev's. He sought to construct a common cultural framework for the 'Yugo-Slavs', in which Byzantine culture was assigned a distinct and controversial place.

According to Dvorniković, Stefan Nemanja's sons, Stefan the First-Crowned and Sava, realised 'an ingenious division' of political roles and a synthesis of civilisational spheres, the first taking his crown from the West, the second taking the church from the East. The importance of their

---

[67] Radojčić 1942: 116–17.   [68] Ćorović 1933: 238–9, 291.

An Improved Edition of Byzantium

'mighty state-building and organisational work' was that, while until then Serbia had continuously wavered between the Greek-Byzantine and Western-Latin political and cultural spheres, 'Stefan and Sava's action, in an apparent inner contradiction, brought about the fortunate reconciliation of these spheres through a formula that provided an orientation line for centuries [ahead], which is: material-technological adherence to the West and spiritual-cultural [adherence] to the East'.[69]

The state the Nemanjićs had created 'at the intersection of East and West', Dvorniković argued, was anything but a mechanistic mix. At base it was 'a Byzantinoid state' – neither a bureaucratic, Roman-law-based Byzantine state nor a feudal one in the Western sense, but something outside these categories. It drew on the '*županian* atavism' that counteracted the 'Byzantine-Oriental theocratic principle' but at the same time was acquiescent to strong leadership. The Nemanjićs, he wrote, were led by the desire to 'erase the Greek name' from the territory of the Serbian state – which indicated 'that there was, although not in the present-day sense, something nationally conscious and opposed to the Greek spirit in the souls of all the strong state-building Nemanjićs – except Dušan'. Thus far it looked like this 'composite' Serbian state could serve as a blueprint for the Yugoslav cultural convergence. With Dušan, however, imperialism entered Serbian medieval history: 'instead of bringing the idea of the "unifier" of the Serbian lands, [Stefan] Nemanja, to completion, Dušan tied to the state framework new Greeks and Albanians'. The essence of the proclamation of the Serbian-Byzantine empire, according to Dvorniković, was 'in the continuity of the Eastern-Christian idea, whose bearer was the Byzantine *basileus*, and the Romaic state nation'. In its internal organisation this empire was a '*mixtum compositum* of ancient remnants and new reformist beginnings'. However, 'this legal-Byzantine and western-feudal state arrangement' was not to last: 'after its healthy beginnings Nemanjić's's Serbia degraded into an artificial Serbian-Greek symbiosis'; as such, it was doomed to fail.[70] Here we can detect close similarities with Mutafchiev's portrayal of the 'organic', proto-national phase of Bulgarian medieval history and the 'inorganic' one following the unbridled infiltration of byzantinism.

On the historiographical field of interwar Yugoslavia there was another important player, exerting a major impact on the Serbian self-perception vis-à-vis the Byzantine empire and, generally, on the direction of Byzantine studies: the Russian émigré community. In 1933 Georgiy Ostrogorski (1902–76), at

---

[69] Dvorniković 1939: 852–3.   [70] Dvorniković 1939: 853–6.

that time a promising young byzantinist and a leading figure in the discipline after World War II (to whom more attention will be paid further on), settled down in Belgrade, where he spent the next forty-odd years researching Byzantine history and the cultural limits of *Slavia Orthodoxa*. A year after his arrival in Yugoslavia, he published an article audaciously titled 'Of What and How Was Byzantium Made'. Ostrogorski has been generally credited for having coined the succinct definition of Byzantium as a product of the synthesis of three elements: Roman statehood, Greek culture and Christianity. The essentially Roman structure and identity of the state (administration, military organisation, law, economic system, state and citizens' self-perception) were its core characteristics, to which the empire tenaciously stuck until its last days. 'In the Middle Age Byzantium was the only state in the proper sense of the word, and precisely because it continued the tradition of the Roman state.' Its culture (language, philosophy, literature, arts and architecture) was Greek, but only in form, as in content it was Christian.[71] Remarkably, Ostrogorski found the Oriental influences in both politics and culture, despite numerous borrowings in arts and architecture, to be marginal, 'lacking deep roots in Byzantine life', and took issue with those, like Charles Diehl, who considered Byzantium an 'Oriental empire'. Iconoclasm, which came about after the great territorial losses to the Arabs, was for him 'an attack of Oriental culture on the Byzantine world, an attack directed simultaneously against Byzantium's characteristic Greco-Christian essence, its Greek culture and art and its Roman law'. The defeat of iconoclasm and Byzantium's spectacular upturn after the mid-ninth century signalled 'the great synthesis between the Christian-Greek culture and the Roman state' and the safeguarding of the ancient heritage through Orthodox Christianity. The 'unequivocally Greco-Roman nature of Byzantium' determined its much more intensive exchange with the West than with the East, with the caveat that 'in general it was not Byzantium which learned from the West, but the West which learned from Byzantium'.[72]

For Ostrogorski, it was crucial that the empire had launched its 'great missionary activity among the Slavs' after decades of mainly military clashes with them, 'precisely at the time of the spectacular flourishing of Byzantine culture, when the Greco-Roman nature of byzantinism was already defined'. He regarded it as highly symptomatic that 'at the pinnacle of its power [Byzantium's] major interests lay in the Slavic lands', not in the East (Asia Minor), from where it drew its military strength. In a political sense the fourteenth and fifteenth centuries were a 'sad era' for the empire,

---

[71] Ostrogorski 1934: 508–10.   [72] Ostrogorski 1934: 511–13.

An Improved Edition of Byzantium 153

but culturally it saw another peak, marked this time by intense preoccupation with antiquity. Until its last days, Ostrogorski affirmed, Byzantium safeguarded its Roman identity and the Greek cultural tradition: 'This, by the way, explains why Byzantium – unlike the West – experienced no explicit Renaissance. In Byzantium no Renaissance was needed, as ancient culture in Byzantium never died but lived on continuously. And the western Renaissance ... became possible only thanks to Byzantium for only in Byzantium could the West find the goods of ancient culture, otherwise forgotten and lost.' 'That which the Slavs adopted from Byzantium', Ostrogorski's coda read, 'were not Oriental elements, but above all what the history of mankind has ever achieved: Christian faith, Greek culture, Roman state principles.'[73] The bottom line in all of this was, obviously, the de-orientalisation of Byzantium and the assertion of its quintessentially European nature and of the Slavs as the heirs to its legacy. Certainly, this rendition appealed to the Serbian proponents of a Serbo-Byzantine cultural symbiosis that endowed the Serbs with an ancient inheritance of paramount European value.

It is no exaggeration to say that the engaged scholarly interest in Byzantium and Serbian- (or Slavo-)Byzantine relations in interwar Yugoslavia was largely the territory of the Russian émigré circle. Most of its members delved into specific sub-fields, especially legal history, as is testified by the work of two prominent legal scholars, Teodor Taranovskiy (1875–1936) and Aleksandar Solov'ev (1890–1971), which focussed on an 'exegesis' of Dušan's Legal Code. Taranovskiy was not inclined to read the Code as a reflection of a highly developed Serbian society, as post-Romantic Serbian historiography tended to do. For him, the provisions placing the rule of law above the tsar (art. 105, 171 and 172) were an expression of Dušan's imperial *legal ideology*, with roots in Byzantine law, rather than an expression of *legal practice*.[74] Solov'ev, for his part, took up the task of dispelling the Serbian provenance of the Code and identifying its Byzantine sources. He also polemicised with Bobchev by arguing that the Slavs did not bring with them a developed system of customary law and that they put together their juridical codices quite late (at the end of the thirteenth century) in the form of a 'mixed system of Byzantine-Slavic law'. Until then Byzantine law had been fully adopted by the Bulgarians as 'sacred, perfect, complete and civilised', with the penal code presenting the only instance of 'serious divergences and contradictions between the Slavic and the Byzantine points of view'. According to Solov'ev, it was

[73] Ostrogorski 1934: 513–14. [74] Taranovski 1931–5; 1926.

unwarranted to assume that the Bulgarian tsars had governed and judged according to the customary law, especially after the Byzantine domination in the eleventh and twelfth centuries.[75] At the same time, Solov'ev made no distinction, in the vein of Taranovskiy, between ideology and practice when discussing the *Corpus juris* of Dušan's 'composite Serbo-Greek Empire' and lent his authority to the thesis about the 'high juridical consciousness' transpiring from it: the Code, he held, pursued the creation of 'a great state, based on the force of the Serbian race and on the Roman-Byzantine tradition, a legal state, in which the conqueror and the conquered would be equal [and] where everyone, including the emperor himself, had to respect the principles of the objective law'.[76]

For his part, Vladimir Mošin (1894–1987), another prominent byzantinist in this circle, identified 'three main waves' of Byzantine cultural and political permeation among the Serbs, which also marked the progressive phases of their civilisational transformation from primitive tribes to carriers of the Byzantine heritage: the first coincided with the introduction of the Cyrillic (religious and legal) literature, the second with the 'nationalisation of the Church' and penetration of Eastern Christianity 'in the deep popular strata' and the third with Dušan's conquests in the south.[77] With this framework, Mošin was instrumental in conceptualising the byzantinisation of Serbia as a process of transition from '"automatic" infiltration of Byzantine traditions and unconscious emulation of Greek culture' into 'intentional borrowing of the Byzantine cultural values'. He was also at pains to demonstrate that the peak of Byzantine influence at the time of Dušan's conquests was only the 'logical conclusion of the previous development of the Serbian political history' associated with King Stefan Milutin's conquests of Byzantine Macedonia.[78] Mošin thus lent additional credibility to the Serbian historians' argument of Serbia's steady advancement, through wilful and geopolitically justified byzantinisation, towards its 'Serbo-Byzantine' condition while shifting the emphasis from the political to the cultural aspects of this process.

Versions of *Byzance après Byzance*

Romania emerged as the great geopolitical victor of World War I in the region. The peace treaties of 1918 fulfilled almost all the dreams of the prewar irredentists of uniting the ethnic Romanians and the territories where

---

[75] Soloviev 1936: 437–45. [76] Soloviev 1936: 437–45. See also Solovjev 1928a; 1928b.
[77] Mošin 1939: 355; 1937: 147–60. [78] Mošin 1937: 148, 158.

Versions of Byzance après Byzance

they lived into a unitary Greater Romania. Romanian nationalism's success was perceived as confirmation of Romania's historical 'mission' as a regional power and civiliser. This very triumph, on the other hand, brought along new problems related to the unification of populations and territories that had belonged to various empires (Habsburg, Ottoman and Russian), encompassed substantial ethnic minorities and came along with different historical, cultural and institutional traditions. The combination of heightened self-confidence as a result of territorial aggrandisement and grave challenges to Greater Romania's national integration boded unremitting dominance of ethnic nationalism in politics and culture, occasionally morphing into quasi-imperial visions.

In Romanian historiography, in contrast to the Greek, the Bulgarian and the Serbian, the fall of Byzantium in 1453 marked not an end but a new, bright beginning: the rise of a fresh Orthodox power, the Romanian principalities which, albeit tributary to the Sublime Porte, preserved internal autonomy until the eighteenth century. As before the war, Nicolae Iorga largely set the frame and the terms of the debate on the Romanian past in a wider, grander than regional, context. The convening of the First International Congress of Byzantine Studies in Bucharest in 1924 and the founding of the Romanian Institute of Byzantine Studies in 1934 were also his initiatives.

In the previous chapter we tried to identify the elements that, in Iorga's view, made the Romanian principalities particularly apt to receive and perpetuate the Byzantine legacy. After the war, he kept expanding on this theme. He saw the Byzantine empire as 'an international formula, consecrated by imperial legitimacy and propped by Roman law and the Eastern Christian Church'.[79] In neither political ('national') nor cultural sense was it a 'Greek' empire, despite the dominance of the Greek language and the prestige of the Hellenic heritage:

> Greek scholars usually make a mistake as bad as the one that considers the Byzantine empire a 'Bas-Empire'. By connecting classical Greece, a completely different world, to Byzantium, which was of Roman descent in both its origins and principles, they attribute to what should only be considered as a stage in their national development an exclusively national, unchangeable, nature that, despite instincts natural to most races, did not exist at all .... Byzantium excluded, until the end, everything related to nationality.[80]

[79] Iorga 1922a: 34–5.   [80] Iorga 1935–6: 18–19; 1939b: I, 329.

156   Between Byzantine Studies and Metahistory

The soberness of such views, however, was not replicated in discussions of, to use Iorga's dramatic style, the 'vast "Romanian Fatherland", a term imbued with a deep ethnic instinct' and 'the role that the Romanians played in the East not as warriors but in the higher terms of culture, of ideas and above all *of conservation of the ancient ideals of unity* and *ancient links with the other world, the West*'.[81]

Iorga's most famed contribution to the field of Byzantine studies was his idea of Byzantium's continuity after the empire's political demise in 1453 – an idea he developed in full in the 1930s. Captured by his felicitous formula 'Byzantium after Byzantium', it provided a new perspective on the institutional and cultural landscape not only of the Balkans but also the entire Near East. 'As a complex of institutions, a political system, a religious formation, a type of civilisation comprising the Hellenic intellectual legacy, Roman law, the Orthodox religion and everything it created and preserved in terms of art', the empire, Iorga averred, remained alive. What is more, it kept on evolving and assimilating new forms of civilisation. Byzantium, he wrote, 'namely that which formed its essence, not only maintained itself . . . but continued its millenary action . . . always evolving, accumulating all that entered its wide area of action. . . . Many new things would come to light, but deep down the unyielding Byzantine continuity would remain'.[82] Although it encompassed a vast area, stretching from Italy to Georgia and Syria, 'the essence of Byzantine life' was preserved mainly in the Balkans. And while the Ottoman empire and the Patriarchate of Constantinople took over many of its functions, the real successors and perpetuators – spiritual and civilisational – of Byzantium were the Romanians:

> For five hundred years we gave asylum to the whole higher religious life, to the whole cultural life of the peoples from across the Danube. Greek Byzantium and Slav Byzantium, which derived from it, thus lived for another half-millennium among us and through us, if not for us . . .. There was a time when the entire Byzantine Balkan legacy seemed destined to pass on to our princes.[83]

The process of creating this 'new Romanian Byzantium'[84] went through stages. The first coincided with the Ottoman expansion, when Byzantine notables took refuge in the principalities and infiltrated the nascent Romanian nobility. Thus, from the fourteenth century, the Romanian provinces came to represent 'the Byzantine and Slavo-Byzantine political

---

[81] Iorga 1920: 49; 1913a: 424 (original emphases).   [82] Iorga 2000 [1935]: 25–6.
[83] Iorga 1914: 11.   [84] Iorga 2000: 166.

Versions of Byzance après Byzance

civilisation in the entirety of its diverse elements', while the Romanian princes assumed the role of 'legitimate heirs of the Eastern Caesars'. The second phase began with the Ottoman conquest first of the independent Balkan states and then of Constantinople. During this period the cultural life of all of southeastern Europe was concentrated in the Romanian lands, which bestowed on the Romanians the role of 'protectors of the Byzantine Church and civilisation' and of 'Christian unity in a world subjected in a political sense to Islam . . . .. *That which was still preserved of the Slavo-Byzantine religious life now passed into the Romanian countries, and there alone*'. During the third phase the Romanian princes 'appeared before all Eastern Christians as the custodians of the tradition of the one-time Byzantine emperors'.[85] The Phanariots picked up the baton as they assumed 'the task of continuing Byzantine traditions within the territory under the authority of the sultan'; they had come to Romania 'not as Greeks tending to Hellenise, but as successors of universal civilisation of the Greek language [who] endeavoured, through the newly established schools, to attract any Orthodox believers to their Byzantine Hellenism'.[86] Thus byzantinism survived until 'the dawn of the nineteenth century', when it was stripped of its essence by the new philosophical ideas, averse to religious influences and historical authorities, and by national consciousness.[87]

In Iorga's reading, therefore, Romania was the real *Byzance après Byzance*, having fulfilled a universal mission and safeguarded the distinctive post-Byzantine civilisation of southeastern Europe. What the Bulgarians and Serbs had long fought for in vain, the Romanians received by right, since deep down they had never relinquished the Roman idea of empire and their Roman self-awareness:

> If this Byzantium could come close to us, thus causing our deviation from the old popular life and from the western life . . . if Byzantium could reign among us, this was neither because of its Greek character nor because of our special devotion to Orthodoxy . . . but because, due to the Roman inception preserved in the instinct of our popular classes, we recognised its Roman basis.[88]

Ultimately, it was the synthesis between Byzantium and Rome, the imperial legacy and the democratic organisation of the popular masses, that shaped the unique character of Romanian civilisation. And it was this synthesis that secured the Romanians' place in world history. It has been suggested that

---

[85] Iorga 1914: 46–50, 52–8 (original emphases); 2000: 129–94, 200. See also Cicance 1971: 219–28; Cândea 1971: 193.

[86] Iorga 2000: 205, 213.   [87] Iorga 2000: 231–4; 1913c: 47–8.   [88] Iorga 1939a: 21–2.

158   Between Byzantine Studies and Metahistory

Iorga's thesis about the Byzantine heritage in the principalities of Wallachia and Moldavia 'remains the only universal vocation produced to this date by the Romanian historiography'.[89] But it was also the solution Iorga offered to the specific problems Romanian historiography faced in dealing with the massive Slavic traits in medieval and early modern Romanian culture and with the *grecismul* of the Phanariots in more recent times.

Most post-war Romanian medievalists and byzantinists had studied with either Iorga or Russo. Nicolae Bănescu (1878–1971), a lifelong aficionado of Iorga, led the Chair of Byzantine History at the University of Cluj (1919–38) and later succeeded D. Russo at the University of Bucharest (1938–47) and Iorga as Director of the Institute of Byzantine Studies (1940–8). Unlike his teacher, Bănescu was not a visionary lured by grand generalisations and syntheses. Having assumed wholesale Iorga's assertions that the first Romanian 'crystallisations of state' took place in the eleventh century in the Lower Danube, Bănescu set out to identify the political and administrative conditions promoting such crystallisations. Since the mid-first century, he argued, Romanity in these lands had never perished: first the 'mother city', Rome, then (with brief interruptions) the 'New Rome' exerted protection on 'the Roman tradition' in this area in the course of a full millennium. Ignoring the lack of any evidence that could make it possible to define the ethnic and political character of whatever formations might have emerged in these lands, given the extremely mixed populations living there, Bănescu confidently argued that Tatos, Sesthlav and Satzas, the three rulers presiding over the process of early 'Romanian state-formation', were Romanians who, until that time, were integrated into the provincial life of the Byzantine *thema* of Parastrion. By rebelling against Byzantium, they had made plain their desire for political independence.[90] At the roots of the medieval Romanian state, Bănescu implied, was an uninterrupted political tradition built on the imperial pattern of Rome and Byzantium. While the Old Rome left its indelible mark on the formation of the Romanian identity, the New Rome played a key role in the maintenance of this national identity by supplying it with a civilisational and organisational model. Bănescu's many years of research on the Byzantine *reconquista* of the northern Balkan lands in the eleventh and twelfth centuries and on the Byzantine

---

[89] Leanca 2013: 293. See Iorga 1935–6 (3 vols.) for 'The Place of Romanians in World History'. Also Iorga 1939b: 161–3.

[90] Bănescu 1921–2: 138–60; 1923.

Versions of Byzance après Byzance

domination of the Lower Danube and the northeastern coast of the Black Sea pointed in the same direction. At the same time, he, like Iorga, doggedly refused to admit that the Bulgarian state ever effectively reigned over the 'Romanian-inhabited' lands north of the Danube, despite solid arguments to the contrary adduced not only by foreign but also by Romanian historians such as A. Xenopol, D. Onciul, C. Giurescu and P. P. Panaitescu. Such refusal was instrumental in claiming national authenticity and direct imperial pedigree in that it revoked, at once, any Slavic share in the Romanian ethnogenesis and a Slavic transmission (and translation) of Byzantine culture to the Romanian lands.

A very different picture of the factors leading to the Romanians' political maturation and of Byzantium's role in it emerges from the writings of George Murnu (1868–1957), a reputed classical philologist who dealt extensively with the history of the Balkan Vlachs. Analysing *The First Appearance of the Romanians in History* (1913), as his study about the earliest mention of the Vlachs in the historical record in 976 (by an eleventh-century Byzantine historian Kedrenos) was entitled, Murnu concluded that the relative social and political autonomy the Vlachs enjoyed in the Byzantine empire was a legacy of their political status in the First Bulgarian Kingdom, not Byzantium. This thesis was already present in his major work, *Kekaumenos and the Romanians in the Eleventh Century* (1905), discussing the history of the Balkan Vlachs in their relations with the Byzantines. In the interwar period, he extended it into a general theory of Romanian-Bulgarian solidarity against Byzantium.[91] Murnu read the Byzantine chronicler Kekaumenos's disparaging attitude towards the Vlachs as an expression of the Byzantine imperialist mentality. This mentality, resting on political, ideological and sometimes economic foundations, was marked by deep-seated animosity to 'other nationalities' (Bulgarians, Armenians, Jews and Western peoples, usually described as 'barbarians') and their aspirations to independence. The 'barbarians' in turn reacted with reciprocal hostility against Byzantine imperialism. Adopting the vocabulary of ethnic psychology, Murnu spoke of 'racial aversions' and 'deep racial instincts' that added to the politically and economically motivated antagonism between the Byzantine Greeks and the other Balkan nations.[92] The 'dictatorial and centralist tendency of the detestable Byzantine

---

[91] Murnu's contributions to the history of the Balkan Vlachs are collected in Tanaşoca 1984.
[92] Tanaşoca 2002: 41.

160 Between Byzantine Studies and Metahistory

autocracy' engendered a long-standing anti-Byzantine tradition, based above all on the 'close solidarity' of ethnic and political interests between the Bulgarians and the Vlachs, which culminated with the Second 'Vlacho-Bulgarian' Kingdom. The Bulgarian tsars of both the First and Second Kingdom had a vital interest in forming 'a single political and military structure' with the Vlachs since they had recognised the Balkan Romanians' numerical power and military valour ('a vigorous, free and freedom-loving mountaineer population' who held the equilibrium between Bulgaria and Byzantium) and, unlike the Byzantines, were ready to reward them with self-government and respect for their 'infallible instinct for ethnic preservation'. (Of note here is the reversal of Iorga's contention about the 'great tolerance of Byzantium' for the local autonomy of the diverse Byzantine populations.) The Vlachs not only participated in all the uprisings against Byzantine oppression but the 'Vlacho-Bulgarian' Kingdom itself was also, according to Murnu, 'the exclusive deed of Romanian will, intelligence and energy'. Instances of the Vlachs' 'solidarity' with Byzantium against the Bulgarians were offhandedly dismissed. They were impractical for Murnu's strategy of factoring in the Vlachs (read Romanians) as the empire's major and ethnically assertive opponent in the Balkans once the Bulgarians lost their 'indigenous vigour' in the late tenth century. As Murnu affectedly put it, the creation of the 'Vlacho-Bulgarian' Kingdom was the occasion when 'the Romanian people for the first time manifested itself in the most brilliant manner in the light of universal history', signalling the beginning of 'the fulfilment of its mission by the definitive founding of the purely Romanian states on the other side of the Danube'.[93]

Here is a distinctive Aromanian perspective to Byzantium and its role in the destiny of the Romanians. In it one can easily detect the points of divergence from the mainstream Romanian narrative stressing the beneficial impact of the empire's presence in the Lower Danube. One can also find strong affinities with the Bulgarian interpretation focussing on Byzantium's 'de-nationalising' oppression and imperialism. To explain it, one ought to consider the evolution, since the early twentieth century, of the 'Aromanian question' in the Balkans, which Murnu and other scholars of Aromanian descent perceived in ways strikingly similar to those advocated by their Bulgarian compeers about half a century earlier. From the latter nineteenth century, the Aromanian intelligentsia aspired to cultural autonomy – that is, national schools and a national church – for

[93] Murnu 1938: 1–21.

Versions of Byzance après Byzance

the Aromanians as a shield against their denationalisation and the contestation of their identity, especially by the Greeks.[94] Once the major Aromanian grievances were satisfied, the attitude towards the 'Greeks' became more nuanced. In a lecture dedicated to the 100th anniversary of Greek independence in 1931, Murnu took care to distinguish between 'two contradictory *psyché*', that of the 'Byzantine race' – the ethnically heterogeneous, oppressive, bureaucratic, sterile, in a word mossbacked political class of the empire– and the authentic, liberal, vigorous and creative, therefore progressive, Greek people. The latter had suffered no less than the Romanians and the Bulgarians under the yoke of this Asiatic-tinged byzantinism, whose later embodiments (even more impure because it served an inferior culture – the Ottoman) were the Phanariots.[95] At the same time, the thesis about the 'Vlach' complexion of the Second Bulgarian Kingdom, promulgated by Iorga, Bănescu and Murnu, set the stage for a historiographic war with the Bulgarian historians with a long-term future.

The younger generation of historians, grouped around *Revista istorică română* (C. C. Giurescu, V. Papacostea, Gh. I. Brătianu, P. P. Panaitescu), hoped to infuse a new spirit into Romanian mainstream historiography by reforming it into a more rigorously 'scientific' and 'objective' field, detached from both sentiment and politics. They were less enthralled by Byzantium and the idea of its 'Romanian' continuation. Constantin C. Giurescu (1901–77), similar to Ioan Bogdan before him and Petre P. Panaitescu in his own day, saw the role of Byzantium in Romanian history as derivative of or else mediated by that of the Slavs. The latter, Giurescu maintained, had influenced the Romanians more strongly than any other population 'in terms of *race, of language, of social and state organisation,* in *cultural* and *ecclesiastical* terms'. Indeed, by being precisely a 'Romanic people of Slavic coloratura', the Romanians represented 'a distinct, characteristic nuance and a possibility for *unique* civilisation and culture among the large Romanic family' – a valuation that flouted Xenopol's, which foregrounded the degrading impact of 'Slavobyzantinism' on Romanian culture, or Iorga who belittled it.[96] The first reliable evidence of the existence of Romanian polities, he pointed out,

---

[94] Murnu was actively involved in lobbying for the Aromanians' cultural and political rights as a member of the Society for Macedono-Romanian Culture and a delegate, on behalf of this society, to the London Peace Conference in 1913 and the Paris Peace Conference in 1919 (Tanaşoca 2002: 31–2). For a contemporary Greek challenge to the Aromanians' Roman origin and kinship with the Romanians, see Keramopulos 1939.

[95] Murnu 1931: 3–9; Tanaşoca 2002: 53–5.   [96] Giurescu 1935: I, 246 (original emphases).

dated from the second half of the thirteenth century, a time dominated by the invasions of the Tartars and Turks. Giurescu did not make much of Byzantium and the Romanian-Byzantine relations during that formative period. Except for religious architecture and art, his remarks on the role of Byzantine tradition in the organisation and culture of the medieval Romanian states were fleeting and showed concern with making no sharp distinctions between direct Byzantine influences and those exercised via the Bulgarian or Serbian courts.[97] This does not mean that Guirescu's historical discourse was anti- or non-nationalist: indeed, he was no less a national prophet than Iorga, whom he severely criticised on mythological grounds but whose championship of Romanians' autochthonism and uninterrupted continuity he shared completely.

Petre P. Panaitescu (1900–67), perhaps his generation's most outstanding historian of Romanian culture, came up with a more straightforward and 'realist' and at the same time essentially sociological interpretation of the origins and value of what he called the 'Slavo-Byzantine' culture of medieval Romania. That this culture was not purely Byzantine but a form of 'popular byzantinism' filtered through the social and cultural conditions of the Slavs was essential for its adoption by the Romanians. In this form it dominated Romanian society all the way from the Middle Ages to the eighteenth century. Its Byzantine origin showed in the Eastern Orthodox faith, a religion of the anonymous masses with a tradition in humility and fraternity; in the predominance of classicism in art and of the concrete over the abstract and intellectualism; in the centralised state as distinct from the Western knightly feudalism; and in the ancient Greek and Roman tradition in literature that was interrupted in the West. This Byzantine culture, however, was created for an empire, for the New Rome, while the Slavs were primarily villagers, with patriarchal and agricultural monarchies, whose potential for assimilating a culture was limited. From the vast Byzantine culture, Panaitescu argued, the Slavs had adopted what they could understand and assimilate as per the level and structure of their society – that is, only its popular forms: 'the Slavic culture is a Byzantine culture for the people', or, since it had an ecclesiastical bent, 'we can characterise it as a religious culture of Eastern-Byzantine origin adapted to an agricultural-patriarchal people. Such was the nature of that culture, in which only the outer garment was Slavic [and] which the Romanians adopted and maintained for nine centuries'.[98]

---

[97] Giurescu 1943: 148, 242–63. See also Giurescu 1935: I, 438, 497; II, 354–5, 367, 382–6.
[98] Panaitescu 1944: 37–41.

Versions of Byzance après Byzance 163

Panaitescu set out to expose the flawed reasoning of all those Romanian historians (and they were the majority) who saw the period of the domination of 'Byzantine and Orthodox Slavonism' as a huge historical misfortune – first, for having severed the links between the Romanians and the 'superior culture of the West', kept them in an inferior position to the other Romanic peoples and prevented any progress; and second, for having severely disrupted the course of development and the cultural destiny of the Romanians as a Latin people. If the Romanians had adopted Byzantine culture in its Slavic form, and not some Western culture, Panaitescu affirmed, it was because it accorded with their social, economic and spiritual conditions that prevailed between the ninth and eighteenth centuries, unlike Western culture, whose technical and urban character was alien to them. Slavo-Byzantine culture 'was thus a necessity' rather than 'a misfortune or disgrace' of history. 'Slavonism (that is, popular byzantinism)', Panaitescu concluded, 'was not the cause for our rupture with the West, but the result of this rupture, produced by the contrast in the economic and social life.' Nor was it lacking, according to him, in significant services to the Romanian people: this culture had stirred the social and moral solidarity of the Romanians, the unity of their three historical provinces and their ability to unite and resist foreign invasions, dominance and denationalisation. The Slavo-Byzantine culture and the identity it conferred on the Romanians, 'ensured the cohesion and consolidation of the people during the hardest times of the past'. The centuries of its domination, Panaitescu opined, ought to be fully rehabilitated as 'a glorious period in our history ... rich in moral values', because 'a culture that is adapting to the spiritual needs of the whole people, in a certain stage of its evolution, is a spiritual good that the inheritors have to respect'.[99]

Panaitescu's reading of the Slavo-Byzantine factor in Romanian history thus not only contravened the prevailing one as it was authoritatively enunciated by Xenopol. His rehabilitation of the Slavo-Byzantine period in Romanian history submitted to a logic that diverged considerably from that of Russo or Iorga in that it built on an organic sociological understanding of the relationship between culture and society. Of particular interest to our topic is his inference, clearly at odds with Iorga's, that byzantinism never reached Romania in a pure and direct form and that its 'Slavicisation' was precisely what made it adequate and effective in the Romanian context. Such reading did not gain large traction with the Romanian medievalists in the decades to come; a 2001 edition of *History of the Romanians*, however, would make

---

[99] Panaitescu 1944: 34–7, 41–50.

164 Between Byzantine Studies and Metahistory

a similar point on behalf of the socio-cultural foundation of Romanians' 'cultural Slavonism'.[100]

A case apart among the younger members of the critical school in Romanian medieval and Byzantine studies is Gheorghe I. Brătianu (1898–1953), another historian combining scholarly and political roles (while coming from the most prestigious family of politicians in Romania), whose interests, like Iorga's, went beyond Romanian history into regional and global history. A trainee of the 1920s illustrious French generation of medieval historians and byzantinists, such as Marc Bloch, Ferdinand Lot, Charles Diehl and Gabriel Millet, Brătianu's original interests lay in the commercial relations of the Byzantine world with the Italian city-states. Soon he came to promote a new perspective on European medieval history and the periodisation proposed by Henri Pirenne, steered not solely by the changes produced in Western Christianity but factoring in also Byzantium, Islam and the East–West interactions. Along the way he sought to combat the time-honoured clichés of Byzantium as the extension of the Roman state's decadence and Byzantine cultural immobility.[101] Brătianu tackled aspects of Byzantine history few historians until then had paid heed to, among them monetary circulation, trade monopolies, public debt, grain supply of Constantinople, municipal taxes, economic protectionism and so on. Originally published in the most prestigious European journals of Byzantine and medieval studies such as *Byzantinische Zeitschrift*, *Byzantion*, *Annales d'histoire économique et sociale* and *Seminarium Kondakovianum*, his works on these issues were later brought together in a volume titled *Etudes byzantines d'histoire economique et sociale*.[102] Brătianu's masterpiece, *Marea Neagra*, offered an account of the history of the Black Sea and its surrounding communities, which tallied with the contemporary historical direction of the Annales school.[103] Similar to Iorga, Brătianu managed to combine this methodologically sophisticated and global perspective with a hard-core nationalist ideological commitment, subscribing, in his symbolic clash with Hungarian and Bulgarian historiography, to doctrines linked to the Nazi geopolitical discourse of the 1940s. In his influential publications and pronouncements devoted to Romanian historical continuity in the lands of post-World War I Greater Romania and the role of historical tradition in the foundation of the medieval Romanian states, Byzantium did not feature prominently;

---

[100] Ştefănescu and Mureşanu 2001: IV, 655. [101] Brătianu 1939: 252–66; 1939.
[102] Brătianu 1938. [103] Brătianu 1969.

An International Byzantium 165

instead Brătianu identified a Western pattern of state formation transmitted through Hungary and Romanian Transylvanian refugees.[104] The political fate of the two most prominent Romanian historians was also similar: arrested by the communist Securitate in 1950, Brătianu was sent to prison without trial, where he died three years later under unknown circumstances.

An International Byzantium

The 1930s saw the rise of a parallel, 'supra-national' paradigm of interpreting Byzantium and the Byzantine legacy in the framework of what was then dubbed 'the new science of balkanology'. Geopolitics and historiography converged again, this time on behalf of an anti-hegemonial regional agenda. In the face of rising international insecurity and a mounting sense of small-state defencelessness, regional solidarity became a coveted option, which achieved provisional materialisation with the conclusion of the Balkan Pact in 1934.

The institutional groundwork for internationalising Byzantine research had been prepared by the four international congresses of Byzantine studies that took place, between 1924 and 1934, respectively in Bucharest, Belgrade, Athens and Sofia. The proscription of Byzantine studies in the USSR after the Bolshevik Revolution gave greater weight to the 'successor states of Byzantium', specifically named in the first issue of the newly founded journal *Byzantion* as Greater Romania, Greece, Bulgaria and the Kingdom of the Serbs, Slovenes and Croats.[105] Foregrounding the link between scientific collaboration and international relations, the Swiss byzantinist Albert Vogt went as far as to define these meetings as 'a great official act of mutual good will, and, why not add, a first hope for pan-European unity': 'At times', he said, 'there was a feeling that Byzantium was reviving and attracting again in its radiance, first the peoples of southeastern Europe, who claimed it to be their common mother, but then also the descendants of those who, in 1204, took Constantinople and destroyed the Empire "guarded by God".'[106] Put more pragmatically, the congresses performed various political, cultural-diplomatic and scientific functions: they were places for demonstrating international reconciliation and cooperation and staging a fraternal scientific community in a period marked by the traumas of the Great War; they pursued recuperation of Byzantine history and culture and, thus, enhancement of a relatively young

---

[104] Brătianu 1940; 1980; 1943.   [105] Graindor and Grégoire 1924.   [106] Maufroy 2010: 233.

discipline suffering from a shortage of recognition in the scientific field; finally, they served the canonisation of the discipline by identifying its authoritative personalities.

For the 'successor states', the stakes of these congresses were even higher. In their official pronouncements the Balkan representatives used to emphasise the formative impact of Byzantium for all Balkan countries, the shared Byzantine foundation and the common civilisational heritage of their national cultures – all of these invariably wrapped in a discourse of fraternity and collaboration impervious to political climate or international tensions. One need not doubt the genuine desire of the Balkan scholars to assert, at forums like that, the civilisational role and European belonging of their peripheral nations by staking claims to the Byzantine legacy and, indirectly, to that of Hellas and Rome. It was precisely on this terrain, however, that the 'successor states' entered into competition. Nicolae Iorga, the initiator of the first congress in Bucharest, chose to interpret the acceptance of his invitation as a homage paid by foreign scholars to 'the cultural role that Romania had fulfilled and continues to fulfil in this part of Europe'. These scholars were called to acknowledge that, despite the vicissitudes of history, 'the Romanians had developed a civilisation of synthesis (not a borrowed one)', in which Byzantium occupied an important place: 'Albeit in less pronounced forms', Iorga said, 'we continued what the Eastern Christian world once was. The essence of Byzantium did not recede with the limitation of our borders.'[107] At the second congress (Belgrade, 1927), the Serbian delegates were at pains to demonstrate that the Serbs were unsurpassed in cultivating further the Byzantine civilisation and to emphasise the influence 'which the Serbian state and culture in the fourteenth and fifteenth centuries exerted on its neighbours'; the Romanian delegates asserted that 'since the year 1400 Romania had taken over and preserved the whole legacy of the Eastern Roman empire'; the Bulgarians held that, more than any other, their country 'bore the stamp of Byzantine culture' and that because of its Byzantine heritage it had 'played a major role in the southeastern part of Europe', while the Greeks did not miss the chance to restate the Hellenic character of the Byzantine empire and Greece as 'the heir of Hellas and Byzantium'.[108] Each congress was accompanied by an extensive 'cultural programme' meant to showcase the most impressive material evidence that could be summoned in support of such claims.

---

[107] Iorga 1924b: 1; Fodac 2006: 511–12. [108] Ignjatović 2016: 186, 195–6, 201.

An International Byzantium   167

Byzantine studies in these countries, the editor-in-chief of *Byzantion*, Henri Grégoire, noted in his report about the Sofia Congress (1934), were a much more critical political issue than in western Europe and 'most Byzantine problems continue to take the form of religious or national controversies'.[109] Justified as this observation had been, it should not be taken to mean that Western experts played no part in these controversies or in the nationalisation of Byzantine studies both as a field of research and as a resource in contemporary political legitimation. Outside the predictable 'Hellenic field' there is no dearth of examples either. To this day, Gabriel Millet (1867–1953), one of the two most renowned French byzantinists at the time next to Charles Diehl, is treated as a leading authority in Byzantine art history by dint of having introduced the concept of 'schools' into the study of Byzantine architecture in Serbia and Greece. Millet was instrumental in solidifying the understanding of Byzantine studies generally as an aggregate of 'schools' defined by national affiliations, which implicitly but effectively undermined a broader, supra-national frame of reference.[110] 'Millet, perceived as an "impartial" foreign scholar of impeccable authority', Slobodan Ćurčić observes, 'ultimately became an undeclared idealised champion of national causes in architectural studies.'[111] Nor did such mouthpieces of Western Byzantine studies show more caution than their Balkan hosts in employing medieval references in support of present national-political agendas. 'The glorious days of Dušan have returned', were Millet's opening words to the congress in Belgrade, in reference to the newly created big state of the Serbs, Croats and Slovenes under the sceptre of a modern Serbian dynasty.[112]

Parallel to the institutional internationalisation of Byzantine studies, in the second half of the 1930s the transnational agenda of 'balkanology' took shape. It aimed to elucidate regional commonalities and orient national academic research 'towards the study of a Balkan organism that had constituted one whole since the most distant times'.[113] A major drive towards 'Balkan aggregation' (next to the Macedonian dynasty and the Ottoman empire), the Yugoslav champions of balkanology held, was the Byzantine empire: it had 'maintained the Roman cohesion of the Balkans while struggling against the particularisms that had emerged after the settlement of the Slavs in the peninsula'. In contrast to the particularistic life of the ancient Greek cities, Byzantium represented 'the Christian continuation of the Roman empire' – it was a Christian, not a national,

---

[109] Grégoire 1935: 259. [110] See especially Millet 1916 and 1919. [111] Ćurčić 2013: 12.
[112] Ignjatović 2016: 214. [113] Budimir and Skok 1934: 2–3.

168 Between Byzantine Studies and Metahistory

empire. The modern Greeks had as much right to claim direct Byzantine origin as the different Romance peoples had with respect to ancient Rome. Once they became aware of their force, Slav particularisms succumbed to the same 'law of Balkan aggregation': the two Bulgarian kingdoms and that of Stefan Dušan sought to impose their own unification of the region while upholding its ethnic diversity. This was a crucial point in the balkanological reasoning: unlike 'Pax Romana' with its 'uniform unity', the Balkans of both the Byzantine and Ottoman eras 'tended towards unity in variations, a diverse unity', in contrast to the situation in the West. This was beneficial in that 'varied commonality is more efficient and more durable than uniform unity, since organised variety has, properly speaking, more "biological" value than unity without variations'.[114] The balkanologists thus tried to reconcile the ethnic plurality of the region, and hence the centrality of the national principle, with the idea of regional 'interconnectedness' and 'commonality', where Byzantium and its legacy were assigned a key role.

The founder of the Institute of Balkan Research in Bucharest (1938), Romanian medievalist Victor Papacostea (1900–62), elaborated further on the prominence of Byzantium as the single most important unifying factor of the Balkan world. On the military and political level, he wrote, its very existence spurred 'more than once a great grouping of Balkan interests'. Even when its social cohesion was weakened, thus opening the way to the emergence of various 'nationalities', the latter did not act in isolation but formed veritable 'Balkan leagues of Serbo-Albano-Bulgarian-Vlach' complexion. National historians erred in treating the Bulgarian or Serbian empires as national states in the modern sense of the word. The heads of these 'associations' were haunted by the idea of a universal empire, which Byzantium embodied, and their initiatives had an 'inter-Balkan character' (even the Greeks often joined the revolts instigated by the Bulgarians against the imperial power of Byzantium). Inspired by the Byzantine model and seeking to replace Byzantium, the Slavic empires acted as unifying forces by 'Balkanising' byzantinism. On the level of culture, administration, and political, ecclesiastical and juridical organisation, Byzantium demonstrated a remarkable capacity to adapt to local and ethnic particularities, safeguarding the proper traditions and customs of the invaders and, above all, transforming the national languages into instruments of culture. In all of this it often took on the appearance of a 'grouping of Balkan interests': the political and cultural model of

[114] Budimir and Skok 1934: 4, 10–11; 1936: 602–4, 607.

An International Byzantium 169

Byzantium was creatively reworked by all Balkan peoples, thus ensuring their mutual affinity and stimulating their originality.[115]

This last metamorphosis of Byzantium, which aimed to underwrite, in the words of Papacostea, a regional 'synthesis drawing on the elements of Balkan interdependence and unity', remained marginal in the interwar Balkan historiographies. But it laid down the methodological premises and served as the basis for institutionalising Balkan studies as a discrete field of research, one that would exert certain pressure on the national framework of history-writing after World War II.[116]

The interwar period was thus marked by a wide gamut of interpretations of Byzantium, which involved a growing number of disciplines (political and cultural history, archaeology, ethnology, linguistics, art and architectural history, law), different interpretative strategies and methods (from rigorously factographic to metahistorical) and competing political agendas and ideological orientations – national, quasi-imperial (or multinational) and regionalist. Byzantine studies became firmly embedded in the academic systems of all four countries, and the overriding foreign, Western and Russian, dominance in defining its orientation began to recede. Still, it was not a privileged terrain for the historians of the day. Even those who, like Lambros, Mutafchiev, Stanojević or Iorga, were trained in this field were busy bringing their expertise to bear on the current debates about collective identity and state formation rather than cultivating knowledge of matters Byzantine. The historiographic emplotments of Byzantium could, in this sense, be more properly seen as a continuation of ideological arguments that had political ramifications. The resultant confrontation between the different historical narrations fed on a set of shared assumptions and ideological concepts which, ironically, underwrote the fragmentation of history into national compartments. Consequently, the positive appropriation of Byzantium was reserved for those of its achievements or imprints that could be effectively nationalised or made to serve a national cause. The only remarkable exception was the supra-national post-imperial agenda of the budding 'science of balkanology', but its theoretical and programmatic acumen was barely matched by actual historical research.

---

[115] Papacostea 1943: iii–xxi. See also Tanaşoca 2002: 174–88.
[116] On the premises of the Balkan studies and their ideological implications, see Mishkova 2019.

CHAPTER 5

Byzantium in Ottoman and Early Republican Turkish Historiography

Christians and Muslims had a long history of contacts in the eastern Mediterranean before the rise of the Ottoman empire. Once the Seljuk Turks migrated into Asia Minor during the eleventh century, the Byzantines did not succeed in recovering their former territories there, except for the plains in western Asia Minor in the twelfth century. The settlement of the Seljuks deprived the empire of much of its remaining eastern territory. From that time on, Byzantium's slow disintegration, culminating in the crusader conquest of Constantinople in 1204, proceeded simultaneously with the rise of the new Muslim power on its eastern border. The restored Byzantine empire following the recapture of Constantinople in 1261 emerged as a fragmented, smaller and weaker, even if intellectually and artistically vibrant state, whose territory continued to shrink until the fall of Constantinople to the Ottoman Turks in 1453. By contrast, the Ottoman state rose from a small frontier principality (*beylik*) in Bithynia (northwestern Asia Minor), first attested in about 1300, to an empire which by the late sixteenth century encompassed the entire eastern Mediterranean, parts of central Europe, Arabia, Iraq and north Africa.

For more than a century and a half the Byzantine and Ottoman states existed side by side. Byzantine rule lasted over a thousand years in Anatolia and the core land of the two empires, centred on the Balkans and Asia Minor, was generally the same. Constantinople remained the capital city, named Istanbul by the Ottomans. The early Ottoman sultans appropriated the major elements and material remains of the heritage of their predecessors and used Byzantine symbols to legitimise their claim to Byzantium's imperial legacy and refashion themselves as *Kayser-i Rum*, the heirs of the Byzantine emperors.[1]

For all that, early Ottoman histories only rarely and briefly touched upon the history of the (late-) 'Eastern Roman empire' (*Rum-i Şarki*). As chronicles and imperial annals written for, and dealing with, a Muslim

---

[1] Bazzaz, Batsaki and Angelov 2013; Angold 2014: 154–6, 160–2.

Ottoman and Early Republican Turkish Historiography 171

dynasty and the affairs at the court, they displayed marginal interest in the pre-Ottoman past and almost none in pre-Islamic history, the 'time of ignorance'.[2] In the seventeenth century, when trade, diplomatic and political relations between the Ottoman empire, France, the Habsburg empire and Venice intensified, scholarly contacts related to science, geography and history increased. This exchange spurred, and was propelled by, intellectual networks in the Ottoman capital, which maintained contact with Europeans with no involvement of the state.[3] It was in this environment that the first two brief historical accounts of the Byzantine empire appeared. Penned respectively by the Ottoman literati Katib Çelebi and Hüseyin Hezarfen, they signalled a break with the erstwhile historiographic tradition in that they presented abridged compilations of European works and rested not on popular Ottoman legends but Latin translations of Byzantine sources. Katip Çelebi (1609–57) wrote a history of Constantinople from the ninth through the fifteenth centuries, using a translation of selected parts of a Latin compilation of four Byzantine chronicles published in Frankfurt in 1587 (and presumably begun by Hieronymus Wolf). Hüseyin Hezarfen (d.1691), the author of a 'History of the Empire of Rum' (*Tarih-i Düvel-i Rumiye*), was probably the first Ottoman historian to write a history of pre-Ottoman times based on Western sources.[4] These, however, were exceptions to the traditional dynastic, imperial-court and biographical orientation of Ottoman historical writing.

The germs of modern Turkish history emerged during the *Tanzimat* (Reorganisation) era between 1839 and 1878, when a top-down Ottoman reformist programme of rationalising the state apparatus and introducing modern institutions common among the 'civilised nations' brought along the infiltration of modern ideas and Western concepts about writing and the 'meaning' of history. Sometimes labelled 'the interrupted Enlightenment phase in the Turkish historical trajectory', this optimistic era was epitomised by the Young Ottomans – the first cohort of Ottoman-Turkish public intellectuals who propounded a liberal-national vision of the political nation, fusing imperial, dynastic, Ottoman, Muslim and supra-national state patriotism and loyalties.[5] The secular concept of

---

[2] Ursinus 1986: 211–12.   [3] Hagen 2006: 249–52.
[4] Ursinus 1986: 212; Yıldız 2013: 48–53. *Rum* is the Turkish derivative of *Rhomaioi*.
[5] Gürpınar 2013: 14–15. The Ottoman-Turkish word for intellectual, *münevver* (meaning enlightened), was first used to distinguish between those with a traditional religious education – that is, those who uncritically accepted past learning as unchangeable fact – and those enlightened with modern or Western education.

172   Ottoman and Early Republican Turkish Historiography

universal history, as developed during the Enlightenment, made its way from the 1860s through several specialised educational institutions modelled along 'Western', particularly French, lines and introducing modernised curricula in history. Substantial chapters or separate volumes on Roman and, to a far lesser extent, Byzantine history were published as parts of world or general histories from ancient to modern times, and a number of European works on ancient history appeared in Ottoman-Turkish translations, including Montesquieu's *Considérations*. In these general historical accounts the history of Byzantium, as distinct from that of Old Rome, received at first scant attention, usually in the form of brief summaries of political events.

The three decades preceding World War I were a politically dire but, in intellectual terms, unprecedentedly fecund time for the empire. Under the combined pressure of military weakness, Christian separatism, economic difficulties and political instability, the self-assured traditional vision of the 'eternally lasting state' of the *Osmanlı* began to crack. Members of the Ottoman elite saw themselves forced to reshape their legitimising ideology and search for new sources of identity, which resulted in the gradual ethnicisation of the notion of political ('Ottoman') nation. These currents were undergirded by a growing interest in the pre-Islamic Turkish past, the foundation of the Ottoman state and the medieval era generally, whereby Ottoman history came to be placed in a new set of historical contexts, while 'history became the model for the solution of present problems'.[6] These tendencies accelerated after the Young Turk revolution of 1908, which heralded a new wave of radicalisation and ethnicisation of politics and intellectual discourses. The loss of the last African territories of the Empire in a war with Italy (1911) and of the remaining Balkan territories as a result of the Balkan wars (1912–13) galvanised the upsurge of Turkish nationalism. With a truncated polity resting almost entirely on Asian soil, the dominant rhetoric of 'preserving the Empire', which was upheld by several generations of Ottoman reformers, ceased to make sense anymore. For a growing number of disillusioned Ottoman patriots, nationalist intellectuals and activists, including the ruling (and up to that point patently 'Ottomanist') Committee of Union and Progress, political Turkism seemed to offer a sense of hope and compensation for the huge physical and symbolic losses.[7] One of the results was the burgeoning of Turcological studies in the 1910s.

---

[6] Neumann 2002: 64.   [7] Ersoy, Górny and Kechriotis 2010: 221–2.

Ottoman and Early Republican Turkish Historiography 173

Such were the circumstances in which Ottoman historiography, influenced primarily by French positivism, began to display considerable interest in the history and institutions of the 'Eastern Romans', not as a part of world or general history but as a prolegomenon to Ottoman history. From the 1870s, 'Westernised' Ottoman historians came to be increasingly preoccupied, alongside its ethnically Turkish character, with the Ottoman state's 'imperial' component that set it apart from the other Turkic states on the steppes of Central Asia. This led some Ottoman writers to contemplate the existence in the 'Land of Rum' (Asia Minor and the Balkans) of an imperial tradition, which would link the Ottoman empire with that of the Second Rome.[8] Such descriptions were driven by a naïve 'comparative approach', meant to foreground the achievements of the Ottomans: 'Whether the rise of the Ottomans was to the benefit of the civilisation of mankind or to its detriment', Ahmet Midhat Efendi (1844–1913), a protagonist of Ottomanism and proponent of the Turkish ancestry of the Ottomans, wrote, 'will become apparent by comparing Ottoman history with that of the Eastern Roman empire.'[9]

Ahmet Midhat authored the first major account of the history and institutions of Byzantium to be published in Ottoman-Turkish in his three-volume *Detailed History of Modern Times* (1885–8), as part of, and in comparison with, the history of the Ottoman empire from its foundation to c.1500.[10] This unprecedented approach was followed three decades later by the other major specimen of Byzantine history in late-Ottoman historiography, the massive 'Introduction' to Mehmed Arif and Necib Asım's *History of the Ottomans* (1919) – the last such history to appear in the Ottoman empire. Both surveys were almost exclusively based on Western works on Byzantium (Edward Gibbon, Louis-Philippe Comte de Ségur, Le Beau, Pierre Grenier). That they reiterated almost *ad litteram* Gibbon's invectives should not, however, be taken as a sign of sheer imitation. These were writers deeply concerned with the national cause of the Ottoman Turks and, as such, eager to serve a didactic task by contrasting the Dark Ages of Byzantine history – 'the terrible Middle Ages of world history', as Midhat phrased it – with the 'enlightened and liberating Ottomans'. For Midhat, the Byzantine empire stood for corruption, lawlessness, extravagance and frivolity – the exact opposite of the early Ottoman community based on high moral values such as decency, concord, obedience and mutual esteem. In this view, the rise of the Ottomans

---

[8] Ursinus 1988: 306–8.   [9] Ursinus 1986: 213–14.
[10] Midhat 1885–8. The section devoted to the 'Eastern Roman empire' is in volume 2, 269–427.

174   Ottoman and Early Republican Turkish Historiography

heralded the dawning of the enlightened, emancipative and progressive Modern Age:

> To save the oppressed of the East and to grant them personal and national freedom as well as religious and political privileges, the [mere] necessity of a general uprising as in Europe was not sufficient; what was needed was rather a champion-like performance [realised] with the appearance of a group of believers [destined] to save the world. It does not need to be emphasised that this group of believers were the Ottomans.[11]

Remarkable here is the retroactive mobilisation of a modern liberal vocabulary on behalf of what the contemporary European liberal scholarship invariably qualified as the most retrograde oppressive regime that had ever existed in Europe.

In a major section titled 'Critical Discussion of the First Part of the History of the Eastern Roman Empire', Midhat castigated Byzantine society and institutions on moral, political and religious grounds. Byzantium was said to have been pervaded by hypocrisy (most of the Byzantine emperors, who were worshipped as God, died an unnatural death), a lack of virtues (due to the influence of the 'Greek priests and philosophers') and defective government ('even the sons of peasants and shepherds were able to make their way to the imperial throne'). Midhat was particularly scornful of the 'most powerful and dangerous institution', the Byzantine Church, for having cultivated fanaticism and superstition and practising 'false belief' through pagan-like idolatry and the use of candles. The moral opposite to the Byzantines thus portrayed were the 'enlightened' Ottomans – the 'true protectors of all religions and peoples' in the empire, the fair nemeses of 'the fanaticism and absurd opinions in the Eastern Roman empire'. In the artless wording of Midhat's recap, 'Only the virtues which the Turks had brought from Central Asia could do away with such immorality as generated in the Byzantine lands by the ancient civilisation.'[12]

The Byzantine-Ottoman comparative framework was made explicit in two essays, 'Historical Comparison between the Roman and Ottoman States' and 'Ancient Greece, Byzantium and the Ottoman State' written by Celal Nuri [İleri] (1881–1938), a prominent Young Turk, journalist and writer. Published at the time of the Balkan wars in a book tellingly titled *History of Ottoman Decline: Providence in History*, they aimed to offer his

---

[11] Ursinus 1987: 238. My reading of Ahmed Midhat's rendition of Byzantine history draws on the observations and translated excerpts by Ursinus.

[12] Ursinus 1987: 240–3; 1988: 308.

Ottoman and Early Republican Turkish Historiography 175

readers 'the explanation to be found in history' for the decline and near fall of the Ottoman empire.[13] A few years later he published another essay, 'Roman and Byzantine', where he maintained that 'knowing Roman history and its successor, Byzantine history, is important for those eager to know Ottoman history'. Nuri took on the task of examining similarities between the Byzantine empire and the Ottoman empire in terms of their 'multinational' populations, state organisation, positions of rulers and subjects, palace ceremonies, and religious tradition.[14] His attempt to apply seemingly less biased forms of comparison, however, did not prevent him from coming to the conclusion that 'the Eastern Roman Empire bequeathed to history nothing but moral decay, discord, passions and rivalries'. The main culprits for the 'disorder and moral decay' that followed the glorious reign of emperor Justinian (527–65) were found to be the Greeks, who had 'brought their language, arts, women and disgrace'.[15]

With the approaching of the final collapse of the Ottoman empire after the Balkan wars, triumphalist comparisons became replaced by despondent ones, which sought the roots of the empire's doom. Celal Nuri saw the primeval cause of the Ottoman decline in the Byzantine (as well as the Arab and Persian) influences, which had befouled the original Turkic purity:

> Byzantium was an epitome of immorality. Like cholera, the Byzantine corruption contaminated the Ottoman Empire . . .. The Turks did not conquer the Byzantine Empire; on the contrary, the Byzantines conquered the Turks . . .. The disease and moral decay that had caused the decline of the Byzantine Empire was now passed on to the Ottoman Empire, and thus the same reasons that had caused the collapse of the Byzantine Empire affected the Ottoman Empire. Being the heir to Byzantium is the main reason for the Ottoman decline. From this point of view, the decline of the Byzantine Empire still goes on.[16]

In his monumental *Ottoman History* (7 vols., 1909–16), Mizancı Mehmed Murad (1854–1917) came up with a similar explanation. He avowed that the mouldering Eastern Roman empire that, mainly for geopolitical reasons, the Ottomans had to incorporate exposed them to the pervasive nefarious influences of the 'Greek disease', which enfeebled the 'health' of their state and led it to its ruin. As Michael Ursinus notes, 'the Sick Man on the Bosphorus had finally come to know who was to blame for his sickness', and 'it had nothing to do with the national character of the Turks'.[17]

---

[13] Nuri 1912–13: 378–87, 388–400.   [14] Nuri 1917.   [15] Nuri 1912–13: 86; 1917: 21.
[16] Nuri 1912–13: 89, 386–7.   [17] Ursinus 1988: 312–13.

176   Ottoman and Early Republican Turkish Historiography

As in the case of Bulgarian historiography, contemporary Greek-Turkish relations weighed heavily on the conceptualisations of Byzantium. There was little in the nineteenth- and early twentieth-century history of these relations that the Turks could positively look to. The Greeks were (next to the Serbs) the first to set off the nationalist fire in the Balkans at the beginning of the century and had continued ever since to expand their territory at the expense of Ottoman lands; Greece brazenly propounded its infamous 'Great Idea' in a quasi-Byzantine shape and coveted Constantinople as its 'restored' capital, always with the support of 'the Europeans'; finally, the Greek-Turkish war of 1919–22 over the heart of the Turkish *vatan* (patria) in Anatolia sealed the view of the Greeks as the Turks' historical other and perennial enemy, an attitude that the Greeks fully reciprocated.[18] In this sense, the above-discussed renditions of Byzantium as the ultimate cause of Ottoman 'sickness' were an attempt at transforming the recurrent Greek-Turkish conflicts into a primordial phenomenon, dating back from at least the battle of Manzikert (1071) between 'Byzantine Greeks' and 'Seljuk Turks'.[19] It is also significant that most Turkish authors defied any claim about a connection between the ancient Greeks, whose contribution to European civilisation they readily acknowledged, and the modern Greeks, whom they saw as the heirs of a people who had lived for centuries under, and whom the Turks liberated from, the 'corrupt Byzantine rule'.[20] The animosity nurtured towards the Bulgarians, Serbs and Armenians as accomplices in the destruction of the empire only expanded the space of extrapolations linking Byzantium with the degradation of the Ottoman state.

There were, however, remarkable exceptions to this manner of treating Byzantium in Ottoman history narratives. Ahmet Refik [Altınay] (1880–1937), often credited as one of the first modern historians in Turkey because of his reliance on Ottoman archival sources, was probably the most outstanding representative of that small group of Ottoman scholars who sought to incorporate the Byzantine legacy in the understanding of Ottoman patriotism. Refik's first venture into Byzantine history was a section in his six-volume *Great World History* (1911–13) – a compilation based on translations from mostly French authors, where the central political-historical narrative was supplemented by a sub-chapter devoted to 'Byzantine Civilisation, Life and Society'.[21] Refik also published

---

[18] Millas 2004. One should note here the rather rare instance in history of two national states having gained their independence after a bloody struggle against the other.
[19] Heraclides 2013.   [20] Yıldız 2013: 186.   [21] Refik 1911–12: 93–257.

Ottoman and Early Republican Turkish Historiography 177

a separate study on 'Byzantine Empresses', essentially a replica of Charles Diehl's, an author he clearly appreciated, *Figures Byzantines* (1906).[22] Still, the initial chapter of this book, titled 'Introduction to Byzantine History', contains Refik's own views about the importance of the Byzantine heritage for the Ottomans, starting from the proposition that the persisting negative connotations of Byzantium 'derived from the lack of knowledge [about it]'.

In tackling Byzantine matters Refik was guided, like most of his contemporaries, by a growing concern with the Ottoman decline and the felt acute need to 'cultivate loyalty to the fatherland and stimulate patriotism as [this is done] in Europe' – a need he deemed most appropriate to satisfy through history lessons. Contrary to the prevailing view that blamed 'Byzantine influences' for the Ottoman misfortunes, Ahmet Refik argued that 'the brightest and most impressive pages of our history are related to Byzantium'. The Ottomans' disasters, he asserted, were the result of the lack of love and devotion for their homeland, while 'commitment to the homeland is achieved by cultivating appreciation for it and by exalting its past. Only the [knowledge of] Byzantine, Ottoman and Islamic histories will give us these great feelings'.[23] Refik, however, did not stop at recognising the importance of the study of Byzantine history and the late-Byzantine authors for the understanding of the early Ottoman history. 'For us, the Ottomans', he wrote,

> there is a great need to know the Byzantine history well and to examine all stages of this history with full attention. The Ottomans created their sultanate on Byzantine soil. Ottoman customs and traditions had experienced considerable Byzantine influences. At the present time our beloved homeland includes lands, over which the Byzantine emperors had ruled for many centuries, and the heritage of all the peoples inhabiting Byzantium.

Moreover, since these were territories, where Byzantine civilisation had flourished, 'there exists a cultural continuum between the Byzantine and the Ottoman empires. Therefore', Refic concluded, 'the Byzantine heritage should be embraced as part of our history.'[24]

Such a reading tallied with the Ottomanist convictions of those Young Turk intellectuals who espoused a 'patriotism of the land', according to which all inhabitants of the state, regardless of language, ethnicity or creed, were considered compatriots – a form of supra-national Ottomanist inclusivism that the proponents of Turkism, such as Ahmet Midhat and

---

[22] Refik 1915.   [23] Refik 1915: 4.   [24] Refik 1915: 14; Yıldız 2014: 107.

178   Ottoman and Early Republican Turkish Historiography

Mehmed Murad, found inacceptable. There was even more to it in that, as Refik warned, 'if the Ottomans fail to claim the Byzantine heritage, the Greek and Slavic aspirations to take hold of Istanbul will turn into reality'.[25] Appropriating Byzantine heritage for Ottoman history was thus seen as a means to both establish an imperial lineage for the Ottomans and thwart the irredentist policies of the empire's Balkan neighbours.

This brings us to another key element that shaped the late-Ottoman discourses of Byzantium: the issue of cultural (ancient and medieval) material heritage, in the modern 'European' understanding of the term as it evolved since the eighteenth century and was adopted by the Ottomans in the later nineteenth century. It has been argued that 'ever since the beginning of Ottoman museology and archaeology, in the second half of the nineteenth century, one of the major issues has been to deal with a discrepancy between the state's cultural identity, on the one hand, and the "foreign" nature of cultural heritage, on the other'.[26]

During the late-imperial period, Ottoman attitudes towards antiquities underwent a dramatic transformation from a general lack of interest in heritage to claiming the state's exclusive right over every site and object throughout the Ottoman lands and ownership of any artefact from the country. This was effected by a series of antiquity bylaws (in 1869, 1874, 1884 and 1906), control over foreign archaeological excavations, upgrading the Imperial Museum (set up in 1869 but opened to the public in 1880) to modern standards and support for archaeological researches carried out by Ottomans. These developments constituted the first steps towards the definition of a 'national' cultural and historical heritage as part of a broader official agenda of defining a civilised modern identity and image for the Ottoman empire, which was addressed not to its own citizens but to a foreign audience, mainly foreign diplomats and visitors. At a time when possessing the archaeological findings came to denote possessing the civilisation, the growing Ottoman preoccupation with antiquities and archaeology was, on the one hand, a response to the aggressive way in which Europeans tried to repossess the objects and monuments lying across the Ottoman lands and, on the other, the only means to produce the 'patrimony' that would generate the cultural link with Europe.[27] As Çiğdem Atakuman formulated it, 'The state heritage discourse and practice in the Ottoman Empire highlighted the territorial possession of the cultural properties sought after by Europeans and asserted control over these properties in negotiating for the recognition the Empire craved in the

---

[25] Refik 1915: 13.   [26] Eldem 2015: 67.   [27] Çelik 2011: 443–79; Eldem 2015: 71–9.

Ottoman and Early Republican Turkish Historiography 179

league of civilised nations as it attempted to restore its loss of authority in other political matters.'[28]

This campaign for recognition was focussed at that time almost exclusively on Hellenistic and Roman antiquities, whereas the Byzantine heritage was largely neglected. One reason was the status of the (surviving) Byzantine monumental remains. Following the fall of the empire, part of their material was reused by the Ottomans in their own constructions, while other buildings were put to different uses, commonly as mosques. (Hagia Irene Church was the only Byzantine church that was not converted into a mosque after the conquest of Constantinople; instead it had functioned as an army depot since the sixteenth century.) Occasionally, as in the case of Hagia Sophia, pre-Ottoman monuments were symbolically appropriated by modifying or reinterpreting their meaning.[29]

In Europe itself the change of attitude to Byzantine monuments was slow to emerge. It was only around the mid-nineteenth century that Byzantine architectural and artistic heritage – in Ravenna, Venice, Sicily and Constantinople – began to feature more prominently in works on European post-classical art and architecture.[30] The increase of knowledge about Byzantine architecture and the historical topography of Constantinople in the second half of the century was almost exclusively the work of German, British, French, Russian and Greek scholars, most notably Andreas D. Mordtmann, Alexander Van Millingen, Edwin Grosvenor and Alexander Paspatis. The interest shown by Western experts in Byzantine artefacts triggered a growing awareness among a small circle of Ottomanist intellectuals, who strove to create a sense of Ottoman political community, rooted in a common fatherland and integrating the heritage of all cultures that had ever existed in Ottoman territories. Combined with the craved recognition for the Ottoman state as a custodian of ancient cultural traditions appreciated by the 'civilised nations', it alerted up-and-coming art historians, such as Celal Esad Arseven (1876–1971) and İhtifalci Mehmed Ziya (1866?–1930), to the need to undertake studies of the Byzantine monuments of Constantinople. It is no surprise, therefore, that the most comprehensive of these studies, Arseven's *Constantinople, de Byzance á Stamboul* (1909), appeared in French, with a preface by Charles Diehl.

As with most of his contemporaries, who touched upon Byzantium as the background to the Ottoman rise to a world power, Arseven was critical of the overall condition of the late-Byzantine society and rulers in terms of

---

[28] Atakuman 2010: 19.   [29] Yerasimos 1990: especially 143–59, 210–14.   [30] Bullen 2003.

180   Ottoman and Early Republican Turkish Historiography

a deplorable state of morals, economic frailty because of excessive spending and political impotence, which had opened the door to destructive foreign interventions. Describing the conquest of Constantinople by the Turks, he admitted the looting of the city as a common practice at the time but also pointed out that the pillage Constantinople had suffered at the hands of the Crusaders far exceeded that of the Turks. The latter actually showed considerable respect for the Byzantine civilisation and took on its imperial dignity, as was evidenced by Mehmed II's adoption of the crescent, which was the sign of the Byzantine empire, as the state emblem, while adding a star to it.[31] Arseven was even more explicit in acknowledging the influence of Byzantine art on both European and Ottoman artistic traditions and criticised those European experts who downplayed its quality and significance. Already during the Seljuk period but especially after the conquest of Constantinople, Turkish architecture, he affirmed, experienced the influence of the Byzantine architectural tradition as was especially visible in the similarities between Byzantine churches and Ottoman mosques. Yet, far from being a 'servile imitation of Byzantine art', Arseven added, in a short time Turkish art acquired 'a unique character', and soon after the capture of Constantinople its Byzantine identity was completely overshadowed.[32]

As a member of the Commission for the Conservation of Old Monuments, set up in 1917 with the task of assembling an inventory of the historically significant monuments in Istanbul, İhtifalci Mehmed Ziya compiled a massive register of Byzantine and Ottoman monuments in Constantinople. In its introduction he sought to broaden his comparative framework by including an overview of the development of Byzantine studies in Europe since the seventeenth century. In a succinct assessment of the Byzantine empire, Mehmed Ziya contended that at a time when European peoples still found themselves in a state of 'barbarity', the Byzantine empire shined with magnificence. Like Arseven, he maintained that, if this empire later lost its glamour and prestige, it was due to the nefarious impact of foreigners, who had penetrated Byzantine society and ultimately led to its fall to the Turks.[33] The most remarkable feature of Mehmed Ziya's study was the connection it professed between Byzantine Constantinople and Ottoman Istanbul. Whereas Arseven put them next to, but largely detached from, each other, Mehmed Ziya built his narrative of the city history by entangling the Byzantine and Ottoman heritage.

---

[31] Arseven 1909: 10, 33–6.   [32] Arseven 1909: 151–3, 169, 176. See also Üre 2014: 86–8.
[33] Ziya 1937: 9, 17.

Ottoman and Early Republican Turkish Historiography

Drawing on written accounts, not least in order to trace lost or crumbling Byzantine monuments, in situ examinations and archaeological works, he came to the conclusion that Byzantine architecture bore more similarities with Ottoman than European architecture.[34]

That said, Celal Esad Arseven's and Mehmed Ziya's overall positive interpretations of the Byzantine artistic legacy, in addition to being limited to a handful of intellectuals, should not be seen as constituting some kind of national re-definition of heritage in the service of creating national consciousness. They are better understood as showcases of a civilisation in competition with European rivals over the appropriation of the Byzantine legacy and as expressions of Ottoman imperial identity. By foregrounding the similarities between Ottoman and Byzantine art and architecture, they asserted both the legitimate right of the Turks to pose as the recipients of the Eastern Roman civilisation and the Ottoman empire's participation in the European cultural sphere.

The 1908–22 period marks a watershed in Ottoman/Turkish history, one that saw the collapse of the Ottoman monarchy and the discrediting of anything Ottoman, the dynastic capitulation to the invasion after World War I and the Turkish war of independence (1919–22), fought by the adherents of Mustafa Kemal (Atatürk), the hero of the National Struggle and the president of the new republic until his death in 1938. With the promulgation of the Republic in 1923 in Ankara, the new regime symbolically and physically dissociated itself from the Ottoman-Islamic past and arduously embraced an outwardly secularist ideology as proof of its commitment to modernity. Thereby Turkish nationalism emerged as the only legitimate and credible political disposition, which meant re-definition of the cultural background of the Turkish nation, if necessary by reinventing its whole history and genealogy, and rendering historical imagination exclusively ethnic-based.[35] To all intents and purposes, this amounted to a cultural revolution waged by 'a state in search of its nation'.[36] A Turkish Historical Society was founded (1930), under Atatürk's patronage, to institutionalise the Kemalist version of history (the so-called Turkish History Thesis), forge a new historical consciousness among the Turks and monopolise historical scholarship. In this it never fully succeeded, yet with the consolidation of the Republican regime in the second half of the 1930s, those who wished to pursue an academic career in Turkey toed the

---

[34] Ziya 1937: 133; Üre 2014: 89–90; Yıldız 2013: 154–63.
[35] Gürpınar 2013: 18–19; Eldem 2015: 81.   [36] Kadioğlu 2009: 122.

182   Ottoman and Early Republican Turkish Historiography

official line and often combined the roles of scholars and politicians, whereas dissenters were marginalised.[37]

Formulated by a Committee for Research on Turkish History, hand-picked by Atatürk (1930), and widely propagated through textbooks and the periodic Turkish History Congresses, the 'History thesis' posited a Turco-centric view of world history by setting forth a new 'myth of origin' that went beyond the disinherited Ottoman past and asserted the superiority, rootedness and ethnic purity of the Turkish nation. It depicted the Turks as a very ancient, homogeneous people of the 'white race', whose cradle was in Central Asia, the progenitors of all the nations of Eurasia, the creators of the major ancient civilisations of China, India, Mesopotamia, Egypt, the Aegean and Asia Minor and the quintessential state-builders throughout the centuries. It had a linguistic analogue, the 'Sun Language Theory', which defined Turkish as the world's oldest language.[38] After the 1930s the 'History thesis' was attenuated by variants of Anatolianism (*Anadoluculuk*) and cultural Turkism, whereby the idea of an 'original Turkish homeland' in Inner Asia continued to hold sway, but the claims to autochthony moved to Anatolia (contemporary mainland Turkey). The Turks now came to feature most prominently as having provided the racial stock for the Aegean and Anatolian societies of the ancient era (the Minoans, Mycenaeans, Trojans and the Hittites), thus dispossessing other rooted ethnicities (Pontus Greek, Armenian, Kurdish) of claims to autochthony in Anatolia and the ancient Greeks in particular of cultural contribution other than that of usurpers of the legacies of earlier and superior civilisations settled in the Aegean region.[39] A softer version of Anatolianism emphasised cultural nationalism and the power of the Turks to assimilate creatively the Anatolian heritage regardless of ethno-racial ownership, short of relinquishing the claim to Turkish autochthony. Looming behind this set of pseudo-scientific assertions was a formidable cultural agenda, which sought to reconcile locally embedded ethnic-based particularism with the transformative programme of 'becoming European'. As Ahmet Ersoy has argued, '[b]y fabricating the image of proto-Turks as prime movers in the founding of great ancient civilisations, the "History thesis" helped "naturalise" and appropriate the entire edifice of Western civilisation, while implicitly contesting the Eurocentric biases and the pro-Hellenic exclusivism of the standard narrative on the origins of

---

[37] Ersanlı 2002: 116.   [38] Ersanlı 1992.
[39] For a discussion of the historical context of these claims, see Erimtan 2008: 141–71; on the Greeks as cultural usurpers, see the Turkish archaeologist Mansel 1938: 83.

Ottoman and Early Republican Turkish Historiography 183

"world history".[40] In this sense it was also a reaction to the dominant paradigm of Western history, aimed at transforming the way in which the Turkish nation perceived itself and its history: 'contrary to the Ottoman attitude of the preceding century, modern Turkey was no longer willing to accept a civilisational model developed in the West; it wanted to create its own'.[41]

In this ideological setting historical investigations drifted heavily towards unearthing and proving the primeval Turkish ethnic roots while privileging territorial and biological aspects of identity. Consequently, archaeology – yet another discipline favoured by the Kemalist regime – focussed almost exclusively on the Sun Language Theory and the links between the Turks and the Bronze Age civilisations of the Sumerians and Hittites. Steeped in ethnocentric nationalism and radical secularism, the 'History thesis' downgraded the Ottoman-Islamic past and rebuked the multi-ethnic, multi-lingual and multi-confessional *ancien régime* as reactionary, backward and cosmopolitan. As Mustafa Kemal had put it years before the thesis took shape, 'the Ottomans had usurped the sovereignty of the Turkish nation. And they continued this usurpation for six hundred years. Now the Turkish nation has put an end to this and taken back its sovereignty. This is a revolution'.[42]

One is struck by the ironic resemblance with the heritage strategy followed by the newly independent Balkan countries, whose elites set out to eliminate the Ottoman features from their budding 'national cultures'. However, unlike the Balkan states, the Republic of Turkey did not result from a secession from the empire but was rather erected on the ruins of a defunct empire. The 'discontinuity thesis' thus presented a formidable historiographical challenge that was dealt with through complex schemes of co-opting and reconceptualising Ottoman history, whereby 'the Ottomans simultaneously were "owned" as "[the Turks'] ancestors" but rejected as the *ancien régime*'.[43] Kemalist historiography, accordingly, did not repudiate the whole Ottoman past but treated it selectively, keeping what it considered to be the glorious and unadulterated 'Turkish' period of the empire – roughly until the 'decline' of the seventeenth century – and rejecting the later periods as a form of degeneration and international humiliation.[44]

In these scenarios Byzantium, if dealt with at all, was usually attributed epiphenomenal (negative) roles and its influence was deliberately alienated

---

[40] Ersoy, Górny and Kechriotis 2010: 57. For the racialist implications of the 'History thesis', see Inan 1941.
[41] Eldem 2015: 82.   [42] Cited in Ersanlı 2002: 141.   [43] Gürpınar 2013: 58.   [44] Eldem 2015: 83.

184   Ottoman and Early Republican Turkish Historiography

from Turkish history. Ziya Gökalp (1876–1924), an ardent exponent of Turkism considered to be the intellectual founder of Turkish nationalism, sought to juxtapose modern Turkishness with the medieval Arabness. In doing so he 'transferred' the Byzantine legacy to the Arabs who 'not only emerged as the political successors to the Eastern Roman Empire but also as their civilisational heirs'. He argued that, whereas the legacy of the 'Mediterranean civilisation' was inherited by Europe and transmitted via the Western Roman empire, '[w]hen the Eastern Roman civilisation was taken over by the Muslims, it was dubbed as the oriental civilisation'. For him, the Muslims and the Arabs imitated and replicated the Byzantines in architecture, music, philosophy and science.[45] As Doğan Gürpınar observes, Gökalp deployed the strategy of portraying the Arabic/Islamic culture as merely a sham of the Byzantine culture in order to discredit their legacy and liberate Turks from their burden.[46]

To understand the reworking of Turkish culture by distancing it from both Byzantine and Islamic/Arabic culture, one needs to bring in another major element that moulded the intellectual climate of the early Turkish Republic, namely the dialogue with European Orientalist scholarship. Partly because of the limited knowledge of the Turkish sources, it was common for this corpus of studies to deny the capacity of the Turks, an 'Asian nomadic nation', to establish a durable and robust empire and, at the same time, praise as authentic the 'Muslim civilisation' of the 'Persians' and 'Arabs' compared to the 'derivative' culture of the nomadic Turks.[47] Herbert A. Gibbons (1880–1934), an American historian teaching at Robert College in Istanbul in the 1910s, became the flagman of this approach with his *The Foundation of the Ottoman Empire* (1916). The tremor this book produced in the Turkish nationalist milieu was in important ways comparable to that of Fallmerayer's *Geschichte der Halbinsel Morea* in Greece a century earlier.[48] Gibbons set out to show that the Ottomans were in fact 'a new race', one formed 'through the blending of wild Asiatic blood with European stock'; that is, Islamised Turkish peoples and Greek and Balkan Slavic converts to Islam. In the ensuing admixture the Christian element was by far the most important, ensuring the continuity of Byzantine administrative practices under an Islamic guise. The Ottoman empire owed its expanding power and creative force to this Islamic-Byzantine amalgam; such a mighty formation, the tacit message went, could not have emerged from purely Turco-Muslim roots, but could only be the result of

---

[45] Gökalp 1923: 40.   [46] Gürpınar 2013: 72.   [47] Bozdoğan and Necipoğlu 2007: 2–3.
[48] Gibbons 1916.

Ottoman and Early Republican Turkish Historiography 185

racial blending and direct lineage from the Byzantine-Christian traditions and statecraft.

Gibbons's theory fell on receptive ears with Western and regional byzantinists, since it tallied with their own theory that the accomplishments of early Ottoman administrative institutions and practices were due not to a Turco-Islamic but to a Byzantine heritage. In the words of Charles Diehl, 'the Turks were neither administrators nor lawyers, and they understood little of political science. Consequently they modelled many of their state institutions and much of their administrative organisation upon what they found in Byzantium'.[49] Nicolae Iorga, too, argued that the Ottomans were almost fully assimilated into Byzantine life except in their religion, the reason being that they lacked the requisite 'forms of life' (*Lebensformen* or *formes de vie*), a key concept in Iorga's understanding of history, for the establishment of an empire.[50] Albeit in less emphatic terms, some of the most authoritative orientalists and historians of the Ottoman empire, from Joseph von Hammer-Purgstall through Alfred Rambaud to René Grousset, came to uphold similar views based on the observable similarities between Byzantine and Ottoman institutions. A general consensus of opinion thus emerged, and became accepted as fact in contemporary European historiography, that the most important Ottoman government, military, legal and economic as well as many social institutions and concepts drew on Byzantine models. Put differently, whatever creative force there was in the Ottomans must be attributed to a 'European' element. The Ottoman empire thus appeared to be a 'Muslim Roman Empire', and the Ottoman Turks the *Néo-Byzantins de l'Islam*, in the formulation of Iorga.

In a considerably attenuated form such views found some echo in the earliest specimen of Republican historiography, such as Hamid and Muhsin's *History of Turkey* (1924), where the foundation of the Ottoman empire was explained in the following terms:

> The Ottoman state, founded by the initiative of a tribe, during the early years of the Empire did not establish contacts with foreign cultures. Occupation of the Balkan peninsula, however, paved the way for a closer relationship with other elements, principally the Byzantines. Istanbul became the capital. Although it was Turkish inspiration and dynamism which made the formation of a state possible, since the mid-fifteenth century, Byzantine culture was more and more influential.[51]

---

[49] Diehl 1919: 305.   [50] Iorga 1934: III, 159–60; 1908: 264. See also Kafadar 1995: 33–4.
[51] Cited in Ersanlı 2002: 127.

186   Ottoman and Early Republican Turkish Historiography

The aforementioned Ahmet Refik highlighted the victories of the Ottoman dynasty in Anatolia and drew attention to some of their members' close relations with the Byzantines. However, Refik's presumed sympathies with the Ottomans occasioned his falling out of favour with the new regime, whereby he was forced to resign all public positions, including his professorship at Istanbul University.[52]

The heyday of the 'discontinuity thesis' in its radical form was short-lived, though. By the late 1930s the view that the Ottoman empire was alien and non-Turkish gave way to a different one with a much longer sequel, namely that 'the Ottoman state is the penultimate of a long line of Turkic states and as such worthy of special attention'.[53] The exertion to thoroughly extract Byzantium from this reframed Ottoman past can only be understood in view of the conjuncture of coveted Turkish ethnic purity, to the exclusion of anything else, and rebuttal of the European claim that Byzantine influences were responsible for the accomplishments of the 'Turks who took on the name of Ottomans'. It was accomplished, with considerable erudition and methodological sophistication, by Mehmet Fuat Köprülü (1890–1966), a highly influential and internationally renowned sociologist and turkologist, praised as the founder of scientific historical studies in Turkey and a prominent Turkish nationalist and statesman, who served as a member of parliament in the 1930s and, after World War II, as minister of foreign affairs and, briefly, deputy prime minister.

Having started as a man of letters and literary historian, Köprülü pioneered a sociologically informed cultural history of literary and political traditions. He was an untypical proponent of the 'Turkish History Thesis' both by dint of his critical scientific method and the emphasis he put on the cultural requisites of nationalism, or what he called 'history of Turkish civilisation', rather than on geographical and genealogical continuums as the basis for rewriting Turkish history. Setting out to rectify the widespread idea that 'the historic role of the Turks was military and destructive [and that] they had no positive role in civilised life', Köprülü identified two questions which he considered vital for establishing the proper place and role of the Turks and the Turkish nation in world history: the question about the nature of Byzantine influence on Turkish and Ottoman institutions and that concerning the foundation of the Ottoman state. He tackled these issues in a series of studies and lectures between 1922 and 1935 and thus opened a new field of research dealing with the social structures of the

---

[52] Ersanlı 2002: 128.   [53] Ersanlı 2002: 130.

Ottoman and Early Republican Turkish Historiography 187

Turks that made possible the establishment of the Ottoman empire. Along the way, Köprülü kept underscoring the importance of scientific method, which he defined as 'genetic and comparative', the use of sociology, which included anthropology, and the widest range of sources.[54]

Professing to follow this methodology, Köprülü embarked, first, on refuting Gibbons's thesis about a Byzantine origin of the Ottoman administrative apparatus by demonstrating the extent to which early Ottoman institutions derived from Seljuk and Ilhanid precedents.[55] In the next years he developed further his argument in an extensive essay titled 'Some Observations on the Influence of Byzantine Institutions upon Ottoman Institutions' (1931). In this work Köprülü took issue with a long line of European scholars of Byzantium, the Ottoman empire and the Middle East – among them Rambaud, Diehl, Iorga, Deny, Scala, Gibbons, Kramer and Sokolov – for having presented no proof for the claim that, especially after the conquest of Constantinople, the Ottomans had borrowed almost wholesale from Byzantine practices. Instead, these scholars had resorted to 'logical deductions' by assuming that the resemblances between given institutions were due to a common – that is, Byzantine – origin, without attempting to trace the origin of an institution through the sources. Köprülü was particularly critical of the byzantinists for discussing these issues with little or no reference to Islamic sources and for not even acknowledging the need to look for such sources.[56] In brief, he accused the European scholars of having failed to follow their own scientific principles and of building their conclusions on unverified assumptions.

By means of applying his 'genetic' approach to (almost exclusively Muslim) sources, Köprülü examined, one by one and in considerable detail, the major public institutions which the Ottomans had allegedly adopted from Byzantium: the government offices and state administration, the taxation system, the military and land tenure system, the concepts of empire and sovereignty, and the organisation and life of the palace.[57] The result of his research led him to maintain that, with few minor exceptions, the said institutions had pre-Islamic Turkish or pre-Ottoman Muslim precedents. Köprülü did not, and could not, demonstrate the mechanisms of transmission of these institutions to the Ottomans; instead, their very existence in the

---

[54] Köprülü 1999: 29. See Leiser, 'Introduction', in Köprülü 1999: 6–7 [1–15]. By 'genetic' (*génétique*), a term adopted from French scholarship, Köprülü meant a methodology of tracing back through the sources the historical stages through which an institution passed in order to get to its 'roots' (Köprülü 1999 [1931]: 33).

[55] Köprülü 1993: 281–311, 385–420, 457–86.   [56] Köprülü 1999: 16–32.

[57] Köprülü 1999: 38–137.

188   Ottoman and Early Republican Turkish Historiography

sphere of Turkish-Islamic civilisation was deemed sufficient to prove their non-Byzantine origin. Köprülü could thus confidently state:

> The analyses I have made here, one by one, of the administrative organisation, financial practices and palace customs of the Ottoman state completely refute the claims of Byzantine influence on these institutions. Byzantine influence was found only in a very limited number of things .... The connections that were made between Byzantine and Ottoman institutions by means of logical deductions based on preconceived ideas and merely looking at external similarities have been demolished .... *The Ottoman state was a Muslim Turkish sultanate that had inherited the administrative traditions of the Anatolian Seljuk sultanate and was partly under the influence of the Ilkhānids and Mamlūks.*[58]

Köprülü's take on the *origins* of the Ottoman state shored up this line of reasoning. It appeared in a book featuring three lectures he delivered at the Sorbonne in 1934 on the occasion of the opening of the Centre for Turkish Studies.[59] There Köprülü not only launched a pointed attack on Gibbons's thesis but went one step further, arguing that the Ottoman state was purely Turkish in nature, not formed from a commingling of Byzantine, Slavic and Turkish peoples as Gibbons had maintained. It was derived from an amalgamation of various Turkish tribes, who lived in Anatolia and who were the inheritors of an administrative tradition which passed to them from ancient Turkish, Seljuk and, to a lesser extent, Ilhanid and Mameluke roots. Of most significance for him was to stress the homogeneous Turkish ethnic origin of the Ottomans and the entirely Turkic background of the Ottoman dynasty. In Köprülü's concluding words,

> The Ottoman state was founded exclusively by Turks in the fourteenth century. It was after this state began to develop into a great empire ruling various elements – after the first half of the fifteenth century – that, as occurred with the Byzantine and 'Abbasid empires, other elements, which in this case were 'Ottomanised', entered the government. Moreover, just as the fact that a significant number of the rulers of the Byzantine empire came from foreign elements is not proof that the Greeks lacked administrative ability, an analogous situation occurring in the Ottoman Empire cannot be used as proof that the Turks lacked administrative ability.[60]

Next to its administrative prowess, Köprülü emphasised several other aspects of the rising Ottoman state which helped explain its swift expansion in the Balkans and Asia Minor, among them the protection and

---

[58] Köprülü 1999: 141–2 (original emphases).   [59] Köprülü 1992.
[60] Köprülü 1992: 86–8. See also Lowry 2003: 5–7.

Ottoman and Early Republican Turkish Historiography 189

security it provided for the peasantry (and which Byzantium was no longer able to deliver), the alleviated tax burden on the conquered populations, the lack of pressure to convert and the 'respect for religious freedom, the privileges of the clerical classes, and the customs and traditions of the various communities'.[61]

The crux in all this was the categorical rejection of the idea that the Ottomans 'did not possess the civilised components necessary to found a state', therefore their polity was nothing more than an 'Islamised continuation of Byzantium'. The Ottoman empire, Köprülü pointed out, 'can be compared, in certain respects, to Byzantium as regards the world-embracing and historical role that it played not only in the Middle Ages but also in the modern period'. Namely, the Balkan Christians became relatively prosperous and enjoyed peace and tranquillity within the framework of the Ottoman empire, as they had done during periods of Byzantine power. The Eastern Church was saved from Latin oppression. It was still possible to find significant and well-established vestiges of the Ottoman empire in the past and even present ethnological landscape of the Balkan countries, in their social institutions and cultural achievements. Turkish language and culture had left profound and prominent traces in the languages, popular literature and customs of the Balkan nations. Indeed, '[i]f research were to be done on Ottoman cultural history, it would become clear that the peoples of various nations in various cities of the Empire, from Baghdad to Pest and from Algiers to Kefe, all lived in a common cultural milieu'.[62] In all these respects the role of the Ottoman empire was comparable to that of Byzantium; this, however, could not be attributed to borrowings and imitations since *the contacts of the Ottomans with Byzantium had no fundamental influence on this development, neither before nor after the conquest of Constantinople*.[63]

It is not that Köprülü denied any Byzantine influence on the 'material and spiritual life' of the Ottomans. However, that influence, he argued, was exerted indirectly, via pre-Ottoman Muslim Turkish states and primarily the Seljuks of Rum (Anatolian Seljuks), whose state had been in contact with Byzantium for centuries and whose institutions and traditions the Ottomans closely followed. Somehow this fact in itself seemed to diminish the importance of the Byzantine influence. Influence, furthermore, did not flow in one direction only, since the Ottomans and earlier Muslim cultures, notably the Sasanid empire, Arab and Turkish dynasties, had also influenced Byzantium.

---

[61] Köprülü 1992: 82–117. [62] Köprülü 1999: 142–4. [63] Köprülü 1999: 145 (original emphases).

190 Ottoman and Early Republican Turkish Historiography

> For seven centuries, from the rise of Islam to the foundation of the Ottoman state, Muslims and Turks had continuous relations with Byzantium. The mutual influences of these two worlds on each other ... constitutes one of the most noteworthy stages of Turkish legal history. *Although Byzantine state institutions exercised no apparent influence on Ottoman state institutions, this is not proof there was no such influence in the pre-Ottoman period . ... However, the most important period in which the Turks were directly under Byzantine influence was, without doubt, the first centuries following the conquest of Anatolia.*[64]

The real issue at stake in these conclusions was not solely to validate the Ottomans' state-building potency in the mirror of European Orientalism. Just as important was to posit the Ottoman empire within the larger context of ecumenical Turkish history, thus mitigating the discontinuity gap the 'Turkish History Thesis' had opened and the anti-Ottoman radicalism of the Kemalist ideology. To be properly understood, Köprülü insisted, Ottoman history must be 'situated and investigated within the framework of general Turkish history, that is to say, in conjunction with the other Anatolian Principalities and as a continuation of Anatolian Seljuk history'.[65] To this effect, at every step and in every respect a Seljuk derivation had to overshadow a Byzantine one and the genuine Turkishness of the Ottomans be confirmed. Similar to the Greek appropriation of the Byzantine, the 'Ottoman' became subsumed within the 'Turkish', thus opening the road to its rehabilitation in post-Kemalist Turkey. And as long as *Rum* began to denote ethnic Greek as descendants of the Eastern Roman empire, making what was previously a religious term into an ethnonym, the polity 'Seljuks of Rum' (*Rum Selçukluları*) was renamed 'Anatolian Seljuks' (*Anadolu Selçukluları*) to underwrite the Anatolianisation of the Turkish *Heimat*.[66]

At the time of its appearance, Köprülü's thesis about the Byzantine influence was seriously analysed by only one orientalist, the German historian Franz Taeschner (1888–1967), and never thoroughly evaluated by a byzantinist. Part of the explanation, according to its English translator and editor Gary Leiser, was that it was in Turkish. Taeschner agreed that Köprülü was basically correct in interrogating the hitherto greatly exaggerated Byzantine influence, especially after the conquest of Constantinople. He also praised him for having brought to light sources which were generally unknown or inaccessible. But, while rightly criticising European scholars for

---

[64] Köprülü 1999: 146–57 (original emphases).   [65] Köprülü 1992: 63.
[66] Gürpınar 2013: 116–20.

Ottoman and Early Republican Turkish Historiography 191

ignoring Islamic sources, Köprülü himself ignored Byzantine sources. In reality, Taeschner maintained, there was a difference between Ottoman state institutions and those in other Islamic lands, which must be explained. Instead, Köprülü had presented only the negative side of the problem, mentioning briefly the possibility of earlier Byzantine influence on the Turks prior to the establishment of the Ottoman state. All in all, Taeschner argued that it was incorrect to reject Byzantine influence on the Ottomans in the manner and to the extent that Köprülü did, pointing to the improbability that 'the political inheritance which [Mehmed II] has assumed should not have claimed recognition in the new institution of the new state'.[67] In time, Köprülü's work evoked wider resonance within the circle of orientalists, but despite the substantial challenge it issued to their interpretations, it appears to have had little or no effect on byzantinists. If, in the following decades, some of his conclusions became integrated into the mainstream of Byzantine studies, this was because of the accumulation of (mostly translated) Islamic sources and published work of Western Ottomanists and Islamicists. Few agreed with Köprülü's view that on the level of 'high culture' – that is, the central administrative and religious institutions – there was little or no Byzantine influence. Even those who, like Speros Vryonis, Jr, tended to see the major 'afterlife' effect of Byzantium on the level of popular culture detected continuity of Byzantine legacy in such important areas of 'formal culture' like agrarian and maritime law.[68] Others have come to more nuanced conclusions by bringing forth previously ignored elements of continuity and Byzantine-Ottoman imbrication during the transition to *Turkokratia*, such as the existence of aristocratic Byzantine families active as entrepreneurs, forms of organising the urban economy and town–countryside relationships, sedentarisation of Ottoman warfare, the 'heritage of autocracy' and so on.[69]

The really profound effect of Köprülü's work, however, was on Turkish historiography. It concerned both methodology, with its strong and weak sides (such as the disregard of Byzantine sources), and the conclusions reached. Subsequent studies of Turkish and Ottoman institutions were basically imitations or supplements, with barely any attempts at

---

[67] Leiser, 'Postscript', in Köprülü 1999: 161; Park 1975: 256. Later critics added that Köprülü sometimes made the same error of which he accused byzantinists, namely the assumption that, because two institutions appeared to be the same (e.g. because of parallel names or allusive description), they, in fact, were identical or had a common origin (Leiser, 'Introduction', 11–12).

[68] Vryonis 1969–70: 251–308; 1991: 17–44.

[69] On major aspects of Byzantine-Ottoman interaction in the socio-demographic, economic and military spheres, see Matschke 2002: 79–113. See also Lindner 2014: 269–77.

192   Ottoman and Early Republican Turkish Historiography

modification until at least the late 1970s.[70] In the Turkish case there has not been an historian who attained the social recognition of the Greek Paparrigopoulos or the Bulgarian Zlatarski, or a corresponding oeuvre of indisputable validity to be considered a master narrative. Yet in important respects Köprülü came close to it. He contributed hugely to the Turkification of Ottoman imperial history and making it a cardinal part of Turkish national history. He also set the stage for a future reconciliation with Islam by distinguishing a progressive ('genuine and pure') 'Anatolian-Turkish Islam' from the alleged obscurantist and dogmatic Islam of the Arabs and rendering it compatible with secular nationalism[71] – a form of arrogation and nationalisation of Islam not dissimilar to the Greek, Bulgarian or Serbian appropriation and nationalisation of Eastern Orthodoxy. At the same time, Köprülü's standards of research were much more sophisticated than those of his Romantic predecessors and opened up, both thematically and methodologically, new scholarly horizons that went beyond the confines of turkology.

Convergence of views was not only a result of direct or diffuse impact, though. The shift of interpretation that the aforementioned art historian Celal Esad Arseven, now a professor of architectural history at the Academy of Fine Arts in Istanbul, underwent under the Republican regime is revealing of the cultural-political forces at play in Kemalist Turkey, intertwining nationalism with modernity. In his classic *Türk Sanatı* (*Turkish Art*), first published in 1928 and launching the concept of 'Turkish art', Arseven reconceptualised Ottoman art by foregrounding both its Turkish 'purity' and uniqueness that set it apart from the Byzantine and other Islamic traditions *and* its trans-historical affinities with European modernism.[72] Whereas in his earlier *Constantinople, de Byzance à Stamboul* he saw fit to put Byzantine and Ottoman monuments side by side and acknowledge Byzantine artistic influences, in *Turkish Art* he made only fleeting references to Byzantine architecture and its influences went mostly unacknowledged or were rejected outright. 'Ottoman artists', he maintained, 'had very different perspectives from those of the Byzantines. Ottoman architecture has no relations with the ailing sadness (*hastalıklı hüzün*) of Byzantine architecture.'[73] In terms both of its preoccupation with an ethnically defined 'Turkish' architecture untouched by any Byzantine precedents and of its overall ideological framing, Arseven's *Turkish Art* constitutes the art-historical counterpart to Fuat Köprülü's

---

[70] Leiser, 'Postscript', in Köprülü 1999: 165–6.   [71] Gürpınar 2013: 95, 112–13.
[72] Bozdoğan 2007: 199–221.   [73] Arseven 1984: 83.

Ottoman and Early Republican Turkish Historiography   193

foundational thesis.[74] Two influential Austrian art historians, Josef Strzygowski (1862–1941), who had revolutionised Byzantine studies with his work on the role of Anatolia in the development of Byzantine art, and his student Heinrich Glück (1889–1930), lent valuable support to this view. In articles published in the journal *Türkiyat Mecmuası* in 1933, both of them contrasted the Turkish and Byzantine art and thus boosted the position of those who denied any link between Ottoman and Byzantine heritages and exalted the assimilative and acculturative powers of the Turks. In this cultural atmosphere, it comes as no surprise that Byzantine archaeology was non-existent and that among the archaeologists and historians, whom the state sent to Europe for education, there were no byzantinists. Excavations of Byzantine sites were conducted by foreign scholars, usually under the auspices of newly founded foreign national archaeological institutions in Istanbul and Ankara.[75]

With the interpretations advanced by Köprülü, a scholar with disproportionate impact both through his work and his disciples, and Arseven, an outstanding art historians, it is not hard to explain why 'a country, which, after 1935, established chairs for Sumerian, Hittitian, Sanskrit, Chinese, Latin, Greek, Hungarian, Russian, Arabic, and Persian at the University of Ankara' and 'which had inherited the entire material culture of the Byzantine empire's core territories', failed to establish a tradition for Byzantine studies commensurate with these advantages and train internationally renowned byzantinists. As Halil Berktay has noted, '[f]or Turkish nationalism, Byzantium has remained "the enemy" defeated at Manzikert in 1071 and then again in 1453; it has been excluded from the country's historical heritage'.[76] The epistemic 'war' behind it was the pursued affirmation of the budding field of Ottoman studies as a sub-discipline of turkology, and Turkish history in particular, against the by then well-established field of Byzantine studies. The scholar generally considered to be the founder of Byzantine studies in Turkey, Şerif Baştav (1913–2010), completed his PhD in Hungary in 1947 and was later occupied mainly with the translation of and commentaries on late-Byzantine texts discussing the Ottomans.[77]

The decade preceding World War II saw the consolidation of an authoritarian single-party regime pursuing a heavily statist and isolationist policy and fostering a homogeneous and reductionist vision of the national past. In contrast to the first decade of the Republic, this period was marked by a rising pro-Ottoman sentiment encouraged by the paternalistic and

---

[74] Bozdoğan 2007: 202.   [75] Akyürek 2010: 208–9.   [76] Berktay 1991: 111.
[77] Delilbaşı 2005: 64.

194   Ottoman and Early Republican Turkish Historiography

state-centred aspirations of the regime.[78] After Atatürk's death in 1938, the rehabilitation of the Ottoman past gained new impetus and by the early 1940s scores of publications about Ottoman history appeared. Almost all of them glorified the 'classical period' of Ottoman history (until the reign of Suleiman, 1520–66) as a golden age of power and perfect symbiosis between state and society. Decline, when it came in the eighteenth century, was averred to have resulted from the influx of 'foreign elements' and the increasing power of the reactionary *ulema* – a strategy that allowed the Turkish nation to take credit for the early Ottoman empire's cultural achievements and battlefield victories while escaping blame for its later failures.[79]

Moulding the image of the Ottoman empire in the Byzantine mirror continued to be vital for the reworking of the Ottoman past along such lines. This is exemplified by the work of Ömer Lütfi Barkan (1905–79), one of the founding fathers of Ottoman social and economic history and a major intellectual figure straddling the pre- and post-World War II decades. Barkan did not delve into *stricto sensu* Byzantine *problematique*, nor did he ever write a major book presenting a more comprehensive and synthetic approach to Ottoman history. His seminal essays, utilising state-archival documents, however, were essential in shaping for many years mainstream Turkish historiography on Ottoman land tenure system, price and population movements, and the status of the peasants.

What Köprülü considered as 'improvements' on the social situation in the region following the Ottoman conquest Barkan translated into a theory of liberation from Byzantine feudal oppression. We have seen how some pre-Republican authors, such as Ahmet Midhat, lionised the 'enlightened and liberating Ottomans', who had 'save[d] the oppressed of the East, grant[ed] them personal and national freedom as well as religious and political privileges'.[80] Barkan, however, undergirded such rudimentary statements with archive-based methodology and socio-economic arguments. He went to great lengths to prove that Ottoman society in the 'classical age', unlike the Western or the Byzantine, was 'non-feudal', a unique form of social contract between the ruler and the ruled and a system of perfect solidarity, within which every member and every activity was directed towards serving the state and where the state, in turn, secured the fair treatment and freedom of the inhabitants of the empire. In Barkan's words, in the Ottoman empire 'we observe how the

---

[78] Mishkova, Turda and Trencsényi 2014: 307–8.   [79] Ersanlı 2002; Danforth 2016: 11–12.
[80] Ursinus 1987: 238.

Ottoman and Early Republican Turkish Historiography

willpower of a colossal and omnipotent state . . . could manipulate all sorts of economic, social and demographic forces in order to create its unique form of order and harmony'.[81] The image of the 'classical' Ottoman state as an unparalleled historical entity, exalted for its exemplary virtues and superior capacity to maintain immaculate social harmony and freedom, was destined to become an enduring form of orthodoxy in Turkish historiography.

The antagonistic background to this presentation was provided by the Byzantine, as a version of the Western, feudal states and the 'inordinately more primitive regime of the infidel, which represented a terrible and destructive force of oppression for the peasant classes'. As a natural result of the conquest and annexation of Byzantium and the Balkan countries, Barkan wrote, the Ottoman empire abolished the obligations that were 'arbitrary and reminiscent of the powers of the slave-owner over his slaves' and replaced them with a fair tax system regulated by law; the peasants in these countries 'were instantly and fully liberated from serfdom; from being the slaves of numerous petty lords, they achieved the status of the protected *reaya* of a great Empire'; the 'immense improvement in their legal and social condition', which amounted to 'a great land reform on an international scale' and entailed 'immediate obtainment of their freedom', helped explain 'the miraculously rapid and irresistible rise of the Ottoman empire'.[82] The Ottoman conquest of Byzantium and the Balkan states thus appeared as an anti-feudal revolution executed by a benevolent Ottoman state to the benefit of a previously enslaved population, now turned into 'free peasantry' – the backbone of the future 'classless' and state-centred Turkish Republic. Before long, another lasting trope, that about the empire as a 'paradise of cultural pluralism', where the *Rum* (its Orthodox Christians subjects) thrived, would be incorporated into the 'national history' and the mainstream Turkish narrative.

---

[81] Barkan 1980: 725–88, as translated in Mishkova et al. 2014: 309–12.
[82] Barkan 1980: 758. See also Berktay 2009: 53–4.

PART II

Metamorphoses of Byzantium after World War II

CHAPTER 6

From Helleno-Christian Civilisation to Roman Nation

The civil war in Greece (1946–9), which ended with the defeat of the Greek Left, ushered in a period often described as being shaped by conservatism, communist phobia and anti-intellectualism. The prevailing climate forced non-compliant scholars to remain silent or seek refuge abroad. History-writing continued its pre-war course, untouched by the developments that swept through much of European historiography after 1945. On the whole, the work conducted in Greece from the 1950s onwards was confined to fields that were 'ideologically safe' – the Greek War of Independence (1821–8), the history of Greek Macedonia and the old question of Hellenic continuity.[1] The time of the military dictatorship in Greece (1967–74) breathed new life into the awkward fiction of 'Christian Hellenism', enshrined in the 1968 Constitution of Greece and of 'the values of Hellenic Christian civilisation'. As a 1973 history textbook phrased it, 'Hellenism and Christianity are the two basic defining characteristics of the Byzantine civilisation. Byzantine civilisation = Helleno-Christian civilisation'.[2] The idea of 'Greece of the Greek Christians' that pervaded the post-war Greek political discourse did not vanish with the colonels' regime. In 1982 the then Prime Minister Karamanlis could state that, 'Orthodoxy, by enriching the shining cultural tradition of classical antiquity constituted with it the strong spiritual and ethical foundation of Hellenism .... For this reason the concepts of Hellenism and Orthodoxy have been interwoven inseparably in the consciousness of the nation.'[3]

Not that there was no change at all. The defeat of the communist Left in the civil war affected its historical outlook. Until 1945, the Communist Party leadership and left-wing intellectuals showed reluctance to portray modern Greece as the heir to the slave society of ancient Greece or to the 'Asiatic despotism' of the Byzantine empire. This changed with the end of

---

[1] Kitroeff 1989: 270, 272.   [2] Burke 2014: 22.   [3] Cited in Kokosalakis 1987: 45.

the civil war, when the Left saw itself urged to establish its own 'progressive' and 'people-grown' version of historical continuity in response to the accusations of unpatriotic action coming from the victorious Right. The language of class in the party documents was gradually abandoned in favour of the abstract notion of 'the people'. When speaking of Byzantium, they referred to 'the dominant Graeco-Roman ethnie [*graikike laoteta*] that spoke the same language, shared the same religion and lived in the same area' and whose transformation to a nation during the declining phase of the Byzantine empire was reflected in 'the people's epic'.[4] As critics from within the left-wing circles in exile noted already at the time, such an understanding of the trajectory of the Graeco-Roman *ethnie* betrayed a genuinely conservative, racist claim to continuity. The critique targeted as much the masterminds of the official party line as it did left-wing historians, such as Nikos Svoronos, to be discussed later, who translated this narrative into a communist version of the 'three-thousand-year-old continuity' of the 'Greek people'.[5]

Such was the domestic background to the impassioned debate on the historical premises of Greek identity, which erupted in the late 1960s and spilled into the 1980s and whose resonance in the field of historical Greek studies is in many ways comparable to that of Fallmerayer's intervention in the 1830s. The protagonists, who set the terms of the debate, were several distinguished British byzantinists, all of them holders of the Korais Chair of Modern Greek and Byzantine History, Language and Literature (University of London, King's College), on the one side, and Greek and Greek-American scholars, on the other.

In 1962, Romilly Jenkins (1907–69), Koraes Professor (1946–60) and director of the Byzantine institute at Dumbarton Oaks (1960–9), delivered two lectures at the University of Cincinnati, Ohio, titled 'Byzantium and Byzantinism', which presented a recapitulation of sorts of his lifelong studies. There he questioned the connection between Byzantium and Greek antiquity, with the full consciousness of assailing the Greek 'national mythology'.[6] The Byzantines, Jenkins argued, were the Romans and the new chosen people, who constituted the Roman empire and the New Jerusalem. In the greatest epoch of Byzantium, 'pride in, and sense of belonging to, the superior culture of Hellas was not in any way connected with a sense of Hellenic nationalism, in the late medieval or modern sense

---

[4] Koufou 2008: 302, where the author quotes from the *Draft Programme* of the Communist Party of Greece of 1954, featuring the revision of the party's historical approach.

[5] Koufou 2008: 303.   [6] Jenkins 1963.

of that word'. It was only in the thirteenth century, in the face of declining power and prestige, that some educated men began, *pari passu* with contemporaries in western Europe, to turn away from the concept of Roman universality and back to the specifically Hellenic, as opposed to the Romano-Hellenistic, legacy. Yet, the myth of direct descent and heritage from the Hellenes of old that emerged at that time, 'though potentially very strong for a future Romantic age, exercised little influence at the end of the Middle Ages, when it was confined to some scholars and antiquaries . . . and made very little progress, even among educated people, during the earlier centuries of Turkish occupation'.[7] The chief nourishers of this myth were educated Europeans, 'who had made capital of the genius of the Ancient Hellas, but had remained abysmally ignorant of the medieval history of the Near East'. It was Romantic Europe that reassured nineteenth-century Greece of its classical ancestry, and Greece cannot be blamed for having accepted this assurance.[8] Finally, and in the vein of Fallmerayer, Jenkins debunked the 'claim to historical, that is, racial continuity' between the ancient Greeks and the Byzantines and asserted the wholesale extinction of the ancient Greeks following the Slav invasions and the Albanian migrations in Macedonia, Hellas and Peloponnesus.[9]

It is at the same time remarkable that Jenkins was not an admirer of Byzantium. He held a patently orientalist vision of it, juxtaposing eastern 'faith', penchant for self-delusion and 'immutability' to western pursuit of 'truth', 'element of revolt' and affinity to progress. He deemed Byzantium's political ideology to be 'antagonistic to everything which western civilisation has stood for since the Renaissance', and Byzantine letters and art as bearing witness to yet another caesura, namely that the educated Byzantine 'could never see the Hellenic heritage with fresh eyes, and thus could never understand its true significance and splendour'.[10]

Two years later, in 1964, in his inaugural lecture as successor to Jenkins in the Korais Chair, titled 'Byzantinism and Romantic Hellenism', another renowned British byzantinist, Cyril Mango (1928–2021), set out to interrogate the 'assumption of direct historical continuity' from the other end – between Byzantium and modern Greece. He did so not by raising 'the ghost of racial continuity' (for 'all that could be said on this topic has already been said, most recently and eloquently by Professor Jenkins himself'), but by exploring claims to intellectual continuity, specifically regarding political ideology. Mango averred that byzantinism – that is,

---

[7] Jenkins 1963: 8, 11, 18–19, 21.   [8] Jenkins 1963: 21.   [9] Jenkins 1963: 34, 36–40.
[10] Jenkins 1963: 5–6, 14–15, 20, 42.

202   From Helleno-Christian Civilisation to Roman Nation

Byzantine political ideology (and self-image) during the time of the empire's height – 'was much more Biblical than Greek'. Unbroken continuity between the period of late antiquity and the Byzantine early Middle Ages did exist; however, 'the Byzantines in general did not evince the slightest interest in what we understand by classical Greece . . . a truth that has been blurred by much loose talk about "Byzantine humanism" and "Byzantine hellenism"'.[11] Mango challenged the widely held idea that, as the Byzantine world fell politically apart in the thirteenth century, so Hellenism was reborn; at best, one could see it as 'an upsurge – not a renascence – of classical scholarship'. In any event, 'it is clear that expressions of hellenism during these two or three centuries were largely rhetorical; that they were confined to a very small circle of intellectuals and had no impact on the people'. Consequently, there was little 'hellenism' and much 'messianic Byzantinism' among the Greek-speaking Christians during the period of Turkish rule. The ideology of modern Greece, or 'romantic hellenism', was imported from the west in the eighteenth century in the form of forged ancient ancestry. In the next century, however, it was overruled by the 'Great Idea', which was both messianic and nationalist.[12] Mango thus found both continuity and discontinuity, but in unequal proportions:

> We have followed one clear line of continuity from imperial Byzantinism to messianic Byzantinism and thence to the Great Idea, noting at the same time how this concept became perverted, robbed of its original significance and made to serve the ends of nationalism. In all other respects, however, we have found that Byzantinism, as a system of thought, had nothing in common with the hellenism of the nineteenth century; nor have we discovered a line of filiation leading from the one to the other. Hellenism, both romantic and national, was not of indigenous growth; it was implanted from abroad, and in being so implanted, out of its natural context, it produced a break in continuity.[13]

Long after having been assailed in both daily press and scholarship 'not only as an ignoramus, but, worse, as a traitor for having challenged the dogma of the unbroken continuity of Hellenic culture',[14] Mango returned to this topic by looking into, and discriminating between, the small and closed caste of highbrow Byzantine authors – the conduits of the classical tradition, writing in an artificial language and 'effectively obliterat[ing] the reality of Byzantine life' – whose texts scholars of Byzantium most often read; lowbrow Byzantine literature (chronicles, saints' lives, legal and

[11] Mango 1984: 32–3.   [12] Mango 1984: 35–41.   [13] Mango 1984: 42–3.   [14] Mango 1984: 3.

From Helleno-Christian Civilisation to Roman Nation   203

canonical enactments, etc.), where 'the conceptual world of Byzantium can most fully be appreciated' but where 'the hellenic tradition plays a very minor role'; and the lowest stratum of Byzantine culture, that of the illiterate folk – a field pre-empted by folklorists 'whose methods are a puzzle to the historian' as the evidence they used to show a survival of classical antiquity in the consciousness of the popular masses could rarely stand up to closer scrutiny.[15] 'I persist in the belief', Mango concluded, 'that the true culture of Byzantium ... was dominated, not by classical antiquity as we understand it, but by a construct of the Christian and Jewish apologists built up in the first five or six centuries A.D.'[16] It was this view of the world – one specific of a thoroughly medieval society – that bestowed on Byzantium 'a distinctive place in the history of thought' or, as Mango put it elsewhere, 'it is the discovery of [Byzantium's] true self behind its antique mask that ought to occupy those of us who pursue this discipline'.[17]

Transpiring here are the institutional stakes – the 'war of faculties' – which drove this whole polemic. Because of the long-standing European and American academic dominance in the field of classical studies, Antonis Liakos deftly observes, classicists could afford to ignore the appropriation of Greek antiquity by modern Greek national history. Byzantine historians, however, did not have the same advantage because of their dependency on the classicists: Byzantine studies were housed in their departments, and were considered their extension, but with somewhat lower prestige. Nor were they in a position to ignore the idea of a Hellenic Byzantium that Byzantine studies in Greece were promoting with financial support for academic chairs by the Greek state. 'On one level, the debate that started in 1962 was a revolt of Byzantine historians which was aimed both at the hegemony of the Classicists who saw Byzantium as a corrupted extension of Classical Greece, and at the Greeks who had appropriated Byzantium as a period of Greek history.'[18]

Donald Nicol (1923–2003), the founding editor of the journal *Byzantine and Modern Greek Studies*, was next in the row of Korais Chair holders to take up the issue. Resonating Mango's train of reasoning – and the disciplinary interests involved – in his inaugural lecture, titled 'Byzantium and Greece' (1971), he tackled three questions: how Greek were the Byzantines, how Greek were the Greek inhabitants of the Byzantine empire and how Byzantine did the inhabitants of Greece become?[19] Nicol's answer to the first question was that, since nearly all

---

[15] Mango 1981: 49–57.   [16] Mango 1981: 57.   [17] Mango 1984: 18.   [18] Liakos 2008: 218–19.
[19] Nicol 1986: XV, 2.

204 From Helleno-Christian Civilisation to Roman Nation

literature was in 'artificial Greek', whereas demotic Greek was not the only spoken or even the majority language in the multi-racial empire during its golden age in the tenth and eleventh centuries, 'to call the Byzantine Empire the Greek Empire is misleading'. It was only in the last centuries of Byzantium that some literati began to use the word 'Hellene' as a term of self-congratulation, primarily by way of marking themselves off from the Latins and the Turks. A national or ethnic sense of the term 'Hellene' was slow to develop and became regularly employed only after the fall of Constantinople in 1453; the Byzantines of an earlier age 'did not think of themselves as being Hellene in any racial sense . . . nor did they worry their heads about whether the inhabitants of Hellas were the lineal descendants of Pericles'.[20] Nicol linked the answer to the second question – how Greek were the Greek inhabitants of the Byzantine empire? – with the effect of the Slav occupation. Unlike Jenkins, and while acknowledging the importance of the Slav invasions, he assumed a predomination of the Greek element in Greece on the evidence of the survival and continuity of the Greek language, which implied a continuity of the Greek mentality. Nicol wryly devolved the issue of the composition of Greek blood on the chemists, while pointing to the racial mixture of the ancient and Byzantine Greeks.[21] Finally, on the question of the Byzantine nature of the inhabitants of Greece after the 'dark age', Nicol presumed their complete 'byzantinisation' and late-medieval Greece as a 'thoroughly Byzantine province' in spirit and culture, where hellenolatric intellectuals like Plethon were 'odd men out', unhonoured by contemporaries and unknown to later generations.[22]

The Greek counter-offensive followed almost immediately with several ripostes by Greek and Greek-American scholars, published in *Balkan Studies*, an English-language journal committed to publicising the Greek version of history. Notable in these reactions is the full accord between émigré Greek scholars writing from the outside and those working within Greece on behalf of restating and enhancing the mainstays of the Greek grand narrative.

Interestingly, George Georgiadis-Arnakis (1912–76), a professor at the University of Texas, Austin, launched his polemic with Jenkins by defying the assertion about the 'Eastern' character of Byzantium and, insofar as 'the Modern Greeks identify themselves as Byzantium's direct cultural successors', of modern Greece, too. He ransacked selected sources for evidence that 'Byzantium was emotionally closer to the West than to the Islamic

---

[20] Nicol 1986: XV, 5–8.   [21] Nicol 1986: XV, 9–15.   [22] Nicol 1986: XV, 15–19.

Orient' and that Greece had always been led by the perennial desire to 'identify herself with the West' and keep its distance from Russia and the Slavs.[23] The revival of Hellenism in modern Greece might have come from Europe, as Jenkins had contended; however, 'interest in Ancient Greece never ceased to exist among the people'. Arnakis posited 'continuity of cultural tradition' rather than blood relationship as 'the keynote of Modern Greek historiography', yet biological continuity lurked compellingly behind his observation that ancient folklore could survive down to the present time 'only because an important segment of the Ancient Greek people, and its descendants from Hellenistic and Roman times, was able to live, despite war, devastation, and pestilence, and so (admittedly with Slavic and Albania admixtures) to father the Modern Greek nation. Very important in this respect was the role of native Greek women'.[24] Certain blatant nationalist clichés also floated up, as when Arnakis affirmed that 'Modern Greece never claimed the right to control the various non-Greek peoples that had been subjects of the Byzantine Emperors' and that, far from being a 'longed-for return to the Empire of Medieval Byzantium' as Jenkins maintained, the Megali Idea 'was rather the urge to achieve independence and unification of the Greek people'. The coda could hardly have been more outspoken: 'One main stream receives Ancient, Medieval, and Modern [Greek] elements and combines them into a harmonious whole, rendered mellow with the passing of time – thus forming the oldest existing cultural tradition in the Western world.'[25]

The heavy artillery on behalf of the Greek position, however, was harnessed by Apostolos Vakalopoulos (1909–2002), the most influential twentieth-century historian of 'neo-Hellenism'. By the time Vakalopoulos took on a rebuttal of Jenkins and Mango on the pages of the *Balkan Studies* journal in 1968, he had begun publishing his six-volume *History of Modern Hellenism* (1961–87), described as 'one of the most ambitious efforts of Greek historiography of our century'.[26] His understanding of the term *neos Ellinismos* built on Paparrigopoulos's, asserting the existence of a primeval Greek consciousness and an awareness of the historical roots of the Greek *ethnos*, which were only temporarily submerged before being 'rekindled' in 1204 as Byzantium became dismembered by the Latins. Vakalopoulos embarked on fleshing out this concept by weaving the results of detailed investigations into a vast synthesis of unbroken Greek continuity.

---

[23] Arnakis 1963: 384–90.   [24] Arnakis 1963: 388, 394.   [25] Arnakis 1963: 387, 394.
[26] Mango 1968: 257.

206   From Helleno-Christian Civilisation to Roman Nation

The first volume of the history of neo-Hellenism, later translated into English under the title *Origins of the Greek Nation: The Byzantine Period, 1204–1461*, surveyed the crystallisation of modern Hellenism during the last three centuries of the Byzantine empire – a topic he returned to in his rejoinder to Jenkins and Mango, evocatively subtitled 'Remarks on the Racial Origin and the Intellectual Continuity of the Greek Nation'.[27] After having dealt with the successive migrations of Slavs, Albanians, Vlachs, Latins and Turks, Vakalopoulos came to the conclusion that 'in the case of Greece the meaning and influence of the invasions and colonisations of foreign tribes have been unduly stressed .... Despite its changes through the centuries the ancient Greek anthropological nucleus has remained' – a statement he found support for in Count de Gobineau, 'the founder of the racial theory, [who] does not refute the existence of this ancient Greek nucleus in modern Greeks', and other foreign scholars 'who support the racial continuity of the Greek nation'.[28] Later-day Greek critics had good reason to pronounce Jenkins's racial arguments to be beyond the pale of acceptance. At the same time, they remained strikingly mute about the racist premises of many earlier proponents of Greek continuity, whom Jenkins sought to confront on their own ground, and about the racial allegations (occasionally coded as 'demography') of his contemporary detractors.[29]

Turning to cultural continuity, Vakalopoulos called upon the usual arsenal of Romantic and post-Romantic resources: the use of the Greek language and texts (assuming, despite the lack of conclusive evidence, that 'an overwhelming majority of the inhabitants of the Byzantine Empire spoke the Greek language'), folklore and 'folk mentality' (detecting 'many survivals of ancient conditions, customs, manners, etc., a sort of historical fossils' in modern life), and the Acritic ballads and forms of art (purportedly testifying to 'survivals of ancient Greek cultural elements, which from the far off past have not ceased to inherit from generation to generation in popular artistic circles') – all of these indicating, pace Mango, that 'Byzantium was not "biblical" but Greek, at least in substance'.[30] A series of tenuous statements followed suit: that during the Middle Ages, Athens never ceased to be a centre of 'vital Hellenic culture'; that 'the revival of ancient Greek influence in no way provoked the opposition of the Christian Church'; that by the early sixteenth century the Greeks 'were keenly aware of their nationality at a time when national consciousness in

---

[27] Vakalopoulos 1961; 1970.   [28] Vakalopoulos 1968: 103–10; 1970: 1–16.
[29] See especially Vryonis 1978: 242, 247–8; 1999: 25–6.   [30] Vakalopoulos 1968: 110–12; 1970: 18.

From Helleno-Christian Civilisation to Roman Nation   207

Europe was still inchoate'; that the 'Great Idea' seeking the emancipation and unification of the Greeks 'was a shining ideal for the enslaved Greeks from 1204 until the beginning of the twentieth century'.[31] Throughout, Byzantine was used as synonymous with Hellene in the sense of modern Greek – or as Vakalopoulos put it in the revised edition of his *History* (1974), the Byzantines 'were not Romans, but Greeks [who] had not realised this themselves'.[32]

Through the 1970s the spirit of *ethnikismos* continued to pervade the work of most Greek and Greek-American historians of Byzantium and modern Greece. When talking about Hellenism, an ineludible theme in any discussion of Byzantium, many professed to disavow racial determinism and foregrounded instead 'language and culture'. Peter Charanis (1908–85), a long-time professor of Byzantine history at Rutgers University and author of numerous studies on the demographic composition of Byzantium, contended that 'those who passed under the ethnic of "Romans" were in reality Greeks, i.e., Greeks in language and culture':

> The Romans of the Byzantine empire then were Greeks and these Greeks constituted the medieval phase of the Greek people. For a little while in the course of the thirteenth century and again towards the very end of the empire Greek intellectuals tended more and more to use the term 'Hellenes' in place of that of Romans in their references to the Greek people, but this . . . should not be taken to mark the beginning of the Greek people. The formation of the Greek people goes back, of course, to antiquity; it began to assume its medieval character during Roman times, after the triumph of Christianity.[33]

Eventually culture was trumped by race, though. The massive waves of Slav invaders, Charanis stated, were 'completely absorbed by the Greek race', leaving behind only some Slavic place names. This became possible because in Greece 'the original ancient inhabitants' remained sufficient in magnitude to impose themselves on the Slavs, so that 'one cannot speak of the disappearance of the ancient Greek race'.[34]

Speros Vryonis, Jr (1928–2019), another eminent Greek-American byzantinist, promoted a patently essentialist view of the role Greek culture played in Byzantine identity, arguing, like Vakalopoulos, that the Byzantines were some kind of oblivious Greeks. The rise of Byzantine civilisation to a world civilisation, he averred, was due to its 'hybrid, Hellenic and Christian, character'.[35] In this long-cherished 'Helleno-Christian' formula there was

---

[31] Vakalopoulos 1970: 19, 26, 42–3, 256; 1968: 119.   [32] Vakalopoulos 1974: 87.
[33] Charanis 1978: 88, 92.   [34] Charanis 1949: 258; 1970: 1–34.   [35] Vryonis 1992: 20–1.

208   From Helleno-Christian Civilisation to Roman Nation

no place for Roman strands, let alone identity. In fact, Vryonis condescendingly dubbed those who took the label 'Roman' seriously proponents of the 'legalist school of names' – scholars who believe that 'a people are what they call themselves' and who 'emphasise the absoluteness of the name rather than of the actuality'. And 'the actuality which lurked beneath the name *Rhomaioi* as used by the Byzantines was most often the Greek-speaking and Greek Orthodox population of the Empire'; all others were ethnic minorities, liable to identification by individual ethnic designations.[36] Vryonis, accordingly, saw himself as having every right not only to refer to Byzantines as 'the Greeks' but also to make the sources that he quoted talk about Greeks or the Greek nation when they did not.[37] Conversely, he applied a strictly nominalist reading of the terminology Byzantium's neighbours used to designate the Byzantines and their state by some form of the word Greek, which he confidently took for indicating ethnic identification. The use of the term 'Hellene' 'with a contemporary ethnic connotation', he further held, had begun in the ninth century and, after the destruction of the political unity of the 'Greek political world', came to function as an 'ethnicon that denoted Greekness more directly than the term Rhomaios'.[38] As Anthony Kaldellis drily puts it, when Greek scholars force the ethnonym 'Greek' into texts where it does not exist (or, one may add, when they interpret it as an ethnicon regardless of the context), they do it in good faith, bespeaking 'their participation in a nationally oriented discourse that valorises modern ethnonyms'.[39]

A remarkable instance of substituting Greek for Byzantine on account of continuity of race, cultural forms and collective identity is presented by the work of Dionysios Zakythinos (1905–93), perhaps the most prominent byzantinist in Greece during the first three decades after the war and a leading representative of the Greek academic establishment both before and after the 1974 watershed (among his many posts were those of a director of the Centre of Byzantine Studies at the National Research Foundation, president of the Academy of Athens, secretary general, chairman and later honorary president of the International Association of Byzantine Studies, and an MP). What should concern us here are not his specialised writings on Byzantine history, but his interpretation of the

---

[36] Vryonis 1978: 248–9; 1999: 27.   [37] Kaldellis 2008: 114; 2012: 389.

[38] Vryonis 1999: 29–30, 32–3; see also Vryonis 1967, where the enormous importance for Europe of Byzantium as a civilisation is constantly stressed, as is the predominantly Greek character of this civilisation. On the Latin origin and the use and meaning of 'Greek(s)' in Serbian and Bulgarian texts, see Maksimović 2008: 219–31.

[39] Kaldellis 2008: 114.

From Helleno-Christian Civilisation to Roman Nation 209

connection between Byzantium and modern Greece, especially as it was articulated in his *The Making of Modern Greece: From Byzantium to Independence*, a compilation of translated excerpts of Zakythinos's publications from the 1950s through the 1970s. Already on the opening page of this book the author made plain his frame of reference:

> For the Greeks the fall of Constantinople drew the dividing line between the two main periods of their history. By creating the world monarchy of Alexander and its succession states, the Hellenistic kingdoms, the Greeks had prepared the way for the eventual rise of Imperial Rome and for the triumph of Christianity. Culturally, Greece had dominated Rome and had framed the moral standards of the new world government. When the walls of Byzantium were breached by the Turks, this great construction of Greek political thought, which had governed the development of the ancient and medieval world, was finally shattered. Deprived of its political independence, the Greek nation entered on the most critical period of its history.[40]

The interpretation that followed evinced basic assumptions of the Greek national mythology: it equated culturally and politically Byzantium with Greece (Byzantium featured as 'the medieval Greek state' or 'Byzantine Greece', and 'Byzantine' was substituted by 'Greek' in description of both cultural and political phenomena); transmogrified the Greek-speaking Orthodox of the empire into Greeks; and maintained that, through their 'learned' and 'popular' traditions, the Greeks had preserved and transmitted to modern Greece both the 'vigorous Hellenic humanism' and the universalist principle of the Byzantine empire – the two 'sources of inspiration' for the Greeks during the *Tourkokratia*, which formed integral, even if contradictory, parts of the 'Greek consciousness' and the 'Greek intellectual tradition'. The gist of his argument was that 'in Greek tradition there are no gaps in the Greeks' consciousness of their own nationhood'.

> In contrast to other non-historically-minded racial groups, the Greeks are a 'historical' nation, not merely because they have preserved unbroken their consciousness of their historical continuity but also because they have transmitted their conception of this to others. An isolated race, without kindred . . . they based their independent existence not on their mass or on their compactness but on the clarity of their historical self-consciousness.[41]

Zakythinos's defence of the unflinching national awareness of the Greeks across millennia mingled racial, cultural and identitarian claims in a conceptual hodgepodge, with little heed for defining or discriminating

[40] Zakythinos 1976: 1.   [41] Zakythinos 1976: 150–1, 187–8.

210   From Helleno-Christian Civilisation to Roman Nation

between them. A series of controversial propositions followed suit: that the term 'Romaic race' (*genos*) was an 'expression of the Greeks' feeling of themselves as a national and moral community'; that Orthodoxy 'symbolized the union of Faith and Nation'; that the fusion of race and faith augured 'the fourth age of Greece' as it was first conceived by Spyridon Zambelios in 'a daring vision of the universal Greek empire of the East'; and so on.[42] Underlying such declarations was Zakythinos's understanding of Byzantium as 'a triumphant expression, cultural as well as political, of Hellenism'. The stage for it was set with the 'total disappearance of bilingualism and the demise of the [eastern] Roman Latinity', which 'progressively transmuted the Romano-Byzantine *Staatsnation* into a Hellenic *Kulturnation*'. By fusing Hellenism and Christianity (this endeared formula!), the Byzantine culture produced a symbiosis and a civilisation with powerful acculturating radiance. The Slavic Christian culture was 'its creation, its invention, a deliberate human act': by inventing the Slavic script, the empire sacrificed the ecumenism of the Greek language for the sake of the universality of its culture.[43] What this Hellenocentric interpretation of the 'Byzantine synthesis' basically meant, then, was the acculturation of the 'bastard' Slavic culture by the 'congenital' Byzantine (i.e. Greek) civilisation. How the 'Slav' historiographies reacted to this provocation will be discussed shortly. Worthy of note here is that the next generations of Greek byzantinists would refer to Zakythinos – a scholar whose oeuvre straddled Byzantine and Modern Greek studies and whose numerous positions of power ensured its diffuse impact – as *megalos daskalos*, the 'great teacher'.[44]

Post-war Marxist versions of Greek historiography contributed with a few bricks to the imposing edifice of perennial Hellenism. Nikos Svoronos (1911–89), the most outstanding Marxist historian of the second half of the twentieth century, spent some thirty years in exile in France, where he connected with the Eurocommunist trend and the French historical tradition. In 1953 he published *Histoire de la Grèce moderne* (translated into Greek in 1976), where he adopted wholesale the continuity canon but shifted the focus from state and elites to 'people' and folk culture. 'The anonymous folk creativity', he wrote, 'brings together in a living combination elements from all periods of the three-thousand-year history of Hellenism and expresses clearly the continuity of the Greek civilisation.'[45] Significantly, although Svoronos foregrounded the history

[42] Zakythinos 1976: 188–200.   [43] Zakythinos 1980–1: 43–4, 51; 1967: 7–26.
[44] See, for example, Nystazopoulou-Pelekidou 1994: 172–5.   [45] Svoronos 1953: 25.

of society, and the socio-historical method generally, and differentiated on this basis between ancient, medieval and modern phases in the evolution of the Greek nation, this did not lead him to relativise the notion of Hellenism as a latent cultural entity, spanning these epochs with its core intact and the 'Greek people' (yet another abstraction, distinct from 'society') as its caretaker and carrier. Indeed, his view of Hellenism was as patently metaphysical as that of his conservative opponents: 'Hellenism as a metaphysical entity, as a *sui generis* ("alone of its kind") essence', he held, 'does not participate in the changes of the environment and as a result, it remains continuous, coherent and unchanging in its qualities.'[46] The transcendentally ordained Greek endurance was thereby embellished with a Leftist version.

More than anything, the convergence of conservative-nationalist and Marxist historiographic narratives in a profoundly polarised society reveals the authority of the dominant discourse on Hellenic continuity in post-war Greece. It comes with a cost, though, for, as Aziz Al-Azmeh observes, 'writing of history in terms of transhistorical nominatives, like Hellenism or Islam inevitably becomes a history of repetition and re-enactment, that is to say, a typological history of types and figures, a genealogical history subject to all the conceptual distortions of genealogies as studied by ethnographers'.[47] The debate on Greek continuity, which spread across three decades, embroiling, next to those directly involved, most historians of Byzantium and modern Greece in Britain and the United States, continued to reverberate at the threshold of the twenty-first century.[48] On the side of its Greek protagonists, it evinced the pervasiveness of an essentialist and ethereal notion of Hellenism, an unflinching, if nebulous, persistence of Greekness across time and space, with Byzantium being (often explicitly) equated with 'medieval Hellenism'. Its traces can be detected in the work of internationally influential byzantinists, like Hélène Ahrweiler (née Eleni Glykatzi, 1926), who does not explicitly or obviously pursue a Greek nationalist agenda, yet whose teleological views of Byzantium as the medieval Greek state and of all Byzantine attempts at imperial restoration, from Justinian to Michael Palaiologos, as precursors of the 'Great Idea' have been lavishly appreciated back home.[49] The transference of the battle from the sphere of ethnic continuity and racial purity to the ideologically safer terrain of culture (basically language and education) and historical continuity more often than not served to veil the

---

[46] Cited in Liakos 2008: 211.   [47] Al-Azmeh 1998: 199.
[48] See, for example, Magdalino 1992: 1–29; Rapp 2008: 127–47.   [49] Ahrweiler 1975; 2000.

212   From Helleno-Christian Civilisation to Roman Nation

real stakes: in the words of a contemporary, 'biological continuity is what many Greeks really want when they say "language and culture", disclaimers to the contrary notwithstanding'.[50]

The fall of the military dictatorship in 1974 marked the end of a sixty-year period of political turmoil and cleavage, which had begun with World War I. The hitherto suppressed research, due to political intolerance, on modern and contemporary Greek history was among the prime beneficiaries of the liberalisation. The generation of historians who came to maturity briefly before and after the junta were chiefly engaged with the history of the Ottoman period and nineteenth- and twentieth-century Greek history. Criticism of nationalism, which gained momentum in the 1990s and took the form of deconstruction of grand historical narratives, originated from within this community. Notable in the following decades was the influence of cultural studies on debates about the formation of modern Greek identity, where the core of the traditional national ideology – the close relationship between 'Hellenism' (the national essence) and Orthodoxy – was problematised and attention shifted towards exploring the mechanisms of constructing national ideology itself and the way nationalism has shaped attitudes to the past.[51]

For quite some time, the effect of these new currents, concerned as they were with phenomena intrinsic to the modern world, on Byzantine studies and the conceptualisation of Byzantium was at best tangential. Critical theory-based perspectives on the construction of the national narrative and identity elicited no substantial changes in the official version of Greek history, nor did their insights have a visible impact on the mainstream approach to Byzantine history. A radical revisionist stance from within the Byzantine studies field came about with considerable delay and originated in the 'margins' of national historiography, from a diaspora Greek historian. In the last couple of decades, Anthony Kaldellis (b. 1971), a prolific Greek-American cultural historian of Byzantium, has mounted a strong and vehement revisionist challenge to the received wisdom about 'Byzantine identity', which seeks to supplant both the modernist paradigm of nation-making generally and the Greek nationalist discourse about Byzantium. 'Fiercely iconoclastic, tearing down orthodoxies that have stood for centuries', as a lauding reviewer describes it, Kaldellis's scholarship systematically strives to prove that what we call Byzantium was not 'a universal, Christian, multiethnic empire', as all

---

[50] Kaldellis 2007: 113.   [51] Liakos 2004: 351–64.

From Helleno-Christian Civilisation to Roman Nation

think today, but 'the nation-state of the Romans. It was as much a nation-state as any in the modern period'.[52]

Kaldellis launched a strident polemic aimed at demystifying the politics, ideology and interests laying behind the denial of the empire's Romanness and bringing out the resulting 'distortions and strategic misunderstandings' of its structure and history. Provoked initially by the papacy and the German emperors in the eighth century, the occlusion of Byzantine Romanity was later procreated by Enlightenment thinkers, Greek nationalists and Western byzantinists, whose pursuit was 'not to promote understanding but to prevent Byzantium from getting in the way of ideological projects'. Byzantine studies was complicit in this obfuscation, for, 'as a western artefact, it was designed to buttress and promote western ideological claims', specifically the Western medieval views of Byzantium. Byzantine scholarship, Kaldellis contends, has shown itself utterly unselfconscious and unreflective of this fact, as it 'has never critically examined the origins of its basic assumptions and does not know its own history'. Indeed, the field suffers from a type of 'cognitive dissonance': 'while knowing that Byzantium was the Roman empire and that the Byzantines called themselves Romans, it carries on as if neither statement were "really" true'. Stripping the empire of its Romanness and enforcing a Hellenist reading of Byzantium Western historiography opened the door to its official Hellenisation in Greek national discourse and to the Greek nationalist historians' claim that Byzantium was 'really' the medieval phase of the history of the Greek people. 'For different reasons, therefore, both western and national Greek historiography have an interest to engage in denialism', rendering Byzantium 'a field colonised by polemical western and nationalist modern Greek claims'.[53] In terms of method and theory, Kaldellis berates Byzantine studies for its lack of focussed and theoretically informed engagement with ethnicity and dependence on nationalist historiographical traditions. A notoriously conservative field, he states,

> from the nineteenth century onward, it displays a continuous tradition of identifying the constituent ethnic groups of the empire in fixed racial or national terms. Much of this scholarship consists of, or relies on, the national historiographies of modern countries that have ideological stakes in identifying members of their nation in the Byzantine 'mix'. Countries that are geographically situated in territories of the empire still promote

---

[52] Kaldellis 2012: 390.

[53] Kaldellis 2019: 3–37; 2012: 387, 391; 2007: 43; 2014: 208. The few byzantinists Kaldellis singles out as having taken Byzantine Romanness seriously are Hans-Georg Beck, John Bury, Steven Runciman and more recently Chris Wickham (Kaldellis 2019: 32–5).

official historiographies that rely, whether explicitly or in more coded ways, on racial views of the past and these are injected into the international conversation about Byzantium. The stakes for them range from establishing the continuity or purity of the nation to documenting its claim to specific territories and highlighting the greatness of its past.[54]

Kaldellis's own iconoclastic views about the sources of Byzantium's Roman identity had undergone an evolution: from a largely civically anchored notion of the Byzantine, which stressed continuity of Roman republican notions and practice of government,[55] towards one defined primarily by ethnicity. 'Inclusion and exclusion – Roman and non-Roman', reads his 2019 book, 'were defined and perceived in Byzantium primarily on ethnic grounds, not legal ones.' The key indicia of this Roman ethnicity – 'belief in a shared ancestry and history, a common homeland, language, religion, cultural norms and traditions, and an ethnonym to tie it all together' – were irrespective of class, gender or occupation; *Romanía*, or Kaldellis's titular Romanland, was a 'state named after a people'.[56] Kaldellis does not try to distinguish between ethnicity and nation; to him, 'the Romans of Byzantium constituted – and were aware that they constituted – a nation. This made their state, which they called Romanía, into a nation-state'. Slavs, Bulgarians and Armenians were 'minorities', such that all modern nations harbour, and who were not accepted as Romans unless they assimilated to the national norms of the Roman society.[57]

Byzantium, then, was definitely *not* an empire and, according to Kaldellis, we would do well to stop calling it this. It was not 'multi-ethnic' either as there were no ethnic divisions or fixed social classes to fracture the consensus it was made of.[58] As for language – the main argument that has authorised the rebaptism of the *Romaioi* as Greeks – for most of their history 'the Byzantines did not think that their language made them Greeks; to the contrary, their ethnicity as Romans made their language "Roman", or Romaic'. It would be more correct to say that 'the Byzantines had *two* Roman languages, one the language of their ancestors (Latin) and another their language in the present (Romaic)'.[59] Orthodoxy itself is deconstructed as the defining characteristic of Byzantium underpinning its portrayal as an ecumenical state committed to 'universal' values. The 'universal empire', Kaldellis tells us, is a rhetorical fantasy, the 'family of nations' is a diplomatic fiction and the 'Byzantine

---

[54] Kaldellis 2019: 46.   [55] Kaldellis 2015.   [56] Kaldellis 2019: 46–7, 54, 93.
[57] Kaldellis 2019: 47–8, 286; 2012: 391–3; 2007: 74–82.
[58] Kaldellis 2019: 196–268; 2007: 84–100; 2012: 400–1.   [59] Kaldellis 2019: 97–106.

From Helleno-Christian Civilisation to Roman Nation   215

Commonwealth' is a fundamentally flawed notion, corresponding to nothing in the Byzantine worldview and being instead 'the product of a modern Slavic and orthodox bias'.[60]

An out-and-out heterodox reading like this almost inevitably entails taking a stance on Hellenism in Byzantium – 'as fraught a concept within Byzantine studies as the Byzantine tradition is to Greeks today'.[61] Kaldellis approaches Byzantine Hellenism primarily not in terms of Greek *continuity*, but in terms of Greek *identity* 'as discursively constructed'. In view of his main argument of Byzantium's Romanness, he is expectedly critical of the rampant tendency among modern Greek and Greek-American historians, such as those discussed earlier, to see the Byzantines as Greeks of a sort, regardless of whether they thought so or not, and to narrow identity to language. He assumes a 'national Greek consciousness' in the classical period (based on a shared belief in a common language, religion, way of life and ethnic descent) and its survival until the first centuries AD, when the Greeks were absorbed by the Romans and ceased to believe themselves to be Greeks, while Hellenism was condemned as the equivalent of paganism. The sense of ethnic Greek identity became extinct and the Greeks became Romans: between the fifth and the eleventh centuries, 'Hellenic identity went into abeyance'.[62] This, Kaldellis cautions, does not mean that there was no continuity. In language and culture, even biology, it was considerable. However, continuity existed at a level of practice that did not typically translate into identity. The Roman name was no trivial matter; it reflected a profound transformation in identity and consciousness. 'The Byzantines were Romans who happened to speak Greek and not Greeks who happened to call themselves Romans . . .. Many Byzantine practices were inherited from Greek antiquity, but this does not entitle us to call them Greek when the Byzantines understood them as Roman.'[63]

Then how about the widely purported '(proto)national Hellenism' in the later Byzantine period? The reception of Hellenic *paideia* in the eleventh and twelfth centuries, Kaldellis maintains, inaugurated an elite Hellenism of philosophical and cultural (classicist) kind; it 'was in many ways a fantasy' expressed in fiction, from which 'no integrated collective Hellenic identity emerged'. The Greek identity-claims that began to appear after 1204 had a different source: they were the result of 'the fourth wave of European colonialism in the Levant', a reactive anti-Latin Hellenism that served to mark off Byzantine culture from the West. On

---

[60] Kaldellis 2019: 106–13; 2007: 100–11.   [61] Cameron 2014: 48.
[62] Kaldellis 2019: 116; 2007: 114–15, 173.   [63] Kaldellis 2007: 112–13.

216   From Helleno-Christian Civilisation to Roman Nation

the question of whether we can speak of national Hellenism in the thirteenth century, Kaldellis takes a categorical 'denialist' stance: the Hellenising experiments characteristic of that time were not diffused and there is little evidence that at Nikaia the Byzantines developed a Hellenic consciousness, as it is conventionally asserted. As for the late-fourteenth- and fifteenth-century texts that flatly called the Byzantines *Greeks* and are so often cited by scholars as proof of a rising Hellenic self-consciousness of the Byzantines, almost all of these were written by Byzantine converts to Catholicism, who had adopted a Western outlook.[64] Their Hellenist rhetoric failed to move the majority of Byzantines from their Orthodox and Roman positions; reconstituted as a religious community in the framework of the Ottoman empire, they retained their Roman-Orthodox identity down to the nineteenth century. National Hellenic identity, Kaldellis holds, originated in the West's ideological and military attack on Byzantium and was then modified and ameliorated by post-Byzantine thinkers operating in an Italo-Byzantine context. Ultimately, it was this diasporic construct that took over the Greek homeland in the nineteenth century: 'Modern Neo-Hellenism', he concludes, 'began as a western colonial imposition and became a diasporic construct that returned to Greece in the late Ottoman period.'[65] In both its medieval inception and modern reincarnation, Greek national identity, therefore, appears as being largely the product of Western intervention – a thesis redolent of Cyril Mango's.

There is much to be commended about Kaldellis's anatomy of Hellenism as a metaphysical constant and concentration on the 'accumulated modalities of its use' – on its constructedness and changes as well as susceptibility to reinterpretation and reversal in the history of its reception. He is less meticulous and discriminating in applying a similarly non-essentialist approach to Byzantine Romanness and the Latin West, while his take on Roman nationhood leaves some important questions untouched and some arguments flimsy. Yet one cannot but pay tribute to Kaldellis's stalwart engagement with big issues and dogged attempts to invigorate Byzantine studies by redefining basic concepts and perspectives.

Strikingly, then, inside Greece, Kaldellis's scholarship has been met with conspicuous silence. Of his numerous books, only one, arguably the least polemical, has been translated into Greek. Perhaps the unusual blend between an 'anti-modernist' thesis of nation-state-making and a sapient critical approach to nationalism has baffled both constructivists and

[64] Kaldellis 2014: 208, 220–6, 232.   [65] Kaldellis 2014: 227–36.

From Helleno-Christian Civilisation to Roman Nation 217

'primordialists' back home. A forceful critique, from mainly theoretical premises, was issued instead by another Western-trained Greek byzantinist, Ioannis Stouraitis (b.1976).

Drawing on the insights of contemporary social anthropology and sociological theory of constructivist hue, Stouraitis insists on the conceptual distinction between ethnicity and nationhood with reference to a medieval context. Put briefly, whereas ethnicity in the pre-modern era bespeaks an apolitical vision of community, nationhood stands for a sovereign, politically united community, the loyalty to which requires cultural homogenisation and an operative ideology that only a modern state can effectuate.[66] From such premises, Stouraitis takes issue with Kaldellis on basically two grounds: first, for having failed to account for the identity differentials between the Roman ruling (and educated) class and the mass of (largely illiterate) population in the provinces; and second, for having conflated the concepts of *ethnie* and nation by selectively attributing nationalistic traits to ethnic identities.[67] Whereas Stouraitis admits the existence of a political (regnal) and cultural (education-based) Roman identity for the upper class, this identity for him was neither national in the modern sense (i.e. aimed at cultural homogenisation and broader political participation) nor shared by the wider social strata.

On the issue of Hellenic identity in Byzantium after late antiquity, Stouraitis's argument chimes in partially with Kaldellis's. Up to the thirteenth century, he concurs, the Eastern Roman ruling elite did not employ Greek ethnic discourse to circumscribe its self-identification. An ideological tendency within certain circles of literati to identify ethnic Romanness with Hellenic ethno-cultural identity became apparent from the mid-eleventh century onwards. Before 1204, however, it cannot be taken to document the existence of an intellectual movement that envisaged a substitution of Romanness as an identity of political culture and status by Greek ethno-political discourse. After the Latin capture of Constantinople, the historical construct of unbroken continuity with ancient Rome and the vision of *translatio imperii* suffered a heavy blow, which forced a part of the Byzantine elite to look for an alternative historical source of legitimacy for its Romanness. Unlike Kaldellis, Stouraitis reads the claims that the *Romaioi* were the descendants of the historical people of the ancient Greeks as being inspired by a distinct political goal and having little to do with an ideological movement of Greek proto-nationalism. The main aim of this claim was to add an

[66] Stouraitis 2018: 124–7; 2017: 71–2.   [67] Stouraitis 2017: 73–82; 2018: 127–34; 2014: 185–206.

218 From Helleno-Christian Civilisation to Roman Nation

ethno-cultural dimension (Latins/Greeks) to the traditional geopolitical vision of *translatio imperii* from the West to the East and to define the bearers of the historic Hellenic culture as the only 'true' Romans. In late Byzantium, Hellenic ethnicity and Romanness were not two distinct identities but constitutive parts of one and the same identity – that of the contemporary *Rhomaioi*. As their historical homeland, the cradle of their civilisation, they saw neither ancient Rome nor ancient Greece but Constantinople, the city where the best from the ancient *genê* of the Romans and the Hellenes had mingled to give rise to a new people, the *Rhomaiōn genos*.[68]

So, to the idea of identity and nationhood as 'top-down' rhetoric or elite experimentation is opposed that which insists on demonstrating how social, economic, cultural and political factors generate (or render irrelevant) 'national self-awareness' and on taking stock of the conditions making possible its universal entrenchment. Kaldellis's contention of how the Byzantines envisaged their Romanness would have certainly gained in persuasion had he qualified his claim to a monolithic Roman identity by heeding the role played by competition over status and culture between different vested interests in defining the contents of this Romanness. As to pre-modern ethnicity, recent research suggests that it is better understood as a process of identity negotiation whereby groups are seen to stake claims to social power usually via politicisation of a particular kind of identity. Such ethnic (self-)ascriptions are heavily context-based, so much so that one may speak of multiple ethnic identities according to circumstances. The methodological recommendation that ensues from this is to focus research on ethnicity as the process of situational identity creation and negotiation, rather than on ethnic statements as illustrations of 'ethnicity in action'.[69]

---

[68] Stouraitis 2014: 210–20; 2017: 85–8.

[69] See especially Derks and Roymans 2009: 1–10 and the contributions of Catherine Morgan and Dick Whittaker therein. Page 2008, which explores insightfully the evolution of the 'Byzantine Roman' identity in the chaos of the post-1204 Byzantine world, illustrates at the same time the tension between such a situational approach and Anthony Smith's rather essentialist understanding of ethnicity that the author has taken on board.

CHAPTER 7

Towards 'Slavo-Byzantina' and 'Pax Symeonica'
Bulgarian Scripts

If the study of the Byzantine empire per se was largely left to the Greeks, the 'heirs' of the other participants in the 'Byzantine ecumene' resigned themselves to discrete national slots, from where they appraised their distinctive contributions to the 'common patrimony'. To the Hellenocentric interpretations the other regional historiographies reacted with a series of studies illuminating creative 'national' adaptation and fertilisation of the Byzantine civilisation. Since most of these countries fell into the eastern half of the post-war world, where Stalinist Soviet historiography now set the tone for the sister Marxist, especially Slavic, historiographies, it is worth throwing a glance at the way 'Byzantine influence' came to be interpreted after the resumption of Byzantine studies in the Soviet Union.

The influential *History of Early Russian Culture*, published in 1951 under the auspices of the Soviet Academy of Sciences, harshly criticised the old bourgeois scholarship for having viewed Russian-Byzantine relations 'as *unilateral* influence of Byzantium, as a *contribution* made by a leading civilisation to the life of a "retrograde", "barbaric" land, as the *grafting* of the imperial culture upon Russia, as imitation of Byzantine models by the Russians'. Against such 'reactionary, false and tendentious' views, the Soviet authors reacted with a contention that would soon be taken on board, with minor adjustments and variations, by the historiographies of Bulgaria, Yugoslavia and Romania:

> Observing this process, we see how boldly Russian culture *takes* in new elements, how it assimilates progressive and enriching elements of the other nation's experience, elements that contribute to its growth and correspond to the needs and the level of development of the Russian society. It is no accident that in its cultural construction the Kievan state turned towards the culture of Byzantium, the most *advanced* country of medieval Europe, towards the *most complicated and highest 'models'*. This culture was a *match* to the Russian people and corresponded to the *high requirements* of its

220 Towards 'Slavo-Byzantina' and 'Pax Symeonica'

development. No less indicative is the active and creative character of this reception – Russia employs the borrowings from Byzantium for the struggle with it, for the strengthening of its independence from 'East Rome'.[1]

In his opening speech to the Congress of Soviet byzantinists in 1950, academician Evgeniy Kosminskiy noted that, while bourgeois scholars falsified history by speaking almost exclusively of influence exerted by Byzantium upon the other Slavic peoples, Soviet byzantinists were bringing out the influences produced by Slavic and oriental peoples upon Byzantium.[2] Thenceforth, extolling the 'rejuvenating' role played in Byzantine history by the Slavs and their culture would become apparent in all domains. Meanwhile, *Vizantiyskiy vremennik* resumed publication, but was required to publicly denounce 'antipatriotic ideas of bourgeois cosmopolitanism [that had] penetrated into Soviet Byzantine studies', clearly dissociate itself from the pre-revolutionary 'objectivism' and 'narrow empiricism' and replace it with true Marxist-Leninist objectivity.[3] The first Soviet synthesis of Byzantine history from such positions, translated into several European languages, Mitrofan Levchenko's *Istoriya Vizantii*, identified the 'inextricable contradictions of the Byzantine social system', the combination of strong remnants of slavery and feudal relations of serfdom in particular, as the main cause for the 'progressive decline and fall' of the empire. This was, in effect, a quasi-Gibbonian reading of Byzantium's historical trajectory, where the empire's timeworn image of an agonising victim of parasitism, excessive bureaucracy, profligacy and ritualism was cast in the Marxist-Leninist dualism of an opulent corrupt elite and brutally exploited working masses. 'No government [in medieval Europe]', Levchenko wrote, 'held the people in such a tutelage as Byzantium, which stifled any desire for proper activity and posed great many obstacles to the development of the productive forces . . .. Nowhere in Europe were class contradictions as acute as in Byzantium.'[4] The problem of how the empire managed to survive for over a millennium in this precarious condition was left unaddressed, whereas the conversion to Christianity and religion generally were reduced to tools of social oppression.

Such were, in brief, the main procedures and paragons that the 'historical front' in communist Bulgaria was supposed to follow. Bulgarian bourgeois historians, including the two leading pre-war medievalists Vasil Zlatarski and Petăr Mutafchiev, came under attack – the

---

[1] Cited in Ševčenko 1956: 168–9 (original emphases).   [2] Ševčenko 1956: 164–5.
[3] Ivanov 2003: 58–9.   [4] Levtchenko 1949 [1940]: 290–2.

Towards 'Slavo-Byzantina' and 'Pax Symeonica'

former for having disregarded the laws of historical evolution and the class-based nature of the Bulgarian feudal society, the latter for having supplanted class analysis with the Byzantine impact, especially when arguing that feudal processes in Bulgaria would not have advanced as much as they did had there not been the contagious example of Byzantium.[5] Monistic Marxist-Leninist reductionism, embellished with extravagant distortions, provided the scaffold of the new national narrative as we see it enshrined in the two- (later three-)volume *History of Bulgaria*, a collective work published in 1954 after 'consultations' with Moscow.[6] It asserted the revolutionary role of the Slavs' settlement in the Balkans, which annihilated the rotten slave-based system and, by reviving the rural community in Byzantium, enabled the transition to the next, more progressive formation – feudalism. A Slavic state was said to have been formed already in the 670s and, when the Bulgars ('proto-Bulgarians') arrived, they entered in alliance with it in the form of a federal Slavo-Bulgarian state for the sake of waging common war against Byzantium and the Avars. The anti-Byzantine wars that followed were an expression, on the one hand, of the Bulgarian feudal class's quest for new lands and, on the other, of the state's intent to unite the Slavic tribes still under Byzantine rule – an aspiration that squared with these tribes' eagerness to free themselves from the Byzantine yoke and gain their independence by joining this Slavo-Bulgarian state. Similarly, Simeon's wars against Byzantium and his ambition to sit on the basileus's throne were both an indication of the increased self-confidence of the Bulgarian feudal class and a demonstration of his determination to free the Slavic populations within the empire. The Christianisation was driven by the feudal class's need for an ideology justifying its rule, therefore Bogomilism played a progressive role, because it mobilised the oppressed masses for struggle against the dominant class. The burgeoning feudal relations also spurred the need for Slavic literacy, which, after several attempts at its creation by the eastern (Russian) Slavs, was ultimately delivered by the 'Slavic brothers' Cyril and Methodius from Thessaloniki. Originally commissioned as Byzantine missionaries, soon they ceased to serve the interests of the Byzantine Church and Byzantine policy and put themselves entirely at the service of the Slavs' enlightenment. The literature created in this script was of a genuinely democratic character since the broad masses could avail themselves of it in their fight against class and national oppressors.

---

[5] Daskalov 2018: 260–4, 267.   [6] Istoriya na Bălgariya 1954: I.

222   Towards 'Slavo-Byzantina' and 'Pax Symeonica'

The official 'History of Bulgaria' is an intriguing specimen fusing neo-Romantic anti-Byzantine sentiment, Marxist-Leninist scholasticism and outright falsifications. Any Byzantine influence on the course of Bulgarian medieval history, other than the wars waged against its retrograde rule, was ruled out of the new master narrative. Simultaneously, the supremacy of the Slavic element in terms of numbers, state-building capacity and socio-economic progressiveness was inordinately magnified.

For the generation of historians whose professional upbringing had begun before the war but who morphed into communist science brokers after the war, however, the theme of the Bulgarian-Byzantine relations was not fully passé. In 1948, Dimitǎr Angelov (1917–96), the foremost Bulgarian byzantinist during the second half of the twentieth century, published an article on 'Byzantine Influences on Medieval Bulgaria'. A student of Petǎr Mutafchiev, Angelov had specialised in Byzantine studies under Franz Dölger in Munich during the war, and after the war experienced a meteoric rise from an assistant (1944) to full professor (1949) in the Department of History at Sofia University. In this article, Angelov raised questions that had bedevilled 'bourgeois' Bulgarian historians since the Revivalist period, namely: how far was medieval Bulgaria the accomplishment of an authentic (*samobitno*), natural development and how much was it the result of more or less forcibly imposed foreign borrowing? To what extent had byzantinism impacted the life of the whole Bulgarian society or was it restricted to certain social strata? Finally, and 'most importantly', how much had the Byzantine influences, 'in their entirety, played a progressive role in the development of the Bulgarian people and culture and to what extent had they harmful consequences'?[7] Angelov did not try to answer all these questions but set out to provide a clue by weighing and evaluating the Byzantine impact on the formation of the medieval Bulgarian state ideology. While he acknowledged the 'emphatically Byzantine veneer' of this ideology, occasionally reaching 'total imitation and literal borrowing of established phrases and formulas', more crucial for him were the dissimilarities ensuing from the differences in the historical development of medieval Bulgaria and Byzantium.

The most important difference, according to Angelov, was the fact that Bulgaria 'had developed earlier and faster in the direction of feudalisation', in that there emerged an autonomous landlord class and serfs in close resemblance to the Western (read normative) type of feudalism, whereas in the Byzantine empire the unlimited autocratic power of the basileus

---

[7] Angelov 1948: 402.

Towards 'Slavo-Byzantina' and 'Pax Symeonica'

continued for a longer time to hold strong against the feudalising processes in the political and economic sphere. Feudalisation in Bulgaria was carried out, Angelov argued on the basis of rather scant evidence, with the assistance of the central power and the ruler himself, in stark contrast with the situation in Byzantium, where the emperor was caught in a strenuous 'fight against feudalism, in all its multifarious manifestations'. In Bulgaria the resistance against the rising feudal relations came from below, 'from within the oppressed and exploited class', and found expression in Bogomilism as 'a protest against the new feudal forms'.[8] In tenth-century Bulgaria, Angelov opined, 'the feudal socio-economic formation was already in a process of total establishment owing to a purely internal, unique development'. All of this implied one thing: that medieval Bulgaria developed ahead of Byzantium. It could not, therefore, have 'borrowed' or imitated Byzantine feudalism (as Mutafchiev thought), since its evolution was driven by intrinsic dynamics and only later did Byzantium, under Slavic pressure, catch up with it.

From such premises Angelov addressed the question of whether the Byzantine ideological influences harmonised with the actual 'inclinations and traditions of the Bulgarian people' or, conversely, were only 'a foreign importation acceptable and appropriate for the ruling strata'. In answering this question, he stressed the distinction between the 'strictly absolutist' and 'autocratic' traditions of the Bulgars, on the one hand, and the Slavs' 'democratic socio-political conceptions', 'deeply rooted predilections for freedom and popular sovereignty' and tenacious resistance to any unlimited personal rule on the other. Angelov's interpretation thus added an ethnic dimension to the conventional social division between the corrupted elite and the virtuous people, while reasserting the long-standing thesis about the socially divisive impact of Byzantium. The assimilation of the Bulgars by the Slavs, he contended, had completely obliterated the former's undemocratic, elitist notions of power; however, with the conversion to Christianity, the ideas of Byzantine absolutism invaded the country, reviving thereby the traditions of the waning Turanism, and laid the basis for the medieval Bulgarian autocracy in its modified ('feudalised') form. These autocratic ideas were in the sole interest of the ruler and a narrow circle of aristocrats and 'Byzantine-modelled' clerics; for the broad popular strata they were 'no more than a hostile, alien, antinational borrowing that had to be rejected'. Bogomilism emerged as a mass expression of this rejection of autocracy and absolutist traditions that had

---

[8] Angelov 1948: 407–13.

224   Towards 'Slavo-Byzantina' and 'Pax Symeonica'

infiltrated the Bulgarian state 'under the impact of the Byzantium-reared Christianity': 'The Bogomils' protest, notwithstanding its purely local, domestic roots and incentives, represented a reaction against the impact coming from the south, a reaction against byzantinism that was enforced in Bulgaria after Christianisation.'[9]

There is a convenient convergence here of politically correct positions – exaltation with the Slav's innate democratism, progressiveness and love for freedom, dislike for the (non-Slavic) 'upper classes' and all sorts of elite (especially religious), relentless class struggle – and the anti-byzantinism bequeathed by a lengthy cohort of historians from the nineteenth-century Romantics down to Mutafchiev. Angelov was nevertheless careful to distance himself from the 'one-sided and wrong' conception of those who considered byzantinism as a totally harmful phenomenon, ignoring the 'positive and progressive' aspects of the Bulgarians' proximity to the superior Byzantine culture and civilisation. The task of the historian was to distinguish between the numerous positive aspects of byzantinism and 'certain regressive and detrimental manifestations and directions associated with the ideology and strivings of the ruling class'.[10] From such a perspective he assessed, in an arbitrary and controvertible manner, the Byzantine strategy of forging the Slavic script and literary code: it was favourable for the Slavs in Moravia, who could employ it as a weapon against Catholic and German influence, and suppressive and assimilationist with respect to the Slavs within Byzantium. In newly Christianised Bulgaria, it played an ambivalent role: it allowed for a degree of ecclesiastical self-government but opposed the spread of Slavic literacy and culture for fear that the country could become a magnet for the Slavs inside the empire – a policy that ultimately failed because of the work of Cyril and Methodius's followers in tandem with the Bulgarian state.[11]

In the late 1970s, when the nationalist drift in Bulgarian historiography was already in full swing, Angelov made a more rigorous attempt at emancipating Bulgarian medieval history from the impact of Byzantium by highlighting its locally modulated adaptations that, in his view, ultimately turned it against the empire itself. The socio-economic aspects of this influence were now subordinated to the 'national' ones, and several important theses, arguably influenced by the work of cultural historians like Ivan Duychev (to be discussed later), became prominent. Angelov saw a 'historical paradox': while the conversion to Christianity had opened the door to Byzantine influence, it had at the same time inaugurated, through

[9] Angelov 1948: 413–16.   [10] Angelov 1948: 416.   [11] Angelov 1963: 11–69.

Towards 'Slavo-Byzantina' and 'Pax Symeonica'

the replacement of Greek language and liturgy, 'a deep and decisive process of strengthening the Bulgarian principle in education and learning, in language and literature'. This process led to the creation of a 'unique and high spiritual culture, which, moreover, was not confined within the borders of medieval Bulgaria, but infiltrated the neighbouring countries and above all Serbia and Russia'. So, 'the Christianisation of Bulgaria opened the door wide to byzantinism at the same time as it created the decisive preconditions for the triumph of the Bulgarian principle [and] for eliminating the foreign influence'.[12] Overall, however, medieval Bulgaria had 'developed and moved along its own road, on the basis of objective laws that, by themselves and without interference from exogenous factors, pushed its course in a certain direction'. However strong the element of imitation, the requirements of the adopting milieu were the truly decisive factor. 'It is most correct to say', Angelov wrote, 'that the impact of byzantinism grew and could be borne precisely because the Bulgarian society had already been mature enough to accept and assimilate it.' If medieval Bulgaria had adopted Byzantine institutions and culture, it was due to a 'historical necessity' with domestic origin:

> The influence of byzantinism presents not a basic and defining factor, but only an additional impact from the outside that found possibility for consolidation thanks to the objectively formed internal conditions. This is the most precise and acceptable formula by which we should explain and evaluate, generally, the role of byzantinism in medieval Bulgaria.

Angelov thus turned Mutafchiev's philosophy of Bulgarian history upside down: the actual vehicle of this history was not (proximity to) Byzantium but the 'historical necessity' of Bulgaria's evolution in feudalism. Rather than political and cultural subservience and deformation, Angelov's 'objective determinism' envisioned the possibility, indeed the advantages, of an osmosis between two dissimilar but equally developed feudal societies, marked not by unilateral influence of a more developed on a less developed culture but by two-way interaction between societies of the same level of development. Instead of focussing, as had traditionally been the case, on the political relations and frequent wars between the two states, he advised the necessity

> to make a detailed and full assessment of the relations between medieval Bulgaria and the Byzantine empire as relations between two feudal societies at a high level of development, which were integrated in the sphere of the

[12] Angelov 1979: 191–2.

226 Towards 'Slavo-Byzantina' and 'Pax Symeonica'

> medieval Orthodox culture and civilisation and which lived in close economic, political and cultural contact in the course of many centuries .... It is important to clarify what was the role of medieval Bulgaria in the life and development of the Byzantine society, what was, figuratively speaking, our proper contribution to Byzantine history ... medieval Bulgaria's influence on Byzantine society and its political, ethnic and cultural history.[13]

Assumed developmental synchronicity and 'historical necessity' thus not only cancelled the possibility for cultural inferiority, as inculcated by the pre-war generation of historians through the notion of (nationally injurious) slavish emulation, but also enabled the exertion of a Bulgarian impact on Byzantium. Most consequential, according to Angelov, was the impact of Bogomilism, which displayed a number of rationalist, humanist and 'sui generis renaissance features'.[14] By 1994, following in the footsteps of Ivan Duychev, he asserted the existence of a medieval Slavo-Byzantine civilisation, in which Serbia, Russia and Romania also had a share, but where Bulgaria served as the mediator to Byzantium: 'It is in Bulgaria that the synthesis between "the Byzantine" and "the Slavic" first and most strongly took place on the basis of a common bond – the Christian religion, combined with traditions of the ancient cultural heritage.'[15]

The charted evolution in Dimităr Angelov's views on the effects of the Bulgarian-Byzantine interaction to a great extent reflects the revisionist shifts that Bulgarian historiography underwent from the late 1940s until after 1989. The first signs of the gradual abandoning of the dogmatic Stalinist interpretation of Marxist theory became apparent in the early 1960s. Gradually, the formation of 'Bulgarian feudalism', increasingly recognised as having followed the Byzantine model, was moved from the ninth to the eleventh/twelfth centuries (the period of Byzantine domination), while its maturation was deferred to the thirteenth/fourteenth centuries. In place of assimilating Bulgarian (and Byzantine) feudalism within western European feudalism, two types of feudalism, western and eastern, were postulated.

The true revisionist rewriting of medieval history, however, came about with the nationalist turn that began in the late 1960s. It, too, was instigated from above, with the Communist Party leadership's call, in 1967, to 'put an end to the nihilistic attitude to our history'. Leading 'bourgeois' medievalists were gradually rehabilitated and their works republished. The main criticisms now levelled against the previously most castigated among them, Petăr Mutafchiev, was that he had underestimated the level of social,

---

[13] Angelov 1979: 192–7.   [14] Angelov 1947.   [15] Angelov 1994: 321.

Towards 'Slavo-Byzantina' and 'Pax Symeonica' 227

economic and cultural development of medieval Bulgaria compared to Byzantium and presented the Bulgarian nation not as a subject of history but as an object of foreign actions.[16] Shored up by Marxist teleological thinking, major segments of the pre-war national narrative celebrating medieval Bulgaria's great rulers, uninterrupted 'state tradition', ethnic continuity and cultural 'golden ages' experienced a triumphant comeback. One reads about 'liberation' of the Slavs from 'Byzantine yoke' in the ninth century and their 'voluntary gravitation' towards the young Bulgarian state; about that state's 'historic mission of defender and unifier of the south-eastern Slavs' (i.e. those settled in Moesia, Thrace and Macedonia – the 'historic Bulgarian lands', as they came to be dubbed in modern times); and about the steadfast policy of the Bulgarian rulers 'to unite all Slavs from the Bulgarian group in their natural ethnographic and state boundaries'. The adoption of Christianity from Byzantium was, on the whole, positively assessed on the grounds of being conducive to the formation of a consolidated Bulgarian ethnic community and the upsurge of Bulgarian culture.[17] As stated in the new version of the official multivolume *History of Bulgaria*, launched in 1981, by the early tenth century the Bulgarian people, already consolidated 'as a monolithic ethnic community', had confirmed its 'unity and will to defend its motherland and freedom'. During the period under Byzantine rule, a small fraction of the Bulgarian society began to lose its identity to the Byzantines; however, 'the Bulgarian people did not let itself forfeit its ethnic and spiritual individuality'. Accordingly, the uprising that led to the reinstatement of the Bulgarian kingdom in 1185 was presented as a 'vivid expression of the repeatedly manifested aspiration of the oppressed people to cast off the foreign yoke and regain its political independence'.[18] Striking here, especially from a Marxist point of view, is the monolithic and homogeneous notion of 'the people', in which the formerly overarching 'oppressed popular masses' and class divisions became dissolved. As portrayed by the official national-communist historiography, 'the people' appeared determined to defend and fortify, together with the feudal lords, the feudal state.

Nowhere was the transmogrification of Byzantium's treatment more apparent than in the interpretation of its impact on Bulgarian culture, starting with the creation of the Slavic script and literature. During the Stalinist period, the invention of the Slavic alphabet was attributed to

[16] Gyuzelev 1986: 6–34.
[17] Emblematic in this vein are, among others, Gyuzelev 1969 and Angelov 1971.
[18] Istoriya na Bălgariya 1981: II, 261–76; 1982: III, 81, 87–8, 92–4, 118–19, 125. See also Daskalov 2018: 392–432.

228   Towards 'Slavo-Byzantina' and 'Pax Symeonica'

'historical necessity': the thoroughgoing feudalisation of the Slavic society – the dominant analytical category in the narrative of that period, which highlighted the all-Slavic, not the Bulgarian, repercussions of the process – and particularly the need to enhance the domination of the feudal class were what Cyril and Methodius were responding to. Although summoned as Byzantine missionaries, they did not act as such but served 'something much greater, much higher-minded that was neither Roman nor Byzantine'; namely, 'on the one hand, to give a powerful weapon in the hands of Slavdom to preserve its nationality, to which the greedy hands of the Byzantines and the Germans reached out, and, on the other, to integrate it with world culture'.[19] The achievement of Cyril and Methodius, who were 'blood related' to the Slavs, should be most correctly understood as resistance to the aggression of Byzantine feudalism and the Byzantine clergy against Slavdom and to 'medieval obscurantism' in general. Their work was welcomed by the representatives of the as yet 'progressive Slavic feudalism', who strove to free their lands from 'Byzantine and German clerical and cultural propaganda' and Slavicise their church.[20]

In the 1960s this ludicrous Slav-centred narrative was gradually replaced by one that emphasised ever more strongly the momentous contributions of the Bulgarian state and Bulgarian writers to the creation and transmission of the literary Slavic culture. This tendency came to a head following a publication by the renowned Soviet literary historian Dmitriy Lihachov (1906–99) of 1969, where he maintained that the old literature of the Southern and Eastern Slavs presented a basic unity and could not be studied separately. The term 'influence' was inadequate to explain the transfer of cultural phenomena from Byzantium to the Slavs, which created this unity. Instead, one should talk of 'transplantation' in a new environment, where the transplanted phenomena acquired an independent life. The vehicle was a supra-national 'intermediate literature', made of a common stock of literary monuments and written in the supranational church-Slavonic language. This literature was close to the Byzantine but with a distinct local layer – a Slavic edition of Byzantine culture, to the creation of which the Bulgarians had contributed most. The clear-cut divisions between the national Slavic literatures came about later.[21]

The reactions from the Bulgarian side, initially quite cautiously articulated, indicated the anxiety most Bulgarian historians felt regarding the

[19] Burmov 1952: 50–9; 1957: 63–70.
[20] Georgiev 1956: 5–6, 18–21. See also Daskalov 2018: 355–8.   [21] Lihachov 1969: 3–38.

Towards 'Slavo-Byzantina' and 'Pax Symeonica'

implicit denial of the Bulgarian culture's distinctiveness, originality and contributions to Slavdom and its being reduced to a conveyor of Byzantine influence. The notion of 'transplantation' was found particularly inadmissible; firstly, because it disregarded the distinction between translated and original Bulgarian literature; secondly, because it was applied solely to Byzantine literature and culture, while eliding the cultural transfer from the already highly developed Bulgarian culture to old Russia; and thirdly, because the old Slav 'intermediate culture' was not to be seen only as an edition of the Byzantine but must also take into account the great Slav input in the growth of Byzantine culture. Defining the old Slav literature and its language as supra-national was also unacceptable, as they were in fact old Bulgarian.[22]

The full appropriation of Byzantium's cultural impact took the form of a Byzantine-Slavic synthesis and came about in the 1970s through the prodigious work of Ivan Duychev (1907–86), the most renowned Bulgarian expert in Slavic and Byzantine palaeography after the war. Much of his work was devoted to the study of 'Slavia Orthodoxa', that is, the Byzantino-Slavic sphere, with special reference to the cultural (above all literary) dimensions of this filiation.

In several fundamental respects Duychev's approach departed from the previous Bulgarian historiographic scenarios. Firstly, his focus was the Byzantine-Slavic rather than Byzantine-Bulgarian relations, distinguishing between the western, southern and eastern Slavs. He applied himself not simply to registering the magnitude of Byzantium's impact but also to defining its nature, the cultural spheres where it revealed itself and the channels through which it became diffused. Secondly, for him not only the national histories of the Slavs but Byzantine history itself were incomprehensible outside the relations between Byzantium and the Slavs. Along with recognising the empire's shrewd policy of assimilating the 'barbarians', one ought to also 'recognise the Slavdom's participation in and contribution to the state, political, economic and cultural life of the Byzantine empire':

> The history of a world empire such as Byzantium cannot be studied in its entirety if we do not take into account its relations with the Slavic world, if we do not establish exactly all that it had given and all that it owed to the Slavs during their long coexistence . . .. Only through patient research into the Byzantine-Slavic relations could we gain [proper] understanding of

---

[22] Petkanova-Toteva 1969: 24–40; Angelov 1969: 51–61.

230   Towards 'Slavo-Byzantina' and 'Pax Symeonica'

a facet of Byzantium's role as a world empire and of the relation of its civilisation to the development of the European civilisation.[23]

Thirdly, in tacit confrontation with Iorga and the majority of Greek historians, Duychev maintained that if Byzantium had continued to live long after its political extinction, it was due chiefly not to the Greeks or the Romanians, but the Slavs:

> If we have to determine precisely what 'Byzance après Byzance' represents, it is appropriate to look at the Slavic world and not only at the population of Greek descent .... Thanks to the Slavs Byzantium continued to live long after it had disappeared as a state. The Byzantine-Slavic relations, in consequence, extend chronologically over a long period well beyond the Middle Ages properly speaking.[24]

From such positions Duychev undertook to throw into full relief the Byzantine-Slavic relations beyond the temporal and thematic limits prevalent until then. He thus intended to disavow both the continuing national-Romantic 'survivals' in the historiographies of the South Slavs, 'which prevent us even today to reach an objective assessment of the Byzantine-Slavic relations', and 'the Greek scholars, who unfortunately demonstrate the same contempt for "the barbarians" and particularly the Slavs that one encounters among the Byzantines [and which] from a historical point of view is not in the least justified'.[25] Most daringly, his approach went against the grain of the standard trend of treating cultural influence as abiding by what Peter Brown has called 'cultural hydraulics' – culture moving from a high-pressure area to a low-pressure area – or what in Duychev's day was known as 'acculturation' or 'cultural imbalance', terms also used by Obolensky and intimated by Lihachov's notion of 'transplantation' of Byzantine culture in Slavic soil.[26]

Confronting a historiographical 'imbalance', where the hostilities between the empire and the South Slavs came to the fore, Duychev advised more serious consideration of 'the long periods of peaceful coexistence, regulated by very stringent treaties' that helped establish economic relations with the young Slavic states – a concern Duychev deemed to have been of great importance to the empire.[27] In a similar vein, he viewed Byzantium's missionary activity less

---

[23] Dujčev 1960: 31–2.

[24] Duychev 1998: 27. Between 1954 and 1972, because of the unfavourable conditions in Bulgaria, Duychev's works were published in French and Italian in foreign editions; Bulgarian translations of some of these articles made their first appearance in 1998.

[25] Dujčev 1960: 32.   [26] Brown 1976: 5.

[27] Duychev 1998: 30–1; Dujčev 1960: 34–41; Duychev 1964.

Towards 'Slavo-Byzantina' and 'Pax Symeonica'

as an expression of proselytising zeal than as a major vehicle for assimilating the Slavs within its confines and for promoting its 'purely political interests' and those of the Constantinople Patriarchate in the budding Slavic states. This exclusive, overpowering religious domination had spurred the resistance of the Bulgarian tsars and led to the imposition of the principle, formulated by tsar Kaloyan, that '*imperium sine patriarcha non staret*'. Duychev saw here the source of a 'tragic conflict' in the historical fate of the Bulgarians: 'they adopted Christianity from, and eventually the cultural influence of, the Byzantine empire, while often struggling and warring against it in order to preserve the integrity and independence of their state. It is hard to overestimate the effect of this conflict on Bulgarian history'.[28]

Central to Duychev's notion of 'Slavia Orthodoxa' was the emphasis on the Byzantine contribution to its making. If Christianisation and the ecclesiastical organisation inevitably uprooted paganism and destroyed the germs of an original pagan culture, the Church of Constantinople at the same time 'laid the foundations of a nascent Slavic civilisation steeped in Christianity' by accepting the principle of national languages. This made possible the development of national cultures in the countries rallied around the Byzantine Church. Drawing on his 'Byzantine' erudition, Duychev made a much stronger case than Shishmanov once did on behalf of the 'great merit of Byzantium' for having encouraged the adoption of national alphabets, the elevation of the spoken tongue to the rank of national literary languages ('an extraordinary cultural invention in the old European world') and the emergence of national Slavic literatures – a merit he considered to have been of 'as great importance for the historical life of the Slavic peoples as for world history generally'. Byzantine literature hugely stimulated this process. The true blacksmiths of the literary Slavic language, Duychev argued, were the translators from the Greek language, on which they fell back in developing the lexica, morphology and syntax of the Slavic tongues. The Greek language thus contributed directly and powerfully to the formation and enrichment of the Slavic languages. Duychev also pointed to the benefits reaped from the translated Byzantine literature in transmitting the culture of classical antiquity and scientific knowledge to the Slavs. These translations, on the other hand, 'perpetuated – for many centuries after the demise of the Byzantine empire – the spiritual heritage of Byzantium, with which the South and the Eastern Slavs had been living almost to the present day'.[29]

---

[28] Dujčev 1960: 41–6; Duychev 1998: 31–3.

[29] Dujčev 1960: 50–7; Duychev 1998: 35–7. Duychev's most elaborate studies of the Byzantine-Slavic relations concern language and literature. See, for example, Dujčev 1961: 39–60; 1963b: 411–29; 1967: 103–15; 1972: 77–100.

232   Towards 'Slavo-Byzantina' and 'Pax Symeonica'

The fecund legacy that the Slavs received from Byzantium was also reflected in a popular current of the Byzantine-Slavic relations – the apocryphal and non-canonical Byzantine literature. Unlike most of his predecessors, Duychev did not consider Bogomilism to be a primarily domestic phenomenon and stressed the importance of the Byzantine apocryphal tradition for the emergence of the Bogomil heresy among the South Slavs, and attributed certain Byzantine-Slavic reciprocity to the hagiographic literature.[30]

Duychev observed similar reciprocity in the social sphere, too. Taking his cue from Russian byzantinists like Ostrogorski and Syuzyumov, he pointed to the decisive role of the South Slavs in the empire's socio-economic development as a result of their settlement in the Balkan peninsula, which he likened to the role played by the German tribes with respect to the Western Roman empire. In implicit polemics with S. Bobchev, however, he considered the juridical relations to be 'an area where the Slavic states had lost at an early date their original character in order to adopt the Byzantine laws'. Finally, in architecture, figurative arts and music the spell of the Byzantine models was overwhelming and lasting, but they had undergone numerous and diverse transformations, leading to the creation of specific Slavic 'national styles'. The ultimate balance sheet was therefore positive: 'artistic creativity constitutes one of the domains of the Slavic civilisation in the Middle Ages where Byzantium had left its strong imprint and rendered fruitful results'.[31] Therefore, both the emergence of the Slavic national cultures and their drive for national originality and independence, in Duychev's reading, were the result of the Slavs' intimate communication with the Byzantines.

> In the course of a rather long period, the metropolis had exerted strong influence on the regions [of the South and Eastern Slavs] and favoured the development of their civilisation. Later these regions, after having developed their more or less proper civilisation, moved away from their metropolis, abiding by centrifugal forces and wending the road of an autonomous development . . .. It is beyond any doubt that the South and Eastern Slavs are indebted to Byzantium for everything that it had taught them.[32]

Duychev's interpretation thus squarely defied Mutafchiev's and declared it 'totally wrong'. Turning to the perennial question haunting the Bulgarian historians before him about the 'de-nationalisation' of the Bulgarian culture and society by the influx of byzantinism, he made an

---

[30] Dujčev 1960: 53–4.   [31] Dujčev 1960: 57–69.   [32] Dujčev 1960: 70.

Towards 'Slavo-Byzantina' and 'Pax Symeonica' 233

unconventional argument. Since the Byzantine empire was not a national state, but represented a 'sublime expression of the Christian civilisation considered to be a universal cultural asset', the Slavs could borrow freely from it 'without the risk of spoiling their ethnic identity or being stripped of national characteristics'. Just as the Christianisation of the Bulgarians did not lead to their de-nationalisation, so the adoption of the (universal) Byzantine civilisation could not lead to 'denying the national civilisation, to the extent that such [a thing] existed at that time'. Far from losing their ethnic self-consciousness, some historical figures 'suffused with the values of the Byzantine civilisation', like the apostles Cyril and Methodius, Tsar Simeon or the last Bulgarian patriarch, Euthymius of Tărnovo, 'found in [this influence] an effective stimulus for their cultural activities on behalf of their kin brothers'.[33] From such positions Duychev took issue with Lihachov's notion of 'transplantation' and endorsed terms like 'mutual influence' and 'remoulding', 'editions' or 'recreation' of Byzantine culture. Far from making a Byzantine replica of their culture, the Slavs 'adopted critically and re-created ingeniously' the Byzantine influence:

> While it is true that the Byzantine penetration had been very strong, it is entirely incorrect to affirm that this influence had been accepted in a purely 'mechanic' way. The conception [upheld by Mutafchiev] that the Byzantine civilisation had an entirely negative effect on the Slavs by 'suffocating' their original cultural development is, in our view, totally wrong . . .. Summing up the foregoing, we have the right to assert that it was precisely the critical attitude towards Byzantine civilisation, its adaptation and remaking by the Slavs in the Middle Ages which determines the real place that it occupied in their evolution and the role it had played in the erection of the medieval Slavic civilisation.[34]

The outcome of all this was a bold redefinition of the character of Byzantium's civilisational orbit:

> The civilisation that we have become accustomed to call Byzantine is, by its essence, that of the whole Mediterranean East. The creators and the custodians of this civilisation are – in addition to the purely Greek population, relatively less numerous at that time – the various other ethnic groups, among whom the Slavs of the Balkan Peninsula and the large Russian areas play an important role . . .. It is redundant to stress . . . the participation and role of the South and Eastern Slavs in the creation and spreading of this culture spatially and chronologically, that is well beyond the frontiers of the

---

[33] Duychev 1998: 39, 47, 52; Dujčev 1960: 70–1.   [34] Dujčev 1960: 70–1.

234   Towards 'Slavo-Byzantina' and 'Pax Symeonica'

empire and centuries after its disappearance as a political and cultural power.[35]

It is thus mistaken to talk about a sphere of influence of a culture created in Byzantium and radiated from there to the Orthodox Slavs. What we are faced with is a culture common to a broad range of peoples in the Mediterranean world, in the creation of which the Slavs partook heavily and which, in the face of the mortal threat by Islam, jelled in a 'cultural Byzantino-Slavic community', a 'Slavo-Byzantina':

> In many cases that which is commonly defined as 'Byzantine' among the Slavs and is assessed as the fruit of a Byzantine, strictly speaking Greek, influence on the Slavs, is [in fact] an expression of the Byzantine-Slavic cultural and grass-root (*bitova*) community .... The culture that we call Byzantine in essence very often deserves to be called, especially during the later Middle Ages, Byzantino-Slavic.[36]

The imperial aspirations of the late-medieval Slavic rulers did not in the least contravene this fundamental cultural commonality: the titles of 'autocrat of Bulgarians and Greeks' or 'of Serbs and Greeks', which Ivan Alexander, Ivan Shishman and Stefan Dušan took on, expressed not aggression but claims to take over the role of the Byzantine empire, enfeebled by the Turkish conquests and inner struggles, in the political life of the European southeast.[37] Under the Ottomans, the Byzantine-Slavic symbiosis continued to evolve. Indeed, by allowing the suppression of the autonomous churches and extending the patriarch's power over all Orthodox Slavs in the Balkans, the Ottomans had produced a 'historical paradox': 'the Patriarchate of Constantinople – although expressing the Byzantine traditions and those of the Greek civilisation – was transformed, due to the ethnic composition of the majority of the population in its dominion, infinitely more numerous than the entire population of Greek origin, into a kind of "Slavic Church"'. Together with the literary tradition, bequeathed from the Byzantine past and carried on by new translations and transcripts, this religious tradition was decisive for the preservation of national individualities, as were religious architecture, figurative arts and music, which perpetuated the 'Byzantino-Slavic heritage from the past'.[38] Here again we see Byzantine culture, now as heritage, playing a nationally edifying role and the (former) Byzantine 'imports' being assimilated by and enhancing the Slavs' 'own national patrimony'.

---

[35] Dujčev 1965: 131–2; Duychev 1963c: 357–8.   [36] Duychev 1963c: 357–8; 1963a: 129.
[37] Dujčev 1965: 140.   [38] Dujčev 1965: 132–40.

Towards 'Slavo-Byzantina' and 'Pax Symeonica' 235

All this signalled a major shift in the Bulgarian historiographic discourse, as it had taken shape since the Revival period, from self-assertive confrontation with Byzantium to its repossession as a common Byzantino-Slavic cultural capital. 'The views of a scholar so remote from parochialism have been acclaimed', wrote Ihor Ševčenko in his preface to *Slavia Orthodoxa*. Significantly, Duychev's views departed also from Obolensky's 'Byzantine Commonwealth' in that his notion of Slavo-Byzantina was not the outcome of diffusion and acculturation but of cross-fertilisation and co-creation.[39] Duychev thus laid the groundwork for the reassessment of the nature of Byzantine culture and its symbolic appropriation, on which the next generations of Bulgarian medievalists would build. Upon his will, Duychev's house in Sofia was turned into a Research Centre for Slavo-Byzantine studies under the umbrella of the University of Sofia, which hosts his rich library, source collections and archive and which today is the central venue for conducting multidisciplinary education and research in medieval history, culture and art in Bulgaria.

In many respects Vasil Gyuzelev (b.1936), one of the leading Bulgarian medievalists in the last quarter of the twentieth and the first decade of this century, has followed the trail blazed by Duychev while turning back to the narrower focus on the Bulgarian-Byzantine interactions. For him, 'in the whole history of Bulgaria there is no external factor that had had such a lasting and comprehensive impact on it as Byzantium'.[40] The spheres that best illustrate the essence, character and tendencies in the Byzantine-Bulgarian relations, according to him, are the military and political conflicts between the two states, the Christianisation of the Bulgarians and the strong sway of Byzantine culture. As both a political and ethnic community, the Bulgarians had emerged through their confrontation with Byzantium over the hegemony in the European southeast. This, Gyuzelev opines, explained the Bulgarians' long-standing negative attitude to the Byzantines and their empire, whom they almost invariably branded as 'Greeks' and 'Greek kingdom', thus defying Byzantium's self-styling as a Roman empire and the Byzantines as Romans.[41] The exertion of the Bulgarian khans and tsars to grab hold of Constantinople, he echoed Mutafchiev, was 'natural' from a geographical point of view, but turned

---

[39] Obolensky 1994. Duychev's treatment of Byzantium, which at the same time asserted Bulgarian individuality, found indirect but compelling support in Browning 1975.

[40] Gyuzelev 2005: 27.

[41] Gyuzelev 2005: 31–2. On the use of 'Greeks' and 'Romans' (*romei*) in Bulgarian medieval literature, see Tapkova-Zaimova 1984: 51–8.

236 Towards 'Slavo-Byzantina' and 'Pax Symeonica'

into a 'painful and pernicious political illusion': it debilitated the forces of the state and the nation, led to social crises and destabilised the main 'pillar of the political, economic and cultural balance in the European East' – Byzantium. The failure of Simeon's and later Stefan Dušan's attempts to destroy the empire was due to the fact that the two states were not yet mature enough to assume the role of defenders of the peninsula against the great dangers – respectively, the Arabs and the Turks.[42]

The Bulgarian state and ecclesiastical model linking kingdom with patriarchate resembled the Byzantine and later became a role model for Serbia and Russia. This model foisted the spirit of the Byzantine Christian universalism on the evolution of the Bulgarian state and became a hallmark of the Second Bulgarian Kingdom, when Byzantium's political, ideological and ecclesiastical influence reached an apogee. After 1204 the Byzantine political doctrine towards Bulgaria changed: the empire abandoned its previous strategic goal of annihilating Bulgaria in favour of ensuring its presence in the Bulgarian royal court mainly via Byzantine princesses and their numerous entourages (seven among the wives of the Bulgarian rulers of the Second Kingdom belonged to reigning Byzantine dynasties) and exerting influence on the aristocracy and high clergy.[43] Even so, the 'unsteady and sickly development' of the Bulgarian state during the later Middle Ages, marked by alternations between steep upswings and periods of stark decline, was not the result of the Byzantine influence that had penetrated deeply into its institutional construction and political mores, as Mutafchiev believed, but 'of the changes in the feudal socioeconomic structure and the rapid and unfavourable changes in the international situation'. After the Crusaders' capture of Constantinople, the Bulgarian Kingdom emerged on the historical scene as the main pillar and defender of the Balkan Orthodox world and, by virtue of being the main ally of the empire of Nicaea, played an important role in restoring the Byzantine empire in 1261.[44]

Against this political background and partly reanimating, partly complementing Duychev's culturalist perspective, in his later writings Gyuzelev refers to a 'Bulgarian-Byzantine reciprocity' and a 'comprehensive Bulgarian-Byzantine symbiosis' as products above all of the church and monasteries, especially those in Mount Athos. He writes about the 'transplantation, transformation, adaptation and Bulgarisation'

---

[42] Gyuzelev 2005: 32, 36–7.   [43] Gyuzelev 2005: 34–6.

[44] Giuzelev 1981: 23–4; Gyuzelev 2009: 121–2. For a more 'patriotically' suffused rendition of the titanic confrontation between Byzantium and Bulgaria, especially during the First Kingdom, over hegemony in the European southeast, see Gyuzelev 1995: 60–88.

Towards 'Slavo-Byzantina' and 'Pax Symeonica' 237

of Byzantine culture, which took place mainly in monasteries, and of its 'diffusion' in Bulgaria and other linguistically and confessionally related countries.[45] Most recently he promoted the term 'dialogue' to substitute for those commonly used in discussions of Byzantine-Bulgarian cultural relations, such as 'influence', 'transfer', 'penetration', 'presence', 'acculturation', 'byzantinisation' and so on, in that it presumes an active process with several fundamental elements: (1) the presence of a radiating and a receiving country; (2) a common religion and church; (3) a common corpus of religious and secular literature; (4) similar architectural forms, analogous artistic themes and means of expression; and (5) transformation of the received achievements as a result of a dialogical process in its specific context.[46] Such dialogue did not preclude political or spiritual conflicts, or what Gyuzelev dubs, borrowing from the Russian semiotician A. Lotman's formulation of the Byzantine-Russian cultural relations, 'the revolt of the periphery against the centre'. In spite of, but sometimes also spurred by, these conflicts, the dialogue between the two cultures continued unabated, being stimulated and accelerated by two fundamental factors: Christianisation and Slavicisation. 'The monastic spirit and character of the Bulgarian interpretation of the Byzantine cultural heritage', Gyuzelev argues, 'marked profoundly and durably the development of Bulgarian culture not only in the Middle Ages, but during the Revival period, too.' Bulgarian medieval literature was, in the most part, of a religious nature, whereas the models of the secular Byzantine culture and high literature, such as the rich and diverse Byzantine historiography, had no impact on it. The Slavicisation of liturgy and Bulgarian literature that began with the arrival of the disciples of Cyril and Methodius in 886 had a twofold momentous effect: it delivered a decisive blow to the political and ideological hegemony of the proto-Bulgarian aristocracy and cultural model and, together with Christianisation, created the conditions for the vast penetration of the Byzantine influence in different spheres. The real greatness of Khan Boris I and his son Simeon was the fact that through conversion to Christianity and Slavicisation of the Bulgarian community, they contributed in the highest degree 'to the destruction of a model of development that condemned the [Bulgarian] state and nation to political and cultural isolation from the cultural Christian universalism that prevailed in Europe at that time'.[47]

Gyuzelev's ultimate balance sheet of the 'Bulgarian-Byzantine dialogue' tallies with Duychev's. From the ninth century onwards, Bulgarian

---

[45] Giuzelev 1981: 37–41.   [46] Gyuzelev 2011: 5.   [47] Gyuzelev 2005: 41–2; 2011: 6–7, 9–10.

medieval culture became 'Byzantino-Slavic in form, in typology and in some manifestations of its development. Its prototype was Byzantine, yet consciously and deliberately selected, modified and tailored to an ethnic and cultural milieu marked by different sensibility and vision of the world, a "barbarian" milieu'. Specificity, the often pronounced anti-Byzantine attitude and the ambition to vie with the empire and its spiritual and political power were those aspects of the Bulgarian intellectual thought that conferred originality and uniqueness on the medieval Bulgarian cultural heritage. Profoundly affected by Byzantium,

> Bulgaria was never assimilated by it and never became either its copy or one of its failed imitations …. It turned into a new, previously unknown model – a prototype for other cultures and communities. This culture presented an organic rebirth of a part of the Byzantine culture, which thereby acquired new historical life, new forms and manifestations.

Between the thirteenth and fifteenth centuries this heavily byzantinised Bulgarian cultural model contributed to the constitution and *longue durée* of the Byzantino-Slavic community in the geographic and ethnic area of eastern Europe, comprising the territories of the Byzantine empire, Bulgaria, Serbia, Walachia, Moldavia, Russia, Ukraine and Lithuania – countries where eminent representatives of the Bulgarian clergy acted as transmitters of the byzantinised Bulgarian cultural model, fertilising the development of East European Orthodoxy.[48] In sum, despite certain affinities with Mutafchiev's interpretation of the political effects of Bulgaria's proximity to and obsession with Byzantium, Gyuzelev's overall assessment of the Byzantine-Bulgarian relations is closer to Duychev's, seeking to balance the imported and the immanent and affirm a certain originality and specific features for the Bulgarian culture vis-à-vis the Byzantine.[49]

The distinctiveness and autonomy of Bulgarian medieval political ideology and culture with regard to the Byzantine sphere of influence assumed a prominent, on occasion hypertrophied expression in the works of Ivan Bozhilov (1940–2016), another prolific Bulgarian medievalist straddling the 1989 watershed. Bozhilov's thrust to tackle medieval history in robust national terms became apparent in 1975, when he set out to demonstrate 'the massive presence of Bulgarians in Byzantium between the sixth and the eleventh centuries'. Selectively using linguistic (toponymic and onomastic) sources, he sought to unravel the 'Bulgarian' filiation of the Slavs who

---

[48] Gyuzelev 2005: 42; 2011: 14.   [49] Daskalov 2018: 484.

Towards 'Slavo-Byzantina' and 'Pax Symeonica'

invaded Greece in the sixth and seventh centuries, the 'Bulgarian' ethnographic preponderance in Macedonia in the fourteenth century and the Bulgarian lineage of individuals or families who had played a role in Byzantine history.[50] Bozhilov's 'findings' resonated with a broad consensus among Bulgarian mainstream historians, so even cogent criticism from the Greek side failed to effect change in the Bulgarian position.[51] In a relatively recent history of 'Byzantium and the Byzantine World', published on the occasion of the twenty-second International Congress of Byzantine Studies (Sofia, 22–27 August 2011), the authors stressed that although not all 'Slavs of the Bulgarian group' (?), who had invaded deep into Byzantine territories in the seventh century, had acquired 'Bulgarian self-consciousness' and a great many of them became assimilated, 'from the point of view of today's national historiography they are also relevant to Bulgarian history' in that they long kept their language and 'ethnic consciousness' (of 'Slavs of the Bulgarian group'?); on the other hand, 'the Slavic tribes in present-day Macedonia, Albania, partly Epirus and Thessaly acquired Bulgarian self-consciousness, even when inhabiting territories outside the Bulgarian state …. Nowhere and on no occasion is there any mention of some indefinite "Slavs", "Slavic-speaking" Byzantines or Hellenes and the like'.[52] That there is no mention of 'Slavs of the Bulgarian group' either the authors left without comment.

Bozhilov's full-fledged conception of Bulgarian history in its relation to Byzantium came to fruition in the 1990s. At its core are two newly coined notions: 'pax Symeonica' and 'Preslav civilisation'. The medieval Bulgarian state, Bozhilov tells us, emerged as a barbarian polity, whose political ideology boiled down to creating a distinct state model with the aim not of replacing or transforming or even interlacing with the Byzantine, but of opposing and coexisting with it. With its Christianisation in 864, the 'freely invading byzantinism', understood (as it was by Mutafchiev) above all as a blow to the Bulgarian identity, political and cultural autonomy, emerged as the biggest threat to the state. Building a counterforce to it became Simeon's main task. To the robust and compelling ideology of pax Byzantina Simeon opposed another Christian political ideology: 'pax Symeonica', which aimed at creating a new *táxis* (order) in the Orthodox community. This ideology was driven by his belief in the Bulgarians as able

> to become equal to the Romans, to even do away with them and take their
> place in the Universe, to become the chosen God protected people, capable

---

[50] Božilov 1975.   [51] Malingoudis 1981: 247–67.
[52] Tăpkova-Zaimova, Dimitrov and Pavlov 2011: 394.

240   Towards 'Slavo-Byzantina' and 'Pax Symeonica'

> to take over the difficult task of defending Christianity ... to extend the
> frontiers of the Christian world and community by including new Slavic
> and non-Slavic peoples. The Bulgarian Christianity, the Slavic liturgy, the
> new literary culture were perfect weapons for achieving these goals. This was
> how the new 'táxis' in the Orthodox world or pax Symeonica had to look
> like.[53]

There is no trace here of the lamentation of Zlatarski or Mutafchiev over the pernicious effects of Simeon's 'Constantinople dream' and a great deal of apologetics of the 'brilliant political thought of the Bulgarian tsar', his 'own oecumenical programme' and 'imperial Great idea', namely 'to create an *Imperium Bulgarorum [et Graecorum]* to substitute for *Imperium Romanorum*'. Far from being a short-lived endeavour, this programme was revived after the restitution of the Bulgarian kingdom in 1186 in the form of *Renovatio* and, after the fall of Constantinople to the Crusaders in 1204, *Translatio Imperii Bulgarorum et Graecorum*.[54] Remarkably, Bozhilov conceived of this empire as a national state bent on unifying politically the 'ethnic Bulgarian territories' and 'all parts of the Bulgarian ethnos'. Indeed, his is the most forceful statement of an imperial version of the national narrative in contemporary Bulgarian historiography.

The cultural ramifications of this new political ideology were no less spectacular in that it undergirded what Bozhilov calls 'Preslav civilisation' (after the name of the Bulgarian capital), the emergence of which he attributes to Simeon's reign. He defends the legitimacy of the term 'civilisation' on the grounds that it exhibited the 'two mandatory pre-requisites' for such an appellation, namely particular features and a space of origin and diffusion. The defining features of the Preslav civilisation were: a specific culture (Cyrillic alphabet, unified literary old Bulgarian language, common literary fund) that 'far exceeded the idea of self-defence [and] of preserving [Bulgarian] identity, since it created a "civilisation within civilisation", which was both Byzantine and Bulgarian'; a capital city, designed by Simeon as a copy of Constantinople – an element of his state ideology, a symbol of a new culture vying with the Byzantine and a residence of a new emperor; a political ideology or 'pax Symeonica' (as described above); a harmonious entity of tsar and patriarch. The ambit of this civilisation comprised a core – the royal palace and the capital city, and two peripheries – an inner one (the major provincial towns and the whole territory of the state) and a supra-national one, which included Serbia,

---

[53] Bozhilov and Gyuzelev 1999: 246, 254–5. See also Bozhilov 1995: 44–5, 47–8; 1993: 38.
[54] Bozhilov and Gyuzelev 1999: 246; Bozhilov 1995: 162, 182, 187–9.

Towards 'Slavo-Byzantina' and 'Pax Symeonica'

Russia, Moldavia and Wallachia and where the major aspects of 'pax Symeonica' (language, literary repository and political ideology) were adopted. Bulgaria did not simply mediate between Constantinople and these states; it took up the duties of Byzantium, 'particularly its missionary activities, but also the dissemination of the Byzantine-turned-Bulgarian civilisation in new territories', whereby 'the boundary of the Byzantino-Slavic community became also a boundary of the Preslav civilisation'.[55] The character of this civilisation was Byzantine, but not quite: Bozhilov saw it as 'a micro cosmos within the macro cosmos of the Byzantine civilisation',

> a new model of Christian civilisation compared to the Byzantine – slightly relocated in terms of geographic and social space and slightly modified in form and distinctive aspects. At the same time, this extended ambit and this new form gave the Byzantino-Slavic, Orthodox model its ultimate shape – unified in its ideational, philosophical and esthetical essence, but diverse in its forms. This new model has sometimes been called Slavia Orthodoxa. But it was the model born in Bulgaria, in Great Preslav, at the end of the ninth and the first decades of the tenth century, a model that can rightly be called 'Preslav civilisation'.[56]

At the end of the day, the notion of Preslav civilisation effectively 'Bulgarised' Duychev's Slavia Orthodoxa and, tacitly, Obolensky's Byzantine Commonwealth on account of 'stubbornly and constantly recalling the initial history of Slavia Orthodoxa, when the models and parameters that moulded Slavdom in the Byzantino-Slavic political, religious and cultural community were established'.[57]

This marks the end point of the spectacular turnaround that the interpretation of Byzantine 'civilisational' influence on Bulgarian history had undergone since the 1970s. On the whole, the positive assessment of this influence – captured by terms such as 'Slavo-Byzantine synthesis' or 'Bulgarian-Byzantine dialogue' – was associated less with Byzantine culture per se (whose pre-eminence was generally acknowledged) than with the creativity of its Bulgarian adaptation and transformation, on the one hand, and the special civilising mission it devolved on Bulgarian culture with respect to all Slavic or Orthodox nations on the other.

---

[55] Bozhilov 1993: 35–45; Bozhilov and Gyuzelev 1999: 262; Bozhilov 2011: 590–1.
[56] Bozhilov and Gyuzelev 1999: 262.   [57] Bozhilov 1993: 46–7.

CHAPTER 8

How Byzantine Is Serbia?

Unlike post-war Bulgaria, where Byzantine studies were carried out in the institutional framework of Bulgarian medieval studies or the so-called Balkan studies, in Yugoslavia research on Byzantium had already become institutionalised in 1948 with the setting up of the Belgrade-based Institute of Byzantinology (*Vizantološki institut*) within the Serbian Academy of Sciences. Its thematic priorities, as before the war, were heavily tilted towards Byzantine-South Slav (especially Serbian) relations in the political, cultural and, increasingly now, socio-economic sphere. Compared to other branches of historiography and to the situation in Bulgaria and Romania, Yugoslav/Serbian medieval and Byzantine studies were less affected by doctrinaire Stalinism, while, already in the late 1940s, the communist leadership was encouraging Yugoslav historians to put Marxist historical theory to a more creative use.[1] On the whole, Yugoslavia's singular geopolitical position after the Yugoslav-Soviet rift in 1948, which licensed the country's self-promotion as a champion of a liberal and decentralised socialism and a broker in a bi-polar world, coupled with its international identity as the leader of the non-alignment movement, go a long way towards explaining the weaker ideological control of the communist leadership on the academic life in the 1960s and 1970s. Consequently, no break with the pre-war tradition in Byzantine studies took place, international academic links with west and east proliferated and professional standards remained relatively unscathed.

But if such a modicum of intellectual freedom helped sustain Byzantine research, its fecund development after the war owed everything to the aforementioned Russian-born émigré byzantinist Georgiy Ostrogorski's personal prestige and dedication to the growth of the 'byzantinological' field in Yugoslavia. Having emigrated to Finland after the Bolshevik revolution, studied in Heidelberg and Paris and taught at the University

---

[1] Gross 1966: 238–45.

242

How Byzantine Is Serbia?

of Breslau (Wroclaw, Poland), in 1933 Ostrogorski moved to Belgrade, which he made his permanent home and where his career as a world-famous authority on Byzantine history became established. His organisational vigour and diverse research interests shaped Serbian Byzantine studies in the next decades and boosted its international visibility. For forty years he headed the Seminar and Chair for Byzantinology at Belgrade University and was at the helm of the Institute of Byzantinology from its founding in 1948 until his death in 1976, while also serving as the editor-in-chief of the Institute's house organ and Member of the Serbian Academy of Sciences. Present-day Serbian historians portray him as the *spiritus movens* of all major initiatives in Byzantine studies during the three post-war decades and the main catalyst for the 'flourishing of Serbian Byzantinology' and its becoming a 'leading area of Yugoslav historical science'.[2]

By the 1940s, Ostrogorski had gained international fame for his *Hauptwerk* 'History of the Byzantine State' (originally published as *Geschichte des byzantinischen Staates*, Munich, 1940), a work that saw several German and English editions and translations into some ten other languages.[3] Even today, many consider it to be the best synthesis of Byzantine history and the standard reference work on the political and institutional developments in the empire. Most of Ostrogorski's extensive oeuvre deals with three main subfields: social, economic and institutional history (to which pre-revolutionary Russian byzantinists had made major contributions); the religious and imperial ideology of Byzantium; and Byzantino-Slavic, especially Byzantino-Balkan, relations. In his social-historical studies, devoted mainly to the agrarian regime and the history of Byzantine peasantry, Ostrogorski professed the existence of a specific Byzantine variety of feudalism and set the terms of the subsequent debates on the issue. His most well-known achievement in the field of state ideology was the (re)construction of the medieval concept of the hierarchy of states, with the Byzantine emperor at its head. His contributions to the study of Byzantino-Slavic relations, which had a lasting effect on Serbian historiography, focussed on the political and cultural relations between Byzantium and Serbia.[4]

For Ostrogorski, the history of Byzantium was not the story of its Greek speakers alone. Nor did he consider the history of the Balkan Slavs to be

---

[2] Radic 1996: 202, 204; Perivatrić 2010: 487.   [3] Ostrogorsky 1980.
[4] For topics and bibliography, see Maksimović 1988: 667; Ševčenko 1991: 582–3; Ferjančić 1978: 269–74.

244 How Byzantine Is Serbia?

merely a chronicle of resistance to Byzantine hegemony. For him, Slavic society and culture were more than just products of the Byzantine political and cultural radiation. While Serbian historians before him did not go further than postulating the ability of Serbian culture to, in the words of Stanojević, 'fully assimilate and adapt [Byzantine culture] to itself and its own properties and needs, adding that which it had itself created until then',[5] Ostrogorski essentially reversed the perspective and sought to cast light on the Balkan Slavs' contribution to Byzantine society and culture. Taking stock of the deep administrative, military and economic transformations of the empire during the reign of Emperor Heraclius (575–641), he attributed the miraculous resurgence of Byzantine military force to the massive influx of Slavic settlers in Byzantine provinces into the imperial army. Unlike other barbarians, who had come into contact with the Roman-Byzantine empire, he argued forcefully,

> The Slavs entered the Byzantine army not as mercenaries, but as peasant soldiers; having settled as such in Byzantine themes, they obtained military estates, much like the Byzantine *stratiotai* of that age, and so established themselves in Byzantium. Thus the new, young forces of the Slavs poured into the new [theme] organisation that was being created at that time in Byzantium, and this explains the remarkable success of the new Byzantine system. Heraclius and his successors created the form, the Slavs filled it with content and gave real strength to the new system that enabled Byzantium to live on for centuries.[6]

The Slavs' contribution to the social regeneration of the empire was found to be as crucial. Ostrogorski did not share the romantic view of Vasil'evkiy and Uspenskiy that Byzantium had borrowed from the Slavs and introduced a new, supposedly specific Slav agrarian arrangement – the rural community with common ownership by all its members and periodic re-divisions of its entire territory. Such a community, he contended, never existed in Byzantium. What changed under the influence of the Slavs' immigration in Byzantium was nevertheless momentous: 'the social character of the Byzantine rural population and the legal position of the peasants themselves'. The regeneration that Byzantium experienced from the beginning of the seventh century, Ostrogorski explained, primarily involved the emergence of a strong class of free peasants, mostly Slavs, and the creation of a new army of *stratioti*.

> It was essentially a social regeneration that put the Byzantine empire on a wholly new social footing, which could only succeed thanks to the Slav

---

[5] Stanojević 1908: 157.   [6] Ostrogorski 1970: 50.

immigration .... Therefore, we come to the conclusion that the social transformation, which Byzantium experienced at the transition from the ancient to the medieval period and which was life-saving for it, was carried out to a considerable extent by the forces of the Slavs .... The new state and social order, built since the seventh century in Byzantium with the help of the Slav element, explains the rise of the Byzantine empire in the following centuries. The decline of the Byzantine state began with the collapse of this order in the eleventh century.[7]

Such an interpretation squared with the contemporary Soviet Marxist interpretation of the transition from slave society to feudalism and the role played thereof by the Slavs. Ostrogorski, in fact, praised the Soviet byzantinists' 'particular insistence' on drawing an analogy between the rejuvenation triggered by the Slavs in the east and that caused by the arrival of the Germans in the west – 'the difference being that the Germans destroyed the decaying Roman empire in the West and almost all traditions of ancient culture, whilst the arrival of the Slavs had no such destructive effect on the old culture of Byzantium, but poured instead constructive forces into its old yet still viable organism'.[8] It is significant that a common thread running through the Soviet-modelled history textbooks in both Bulgaria and Yugoslavia during the post-war years was the attributed 'progressiveness' of the Slavs' impact on the overall 'development' of the Eastern Roman empire. Their arrival was defined as 'colonisation' (by no means an 'assault' or 'invasion of savage barbarians' of the kind the Germans had carried out in the west), thus giving it a civilisational tenor. By spurring a healthy layer of free peasantry, the colonisation of the Slavs regenerated and healed Byzantium, making possible its survival for another nearly 1,000 years. The significance of the Slavs for the Byzantine empire was, therefore, that they actually rescued it.[9]

For Ostrogorski, the beginning of Byzantine decline in the eleventh century was triggered by the progressive replacement of the small peasant property, of the military and non-military kind, by the *pronoia* (the 'fief' in return to service) in later Byzantine society, respectively, of the class of free peasants by an all-powerful landed aristocracy that employed serf labour. Whereas the former presented the chief foundation of Byzantium's power, the latter was one of the major forces responsible for its decay as it pushed feudalisation forwards, which led to internal and external weakening of the state organism.[10] In the treatment of all these phenomena, and especially

---

[7] Ostrogorski 1970: 52–3; 1948: 12–21.   [8] Ostrogorski 1970: 54, 58.   [9] Marković 2011: 58–9.
[10] Ostrogorski 1951. This book was translated into French as Ostrogorsky 1954.

the agrarian relations in Byzantium, the primacy of the material 'base' over the political 'superstructure', to use the Marxist lingo, is evident. Ostrogorski's approach, while shorn of dogmatism, chimed in with the more secular presentation of Byzantine society focussed on the agricultural policy characteristic of the Marxist tradition. It is no surprise that his writings exerted a strong influence not only on Serbian medievalists but also on the historians in post-Stalinist Bulgaria dealing with the evolution and characteristics of Bulgarian feudalism. Later, both his theses – about a Slav-induced rapid and wholesale restructuring in the seventh century and about an economic decline in the eleventh and twelfth centuries – would be criticised by (mostly Western) historians.

Ostrogorski's assessment of the reverse impact, that of Byzantium on the Slavs, and of the driving forces behind Stefan Dušan's imperial designs were of the same historical-materialist hue, which went against the grain of the state-centred political and ideological explanations that had prevailed until then in Serbian historiography. Dušan's imperial ambitions, he maintained, were not the strongest driving force in the wars with Byzantium. The main forces behind, and beneficiaries from, the offensive against Byzantium, which began under Stefan Nemanja at the end of the twelfth century, gathered momentum under Mulutin in the second half of the next century and reached its climax under Dušan, were the Serbian feudal lords (*vlastela*) pursuing land and administrative positions. The replacement of Greek *archontes* and metropolitans by Serbian magnates and church hierarchy was by no means a reflection of some national Serbian policy, as it was previously held: it reflected the aspiration of the victorious Serbian feudal nobility for new positions and new lands.[11] Ostrogorski thus debunked the importance several generations of Serbian medievalists had attributed to the 'national' incentives behind Dušan's expansionist project and foregrounded the role of social class-based rationales. He found it remarkable that the influence of Byzantium and its church on medieval Serbia, considerable from the very beginning, became strongest precisely during the period of the 'supreme rise' of the Serbian state and went hand in hand with its extension on Byzantine territory: 'The conquerors appropriated the institutions they found in force in the occupied territory, they accepted the Byzantine civilisation in all its manifestations, they adopted the customs and fashions of Byzantium.' If under the previous Serbian rulers one witnessed certain institutions and administrative functions of Byzantine derivation, 'in the

---

[11] Ostrogorski 1970: 190–6.

How Byzantine Is Serbia?

Empire of the Serbs and Greeks of Stefan Dušan, the imitation of the Byzantine model became a programme'.[12] This trend was continued and even surpassed in the independent or semi-independent Serbian principalities that emerged in the ruins of Dušan's empire, above all the principality of Serres in eastern Macedonia (1355–71), to which Ostrogorski devoted several studies.[13] But he saw 'no opposition between the maintaining of the old Byzantine forms and the ascendance of the new Serbian element'.[14] This formula might seem to echo the one interwar historians, most expressly Stanojević, advocated, namely that Dušan's state was Byzantine in form and Serbian in content. Characteristically, however, with Ostrogorski it was stripped of assimilative national or providential connotations.

The scholarly methods underlying Ostrogorski's researches were rigorous and traditional: at the basis of his whole work was the painstaking analysis of written sources. This approach and the predilection for topics concerning the social, economic, ideological and administrative phenomena of Byzantine feudalism became emblematic of what came to be known as the 'Belgrade School of Byzantine Studies' – an assiduous and prolific group that counted, among its twenty-odd members, Franjo Barišić, Jadran Ferluga, Božidar Ferjančić, Ljubomir Maksimović, Mirjana Živojinović and Radivoj Radić. In the late 1970s this community professed to pursue far-reaching internationalisation as a major aspect of Ostrogorski's legacy, by which they meant not only closer contacts with a global scholarly community but above all shared professional standards, consistent research concepts and tools, engagement with broader supranational topics, and relativisation of modern ethnic divisions. Medievalist Sima Ćirković went so far as to state that 'the most natural path of the Serbian history's integration in the global medieval studies has always passed via Byzantium'.[15] These desiderata were only partially fulfilled and it also proved beyond the reach of most of Ostrogorski's disciples to match the breadth of his vision or venture beyond the confines of the Yugoslav thematic ambit into general Byzantine history.

Ostrogorski's impact on the new phase of Yugoslav medieval studies was already visible in the first historical synthesis produced in communist Yugoslavia, although it draped his theses in more patent Marxist jargon and tinted others with a new sense of 'Yugoslav nationalism'. The first volume of the *History of the Peoples of Yugoslavia* – 'the first comprehensive

---

[12] Ostrogorsky 1967: 42.   [13] Ostrogorsky 1967; 1965.   [14] Ostrogorski 1965: 51–2.
[15] Ćirković 1978: 281.

248 How Byzantine Is Serbia?

attempt at explaining our past on the basis of historical materialism', as the unidentified group of Yugoslav authors stated in the preface – came out in 1953 in three editions, Serbian, Croatian and Slovenian, and was meant to cover the medieval history of all 'nations' that constituted the socialist Yugoslav federation.[16] As could be expected, it underscored the socio-economic forces as governing all other aspects of the South Slav medieval societies, including relations with Byzantium. The stated 'strong impact of the Slavs on Byzantium' and 'the basis of the empire's military and social strength in the Middle Age' were predicated, following Ostrogorski, on the preponderance of the free independent Slav peasantry and soldiers (*stratioti*): 'the Slavs contributed to toppling down the slave-owning system in the Eastern Roman empire in the same way as the German peoples toppled it down in the west' and furnished the fundament of the theme system, which 'represented the starting point for the development of feudal relations in Byzantium'.[17] Significantly, already in this early post-war version of Yugoslav history, socio-economic determinism receded before preoccupations with preserving the national tradition and nationally generated growth as the only basis for real progress. For example, while acknowledging that feudal order in Macedonia developed faster and deeper under Byzantine influence, the *History* indicated that 'this influence hindered for many centuries the organic domestic social and political development and in the long run led to a significant reduction of [the Macedonian Slavs'] ethnic territory'. Among the Serbs, who retained their self-governance under Byzantine rule, on the contrary, feudalism did not mature until the twelfth century, 'but precisely because the feudal society there was built primarily on a domestic basis and even if this slowed down to some extent their socio-economic development, it enabled the strengthening of the state and national traditions and the building of solid foundations, on which the nation would develop much faster in the next period'.[18] Accordingly, the chapters dealing with the 'fully developed' Serbian feudal state in the thirteenth and fourteenth centuries barely made any mention of Byzantine influence or models, whereas the discussion of art, literature and architecture was filtered through the so-called regional schools, where Byzantine influences appeared meagre against the backdrop of the pre-eminent Slav elements in the overall cultural life.[19]

In the realm of Byzantine studies, on the other hand, the trends towards the de-ideologisation of science and professionalisation of history-writing

---

[16] Istorija naroda Jugoslavije 1953: ix. [17] Istorija naroda Jugoslavije 1953: 90–1.
[18] Istorija naroda Jugoslavije 1953: 127–8. [19] Istorija naroda Jugoslavije 1953: 365–407, 480–92.

How Byzantine Is Serbia?

during the 1960s and 1970s prescribed close engagement with primary sources and recoil from general history. This resulted in the proliferation of fragmented, highly specialised studies, often devoted to 'individual aspects' of larger phenomena and micro-historical case studies.[20] As in Bulgaria, academic history was, and remained, mainly empirically oriented and descriptive. A survey of Yugoslav historiography, prepared by the Association of the Yugoslav Historical Societies on the occasion of the XIV International Congress of Historians in San Francisco (1975), acknowledged 'the maturation of the important Byzantine School (particularly under the leadership of Georgiy Ostrogorski) as one of the great achievements of contemporary medieval studies', but also admitted the 'pronounced involvement with regional and local themes, the insufficient attention to a wider range of subject matter, the predominance of events over structuralist historical research and above all the inadequate development of theoretical historical research'.[21]

Methodologically and thematically, most of Ostrogorski's disciples, before and after his death in 1976, found themselves cast in his long shadow. Editing, dating, establishing the authenticity and attribution of documents, and providing extensive commentaries to the narrative sources, which were collected in the multivolume *Byzantine Sources for the History of the Yugoslav Peoples*, consumed much of their research work – a sustained dedication that earned them the fame of leading representatives of the critical Serbian historiography. Apart from this, Božidar Ferjančić (1929–98), who succeeded Ostrogorski at the helm of the Chair of Byzantine History at Belgrade University and the Institute of Byzantinology, continued to plough the time-honoured field of Byzantine-South Slav relations along lines closely following Ostrogorski's. His major work, *Byzantium and the South Slavs* (1966), couched in an objectivist and detached style and attesting to a massive byzantinisation of Serbian state and economy in the fourteenth century, contributed with small vignettes to an already familiar picture.[22] Almost thirty years after Ostrogorski's book on the principality of Serres, Ferjančić published his own rendition of the same topic, which underpinned but did not add much to or improve upon Ostrogorski's theses.[23] Jadran Ferluga (1920–2004), another key participant in the 'Belgrade School of Byzantine Studies', dealt similarly with another of Ostrogorski's favourite topics – the characteristics,

---

[20] For an annotated bibliography, see Tadić 1965: 62–102. [21] Janković 1975: 13.
[22] Ferjančić 1966.
[23] Ferjančić 1994. Yet Ferjančić also authored a book on Byzantine history (Ferjančić 1974) and several important articles on the late Palaiologoi period.

evolution and spreading of the Byzantine administrative theme system in the South Slav lands.[24] In fact, to this day, critical re-examinations of the illustrious predecessor's legacy are remarkably few. In terms of method, on the other hand, the reticence that the Belgrade school byzantinists demonstrated to fill in the lacunas left by the general paucity of primary sources with 'logical' or wishful conjectures, and the heed they paid to distinguishing between source-based arguments and hypotheses, had a sobering drilling effect on Yugoslav medieval historiography generally.

This is especially evident in the work of the leading historian of medieval Serbia in the second half of the twentieth century, Sima Ćirković (1929–2009), who was also the editor-in-chief of the first volume of the academic *History of the Serbian People* (1981) and author of two comprehensive surveys of Serbian history written after 1989. Already in the early 1970s, Ćirković bemoaned the lack of critical reassessment of the pre-World War II historiography, and of its assumptions, conceptual toolkit and scholarly standards, thence ideological components and nationalistic delusions – a re-evaluation he considered a necessary precondition for a 'modern synthesis of Serbian history'. The core question to such a synthesis, he explained, was whether it should be a history of Serbia or a history of the Serbs; in other words, whether it should be based on a territorial or ethnic framework. Ćirković sided with the second option, but warned that such an option was viable only if historians distanced themselves from the romantic concept of the people as a primordial and immutable entity ('which still rules the spirits') and become led by 'the ever-present critical awareness that the ethnic whole is changing and shifting and that these changes should be described as an integral part of the historical process'. A modern historical work that aspired to relate the historical development of a people should be able to answer questions about the nature of the consciousness in certain periods that kept it together as a social group; the criteria by which its members were separated from other groups; other divisions that competed with the ethnic one; how the people as a social group increased or decreased; how its integration progressed; and so on.[25]

Such a position squared with the sociologically informed structuralist theories of nationalism current at that time in Western social science literature and challenged the dominant complexion of contemporary Serbian historiography. As Ćirković admitted a quarter of a century later, 'contrary to what one might have expected, the socialist period did not emasculate but strengthened the national character of the Serbian and the

---

[24] Ferluga 1976; 1992.   [25] Ćirković 1970: 200–4.

other [national] historiographies in Yugoslavia'; even Byzantine and Ottoman studies, albeit non-national by definition, 'had Serbian themes at their core'. This, he explained, was 'a consequence of the efforts of the communist regime to use historiography as an instrument for resolving the national question': as a constitutive Yugoslav nation, the Macedonians, for example, were encouraged to take on an 'ideological historical perspective that set the beginning of a distinct [Macedonian] nation right after the settlement of the Slavs and explained its whole medieval development through polemicising especially with the Bulgarian, Serbian and Greek literature. The solution of the Montenegrin "question" affected history in a similar way'. All of this, Ćirković concluded, 'revived and strengthened theses from the earlier stages of development of national historiography'.[26] That said, the very fact that, in the 1970s, Ćirković could enunciate a strongly subversive position on the traditional approach to the nation without risking academic ostracism – in fact, he was promoted to academician and allowed wide publicity in the West – bespeaks a substantial difference from the situation in contemporary Bulgaria or Romania, where state-supported nationalism became the new historiographical norm nobody dared to challenge openly. Ironically, in all these countries many 'dissident' historians conceived of their participation in the re-nationalisation of history as a reaction to communist ideological indoctrination and, therefore, as an emancipatory posture. What actually happened, however, was that nationalist resistance to reigning dogmatism replenished earlier dogmas.

Ćirković's historical surveys, pre- and post-1989, proceeded from the above theoretical positions. His syntheses of Serbian history presented level-headed and balanced narratives, largely stripped of analytical excursions, that marked out the historical process through which Serbian 'individuality and identity' crystallised abreast of the chequered fortunes and shifting contours of the Serbian state. He did not devote himself to exploring specifically the Byzantine facets of historical phenomena, although he paid much attention to Serbia's links with Byzantium and to Byzantine influences. He defined the period following Christianisation (around 870 AD) up until the twelfth century as one of 'continuous Byzantine influence [that] left lasting traces on the Slavs in the eastern and central part of the Balkan Peninsula . . . which would characterise them for centuries'.[27] Political intercourses with Venice, the Holy See and later Hungary became much more prominent after 1204, yet Serbia's ruling circles continued to be drawn to Byzantium through marital relations

[26] Ćirković 1970: 285–6. [27] Ćirković 2004: xix.

between dynasties, by conquering territories with Byzantine institutions and law and through increased trade and exchanges of populations and goods. Ćirković never ventured expressly into assessing the impact of Serbia's relations with Byzantium on its internal development (or vice versa), but his treatment of these relations is remarkably dispassionate and down to earth, free of national bias and generalisations based on assumptions. Most importantly, it was steered by an attempt to explain Serbian development by means of notions and realia consistent with the medieval experience instead of modern phenomena, which prevented him from falling into the conventional teleological trap of much medieval national narrative. From such positions Stefan Dušan's empire, for example, appeared not as the apex of Serbian power heading towards unification, a Serbo-Byzantine empire or a 'national' society, but as an 'unfinished society', struggling with regional and ethnic as well as social, legal and administrative differences and where the state's main preoccupation was to maintain the power balance, while resolving conflicts between such autonomous groups. Sparse documentation, Ćirković argues, indicates that Dušan sought to equate his state with the Byzantine empire (rather than supplant it), but also that 'starting with Milutin, Serbian rulers consistently showed that they honoured the supreme power and higher rank of the Byzantine emperors'.[28] The chapters dealing with medieval Serbia in the academic *History of Yugoslavia* (1974), written by Ćirković and Ivan Božić, are remarkable for their eschewal of ideological bigotry and determinism, both Marxist and nationalist, and impartial narrative.[29]

Ljubomir Maksimović (b.1938), a member of the second generation of students of the Belgrade school of Byzantine studies, served as the vice president of the International Association of Byzantine Studies and director of the Institute for Byzantine Studies of the Serbian Academy of Sciences and Arts. In a series of articles over the years he has dealt expressly with the question of Byzantium's entanglement with Serbian medieval history and 'civilisation'. Serbia's place in medieval Europe, Maksimović avows, was largely determined by the country's affiliation with the basic values of Byzantine civilisation: 'This undeniable fact has shaped Serbian history in a decisive way, with consequences that extend to our days', while 'the Byzantine aspect of Serbian civilisation has grown into its distinguishable feature.'[30] This general observation, however, applied only for the

---

[28] Ćirković 2004: 63–74. See also his Ćirković 1995, first published in Italian (1992) and French (1992).
[29] Dedijer, Božić, Ćirković and Ekmečić 1974 [1972].
[30] Maksimović 2008: I (a collection of articles written between 1970 and 2005).

period starting with the great župan Stefan Nemanja (1166–96), the founder of the Nemanjić dynasty, and his decisive turn to Orthodoxy. Prior to it, 'little is known' about the consequences of the Byzantine-Serbian contacts for the situation in the Serbian 'proto-states' (apart from the inclusion of some Serbian-ruled lands in the Byzantine state system and the conferment of Byzantine titles to their rulers seen as subjects to the emperor), whereas 'until the second half of the twelfth century Byzantine Orthodoxy was not the main factor in the political and cultural life of the Serbs'.[31] Even later, when Serbia was proclaimed a kingdom and was granted episcopal autonomy (in 1217 and 1219, respectively), Byzantine influence, Maksimović emphasised, 'albeit of great importance, was not an all-encompassing or omnipotent factor': next to 'the Byzantine aspect' of what he called 'the Serbian medieval civilisation', there were two others: the 'no less significant influences from the West' and 'the native creativity of the Serbs themselves'.[32]

Setting out from Ostrogorski's classic formula, according to which Byzantine civilisation presented the amalgam of three components – Roman state order, Greek culture and Christian faith – Maksimović proceeded to trace their relative presence in Serbian political ideology, ecclesiastical arrangement and culture, starting with the time of Stefan Nemanja, who 'embraced Orthodoxy for political reasons [and] oriented Serbia towards the political ideology and cultural models of the Byzantine world'. Although shaped by the Byzantine model, the Serbian political ideology, he holds, differed from it in a number of ways. Its concept of autocracy and the institution of the sovereign-autocrat derived less from Byzantine theory than from the Old Testament conceptions of the relations between rulers and the supreme power. The vision about Serbia as the 'New Israel', albeit essentially obtained from the Byzantine understanding, 'in practice emphasised the singularity of the country and its independence'. Milutin's conquest of Macedonia led to an abrupt acceleration of the 'byzantinisation' of Serbia, yet 'the Serbian political ideology, marked out by the idea of autocracy that was incompatible with the Roman idea of the universal empire, did not undergo radical change under these circumstances'. Dušan's empire, from this perspective, appears as a 'temporary renunciation of the specific Serbian approach' in that his imperial ideology 'pursued neither the annihilation of Byzantium nor the founding of a new, Serbian or Serbian-Byzantine empire. On the contrary, its main effort was directed towards inclusion in the power system of the Byzantine empire,

---

[31] Maksimović 2008: 191; Maksimović 2003a: 19–21.   [32] Maksimović 2008: i; 2003b: 99–100.

254 How Byzantine Is Serbia?

which was already quite fragmented'. The proclamation of the empire, in other words, was an attempt to conquer Byzantium from within, through Dušan's involvement in the Byzantine civil war as the third claimant to the throne in Constantinople. Yet neither during this period, Maksimović opined, was the Byzantine model taken as an all-embracing civilisational pattern since, with the exception of the court, Byzantine or byzantinised institutions were adopted only in the newly conquered, traditionally Byzantine territories. The legal norms across the state also showed cleavages between Byzantine, Western and common-law norms, while the coastal cities and the most important sources of income – trade and especially profitable mining – 'were fully oriented to the West', as was almost all import and export. Knowledge about the ancient world, on the other hand, was meagre and that which existed reached Serbia almost exclusively through forms imprinted by Orthodoxy.[33]

Thus, Maksimović concluded, 'only one of the three historical phenomena that made Byzantium – the Christian faith in its Orthodox form, was taken over almost in its entirety in Serbia'.[34] However, this did not come about before the second half of the twelfth century. The adoption of the Byzantine model in this case, moreover, 'was not the consequence exclusively of a unilateral imposition of the will of Constantinople, but the consequence of belonging to a world of common values, with clear recognition and respect for their source', as the state-led merciless suppression of the Bogomil heresy and the Serbian opposition to the Councils of Lyon (1274) and Florence (1439) suggest.[35] During the centuries of Ottoman rule, the Serbian Church and the Orthodox faith 'were the only remnants of the past in which the Byzantine heritage was present in some way'. However, both became hallmarks of national identity, and while in a dogmatic and liturgical sense 'the so-called Byzantine heritage' was obvious, 'Byzantium was barely mentioned in discussions of the middle ages' during that period. In the modern Serbian state and society, 'organised according to Western standards', Maksimović went on, 'there was no deliberate imitation of role models that could be described as Byzantine', except perhaps in architecture, with the unimpressive attempt at developing 'a Byzantine-Serbian architectural model'.[36]

Maksimović thus made a sustained effort to relativise the dominant belief about the Byzantine character of medieval Serbia, assert its specific

[33] Maksimović 2008: 192–206; 2003b: 100–2; Maksimović and Subotić 2003: 174–6.
[34] Maksimović 2003b: 102–3. [35] Maksimović 2003a: 14–18; 2008: 211.
[36] Maksimović 2003b: 103–6.

How Byzantine Is Serbia?

position between Byzantium and the West and unravel its historically unique character of a very particular formation.

> Thus, considered in a global way, Serbia remained during all its medieval history halfway between two worlds, western and eastern, but did not constitute a true bridge connecting them. It created its own civilisation by relying on the one as on the other, without losing the essence of its indigenous traditions. It is thus possible to say that Serbia has in fact constituted, in various ways and in different aspects of life, a specific phenomenon of civilisation.[37]

The dexterous exertion at vindicating it aside, the thesis about an 'alone-of-its-kind' Serbian civilisation was not new. In the Serbian context of the 1990s and 2000s, however, the attempts of some Serbian historians to qualify the Byzantine filiation of Serbian culture and balance the traditional overriding preoccupation with Byzantine influences acquired a certain urgency. In the Serbian nationalist discourse, which gained momentum in the 1980s and escalated during the Wars of Yugoslav Succession (1990–9), the Serbs' historical affiliation with the Byzantine empire, captured by the evocative term 'Serbian Byzantium' (*Srpska Vizantija*), came powerfully to the fore, underscoring a sense of distinctiveness and spiritual superiority over Catholic Croats and Muslim Bosniaks. At the hands of clerical-minded conservatives and nationalists gathered around Slobodan Milošević, the Byzantine narrative became a tool of national homogenisation and ethno-religious exclusion, underscoring Serbia's non-Western origins and cultural orientation towards Orthodox Russia. During and after the war there was a boost of monographs on Nemanjid Serbia, and the publication of works of synthesis on the 'national' history during the Middle Ages also gained importance. Hence, non-nationalist historians saw themselves severely pressed between rampant nationalist propaganda, undercutting the ideal of cultural pluralism that Yugoslavia embodied, and the orientalising Western gaze, portraying the conflict as the ultimate causatum of the region's 'Byzantine heritage'. The older-generation byzantinists, like Maksimović, reacted to it with an attempt to counterbalance the 'byzantinising discourse' and tempered warnings that 'the "Byzantine heritage" should be assessed solely on the basis of the results of scholarly investigations'.[38] This, as we have seen, conjoined with an attachment to a sui generis Serbian medieval civilisation made up of Western, Byzantine and indigenous elements. Representatives

---

[37] Maksimović and Subotić 2003: 181; Maksimović 2003b: 103.   [38] Maksimović 2003b: 106.

256   How Byzantine Is Serbia?

of the younger generation of scholars, on the other hand, were far more censorious of both politicised 'byzantinism' and historical ethnocentrism.

One of the most poignant and radical revisions came from an art historian with a career mostly outside of Serbia, Bratislav Pantelić, an author of several polemical articles focussed on the interpretation of the so-called Serbo-Byzantine architectural style, yet touching upon more general aspects. Pantelić argues that

> not only was exposure to Byzantine culture in the Serbian medieval princi-palities far less unequivocal than is commonly supposed, but it produced no lasting effect; even those aspects of Serbian culture that could be regarded as 'Byzantine', such as the Orthodox faith and Cyrillic alphabet, did not define Serbian cultural and national development (although they hindered and ultimately delayed it) .... Rather than a memory or a tradition, 'Serbian Byzantium' was a historical construct developed in the clerical and trad-itionalist circles of provincial Serbia ... [a] myth ... meant to dislocate Serbia's cultural identity from its secular and European sources and repos-ition it closer to Orthodox Russia.[39]

The arguments Pantelić adduces to shore up his heterodox thesis can be summarised as follows. Serbia's material heritage is diverse, marked by the mixture and coexistence of Romanesque and Baroque aesthetics and several 'national schools' as defined by Gabriel Millet. Only a small part of it was Byzantine in inspiration and hardly any of it was properly Byzantine. Serbia's fateful bond with the Byzantine empire is a myth that conceals complex currents of overlapping and interlocking traditions. The influence of Mount Athos, the religious centre of Eastern Christianity, was indeed overwhelming in the Nemanjid domain, but it pertained mostly to the monastic community and the clergy. Similarly, the Roman legal codes, adopted from Byzantium, were largely restricted to canon law and had little if any impact on the wider population; in daily life customary law and other practices and institutions, which were closer to western and central European legal practice than to Byzantine, prevailed. The byzantinisation of the medieval Serbian kingdom that began with King Milutin and reached its high point under Stefan Dušan was adopted by the elites, who had developed a Christian identity, whereas the general population remained untouched by such trends; moreover, it was largely restricted to the traditionally Byzantine regions in the south (Kosovo and northern Macedonia). The only major sphere (besides religious literature) where the impact of Byzantium appears to be incontestable is religious paint-ing. This in itself, however, is not proof of any deep-rooted cultural bonds,

---

[39] Pantelić 2016: 451.

because the Byzantine artistic tradition was the most widely practised in the region in both Orthodox and Catholic contexts, often by highly mobile *pictores graeci* exposed to diverse artistic trends and traditions. Many other cultural connections, regional affiliations and forms of interaction between Catholic and Orthodox South Slavs traversed the fluid and vague confessional and political borders, but are ignored or played down by the Serbian (as well as Croat) historiography.

As regards the weight of Byzantine culture in the modern Serbian national formation, 'the fact remains that the "cradle" of Serbian culture and nationhood was not in Byzantium, or more specifically in medieval Kosovo (as fantasised by nationalists and proponents of "Serbian Byzantium"), but in the Habsburg Monarchy'. It was the educated Habsburg Serbs, fiercely anticlerical and led by pan-Slav sympathies, who brought nationalism and national identity to their unsuspecting brethren in Serbia proper. They had more in common with their South Slav compatriots of the Catholic persuasion (Croats and Slovenes) than with the estranged Orthodox Serbs; 'they did not reflect their purported "Byzantine heritage" in any way. Byzantium to these burghers was nothing more than a faint notion ... with no bearing on the formation of national and cultural identity'. Until World War I, the Serbian national imagery remained Western oriented; 'when Byzantium was invoked it was by way of an association of art and architecture with religion or "nationality"'. Nor were there any echoes ('shared memories') of Byzantium in popular culture – 'the Byzantines were long forgotten'. The scholars who showed some interest in Byzantine history did so with the intention of furthering the study of 'national' medieval history and heritage: 'there is no indication that these academics' interest in Byzantium was motivated by ideology or feelings of cultural or confessional affinity'.[40]

Therefore, Serbia's Byzantine culture, Pantelić recaps, is largely a myth. It was developed in the 1930s by the Serbian clergy as a corollary of *Svetosavlje* ('Saint Savaism') – a localised version of the Russian Slavophile ideology blending ethnic nationalism, Byzantine culture and Orthodox spirituality in a metaphysical union, which has sustained the community of the Serbs over the centuries. Svetosavlje and the Byzantine narrative of Serbian history and identity thus suffused each other. They were furthered by home-grown church intellectuals, firmly rooted in the rustic culture of the 'deeply traditionalist former Ottoman province', who shared a dislike of Western civilisation, fear of modernity and resistance to

---

[40] Pantelić 2016: 436–9, 440–9.

the religious pluralism that was officially proclaimed in the Yugoslav constitution. Boosted by the anti-Western and anti-modern attitudes, which permeated much of the political discourse in the 1930s, 'the clerical conservative triumph effected a dramatic alteration of established perceptions of history and heritage: henceforth, the Serbs were invariably (and primarily) Orthodox and "Byzantine" (and thereby culturally different from the Catholic Croats and Slovenes.)'. The connection of Serbia with Byzantium continued in post-war Yugoslavia with the founding in 1948 of a Byzantine institute in Belgrade, headed by the Russian Georgiy Ostrogorski. In socialist Yugoslavia the notion of Byzantium was stripped of its religious connotations and included in the pool of models drawn from the diverse heritage of Yugoslavia's constituent republics, which were used to promote the country's multicultural identity. After this socialist interlude, Byzantium returned with unusual force during the Yugoslav crisis of the 1980s and the regime of Slobodan Milošević, who viewed the Yugoslav conflict as the ultimate showdown between East and West.[41]

There is much to be acclaimed about Pantelić's 'de-mythologising' poignancy and anti-nationalist vigour, with which he sought to debunk the disparagement of the West combined with the affirmation of one's own 'spiritual' superiority – a combination that, in the words of another critic of the 'Byzantine revival' in Serbia of the 1990s, literary scholar Marko Živković, 'acted as a salve for the spoilt identity of a pariah people'.[42] Rhetorically, however, his vociferous constructivist, anti-clerical and anti-nationalist stance has ushered in an interpretation that in many ways mirrors the one he seeks to rebuff. In his exertion to bring Serbia's cultural identity to 'its secular and European sources', he has come to portray everything Byzantine as regressive, authoritarian, conformist, lacking in creativity and indeed spirituality, 'pro-Russian' (thus anti-European) and ultimately myth-made – and its adherents as 'indeed a different people', an ignorant and superstitious product of the 'deeply traditionalist former Ottoman province' (Serbia proper), manipulated by 'priests of modest or narrowly religious education'. This 'byzantinised' world is made to stand in sharp contrast to the urban, secularist, rational, innovative 'West' that brings enlightenment and cherishes modernity – 'the world of religious pluralism and cultural diversity', whose epitomes are said to be the educated and 'multicultural' Serbs in Habsburg Vojvodina. The outcome of such a crude dichotomy is an ideological counter-image of

---

[41] Pantelić 2016: 433–6, 449–51.

[42] Živković 2007: 156. Pantelić's articles are generally distinguishable by their polemical renunciation of the 'national delusions' underlying much of the older and recent Serbian historiography and by their constructivist approach to nation making. See, for instance, Pantelić 2011: 443–64.

How Byzantine Is Serbia?

'Serbian Byzantium' that not only underplays the Byzantine impact on medieval Serbia but also brushes off nuances and ambivalences. To give one example, the Habsburg (i.e. 'Western')-bred young Serbian Romantics – the purported antithesis of the Byzantine-bred peasants of post-Ottoman Serbia – are approvingly described as having chosen Stefan Dušan as their hero because he had 'established a multi-ethnic empire on Byzantine territory', a reading based on conjecture rather than evidence; their urban culture and Western orientation is praised, but their fairly conservative stance towards language and orthography and populist instrumentalisation of the rural 'Serbian tradition' are ignored.[43]

Interestingly, except for some fleeting references to what he sees as parochial predilections and nationalist dogmatism of Serbian architectural history, Pantelić does not discuss the role of academically entrenched views, and of Serbian Byzantine studies in particular, in moulding the notion of 'Serbian Byzantium'. Such a discussion is at the centre of a no less seditious and assertive criticism levelled from different premises and with a different outcome by Vlada Stanković (b.1973), a representative of the younger generation of Serbian byzantinists at the University of Belgrade. Stanković does not concern himself with the 'afterlife' of Byzantium in the Serbian self-narration and his analysis remains firmly anchored in medieval ground. The main problem for him is the way Serbian historiography and Byzantine studies had tackled this relationship: 'The Byzantine influence on the formation and development of the Serbian medieval state, its ideology, culture, religion, letters and attitudes', he states gruffly, 'has not been studied, presented and understood adequately and correctly'. The prevailing 'narrow national approach' to studying Serbian medieval history has isolated the latter from the complex broader historical context and vindicated its treatment as a 'separate historical development along national lines', dominated by positivistic erudition that 'views the relations between "states" and "nations" in the strictly antagonistic manner'. This 'isolationistic methodological approach', to which also Western medievalists like John Fine and Paul Stephenson are found to be accomplices, leaves the Byzantine context only as the background, where it serves as an important but not predominant part of the décor of the historical stage of medieval Serbia.[44] Professing to deploy 'a changed method of analysis

---

[43] On the ambiguous worldviews of the Serbian Romantic liberals, see Mishkova 2012: 668–92 and 2004: 269–93; Živković 2007: 159–66.

[44] Stanković 2013: 75–9; 2016b: 91–2. Stanković refers to John Fine's *The Early Medieval Balkans* (1983) and *The Late Medieval Balkans* (1987) and Paul Stephenson's *Byzantium's Balkan Frontier* (2000) (Stanković 2016a: xiii).

and a correct model for understanding broader historical context', Stanković asserts that in the twelfth and thirteenth centuries – the time preceding and following the Crusaders' capture of Constantinople, which coincided with the crystallisation of the medieval Serbian state – an essential shift in the political paradigm in southeastern Europe took place, which rested on direct kinship connections of the regional rulers with the Byzantine emperor and his closest relatives. Consequent to the externalisation of Byzantine marriage policy, the region moved from a state-centred to a family-centred model or rulership, whereby the rulers of the polities within the Byzantine sphere of influence became directly connected to the imperial family to a much greater extent than ever before. It was these kinship linkages which created the deep structure for their relations. Hence Stanković's subversive observation that

> Assessing the position of Serbia within the broader Byzantine world by using the notions such as 'independence' or understanding the status of Serbian polity as 'independent' in the highly personalised and intensively interconnected world of southeastern Europe is highly misleading. Instead of separating Serbia – or any other polity in this region for that matter – from the broader historical contexts and its natural historical surroundings, it would be much more correct and rewarding to analyze the structure and mechanisms of functioning of a tightly connected and hierarchically organ-ised political elite that dominated the entire Balkans from the twelfth century until the Ottoman conquest. The shifts of power, the usually ephemeral rise of one region and the decline, temporary or longer lasting of the other, were therefore more internal oscillations within a strongly connected and mutually dependent set of polities governed by tightly knit relatives throughout the last centuries of the Middle Ages in southeastern Europe than the constant antagonistic confrontation of the unrelated 'independent' self-sufficient states.[45]

Stanković thus not only undercuts the status of traditional constructed boundaries as defining the units of historical analysis in the late-medieval Balkans, but also berates the view, 'commonly stated in the predominantly narrow "national" Serbian scholarship', that Serbia in the thirteenth cen-tury was placed somewhere between 'the East' and 'the West'. Illogical as it might appear, Serbia after 1204, Stanković avowed, 'moved toward closer connections with and, save political autonomy, total inclusion in the Byzantine world'. Simultaneously, owing to this new political paradigm – the all-connectivity of the political elite in the Balkans – 'the centrality of

---

[45] Stanković 2016b: 97–8; 2013: 85–93.

How Byzantine Is Serbia? 261

Constantinople in geopolitical sense lost in significance even before 1204, to be emphatically replaced by the regionally dispersed personal centrality of the most powerful members of the ramified imperial clan' after that date. Serbia's rise to an empire should be understood against the backdrop of the 'diffusion of political power within the broadly understood ruling family' and the 'personalised system of mutually connected or dependent regional polities'. In Stanković's words, 'the King Milutin's definite turn toward Byzantium [in 1299] signifies also the real beginning of the creation of the Serbian empire'.[46]

Stanković has reserved the ultimate *coup de grace* for the 'overwhelming, strongly one-sided and unproductive center-periphery discourse' that ought to be replaced by a *regional* approach, similar to the one employed by Patrick Geary and Robert Bartlett to developments in western Europe. He believes that such an approach 'could offer a new perspective in studying geographically fluctuant entities – as were most of medieval polities in the Balkans – and could prove even more useful for better understanding Byzantium and its transformation in the aftermath of the capture of Constantinople in 1204'.[47]

Despite their provocative tenor, Pantelić's and Stanković's methodological critiques failed to trigger a substantive debate among Serbian historians. Yet several recent overviews of the Byzantine-Serbian political relations by a senior researcher at the Institute for Byzantine Studies, Srđan Pirivatrić (b.1966), lay bare an epistemic rift between Serbian medievalists to date. Pirivatrić's methodology chimes in with the fact-dominated positivist erudition, nurtured by the Belgrade byzantinological school, and the narrative trailed by Maksimović. While acknowledging the weight of the Byzantine models on many levels, from the political-theological to the artistic, and the occasional inclusion of the Serbian rulers in the system of imperial family rule, he reasserts the standard view about the state of Nemanja's successors as 'oscillating in the two worlds and the two monarchical conceptions – that of the Byzantine emperor and the Pope of Rome', and which also experienced growing 'attachment to Hungary'. He characterises the lands of Serbian settlement as 'a contact zone, a zone of mutual cooperation, coexistence, overlapping, opposition and conflict between the different authorities of Rome and Constantinople', where the Serbs' relations with these two centres of universal authority depended on the highly changeable

---

[46] Stanković 2016b: 97–8. See at length in this vein Stanković 2012. [47] Stanković 2016a: xiii.

relationship between them and on the fluctuating capacities of Roman institutions to exert real influence over this area. The ideologically motivated ethnic interpretation of the Byzantine Roman empire as the empire of the Greeks rather than of the Romans, promoted in the West, Pirivatrić argues, also became established over time in the Serbian lands 'as a lasting conception of political ideology, independent of the character and strength of the Byzantine imperial authority'. Against this background, he underscores, pace Stanković, the Serbian dynasts' pursuit of independence and 'the final failure of the Byzantine marital policy' with the arrival of Stefan Dušan on the Serbian throne.[48] All in all, Pirivatrić is dismissive of Stanković's admonitions against the 'outdated historiographical narrative built around the strict divisions between medieval polities in southeastern Europe and the equally strict chronological periodisation that fog the actual historical context'.[49] While such upfront critiques have not been resolved in a scholarly debate over theoretical choices, they make it abundantly clear that the former 'Belgrade School of Byzantine Studies' has, to all intents and purposes, lost its erstwhile common base and direction.

On the occasion of the twenty-third International Congress of Byzantine Studies, held in Belgrade in 2016, an impressive three-volume publication, *Byzantine Heritage and Serbian Art*, came out under Ljubomir Maksimović as the editor-in-chief, which featured several dozen Serbian medievalists, art historians and archaeologists. As framed by Maksimović, its intention dovetails with the triangular Byzantine-Serbian-Western cultural matrix by offering 'a comprehensive, analytic, and synthetic overview of Byzantium's influence on Serbian culture ... the basic idea being to present the true results of the union of adopted Byzantine and indigenous Serbian traditions, and the cultural influences of the West'. In contrast, the statement of the editorial board conveys an emphatically emotive inspiration, stressing the deeply internalised imprint of Byzantine cultural legacy on the Serbian self-perception:

> A sense of belonging to [Byzantine] civilisation and of spiritual kinship with it has been strongly present in Serbia, finding its support in the Orthodox faith and the distinctive worldview that proceeds from it, in historical memory and in myths that have, over time, become part of common consciousness .... The Byzantine legacy has profoundly permeated the everyday surroundings and life of the Serbs – through liturgical worship and music, architecture, and painting .... To the Serbs, therefore, the

---

[48] Pirivatrić 2016a: 17–35; 2016b: 223–40.   [49] Stanković 2016a: xvi.

How Byzantine Is Serbia? 263

Byzantine legacy is not merely a living tradition, it is perceived as the backbone of their identity and as something of a 'national patrimony'.[50]

What this high-rostrum academic statement intimates, therefore, is that, despite attempts at deconstructing or, at the least, relativising its mythological base, 'Serbian Byzantium' is how contemporary Serbs conceive of their culture and identity.

[50] Bikić 2016: 9, 11.

CHAPTER 9

Post-Byzantine Empire or Romanian National State?

Like in Bulgaria, between 1947 and the early 1960s, Stalinism dictated the structure and contents of Romanian history production. With few exceptions, the previous authorities in the field were reduced to silence, thrown out of their posts or imprisoned; not before the mid-1960s were some of them, like C. C. Giurescu and P. P. Panaitescu, allowed to re-enter academia. The pre-war history institutes, including the Institute for Byzantine Studies, were disbanded and merged into a new centralised Institute of History. The 'historical front' was assigned the task of reconceiving Romanian history from Marxist-Leninist positions, often at the price of generating new historical myths and producing outright historical forgeries. Class struggle took over the place of the nation as the driving force of historical evolution, and the beneficial connections between Romanians and (mainly Eastern) Slavs were brought to the fore. The Stalinist historiographical canon emphasised the 'amalgamation with the Slavs' as the basis of Romanian ethnogenesis and the Romanian language, whereas the Roman conquest of ancient Dacia – a far cry from 'Western influence' – was vilified as 'yoke'.[1]

De-Stalinisation of the historical craft in a context of relative relaxation of the communist regime from the early 1960s ushered in a new phase of institutional restructuration and reinterpretation of Romanian history. The proclamation of the 'independence' of the Romanian Workers' Party in 1964 signalled the abandonment of 'communist internationalism', relations with the West were resumed, national values underwent rehabilitation and a degree of diversification of historical interpretations was allowed to emerge. Several of the history institutes were reinstated and, on a decision of the Romanian Academy's Section of Historical Sciences, a Romanian Association for Byzantine Studies was set up in 1962. It summoned all major representatives of the pre-war Byzantine studies

[1] For more on this period, see Georgescu 1991: 9–50 and Papacostea 1996: 187–93.

264

Post-Byzantine Empire or Romanian National State? 265

(N. Bănescu, V. Grecu, M. Berza, Em. Condurachi, Al. Elian, E. Stănescu, D. M. Pippidi), while being formally affiliated to the Institute of Southeast European Studies in Bucharest, re-established in 1963.

Four official surveys of national history appeared between 1960 and 1971, yet none of them engaged explicitly with or even suggested any significant Byzantine involvement. The 1969 'History of Romania' referred to Byzantium in passing only five times, the 1971 'History of the Romanians' made no mention of Byzantine influence during the foundational period of the Romanian states and only cursorily commented on the role of Byzantine cultural imprint after that, while the 'History of the Romanian People' (1970) was slightly more generous in acknowledging Byzantine influence in art and architecture. Characteristically, all these national syntheses treated the state formation in Wallachia, Moldavia and Transylvania as a single process and the outcome of a gradual, locally rooted internal evolution with little influence from 'outside' by other polities. The historical narrative was limited to the territory of the contemporary Romanian state, while the 'Balkan Romanians' disappeared from the scene of Romanian history. The communist Romanian state in its first decades sought to distance itself from the Balkan policy of its pre-war predecessor, which promoted the autonomy of the Aromanians and cultivated special links with them on the basis of common Romanity. At the same time, the Slavophile spirit of the Stalinist period began to recede behind a fervently rediscovered Latinity and Romanity of the Romanians, and the history of the church, previously the object of a prohibitive taboo, was once more brought into the limelight.

The ideological thaw proved short-lived, though – 'a parenthesis of recovery between two hypostases of the totalitarian regime'.[2] The early 1970s saw the unleashing of the Romanian 'cultural revolution', which put an end to 'liberalisation' and 'openness', and the beginning of the increasingly autocratic and myopic Ceauşescu regime. In the process, the discourse on the past came to occupy an ever more important place for, as Stalin had said back in 1931, 'history is politics projected onto the past'. During the 1970s and 1980s a large-scale historiographical re-evaluation began, underpinned by nationalist exaltation, cultural megalomania and assertive autochthonism and supplemented by a retrieval of the big names of pre-war nationalist historiography and their works.[3] A genuine personality cult developed around Nicolae Iorga, while several of his former students became prominent in the communist science-planning system.

[2] Papacostea 1996: 196.   [3] Boia 2001a: 74–6.

266 Post-Byzantine Empire or Romanian National State?

Ancient origins, national unity, independence, ethnic continuity and autochthony were the key topoi of this national-communist historical discourse, embellished with claims to protochronism – a notion endorsing the anteriority of Romanian civilisation in specific fields compared with other civilisations. To be sure, there had always been a non-conformist and less politicised type of historians, determined to maintain a certain professional standard, but if they could elude nationalist excesses, they could not explicitly counteract nationalism as the dominant discourse. More often than not they found safety in less exposed and professionally subtler research areas, demanding erudition and highly specialised knowledge, such as the Romanian-Byzantine relations.

Present-day byzantinist Petre Guran has suggested that the reason for the Romanian-Byzantine studies' continuous oscillation between rejection and exaltation of Byzantium is to be found in Romania's double feeling of marginality in relation to Byzantium – that of placing it within its national history (as related to a state and a current territory), which unfolds geographically outside the borders of Byzantium and chronologically at the empire's agonising end. Hence, two topics had dominated the debate: the actual contact of the Romanian countries with Byzantium and the transmission of its cultural legacy to the Romanians. The two themes were reformulated from generation to generation into a compulsive question: how and why did the Romanian countries enter the Byzantine Commonwealth?[4]

Alexandru Elian (1910–98), a student of Demostene Russo and Nicolae Iorga, who served as the head of the Byzantine section at the Institute of History of the Romanian Academy during the 'liberal' 1960s, was among the first to take up this issue in some of his influential studies of the late 1950s and the 1960s.[5] The question that occupied him was whether there existed any *direct* contacts between Byzantium and 'the Romanian population' in the only interface zone, Dobrudzha (ancient Scythia Minor), before the empire abandoned its possessions on the lower Danube in 1335. Elian's answer was that 'until the fourteenth century, due to the silence of the Byzantine sources, nothing can be affirmed about the Romanians other than the Balkan Vlachs'. Eager to find ancestors under 'often misleading [ethnic] names provided by the Byzantine sources', he explained, Iorga and his followers, most notably N. Bănescu, had asserted not only that the ancient inhabitants of the Danubian towns were mostly Romanians but also that the members of the Scythian tribe, who settled in the towns they

---

[4] Guran 2018.   [5] Elian 1958: 212–25; Elian 1967: 195–203; 1964: 98–179.

Post-Byzantine Empire or Romanian National State?   267

had previously pillaged, were of the same stock. They had even claimed that these urban centres, with their Romanian population and leaders who railed against the imperial rule, were 'the first crystallisations of the Romanian State'. It was time, Elian stated, to discard these erroneous interpretations, which were the result of the false method of 'discovering' Romanians under different other ethnic names. 'The best [we can do] is to bow before the silence of the Byzantines, who made no mention of our ancestors before the beginning of the fourteenth century'. It is reasonable to suppose, he continued, that especially after the victories of Basil II, the 'Slavo-Romanian' population between the Tisza river and the Carpathians benefited from the power that Byzantium regained over these areas, and nor should the lasting presence of the Ecumenical Patriarchate at the mouths of the Danube be underestimated. On the whole, however, 'the balance sheet of the Byzantine-Romanian relations during their first stage is certainly not brilliant': they were reduced to incidental contacts between the population north of the Danube and mostly soldiers and merchants coming from Constantinople. More importantly,

> the coexistence of two civilisational areas, even if they were adjacent, like those of the Byzantines and the Romanians before the thirteenth century, did not necessarily imply that significant contacts were established between them. The Romanians were still ill prepared to assimilate the Byzantine civilisation, even in the more modest aspects it could take in countries as distant from Constantinople as the lower Danube.[6]

The second phase of the Byzantine-Romanian relations, Elian went on, began in the fourteenth century with the establishment of the first Romanian states, the principalities of Wallachia and Moldavia. This phase rendered a different picture: at the time when the Romanians had to create the instruments for the various functions of their new states and enrich their material and spiritual culture, an appeal to the Byzantine civilisation was quick to ensue, even if it meant addressing a spiritual heritage rather than a living presence. It was around that time that the Byzantines themselves for the first time became aware of the existence of a Romanian people north of the Danube. The establishment of metropolitan seats in Wallachia (1359) and Moldavia (1401) under the aegis of and bishops nominated by the Byzantine Church inaugurated the official relations between Byzantium and the two fledgling principalities. The nature of these relations, Elian held, was almost exclusively ecclesiastical

---

[6] Elian 1958: 213–16; 1967: 198; 1964: 158–9.

268   Post-Byzantine Empire or Romanian National State?

and remained so until the fall of Constantinople to the Ottomans. Despite its brevity, the presence of the Byzantine clergy, he surmised, 'must have brought to both countries some reflections of the civilisation of an empire which, although dying, did not cease to exercise its millennial prestige far beyond its shrunken borders'. However, on the central problem of the Byzantine-Romanian relations during their second phase, namely whether the two principalities had managed to secure a place for themselves in the Byzantine 'family of states', Elian's answer was negative. He refuted as groundless Iorga's contention, often repeated ever after, that the self-advertisement of the rulers of the principalities as 'despots' indicated close political relations with and (real or nominal) dependence on Constantinople. The little that could be extracted from the sources indicated that if the empire showed some interest in Wallachia, it was due to its growing importance on the periphery of the free world and was linked to Hungary's anti-Ottoman policy, which served Byzantine interests.[7]

Thus, Elian concluded, direct Byzantine influence can explain neither 'the incomparable ascendancy' that the Byzantine civilisation enjoyed among the Romanians during and well after the Middle Ages nor the fact that a great part of the Byzantine heritage passed to the Romanian countries. The Byzantine features found in medieval Romanian civilisation, he asserted, 'are better explained by the Byzantine-Slavonic synthesis already achieved in the Balkan world to which the Romanians were attached with particularly strong ties', among them: the collaboration of the Bulgarians and Romanians within the Second Bulgarian empire, followed by their common resistance to the Tatar domination, and the ecclesiastical relations between Romanians and South Slavs, which led to the use of Slavic language as the official language of both the state and the church in the Romanian principalities; the dynastic links between the early rulers of Wallachia, on the one hand, and the sovereigns of Bulgaria and Serbia, on the other; and finally, the generous hospitality reserved by the Romanians for the Bulgarians and especially the Serbs displaced by the Ottomans. These clerics, writers and artists reinforced the existing elements of the Byzantine-Slavonic synthesis, which were perfectly compatible with the young Romanian civilisation and which began to make their presence felt in Wallachia before the Ottomans reached the Danube. The fourteenth century saw the emergence of a true hesychast international, where Byzantine Greeks and South Slavs fraternised in the ascetic and anti-Latin ideals of Palamism. It was also the age of the itinerant artists and

[7] Elian 1958: 217–19; 1964: 106–10.

Post-Byzantine Empire or Romanian National State? 269

architects who tirelessly travelled over the European southeast, carrying new and often daring ideas and formulas or diffusing oriental monastic art, which asserted itself within the 'Renaissance of the XIV century'. It was this Balkan symbiosis, underpinned by a civilisation strongly impregnated with byzantinism, that soon gained ground in the Romanian principalities.[8]

The third phase in the Romanian-Byzantine relations began with the disappearance of Byzantium:

> If we can speak, in line with the felicitous expression of Nicolae Iorga, of a 'Byzantium after Byzantium', it is chiefly to the north of the Danube that we must look for it, in those principalities where Byzantine civilisation did not cease to assert itself long after the catastrophe of 1453. The legacy of the Palaeologues ... found a favourable ground for its preservation in these Romanian countries which, in many respects, were the only ones qualified to continue the work of Byzantium.

Except for the patronage bestowed by the Romanian princes on Athos, Elian did not elaborate on other elements of this continuity before the age of the Phanariots, to which he attributed the 'blossoming of the Byzantine idea in Greek-Romanian circles towards the end of the eighteenth century'. For him, the ancient Byzantine elements brought to Romania first by the South Slavs and then by post-Byzantine Hellenism rendered the unique character of the ancient Romanian civilisation, which was brutally brought to an end in 1821.[9]

Elian's reading of the Romanian-Byzantine relations – enunciated before the onslaught of the 'national-communist' discourse – is remarkable above all for its demythologising flair. First, it displays extraordinary restraint, in view of the paucity of conclusive evidence, in determining the ethnic filiation of the north-Danubian populations, whom the Byzantines encountered before the fourteenth century, and renounced as ill-founded Iorga's speculations about 'popular Romanias'. Such moderation proved exceptional in the following decades. In the 1970s and 1980s much of the interwar nationalist propositions returned with a vengeance. Accordingly, Elian's assertion that the direct connections between Byzantium and the Romanians, save those to the south of the Danube, were relatively few and without important consequences was impugned by historians eager to prove the ancientness and continuity of the Romanians in the territories where they now lived. The lack of reliable written sources

---

[8] Elian 1967: 198–200. [9] Elian 1967: 222–3.

270   Post-Byzantine Empire or Romanian National State?

to this effect was offset by attributing Romanian identity to archaeological material; in other words, treating archaeological cultures as ethnic groups. Illustrative of this method is the work of Dan Gh. Theodor (b.1933), who took great pains to show that the roots of Iorga's Romanian 'Byzantium after Byzantium' lay further back in history, at least since the fifth century. By equating continuity of life as attested by archaeological findings with Romanian ethnic continuity across what was often dubbed Carpatho-Danubian-Pontic space, Theodor held that 'nowhere had the Byzantine civilisation left so many traces in history and civilisation, in the material and spiritual culture of a people as it had here, in the area between the Danube, the Black Sea and the northern Carpathians ... so that it can rightly be considered as the only direct heir of that brilliant and unique eastern Roman Empire in the Middle Ages'. Between the fifth and eleventh centuries, he argued, 'Byzantium was so organically integrated into the constitution of ancient Romanian material and spiritual culture that the entire subsequent evolution of the medieval Carpatho-Danubian-Pontic civilisation bore its initiating seal'.[10] (At the same time, the early Slavs, who in the 1950s and 1960s were viewed as the political and military rulers of the local population and were given the status of the third component of Romanian ethnogenesis, had disappeared completely from the Romanian ethnogenetic plot by the 1980s, as Theodor's work also attests.[11]) Theodor thus fused protochronist and ethnocentric claims in order to postulate a prestigious Romanian-Byzantine symbiosis of over a millennium's duration, which coincidentally 'explained the uninterrupted perseverance of Romanianism in these lands with its deep and strong roots in the ancient Dacian hearth' and attested to 'the unity of the whole Romanian territory'.[12]

Elian's other affirmation – that Byzantine influence on the Romanians was effected through the mediation of the byzantinised South Slavs – had by then become a generally accepted but variously interpreted fact. In a vein reminiscent of Panaitescu's thesis on behalf of 'Slavonism' as a form of 'popular byzantinism', the Romanian post-war historiography before the 1970s was on the whole unanimous in acknowledging the 'nationally beneficial' and elevating aspects of this symbiosis. Next to Elian's, one may quote as illustrative the work of a contemporary authority in medieval and early modern Romanian culture, Mihai Berza (1907–78), another disciple of the pre-war critical school of history and director of the Institute of Southeast European Studies in Bucharest. Berza attributed the emergence of the prejudice against what he preferred to call 'Slavo-Romanian culture' or

---

[10] Theodor 1981: 7, 87.   [11] Curta 2001: 373–4.   [12] Theodor 1981: 87.

Post-Byzantine Empire or Romanian National State?   271

'Romanian culture of Slavic language' to the national revival era, marked as it was by the spell of the Latinist school and the more intensive contacts with western Europe. 'This point of view is now completely obsolete', he wrote, 'and no one talks anymore about Slavic "dark ages" or incompatibility between the Romanian spirit and the Slavic garment.' By the tenth century, when the Romanians adopted the Slavic rite, Berza explained, Latin was a dead language for them and the rupture with the West had long been completed. Embracing Orthodoxy in its Slavic form was not only a necessity imposed by geography but a requisite for the preservation of Romanian identity vis-à-vis the Catholic states. The adoption of Slavic as the official language, furthermore, opened a new thoroughfare to the riches of Byzantine civilisation and to the literary production of the Slavs themselves. 'The Romanians, who knew how to preserve it and even transmit it to a certain extent to the Slavic peoples, drew from this fund of Slavo-Byzantine culture food for their own spiritual life and used it, for several centuries, as an instrument for their intellectual formation.'[13] Berza stressed the richness of the 'Slavo-Romanian literature' and the importance of the Byzantine sources, on which it drew and which had produced a 'great many essential works of the Orthodox spirituality'. For him, this Slavo-Romanian culture on Byzantine basis was the indisputably dominant high culture in literature, church, state administration, court and in the upper layers of society, but also the 'common culture of the three historical provinces', even if the contribution of the Transylvanian Romanians to it was less important than that of the other two because of their specific sociopolitical condition.

The early 1970s were marked by two events that help us grasp the then state-of-the-art discussions of Romanian-Byzantine relations. The centenary of Iorga's birth in 1971 was honoured, in addition to a second edition of his *Byzance après Byzance* (prefaced by Berza) and a Romanian translation, with several edited volumes dedicated to his seminal contributions to Romanian historiography, including one commemorating him as a 'historian of Byzantium'.[14] The following year, the XIVth International Congress of Byzantine Studies took place in Bucharest, featuring as one of its central themes 'Byzantium and Romania'. The historian of Romanian culture and Iorga's aficionado, Virgil Cândea (1927–2007), opened his overview of the Romanian contributions to this theme with the following emotive statement:

> For Romanians, the realities of the Lower Empire are too deeply integrated into their own institutional and cultural traditions to consider the Byzantine

---

[13] Berza 1970: 485–506.   [14] Stănescu 1971.

272 Post-Byzantine Empire or Romanian National State?

world only from the distance of an object of scientific research or contemplation of the past. The evocation of this world is hailed by us with affection and pride because we feel Byzantium as largely ours, therefore we deem any sign of appreciation of its values as a tribute to the very origins of Romanian civilisation.[15]

The Romanians, he went on, were intimately linked to the Roman empire in both its western and eastern hypostases. While Rome moulded their ancestors as a Latin people through the Daco-Roman symbiosis, gave them the language and introduced them to one of the highest civilisations of the ancient world, from the area cultivated by Byzantium the medieval Romanians took institutions, ideas, literature and art and developed them according to their own creative virtues, merging them in a synthesis 'which bears the stamp of a vigorous originality'. So, the ethnographic and linguistic bearers of Latinity in eastern Europe across two millennia proved also to be 'the most faithful keepers of the Byzantine permanencies in this part of the world, ensuring their survival after the fall of Constantinople'. The phenomenon of Romanian civilisation itself was only conceivable by virtue of these epochal encounters with ancient Rome and medieval Byzantium.[16]

The reports presented to the Congress, which dealt with different aspects of Romanian-Byzantine relations, demonstrated a fundamental convergence of opinion on their paradoxical nature, namely that the indirect impact of these relations on Romanian realities was deeper than that effected by direct contacts. Having examined the political relations between the Romanians (an ethnic ascription that from the 1970s onwards was indiscriminately applied to the motley populations inhabiting the territories of present-day Romania after the Roman withdrawal) and the empire between the ninth and the fifteenth centuries, byzantinist Eugen Stănescu (1922–89) drew attention to the moment when 'the real Byzantium disappeared and its place was taken by an ideal Byzantium that was going to last through its institutions, literature and art'. Yet he also stressed, pace Elian, the importance of 'the keen interest that Byzantium had in this space [of today's Romania] already before it re-established its northern border on the Danube', the subsequent direct contacts of the empire with 'the first feudal Romanian states' (as he called the plurality of unstable political formations between the eleventh and the thirteenth centuries) and the 'complex and dramatic' relations between a shrinking Byzantium (reduced to a sheer 'Balkan state forced

[15] Cândea 1972: 13.   [16] Cândea 1972: 13–14.

Post-Byzantine Empire or Romanian National State? 273

to fiercely defend its precarious and endangered independence') and the budding independent Romanian states – contacts that, as Cândea put it, 'showed the oldest foundations of our integration in the area of Byzantine civilisation'.[17] The principalities' independence from Hungary and the prospect of their internal consolidation, which were laid at the door of the two newly established metropolises, was what ultimately defined the positive balance sheet of the Romanian-Byzantine relations, and the positive assessment of Romanian byzantinism generally, before the empire's extinction.

This brings us to the central problem that percolated through the papers submitted at the Congress and which continued to structure the main debates in the following years: the dichotomy between autochthony – foreign influence and the interaction between what Iorga had once called 'Byzantine forms and Balkan realities'. A formulation proposed by the abovementioned Berza captures the methodological approach to these issues that came to prevail: 'Instead of the former "influences", which risked transforming culture into a mosaic of borrowings due to the hazards of history, current research is trying to reveal the modalities of an active reception and the original results of the effort at assimilation.'[18] The concept of 'active reception' of Byzantine culture smoothly established itself in cultural, art and architectural studies and was fully consummated in Răzvan Theodorescu's (b.1939) studies, testifying to the maturity of the receiving culture.[19] The adaptation of the Byzantine institutional 'model' and political ideology, however, proved a more contentious matter. Its politicisation should not surprise considering the central place of the state in the mind-set of a nationalist or totalitarian regime. In striking similarity to the Bulgarian discussions around the same time, the function of the Byzantine imperial idea, or more broadly the ideological construction of a Byzantine model of power in the Romanian countries, became a key problem, with which the brightest Romanian byzantinists grappled during the 1970s and 1980s. Hanging over that whole debate was the long shadow of Nicolae Iorga, who had portrayed the sixteenth-century Romanian rulers as the 'natural and legitimate descendants of the Byzantine emperors' and in the same breath affirmed the 'original conception' and the 'local tradition' of Romanian statehood.

While Petre Năsturel (1923–2012) revamped Iorga's vision,[20] Dumitru Năstase (1924–2013) radicalised it. Basing himself on rather fragile

---

[17] Stănescu 1974: 393–43; Cândea 1972: 16. [18] Berza 1970: 500.
[19] See especially Theodorescu 1974. [20] Năsturel 1973: 397–413; 1986.

274   Post-Byzantine Empire or Romanian National State?

evidence, which he detected with great ingenuity but took out of context, Năstase went out of his way to demonstrate the effective existence of imperial ambitions of the Romanian rulers under Ottoman domination. Already before the fall of Constantinople, during the second half of the fourteenth century, he avowed, the Romanian princes raised their first claims of an imperial nature, based on the idea of taking over the imperial-Orthodox and South Slav legacies. After the disappearance of Byzantium and the other Christian states south of the Danube, the voivodes of Wallachia and Moldavia remained the only Orthodox rulers to fight the Turks. In giving their struggle a sense of providential mission, they emphasised the imperial rank they had already assumed, while claiming a Byzantine succession in the broadest ecumenical sense. Although forced to accept the suzerainty of the sultan, they never renounced the imperial status, but made certain adjustments, dictated by the new set-up, 'which would give the concept a typical *crypto-imperial* character, manifest throughout the duration of the Ottoman domination'.[21] Năstase thus moved the beginnings of the imperial conception of the Romanian princes two centuries earlier than Iorga and made it cover a field much larger than the cultural and ecclesiastical 'imperialism' of the Moldavian and Wallachian voivodes, to which other historians had turned – a situation that, he said, 'completely changes the terms of the problem of Byzantium's survival'. Năstase dubbed his proposition 'the Christian Crypto-empire under Ottoman domination, a real *imperium in imperio* . . . whose ground-works had been laid long before the fall of Constantinople [and which] was to be operational until 1821'. The Romanian princes envisaged the realisa-tion of this imperial idea through stages: by uniting all Romanian territor-ies under one single sceptre (which Năstase described as 'the medieval phase of the Romanian people's fight for national unity'), they created a solid base for a liberation offensive in the Balkans (which failed to materialise). There was thus no opposition between local and imperial, 'the national idea' and 'the imperial idea', but two complementary aspects of a single mission. Albeit pursued briefly as actual policy only by Michael the Brave, this was the 'permanent aspiration' and '*traditional* project' of all Romanian princes, the Phanariot included. From this point of view, Năstase concluded, 'the imperial ideology of the voivodes had always considered the Romanian territories as one single national entity, a large "Romanian land" covering the Romanian ethnical and historical area as a whole'.[22] As a later critic would note, Năstase's contention came down to

---

[21] Năstase 1981: 234–7; 1988: 207–8.   [22] Năstase 1981: 237–41, 246; 1988: 209–11.

Post-Byzantine Empire or Romanian National State?

a bunch of hasty peremptory statements 'without convincing arguments and at odds with the historical sense, but true to the contemporary ideological environment of Ceauşescu's neo-Stalinism'.[23]

Alexandru Elian, as we saw, had already challenged the 'imperial' interpretation as originally formulated by Iorga by stressing the South Slav mediation, thence indirect transmission, of Byzantine institutions and mentalities. There followed several comprehensive studies devoted to the institutional and ideological transfer from Byzantium, most notably Valentin Al. Georgescu's *Byzantium and the Romanian Institutions until the Mid-Eighteenth Century* (1980) and Andrei Pippidi's *Byzantine Political Tradition in the Romanian Principalities in the 16th–18th Centuries* (1983), which controverted the idea of Byzantine imperial continuity through the Romanians. A historian of law and institutions, Valentin Georgescu (1908–95) traced the elements of Byzantine institutional borrowing and their local adaptations from the ninth through the mid-eighteenth centuries across a broad range of institutional and legal arrangements, with a special focus on the structuring of the state and royal power and the *idées-force* behind it.[24]

Georgescu commended the 'exemplary rigour' with which Elian had dealt with the Romanian-Byzantine contacts before and shortly after the fall of Constantinople. He concurred with the view that the institutional impact of Byzantium on the Romanian principalities during that period was mediated by the Slavs and related to the place of the church in the state, and that only after the collapse of the empire did it become wider and deeper. Georgescu saw his own contribution in demonstrating that 'everywhere and always the impact of Byzantium, both direct and indirect, was transformed into local creations'.[25] This was the leitmotif of his book on Byzantium and the Romanian institutions, where he rebuked the notions (and theories) of imitation and diffusionism in favour of 'innovative local syntheses', where Byzantine institutions and norms acquired 'new qualities', corresponding to the different functions they came to serve and the 'Romanian development laws' they had to abide by. Georgescu readily admitted that 'after 1500, the Romanian lands were an area of strong and fertile development of a series of Byzantine forms, structures and values', transmitted by the Greek diaspora, the Phanariots and the 'Ottoman permeability for Greek-Byzantine continuity and preponderance'. However, he insisted that 'it would be wrong to see in the Romanian countries a "true Byzantium", a "Byzantium brighter than that on the banks of the Bosporus"', because 'Romanian realities' always imposed

---

[23] Tanaşoca 2014: 18.   [24] Georgescu 1980.   [25] Georgescu 1974: I, 482–3.

276   Post-Byzantine Empire or Romanian National State?

themselves – even on the Phanariots, notwithstanding the 'late and monotonous manipulation of Byzantine slogans' they indulged in.[26]

This, he held, was especially the case with the purported deep implication of the Romanian princes 'in the myth of the imperial resurrection of Byzantium', as inculcated by Iorga and embellished by Năstase. The Romanian princes, led by realism, a sense of proportion and 'national' responsibility, did not succumb to it: they never put forward their candidacy for the succession of the *basileus*, neither directly as the Bulgarian and Serbian tsars had once done nor through the ideological game of a *translatio imperii* in favour of a third Rome. The closest they ever got to the role of the onetime Byzantine emperors concerned their policy of cultural ecumenism and Christian solidarity with the peoples of the region and further afield. Georgescu exerted himself to demonstrate that the infiltration of the royal power with undoubtedly Byzantine elements was, in the last resort, 'non-imperial' or even 'anti-imperial': autocracy served exclusively to legitimate the internal sovereignty and independence of the princes; for them it made sense solely as an instrument in the pursuit of autonomy and finally independence. An early 'vocation for independence' had precluded any tendency towards supranational unity.[27]

Some later students of Romanian medieval state-building would demur Georgescu's anachronistic application of modern concepts, inflating the significance of the opposition between universalist imperialism and local aspirations for national sovereignty.[28] In tune with the rampant nationalist slant of the time, Georgescu strove above all to highlight the particularity of the Romanian political tradition and its 'capacity for selectivity, reinterpretation, fruitful adaptation and search for new solutions for Romanian problems . . . which had diversified the Byzantine heritage in a notable and original way'. As he saw it, the actual meaning of the formula 'Byzantium after Byzantium' suggested the idea of 'non-Byzantium', whereby the nations of southeastern Europe, the Romanian in particular, had always defined themselves in relation to Byzantium but often against it, seeking 'to fashion their own non-Byzantium'.[29] In the final analysis, the ideal of the national state took precedence over the imperial ideal.

Andrei Pippidi (b.1948), Iorga's grandson and author of the most important monograph on the Byzantine political tradition in the Romanian lands, sought to reinterpret the notion of 'Byzantium after Byzantium' from different premises. He pointed to two different

---

[26] Georgescu 1980: especially 287–9.   [27] Georgescu 1980: 126–7.   [28] Pippidi 1983: 14.
[29] Georgescu 1980: 289, 295–6.

Post-Byzantine Empire or Romanian National State? 277

kinds of exaggerations to which historians were prone when assessing the role of Byzantine influence in medieval Romania: overrating the tension between Byzantine universal imperialism and local aspiration to national sovereignty (Valentin Georgescu's viewpoint), and the opposite error of attributing to Byzantium most of the cultural and political characteristics of the medieval Romanian principalities (as typified by Dumitriu Năstase). For Pippidi, it is beyond any doubt that from the fourteenth century until the fall of Constantinople Wallachia and Moldavia belonged to an international community, where the Byzantine hegemony remained uncontested and where the traditional conception of nominal dependence on the Byzantine empire continued to exist. A minor power from an economic and political point of view, Byzantium of the fourteenth and fifteenth centuries was nevertheless invested with intellectual and cultural prestige, which continued to exert its authority on the Romanians. The confrontation with and later subjugation by the Turks had as an unexpected consequence the strengthening of the Byzantine sway not only on the character of the Romanian civilisation, which was gradually detaching itself from the West, but also on the political ideas capable of evoking emotive reaction.[30] Pippidi, however, expressed reservations about the prominence of the Byzantine imperial model as a key to the history of the Moldavian and Wallachian principalities, advancing two arguments: firstly, the Romanian princes rarely undertook anti-Ottoman expeditions, which indicated that the dream of resurrecting the empire was not in the centre of their policy; secondly, the duality of the Moldavo-Wallachian monarchy fitted badly with the idea of *translatio imperii*. Since the beginnings of the Romanian political thought were deeply affected by the Ottoman aggression against Byzantium, two fundamental political themes steered the national energy: the idea of centralisation and the problem of independence. There was no intention to claim the succession of the Byzantine emperors, but to continue and imitate them locally – 'a symbolic affiliation to Byzantium', reflecting a compromise between a political ideal and reality. 'The observance of the Byzantine tradition as an ideal form of government became a myth, a political model'.[31]

For Pippidi, this was the crux of the matter: the impact of the Byzantine model on the Romanians, he stated, 'is best captured in the representations

---

[30] Pippidi 1983: 8–9. [31] Pippidi 1983: 9–10, 14, 17.

278   Post-Byzantine Empire or Romanian National State?

(image, myths and ideas)'. At the centre of his interest in these relations is the analysis of the effects of the Byzantine *idea* as an inspiring *myth* for the Romanian culture and civilisation, where the influence of middlemen Greeks, Bulgarians and Serbs played an important role. The Romanian princes, who ruled as autocrats, imitated Byzantium in the ceremonial, ritual and insignia of power, but they had no ambition to revive an obliterated state of affairs. The characteristic features that their political programme picked up from the Byzantine tradition were protection of the Orthodox Church – a mission 'which can be called *imperial vicariate* and which was manifested in the generous help given to religious foundations in the Orthodox East, thus enabling the Greeks, the Bulgarians and the Serbs to preserve their spiritual, cultural and ethnic identity'; rule according to ancient examples, in a spirit of concord; and struggle against 'pagan languages'. 'In these three forms, solidarity with the Southeast European world and, implicitly, fidelity to the common past become manifest.'[32] Building on Iorga's conceptual framework, Pippidi underlined the positive contribution of the Byzantine tradition to Romania's political and religious life but also stressed its reinterpretation and functioning on a different set of principles, as well as the Ottoman inflections, which made it difficult to define it as a Byzantine heritage per se.

Pippidi drew attention to two Romanian paradoxes with origins in the Romanian-Byzantine association. First, although they were of Latin origin, Romanians embraced a confessional identity that departed from their ethnic source; moreover, since the legacy they took over from Byzantium was that of the late Paleologue period, marked by strong resentment against the Western world due to the indifference it had shown in the face of the Ottoman onslaught, this hostility had coloured the attitude of the Romanian clergy and scholars, who remained highly suspicious of Latin culture and Catholic expansionism over the course of three centuries. Another paradox was that, even though they came to know Byzantium close to its end, the Romanians kept its memory longer than their neighbours, whose parallel experience took place further back in time. This made one think, as Iorga had once put it, of 'those leaves that still grow for some time on uprooted trees'.[33] At the end of the day, the progressive divergence between lived realities and mental representations turned the Byzantine tradition into an 'idée-force and a dream, a myth created by deep nostalgia'. From the mid-seventeenth century the allure of this myth began to wane as the Romanian rulers, the Phanariot included, increasingly

---

[32] Pippidi 1983: 96–7, 268.   [33] Pippidi 2004: 27.

Post-Byzantine Empire or Romanian National State? 279

turned to western European modernity to the detriment of Byzantine traditionalism. From that moment on, Romanian intellectuals started to see a difference between the myth of the Roman empire as an ancestor of the Romanians, which supported their aspiration for national independence, and the myth of the 'Greek Christian empire', which the Greeks wished to restore at its former height as an empire for all the Christians living under the sultan's domination.[34] Erudite, perceptive and balanced, Pippidi's book serves to this day as the standard reference study of Byzantium's political afterlife in medieval and early modern Romania.

From a different perspective, one that sought to throw into relief the deeply ambivalent contribution of Byzantium to the construction of Romanian *identity*, these same issues were tackled by another byzantinist saddling the 1989 political divide, Nicolae Şerban Tanaşoca (1941–2017). Essential to understanding Tanaşoca's position is, similar to George Murnu's several decades earlier, his Balkan-Vlach origin or what Petre Guran has called 'the Aromanian vein of Romanian Byzantine studies'.[35] In a far echo from the seventeenth-century humanists of the Latinist school (to whose anti-byzantinism he also turned his pen), Tanaşoca emphasised 'the hostility of the Byzantines towards the Romanians' aspiration to preserve and affirm their Romanesque identity'. He upbraided the empire for having excluded the Romanians ('Vlachs') from the legitimate heirs of Rome, having rebuffed the Romanesque identity they professed and the political freedom they aspired to and assimilated them with the barbarians. In fact, he held, from its Roman past the empire, which transferred itself to the Greek world, kept only the name, the principle of unity and the legitimation of its aspiration to mould politically the world under its aegis, while 'being in reality a Hellenistic Empire of Greek language and Christian religion'. 'In the attitude of Byzantium towards the Romanians, the descendants of oriental Romanity, who were hostile to Hellenisation and related to the western Latin Christianity', Tanaşoca wrote, 'we find the echo of this old antinomy'. For the Romanians, in turn, the Byzantines were nothing other than 'Greeks' and their empire was, at all times, 'the Greek kingdom' – an implicit subversion of the Byzantine claim to the universality and succession of Rome, which he believed the Romanians had transmitted to the Slavs and Bulgarians. Consequently,

[34] Pippidi 1983: 15, 123.   [35] Guran 2018.

280   Post-Byzantine Empire or Romanian National State?

> The crystallisation of the Romanians as a new Romanesque people, the Romanian ethnogenesis owes to Byzantium no positive formative principle of identity affirmation under the guidance of the empire and in the spirit of its tradition, but a negative one of rejection, marginalisation and isolation . . . . Considered barbarians and called Vlachs, the Romanians kept and affirmed their Romanesque identity against Byzantium, which abandoned and repudiated them.[36]

Eventually, if the Romanians proved able to withstand the efforts at their political submission and ethnic assimilation by 'the Greek Empire of Constantinople', it was because their resistance was 'spiritually supported, both in the north and the south of the Danube, by the proud consciousness of Romanity, a sign of nobility and Europeanness'.[37]

Tanaşoca did not let pass without 'serious reservations' traditional 'pro-Byzantine' historiographical stances such as the praise heaped on 'ecclesiastical Byzantinism' (the Romanians' actual interface with Byzantium according to him) for its role in preserving the Romanians' national being. The Byzantine complexion of the Romanian Church, he contended, had little to do with maintaining the nationality of the Romanians. Initially the Romanian lands were gravitating towards Rome rather than Constantinople. The early byzantinisation of the church and Romanian civilisation, undertaken through the Slavicised and Christianised Bulgarians, also entailed Slavicisation of Romanian religious and cultural life – a phenomenon that Tanaşoca, in contrast to P. P. Panaitescu or M. Berza, saw as 'the result of a conquest, the effect of violence, which isolated the Romanians from the rest of the Romanic, Western world'. The elevation of the Romanian churches in Wallachia and Moldavia to the metropolitan rank marked their definitive option for Orthodoxy and byzantinism, but it also underscored 'the strictly Romanian national meaning of the ecclesiastical inclusion in the Byzantine sphere' in that it confirmed their political independence. Echoing Iorga, Tanaşoca stressed the 'fundamental difference' in relation to Byzantium between the situation of the Romanian countries, whose adherence to byzantinism 'had as its main purpose the safeguarding of [Romanian] independence and national being', and the situation of Russia or the Slavic states in the Balkans, 'where the Byzantine idea became the germ of future medieval imperialism'. The Romanian princes inherited from the Byzantine emperors the unique function of defenders of the Orthodox faith and protectors of the whole cultural and spiritual life of

[36] Tanaşoca 2003 [1985]: 5–8.   [37] Tanaşoca 2002: 21.

Eastern Christianity. However, they espoused 'a rigorous Orthodoxy different from that in Byzantium' because it lacked any tendency to subordinate the church to the exclusive benefit of the Romanian state, and because the spirit of authentic Orthodox 'international' that the Romanian rulers promoted distinguished it from the dominant Byzantine Hellenism. Later, the thrust towards modernisation was spearheaded by the Greek-Catholic (Uniate) Transylvanians, who rekindled the flame of neo-Latin enthusiasm and impelled the 'liberation of our Latin and Roman being from byzantinism, now considered from a modern western and national point of view ... Byzantinism was rejected both in the name of the national idea and in the name of the values of freedom and democracy'. In the nineteenth and twentieth centuries, Tanaşoca concluded this part of his argument: 'the Romanian Church remained, in line with tradition, in the service of God and the nation and by raising itself to patriarchal rank succeeded to consecrate the fulfilment of the Romanian unitary national state within its natural borders'.[38]

As to the impulse the Byzantine model gave to the creation of the Romanian state and Romanian political thought, Tanaşoca's position concurred with that upheld by Georgescu: the Byzantine aspect of the Romanian monarchy reflected the aspiration to autocracy and 'perfect autonomy', but 'no yearning for expansion or desire to replace the Empire, as was the case in Bulgaria or medieval Serbia'; the Romanians adopted and adapted to their national needs the Byzantine political ideology of autocratic power in order to legitimise their full independence. Unlike his peers, however, Tanaşoca sided with Iorga in seeing in this medieval 'Romanian' conception of the purpose of the state 'the foreshadowing of the modern conception of the national state'.[39] With the hardening of the Ottoman domination in the eighteenth century, he went on, the Romanians experienced a new form of 'post-Byzantine byzantinism', one fancied by the Phanariots, which was based on the strange alliance between the Ecumenical Patriarchate, the Greek archons and the Ottoman empire. Attacked by both conservative and revolutionary forces, this new 'Greek-Turkish byzantinism' spelled the end of the 'Byzantine idea': 'As far as the Romanians are concerned, the modern stage of their history begins, in the field of culture, with the repudiation of byzantinism in the name of progress, democracy and national spirit.'[40] Finally, discussing the role of the Byzantine idea in the Romanian literary creation – 'the highest form of manifestation of the national soul' – Tanaşoca maintained

---

[38] Tanaşoca 2002: 11–19.   [39] Tanaşoca 2002: 20–4.   [40] Tanaşoca 1997: 139–40.

282   Post-Byzantine Empire or Romanian National State?

that 'the Byzantine literary model stimulated and influenced the Romanian literary creation less than one might think and is claimed'. It was not the Slavic texts of Byzantine inspiration but the 'Latin literary tradition of the West' that provided the models for the literature in the national language, and the great flourishing of Romanian literature in the modern period 'took place under the sign of reunion with the Roman idea and the Western world, of reintegration in Europe and repudiation of Byzantium'.[41]

So, while fending off the hypertrophied claims of what he later defined as 'Ceauşescu's neo-Stalinism', Tanaşoca's interpretation squared with the regime's calls for 'revival of national sovereignty', glorification of the telos of the nation – its independence and unity in political and cultural terms, and insistence on the Romanian uniqueness that, in the ardent words of the national historian A. Oţetea, 'synthesised the East and the West and harmonised all borrowed elements with the instincts and needs of its soul'.[42] In his writings one detects traces of the 'anti-byzantinism' of the Aromanian strain in Romanian historiography, which hark back to G. Murnu's interwar theses, being stripped, however, of any major sense of Romanian-Bulgarian anti-Byzantine solidarity.

After 1989, the imperative to validate the Romanians' intrinsic Europeanness acquired new urgency. The 1990s were marked by consistent attempts by both the Central European post-communist aspirants to the European Union club and Western analysts like Samuel Huntington to relegate the countries 'marked by the indelible seal of obscurantist byzantinism ... to a civilisation other than that of the countries of Europe itself'.[43] To debunk this rampant view, Tanaşoca employed a two-pronged strategy: to show that these countries, and the Romanians in particular, 'are less "Byzantine" and more open to influences from Western Europe than is believed, and that, in turn, Western Europe itself is much more "Byzantine" than it likes to admit'. The already adduced arguments supporting the first strategy now assumed a different twist: although byzantinism is a characteristic of Romanian civilisation religiously, culturally and artistically, it neither opposes nor diminishes Romania's political vocation to join the European Union. Tanaşoca shifted the Western orientalist perspective from Byzantium to its Muslim successor, stating that it was not the Byzantine empire, which 'throughout a millennium was a factor in the Europeanisation of the countries of the East and a bulwark of European civilisation', but the

[41] Tanaşoca 2003: 24–7.   [42] Oţetea 1965: 1222.   [43] Tanaşoca 2003: 30.

Post-Byzantine Empire or Romanian National State? 283

Ottoman empire, which 'for centuries wrenched the Orthodox countries of the South-East from Europe and marked them with its seal, causing the first really serious fracture of the European unity. The Ottoman Empire compromised byzantinism, which it emulated and altered, trying to make it an instrument of its domination and divert it from its European function'.[44] On the whole, however, Tanaşoca continued to lay stronger emphasis on the 'Roman idea' as guiding Romanian history, at the expense of the 'Byzantine idea': the latter, he affirmed, is 'certainly an important element in the Romanians' identity, but a secondary and accidental one'.[45]

Whereas, as already noted, during the first, 'internationalist' decades of communist historiography the Balkan Vlachs were largely excluded from the discussions of Romanian history, from the 1970s, as Tanaşoca points out, 'there has been a surge in concern for the integration of the history of the Balkan Romanians into national Romanian history'.[46] Medievalists, most of them representatives of 'the Aromanian vein of Romanian Byzantine studies', such as Eugen Stănescu, Stelian Brezeanu, Petre Şerban Năsturel, Tudor Teoteoi, Radu Ştefan Ciobanu (Vergatti), Sergiu Iosipescu and Tanaşoca himself threw themselves into this task, mostly through specialised linguistic and historical researches. For these scholars, as for their predecessors, the survival of the Romance language in the region presented sufficient evidence for the Romanian continuity of Latin stock and the ethnogenetic unity of the Balkan Vlachs with the Romanians to the north, despite their different historical trajectories. Preoccupation with 'Balkan Romanity' necessarily linked up with the question of political continuity as the emanation of ethnic continuity. For, as Lucian Boia observes, 'what gives the Romanian complexes is the absence, for a thousand years, of a Romanian state, the lack of a political tradition deeply rooted in time, comparable with that of the neighbouring nations'.[47] Consequently, the focal point of the engagement with Balkan Romanity remained the 'Romanian-Bulgarian empire' of the Asenids.

With varying vehemence Romanian historians castigated the rejection of the key role Romanians played in the anti-Byzantine uprising at the end of the twelfth century and the Romanian ethnic origins of the Asenids by successive generations of Bulgarian historians (among them P. Mutafchiev, V. Gyuzelev, I. Bozhilov and I. Duychev). Tanaşoca, in particular, added

---

[44] Tanaşoca 2003: 130–3.   [45] Tanaşoca 2013: 266–7.   [46] Tanaşoca 2001: 103.
[47] Boia 2001a: 124.

284   Post-Byzantine Empire or Romanian National State?

to the stakes of the debate by highlighting the importance of the relations between Balkan Romanity and Byzantium for the construction of Romanian identity. For him, the Asenids' rebellion and the restoration of the Bulgarian kingdom were expressions of the political maturation of the Balkan Vlachs and the vitality of their 'Romanesque identity consciousness'; the latter became a political idea and an instrument for national liberation in the twelfth and thirteenth centuries and undergirded the rise of the Romanian principalities in the fourteenth century. Outstripping the early twentieth-century historian Dimitre Onciul and his follower Ştefan Ştefănescu, who saw the Second Bulgarian empire as the catalyst of the state formation in Oltenia and Wallachia, Tanaşoca held that

> The evolution of the South Danubian forms of independent political life has to be linked to the general evolution of all Romanian communities, both north and south of the Danube, in a single direction. Just as in the case of the north Danubian political structures led by *knezes* and voivodes, the southern Asenid Vlachs, like the other Balkan Vlachs, tended to evolve in the direction of independent political life . . .. The appearance of the Asenid state is the first manifestation of this *pan-Romanian* tendency to develop an independent political life.[48]

As French byzantinist Vincent Laurent wrote, the role of the Vlachs in the formation of the Second Bulgarian empire is so important for the Romanian historians 'because, by proving that this empire is of Romanian foundation and dynasty, the Romanian historians would demonstrate by the same token the extreme political vitality of their Balkan ancestors and the permanence, so crucial on the eve of the formation of the first [medieval] national state, of the contact maintained between the two banks of the Danube'.[49]

From a Romanian point of view, the ultimate outcome was disappointing, however, because the reign of Ivan Asen II reactivated the imperial traditions and expansionist tendencies of the First Bulgarian Kingdom, inherent in the Byzantine model after which it was tailored. The attendant return to Slavism led to the complete Bulgarisation of the Asenid dynasty of Romanian origin and their Vlach subjects. 'Thus, Orthodoxy and

---

[48] Tanaşoca 2001: 122. Tanaşoca evokes Vasil Zlatarski's controversial characterisation of the period before 1185 as an age of Hellenisation in Bulgarian medieval history as an indication of the 'severely decreased capacity of the Bulgarian political initiative before the Asenid uprising'. Unlike the Bulgarians, the Romanians in the twelfth and thirteenth centuries 'had the power and the capacity to lead an anti-Byzantine movement' (Tanaşoca 2001: 126).

[49] Laurent 1948: 246.

Post-Byzantine Empire or Romanian National State?   285

Byzantinism, which for the north-Danubian Romanians were supporting factors for their medieval states', Tanaşoca summed up, 'were perceived in the opposite way by the south-Danubian Romanians. To the latter, both Orthodoxy and Byzantinism diminished them through the power of Bulgarisation that they entailed.'[50]

---

[50] Tanaşoca 2001: 132. See also Tanaşoca 1981: 581–94. Although less inclined to dramatise the Romanian-Byzantine relations, the studies of Stelian Brezeanu (b.1941), the other most prolific writer on the Vlach-Byzantine relations before and after 1989, follow similar trail. See Brezeanu 1999.

CHAPTER 10

In the Fold of the 'Turkish-Islamic Synthesis'

In the aftermath of World War II, Turkey, together with the other regional Western ally, Greece, acted as a cold-war security shield for the West. And, as in Greece, resorting to ethnic nationalism and religious identity as antidotes to the luring rhetoric of communism became a favoured political strategy. Within this political environment, the fundamentals of the Turkish History Thesis remained unassailable, even if by the 1940s, following the death of Mustafa Kemal in 1938, its high tide had passed. In the next decades it continued to hold sway and was never officially withdrawn as part of the dominant ideology. Subsequently, references to Byzantium in the national-historical treatises, if featuring at all, were negligible and entirely within the pre-war interpretative frame charted by Mehmet Fuat Köprülü, Celal Esad Arseven and Ömer Lütfi Barkan in the matter of, respectively, political, art and economic history. The number of papers related in some way to Byzantine history, architecture or archaeology, presented at the Turkish History Congresses during those years, was very limited, and most of them were reports on excavations of Byzantine sites and monuments.[1] A limited advance, which had begun during the war, occurred in art history. Between 1941 and 1944, Steven Runciman gave lectures on Byzantine art and history at Istanbul University. After his departure, an Austrian art historian and a German art historian, Ernst Diez and Philipp Schweinfurth, taught Byzantine art there until 1956, when Semavi Eyice, the first Turkish scholar to deliver lectures in this discipline, took over and in 1963 established a Chair of Byzantine Art History at the Faculty of Literature at the same university. But although this institutional innovation paved the way for more systematic explorations on Byzantine art and architecture, these researches failed to integrate the Byzantine legacy into the historical evolution of Ottoman and Turkish architectural and art history.

---

[1] Yıldız 2011: 68.

In the Fold of the 'Turkish-Islamic Synthesis'

Surprising in this context is the Turkish government's invitation, addressed to the International Association of Byzantine Studies (set up in 1948), to hold the Xth International Congress of Byzantine Studies in Istanbul in 1955. However, it was intended not as a sign of recognition of the importance of the Byzantine legacy for Turkish culture and history but as a performance of cultural diplomacy. The opening address of the deputy minister of education was suggestive of the way Turkey wished to present itself to the wider world. Celal Yardımcı indicated that the Turkish nation was the heir and protector of the millennial Byzantine civilisation and its antiquities, and along with the Turkish monuments and heritage, it embraced them all as the cultural heritage of humanity. He pointed up Istanbul's importance as the cradle of the universal Byzantine and Turkish civilisations and described the conversion of Hagia Sophia, a place of worship for the Turkish nation for 500 years, into a museum in 1934 – an act that, in actual fact, reflected the early Kemalist regime's ambition to suppress Turkey's Islamic past, as a testament to the Turkish nation's sincere commitment to preserve the cultural heritage of all civilisations.[2] The one tangible effect of summoning the Congress in Istanbul appears to have been the considerable sum allocated on its eve by the Turkish National Assembly for the cleaning and conservation of Byzantine and other historical monuments in the city and around Turkey. But President of the International Association of Byzantine Studies Henri Grégoire's exhortation that an institute of Byzantine studies be founded in Turkey would remain unfulfilled until 2015.

From the 1950s a more conservative and Islamic understanding of Turkish history started to ease its way back into mainstream culture. In the next two decades the secular-ethnic and Islamic-ethnic currents competed and sometimes pragmatically overlapped, gradually crystallising in an assertive mix of Turkish nationalism and Islamic identity. In contrast to the Kemalist and racialist visions of Turkish history, which attempted to link all past cultures of Anatolia with pre-conversion Turks, the proponents of the new identity politics among historians – İbrahim Kafesoğlu (1914–84), Osman Turan (1914–78) and Mehmet Altan Köymen (1914–93) – endeavoured to construct a new historical imagination that would reconcile the Turkish nation and culture with Islam by incorporating pre-Islamic Turkish history into the post-conversion Turkish history. In a series of works, among them Turan's contribution to *The Cambridge History of Islam* (1970), they advanced the idea that the history of the Turks in Anatolia began when the Islamicised

---

[2] Actes 1957: 48–50; Bayrı 2019: 123–44.

288   In the Fold of the 'Turkish-Islamic Synthesis'

Oğuz Turks defeated the Byzantine army at Manzikert in 1071, thus turning the battle into one of the foundational and mythical moments of Turkish history. A seminal outcome of such reinterpretation and the ensuing reconceptualisation of the Kemalist historical canon – or what in the 1980s was labelled the 'Turkish-Islamic synthesis' – was the full restoration of the Ottomans and their central position in the course of Turkish history. Henceforth, 'the most celebrated epic events in Turkish history, arguably the Battle of Manzikert, the Conquest of Constantinople, and the Independence War, were to be imagined as instances that are linked to each other within linear progression'.[3] All this is strikingly reminiscent of the reinterpretation of Greek history in the nineteenth century through the incorporation of the previously disdained Byzantine empire into its grand narrative. Mid-twentieth-century Turkish historiography undertook to mend the precarious thread running directly from the pre-Islamic Turks to the Kemalist Republic by incorporating the Ottomans as the bridging link and Ottoman history as the crux – an operation that made it possible to envisage, in the manner of Hellenism in the Greek narrative, 'an essence of Turkishness traceable through history and Turkish states bearing the "essence of Turkishness"'.[4] Following the military coup of 1980, the Turkish-Islamic synthesis – essentially a religiously conservative form of nationalism – became the mainstream legitimising ideology of the regime, undergirded by the US 'Green Belt' doctrine seeking to boost various forms of Islam in the region against the Soviet threat.

In this context the representations of Byzantium, its history and its relations to Turkish history remained marginal themes. In what might be tentatively called Turkish-Byzantine studies after World War II, Byzantine history occupied even less of a place than Byzantine art and architecture, which were typically subsumed within 'heritage studies'. Yet, the 'emphatic rejection of the Byzantine cultural legacy in Turkey', as Nevra Necipoğlu describes it,[5] was not only the outcome of the ideology and the cultural hierarchy underpinning the Turkish History Thesis and its offshoot, the Turkish-Islamic synthesis. In a situation of recurrent conflicts with Greece (the most explosive ones after World War II being the continuing clash over Cyprus and the Turkish demands in the Aegean, which led to the brink of war in 1987), the assimilation of Byzantine history into the Greek master narrative coupled with the appropriation of Byzantine heritage as

---

[3] Gürpınar 2013: 104. For the relevant Turkish-language works of the mentioned authors, see Gürpınar 2013: 255–6 (notes 128, 131–3).
[4] Gürpınar 2013. On the 'Turkish-Islamic synthesis', see Taşkın 2007; Çetinsaya 1999: 350–76.
[5] Necipoğlu 2013: 76.

In the Fold of the 'Turkish-Islamic Synthesis'

an integral part of the Greek cultural identity made it hard for the soaring Turkish nationalism to compete for or take pride in partaking in a common historical tradition with the Greeks.

Until the 1970s, Mehmet Fuat Köprülü's interpretation of the Turkish-Byzantine relations remained unchallenged, with barely any attempt at modification. It is at the same time significant that the main contributions that earned him the status of a paramount national historian were also those which prepared the ground for the incorporation of the Ottoman and Islamic heritage as a cardinal part of Turkish national history. The Turkification of Ottoman imperial history was one of them, which enrooted the belief that everything Ottoman was fundamentally Turkish. Another was the affirmation of a progressive ('genuine and pure') 'Anatolian-Turkish Islam', which set the stage for reconciling Islam with Turkish nationalism. On the whole, although the state-supported 'Turkish-Islamic synthesis' gained ascendancy, Turkish scholarship in historiography and social science in the 1970s and 1980s continued to bear and reproduce many of the premises, self-images and self-representations of Kemalism. They proved resilient enough to withstand the critical historiography on the Kemalist regime, typically associated with the New Left, which emerged in the 1970s and flourished in the 1980s.[6]

Halil İnalcık (1916–2016), the don of Ottoman historical studies from the 1970s onwards, was among the first, and the very few, who ventured to modify Köprülü's extremely particularistic position. Noteworthy is that his career developed primarily in an international context: he held several academic positions in the USA before joining the faculty of the University of Chicago as a professor in Ottoman history (1972–86). In his early works from the 1950s, he upheld the idea that in the early Ottoman period (until the sixteenth century) Ottoman conquest was assisted and facilitated by the strategy of accommodation of non-Muslim populations – what came to be dubbed *istimâlet* (trying to persuade, gain goodwill); that is, the policy of granting differentiated concessions to the Christian population in order to incorporate them into the Ottoman administrative system.[7] There is a certain ambivalence in İnalcık's position, however. While denouncing Gibbons's theory as 'groundless speculation', he seemingly adopted its underlying argument when stressing that a common background tied together the Byzantine frontier troops with

---

[6] 'The Kemalist narrative was the ur-ideology and the "root paradigm" of modern Turkish political culture from which all the modern ideologies from socialism to Islamism derived their premises. This is also true for the Kemalist representations of Turkish history' (Gürpınar 2013: 129).

[7] İnalcık 1954: 104–29.

290 In the Fold of the 'Turkish-Islamic Synthesis'

the Muslim *gazis* (warriors for the faith) and that this led to assimilation. It in turn shaped what he described as 'a true "Frontier Empire," a cosmopolitan state, treating all creeds and races as one, which was to unite the Orthodox Christian Balkans and Muslim Anatolia in a single state'.[8] At the same time, as Heath W. Lowry has observed, when positing that Holy War and colonisation were the dynamic elements in the Ottoman conquests, and that 'the administrative and cultural forms adopted in the newly conquered territories derived from the traditions of near-eastern [Turco-Islamic] politics and civilisation', İnalcık totally rejected that aspect of Gibbons's work which argues for the non-Turkish nature of the Ottomans' institutional base.[9] The change of heart becomes more graphic in later works, such as İnalcık's important contribution to the 1994 volume he coedited with Donald Quataert on the economic and social history of the Ottoman empire, where he abandoned both his earlier depiction of the early Ottoman state as 'a cosmopolitan state, treating all creeds and races as one' and the emphasis on the accommodationist practices of the early Ottoman emirate. Instead, and in keeping with Köprülü, he stressed the basic Turkish origins of the state and de-emphasised the interactive symbiosis which typified the early Ottomans.[10]

İnalcık is more consistent in arguing that the agrarian structure of the Ottomans was to a large extent modelled on the Byzantine and that a number of local practices were preserved for centuries. For him, it was only logical 'that the agrarian, economic and fiscal policies undertaken in areas which came successively under Roman, Byzantine and Ottoman rule share striking similarities'.[11] Specifically, he picked up on Ostrogorski's intuition, by that time unsupported by Ottoman sources, about the continuity between the Byzantine *pronoia* and the Ottoman *timar* systems, and augmented it by highlighting the fundamental continuity in peasant family farming, customs regulations and commercial taxation. The greater parts of the laws which Mehmed the Conqueror collected in the famous codes bearing his name and 'the whole system of taxation and landowner-ship found in the registers', İnalcık argued, 'were simply the product of the previous reigns'; 'local taxes and practices were made laws of the Ottoman state . . . and only laws too obviously contrary to the Ottoman religious and administrative principles were abolished . . . . It becomes apparent that the Ottoman law system as well as these local elements became the main instruments in the survival of the Byzantine institutions under the

---

[8] İnalcık 1973: 5, 7.   [9] İnalcık 1973: 8; Lowry 2003: 7–8.
[10] İnalcık 1994: 11; Lowry 2003: 8–9.   [11] İnalcık and Quataert 1994: 143.

In the Fold of the 'Turkish-Islamic Synthesis'

Ottoman regime'.[12] In his later writings, İnalcık attenuated this view by stressing the weight of Islamic jurisprudence and the 'old-established practices in near-eastern Islamic empires'. Thus he asserted that the sultanic law code, which administered the relationships in Ottoman landholding and taxation, was 'actually a combination of Islamic and local practices related to the Roman-Byzantine legacy. In fact, the system was closely analogous to that of previous Islamic and Byzantine states, and there was no reason for the Ottomans to revolutionise tested methods'.[13] There was also little trace of Barkan's triumphalist visions of social revolution and Ottoman 'liberation' of the Balkan peasants. İnalcık readily admitted that 'the Ottoman invasion deprived the Balkan peoples of their national cultural institutions and of the ruling class which embodied them'. He could not, however, resist pitting the 'anarchy of the Balkans' against the 'dynamic unifying force' of the invading Ottomans, and the arbitrary rule of Byzantine and Balkan lords against the Ottoman regime as one that 'represented a strong and impartial central administration which extended to the peasants effective protection against feudal lords'.[14] Even so, for him the former territories of Byzantium instantiated a sphere of continuity rather than of social or religious revolution.

Most of the studies that touched upon the Turkish-Byzantine relations were focussed on the emergence of the Anatolian Seljuk state. A representative of the younger generation of historians, Taner Timur (b.1935), sought to disprove two readings that were prevalent in his view. One had originated with that strand of Western scholarship – the 'many byzantinists, including "Marxists", and other historians influenced by them' – which portrayed the invading Turks as standing on a very backward developmental level, who demolished the highest civilisation of their time and whose invasions of Anatolia and the Balkans reversed the Byzantine empire's autonomous historical evolution into 'classical feudalism' and the modern age. The historical role assigned to the Turks in this scenario was plainly destructive, while the Ottomans, carriers of Islamic ideals and forms of organisation, were said to have established an order fundamentally different from the Byzantine-Christian one, which explained the historical divergence of European and Oriental trajectories. In a legitimate reaction to such a reading, Turkish historians had fallen into a reverse chauvinism and tried to explain all the civilised elements they saw in the Seljuk and Ottoman states with 'Turkishness' or 'Islam'. What Timur endeavoured to achieve instead was to show that the study of the

---

[12] İnalcık 1960: 237.   [13] İnalcık and Quataert 1994: 105.   [14] İnalcık 1976: 34–5.

292 In the Fold of the 'Turkish-Islamic Synthesis'

Turkish element alone was not sufficient to understand the Seljuk sultanate. Knowledge of the Byzantine state structure was also necessary in order to compare the two 'social formations' rather than tracing, as Köprülü had done, dubious legal ancestry that pitted one narrow institutional genealogy against another. Indeed, Timur was convinced that there existed a 'Turkish-Byzantine synthesis' between the eleventh- and twelfth-century Byzantine society in Anatolia and the budding Turkish-Seljuk society, a phenomenon he derived from a theory of common material determinants defined in rigorous Marxist terms – above all, convergent 'relations of production' (agrarian structure and class formation) and a corresponding state and legal 'superstructure'. He saw the Turkish conquest of Anatolia and Istanbul (like most Turkish historians, Timur consistently avoided the use of the name Constantinople) as analogous to the invasion and destruction of Rome by the Germanic tribes. For him, the Germanic tribes and the Turks were heirs, respectively, of west and east Rome.[15]

The Seljuk Turks, Timur explained, came to Anatolia at a time of acute social contradictions inherent in the developing Byzantine feudal society. The 'rural commune' and the free peasant property were in a state of decline, to which the central government reacted by resorting to a new measure – the *pronoia*, which was similar to the Seljuk iqta and the Frank 'beneficum' system. Byzantium and the Seljuk Turks, therefore, were undergoing a similar process of feudalisation, yet the social foundation of both at the time of the Turkish invasion of Anatolia was still communal and patriarchal, and it provided the backbone of the 'Turkish-Byzantine synthesis':

> In fact, socio-economically, the Ottoman state was based on communal-patriarchal relations like the Byzantine state. Byzantine-Ottoman continuity in terms of relations of production has been abundantly revealed by contemporary historians. The difference arises from the fact that the Turkmen tribes, who had not completely severed their tribal ties, represented only the primitive forms of feudalism . . .. During the transition to classical feudalism, the Byzantine state collapsed, replaced by the Turkish state with the same structure – but with the 'energy' of a new nation, as Hegel once stated.[16]

Like most Turkish historians, Timur saw the Ottoman empire as the reconstitution, on the basis of a new dynasty, of Seljuk state power. 'The Ottoman state', he wrote, 'was founded on the Seljuk state model. In fact,

---

[15] Timur 1979: 53–4. [16] Timur 1979: 71–8, 293–4.

In the Fold of the 'Turkish-Islamic Synthesis' 293

it is possible to characterise it as a new dynasty regaining central power rather than seeing it as a new state. Just as in Byzantium, dynasties changed, but the structure and continuity of the state did not'. Moreover, similar to the Byzantine central authority, the Seljuk-Ottoman centralised bureaucratic structure was instituted on the basis of its privileged relations with an independent peasantry, from which it extracted the bulk of its tax revenues. As in Byzantium, Timur concluded, 'the "despotic" character of the Ottoman state' – that is, the heavily centralised power structure – and 'its anti-feudal character are two sides of the same phenomenon'.[17]

Çağlar Keydar (b.1947), who had specialised in the agricultural transformation in modern Turkey, also contested the view that the Ottomans should shoulder the 'blame' for having diverted Byzantium from its natural evolution from a feudal social formation to a modern European society. The model for Ottoman land legislation, he maintained, was the Land Code dating from the post-Heraclian era, which recognised the independent cultivators as the foundation of the Byzantine social structure, prescribed the protection of the peasants' landed property and established the villages as a communal unit with fiscal responsibility. In later periods of Byzantine history, the Land Code remained an ideal model increasingly diverging from the actual agrarian structure. After the eleventh century the fragmentation of authority and the subjugation of the peasantry to dependent status advanced conjointly to destroy the social basis of the empire. It was Ottoman centralisation some three centuries later which succeeded in restoring the basic contours of the classical Byzantine agrarian structure, thus bringing it closer to the ideal picture of the Land Code: all land was reconverted into state property (which did not cause any juridical problems, since land in the Byzantine empire had also been formally in the ownership of the state) and the Ottoman state ensured the perpetuation of a land regime based on inalienable land holdings possessed by independent peasant families.[18]

In addition to refusing to acknowledge a complete historical break between Byzantine and Ottoman empires, both Timur and Keydar, therefore, upheld the existence of a substantial difference between medieval Europe and the Byzantine empire, which the Ottomans partly exemplified and partly inherited. It was this difference that constituted the basis for the Byzantine-Ottoman continuity and convergence. Such views, next to İnalcık's during that period,

[17] Timur 1979: 101, 294.   [18] Keydar 1987: 11–12.

294 In the Fold of the 'Turkish-Islamic Synthesis'

chimed in with those laid out in a contemporary collective volume, *Continuity and Change in Late Byzantine and Early Ottoman Society*, featuring only Western scholars. Its underlying argument was that the Ottomans were successful precisely because they were capable of integrating existing cultural and social institutions into their imperial framework.[19]

Typologically close to this interpretation is the important book of Cemal Kafadar (b.1954), a Turkish-born and North American-trained Ottomanist, on the emergence and growth of the Ottoman state. His starting point was the observation that long periods of coexistence of Christians and Muslims, such as in Anatolia and Iberia, 'shape[d] peoples and cultures on either side in profound ways, and not just in the sense of developing a sense of enmity or in the mechanical sense of "influences" as cultural commodities taken from one side to the other'. But, he adds, 'taking one's commingling with the "other" seriously in the historical reconstruction of heritages seems to demand too much of national historiographies'.[20] Kafadar underscores the inclusionary nature of the frontier society from which Osman's *beylik* (principality) in western Anatolian Bithynia emerged and the combinations and permutations of ethnic, religious, tribal and political groups that made it live. 'Inclusivism', a salient notion in Kafadar's approach, was characteristic of both Islam and Christianity and left its indelible mark on the early Ottoman society. Berating exaggerated 'Turkishness' in the foundation of the Ottoman empire, he promoted the view of consociation with the Byzantines. In fact, one of the unstated intents that informs his work is associating the origins of the Ottoman state with Europe through Rum, that is, Byzantium.

A brief digression seems appropriate here. In 1988, the then Turkish prime minister, and later president of Turkey, Turgut Özal published, in French, a book titled *Turkey in Europe*, which carried his name and dealt with the history of Turkey from distant times to the present. This unusual act took place at the time when Turkey was campaigning actively for admission into the European Community as a full member. In the perspective of our topic, what makes this apparently non-professional work worth mentioning is the official endorsement it lent to treating history as an active argument in current politics and, more specifically, the light it throws on the role Byzantium plays as a realm of engagement between Turkey and 'the West'.

---

[19] Bryer and Lowry 1986.   [20] Kafadar 1995: 19–20.

In the Fold of the 'Turkish-Islamic Synthesis'

Embarking on a humanistic reading of the Turkish History Thesis while upholding its original premises – namely to create an honourable 'European' image for the Turkish nation – Özal claimed that European civilisation had its origins in Turkey and in the Anatolian civilisations which developed there. Greek civilisation and Hellenic consciousness were derivative of this unique composite Anatolian civilisation, whose creators, transmitters and most direct heirs were the Turks.[21] The rise of the Ottoman empire is explained along the following lines. When the Muslim Turks, distinguished as they were by 'their talent for synthesis and their ecumenical character', conquered Anatolia, they re-established its 'unity and independence' and formed a new cultural synthesis – one that blended Central Asia, Islam and Greek rationalism into a mystical humanism peculiar to Anatolia. It was this 'profound and powerful cultural amalgam' that 'created the strongest multinational empire of the past by uniting the different communities or "nations" in tolerance'. Central to this part of the book is the assertion, supported by an analysis of the governmental institutions of the Byzantine and the Ottoman empires, that the political, social, economic and military structure and institutions of the Ottoman empire had been inherited from Byzantium: having accepted and embraced all the cultures of Anatolia by virtue of their 'synthesising, ecumenical approach', the Muslim Turks 'were able to blend with the Greeks and inherited from them the legacy of Byzantium'.[22] Özal made plain the actual intention behind such an unorthodox reading (from a Turkish point of view) when stating: 'Today Byzantine culture is considered unquestionably to be a part of Western civilisation. In so far as we have shown that there were numerous similarities between the Eastern Roman Empire and the Ottoman Empire, one could conclude that Ottoman culture is also a part of Western culture'.[23] The whole book aimed to inculcate the message that Turkish culture is European through and through, therefore Europe is morally obliged to include Turkey, the cradle of Western civilisation, as a full member of the European Community.

This appeal and Özal's reinterpretation of Turkish history along universally humanistic and secularist lines had a foreign address, whereas at home the regime eagerly cultivated a mix of Islamic conservatism with Ottomanist nostalgia, wrapped in the narrative of the Turkish-Islamic synthesis. Remarkably, with the exception of Taner Timur, all proponents of the Byzantine-Turkish continuity versus Turkish particularism referred

---

[21] Özal 1988: chapters 1–3.   [22] Özal 1988: 141–52, 167–8, 340–1.   [23] Özal 1988: 169.

296   In the Fold of the 'Turkish-Islamic Synthesis'

to above were affiliated with academic institutions outside Turkey and published primarily or solely in English.

Within Turkey, on the other hand, some historians brought Köprülü's argument to extremes by denying almost any Byzantine influence. Notable among them is the aforementioned Osman Turan, one of Köprülü's students and a propagator of the Turkish-Islamic synthesis who specialised in the Seljuks of Anatolia. Turan's argument ran as follows. In the sixth century, when Byzantium was at its strongest, it broke away from the old sources of civilisation and entered a phase of gradual decay. The Islamic expansion in the Mediterranean was an essential factor in the Byzantine decline: not only did the empire lose areas in the Near East and important Mediterranean islands, but the influx of Turkish and Slavic peoples also led to disruption in the relations between Europe and the Byzantine empire. As Anatolia became the scene of fighting between Arabs and Turks, on the one hand, and Byzantines, on the other, the decline was exacerbated particularly in Central Anatolia, where population density fell, trade shrank and cultural development stagnated. In general, Turan considered Eastern Anatolia to have been more developed than the rest of Asia Minor, except for the coastal areas, and the Syrians and Armenians at a higher level of civilisation than the Byzantines. Such (poorly corroborated) observations led Turan to conclude that since the seventh century Asia Minor had been in a state of economic and civilisational decline and that the central regions were almost deserted when the Turkish nomads moved there.[24] This made it easier for Turan to discard both the effects of Seljuk-Byzantine interaction and the accommodationist practices as 'methods of conquest'. Instead he foregrounded what has become a recurrent romanticised trope in Turkish historiography: the 'great religious tolerance' of the Seljuk and Ottoman Turks and their 'fair and efficient administration', contrasted with Byzantine and Western intolerance and oppressive rule. Armenians, Georgians and Christians in Anatolia, who 'hated the religious pressure and the assimilationist policy of Byzantium', found under the Seljuks' administration the religious freedom they sought. 'Thanks to the characteristically Turkish religious freedom and just administration', Turan maintained, 'the Seljuk state won the loyalty of the local people and grew stronger . . .. The Turks of Anatolia established a harmonious life among the different races and religions.'[25] The alleged harmony, however, did not involve even partial convergence between Byzantine and Turkish institutions in either state organisation or agricultural structure because the

---

[24] Turan 1980: 156–60; 1970: 257–8.   [25] Turan 1970: 236, 255.

In the Fold of the 'Turkish-Islamic Synthesis'   297

Seljuks had no need of it: whereas Köprülü assumed some Byzantine influence via the Saljuks state, Turan claimed that,

> The Arabs had achieved a synthesis of Islamic civilisation through their contacts with the Christians of the Near East; such a synthesis was not possible in the Seljuk territories, because by that time Islamic civilisation already existed in an advanced stage . . . . Therefore, Seljuk civilisation is an extension of Islamic Turkish culture to this region, rather than a synthesis with Anatolian elements.

Hence, when the sultans abolished private ownership of land by declaring Turkish Anatolia state property and left the peasants as large a portion of land as they could work, they were acting in accordance with ancient nomadic practice and the Islamic law of conquest. This state system under the control of military administrators, which was the basis of the Seljuk and the Ottoman agricultural and land policy, 'contributed to the establishment of a strong and harmonious social order, and prevented the formation of a landed aristocracy, on the one hand, and a servile peasantry, on the other. This social order lasted until the middle of the nineteenth century without basic change'.[26] Turan thus not only cancelled the possibility for convergence, which Timur argued for, but also revamped the Barkanian thesis about a 'degenerate' Byzantium and a rapacious feudal regime until the Ottoman order brought the liberating social revolution on its wings.

A far-fetched and idyllic theory, presenting an essentially non-violent and mutually beneficial process of Ottoman state formation and expansion, was proposed by the historian of the Ottoman empire Mustafa Akdağ (1913–72). He claimed the existence of a 'Marmara-basin economy', which emerged as an integrated unit at the time of Osman I (1280–99). The state Osman created gave political expression to that economic reality and expanded it along routes that linked the Marmara basin to other regional economies.[27] Even though the theory was soon demolished by İnalcık, in his later book, *Turkey's Economic and Social History*, Akdağ reiterated in all seriousness and even stronger terms the advantageous effect of and well-nigh voluntary submission to the Turkish conquest of Byzantium and the Balkans:

> It is clear from both Byzantine and Turkish sources that Turks and the people of Byzantium intermingled with no animosity of either religious or national nature, and procured their mutual needs from one another . . .

---

[26] Turan 1970: 254–5, 258.   [27] Akdağ 1949: 497–571 [1950: 319–418].

298 In the Fold of the 'Turkish-Islamic Synthesis'

Anatolian Christians, who suffered much poverty under Byzantine rule and on the eve of the Manzikert victory, benefited from the economic vitality and prosperity that came about when these lands passed to the Turks. Villages, towns, and cities became more populous and prosperous. Even if it were true that some Christians left their places and homes out of fear during Turkish conquests and fled here and there, this can be considered only for limited strata of the rich and for some of the ecclesiastical class.[28]

The Greek historians' contribution to the debate on the Byzantine-Seljuk-Ottoman continuum deserves to be considered briefly. As early as 1947 the aforementioned byzantinist George Arnakis castigated Köprülü's view that the Osmanlis were the very incarnation of everything Moslem and Turkish as a manifestation of modem Turkish 'ethnicism'. He emphasised that if the Ottomans proved capable of organising a 'model state', to advance and rapidly spread into Europe, this was 'largely due to the administrative experience and the civic traditions of the citizens of Brussa, Nicaea and Nicomedia'; that is, of the indigenous Greek population of Bithynia.[29] Arnakis, therefore, endorsed Gibbons's view about the non-Turkish origins of the Ottoman state. In his landmark work on medieval Anatolia, another above-discussed Greek-American medievalist, Speros Vryonis Jr, took up the task of surveying those demographic, social, religious and cultural changes in Asia Minor which, over four centuries, transformed what was a 'Hellenic Orthodox peninsula' into a predominantly Islamic one dominated by a Turcophone political elite. The results of his research, drawn from the rather scarce information on the demographic situation in Anatolia, contradicted Turan's sweeping assertion of continuous population decline and the steadily deteriorating state of trade and crafts prior to the Seljuk invasion.[30] In contrast to Turan, Vryonis described a picture of massive violence and deliberate destruction of the Byzantine institutional structures that accompanied the process of Islamisation of Anatolia. Whereas Turan saw the relationship between Byzantium and the Islamic world as a contest for supremacy between two different civilisations, leaving no doubt which was superior because of its vitality, Vryonis, who argued on behalf of the significance of Hellenism in Anatolia, deplored the fall of Byzantium in Asia Minor as 'something more than a negative historical event' that led to the subjugation and absorption of the viable Byzantine society there.[31] Elsewhere, Vryonis discussed the continuity between the Byzantine and the

---

[28] Akdağ 1974: 463, 473, cited in Kafadar 1995.   [29] Arnakis 1947: 246.
[30] Vryonis 1971: 25, 30, 33, 42.   [31] Vryonis 1971: 498–501. See also Strohmeirer 1984: 205–12.

In the Fold of the 'Turkish-Islamic Synthesis' 299

Ottoman society which, according to him, did not operate on the level of formal Ottoman institutions and culture, as they were Islamic, but on the lower institutional and popular level of culture. Following the conquest, he argued, Ottoman society adapted itself socially and administratively to the conquered culture. The Turkish society of the time, 'although Muslim in its formal expression ... was strongly Byzantine in its folk culture [and] Byzantine influence was particularly strong in agricultural and village life, but also in the cities with their craft and commercial traditions'.[32]

It has been suggested that the clash of interpretations and, in general, the difficulties ottomanists and byzantinists have experienced in relating to one another 'stem less from the differences in source bases than from the fact that the relevant fields have been "adopted" by Turkish and Greek nationalist historiography respectively . . .. If the history of the Byzantine Empire was the preserve of the Greeks, that of the Ottoman Empire was to a large extent left to the Turks'.[33] Attempts to straddle and reconcile the two traditions, on the other hand, have not necessarily led to sound propositions. In our day, the Greek-Canadian turkologist Dimitris Kitsikis (b.1935), a zealous propagator of the notion of 'Hellenoturkism' as both an ideology and a phenomenon of culture, aspires to trump the two warring positions. Digging for the historical foundations of his project, he argues that the Ottoman empire was in reality a 'Turkish-Greek Empire', the result of 'the co-habitation and interdependence, since the eleventh century A.D., of the Greek and Turkish peoples and cultures'. In his reading, the conflict between 'the two worlds' resulted not in the disappearance of one of them but a metamorphosis of Byzantium into a new Turkish polity, on the basis of which a neo-Byzantine Turkish-Greek confederation comprising Greece, Turkey and Cyprus should be built.[34]

One might disregard such pronouncements as illustrative of bald-faced manipulation of history on behalf of a political agenda. The fact remains, though, that ninety years after the appearance of Köprülü's treatise there is still no consensus in historiography on the extent to which the Turkish-Islamic heritage or the Byzantine model was decisive in moulding the Ottoman state. Relative accord among Turkish scholars exists only on the (asymmetric) presence of three main strands of tradition: the Turkish-Central Asian, the Islamic and the Byzantine traditions transmitted mostly through the Seljuks.[35] But while the former two are part of the national history of the Turks, classical Greek, Roman or Byzantine history is not,

[32] Vryonis 1969–70: 307.   [33] Faroqhi 2004: 7.   [34] Kitsikis 1996.   [35] Strohmeirer 1984: 217.

300 In the Fold of the 'Turkish-Islamic Synthesis'

although major sites of these three civilisations are located in Anatolia and Thrace. As Suraya Faroqhi observes, those writers on history, often from outside the academic community, who have emphasised continuities between the history of antiquity, Byzantium and the Ottoman period remain a small minority. For the most part,

> such continuities, mostly on the level of popular culture, have attracted the interest of journalists and literary figures opposed, in one way or another, to the notion of a Turkish-Islamic synthesis without the slightest leavening of cosmopolitan traits. Given the formidable barriers between academic and non-academic intellectuals in present-day Turkey, such currents have had almost no impact upon established Ottoman historiography.[36]

Present-day Turkish byzantinists indeed show reluctance to resume the debate. When writing on the present and future of Byzantine studies in Turkey, Melek Delilbaşı (b.1947), one of the few professional Turkish historians of Byzantium, elides the issue and emphasises instead the importance of the Byzantine sources for Turkish history (starting with 'the Huns in the fourth century, later the Avars, Sabirs, Bulgars, Patzinaks, Seljuks and finally the Ottomans') and of the late-Byzantine historians for the early years of the Ottoman state and its later phenomenal expansion in the Balkans. 'It is almost imperative for Turkish historians', she pleads, 'to study Byzantine history and culture which comprise a significant part of a thousand year evolutionary process in Anatolia; Turks and Byzantines shared the same lands, ruled over the same peoples and mutually influenced each other over the centuries.'[37] In her own work, on the other hand, Delilbaşı has focussed on the demographic and social changes in the Balkans during the transition from Byzantine to Ottoman rule on the premise that 'undoubtedly, guiding for the Byzantine scholars are the works of famous Ottoman historians such as Barkan and İnalcık'.[38]

High school textbooks offer a shortcut to the official historical narrative peddled among the broader public. The almost eternal presence of the Turks in Anatolia (at least from the fourth century), a felicitous Seljuk invasion in the eleventh century and subsequent thriving of the region under their rule, an overwhelmingly negative view of Byzantium as incompetent, unable to ensure the wellbeing of its subjects, plagued by fights for the throne and dangerously open to the involvement of women in the affairs of the state – such are some of the themes undergirding the message that the Byzantine empire did not have a legitimate right to rule, hence the

[36] Faroqhi 1992: 228–9.   [37] Delilbaşı 2005: 69–70.   [38] Delilbaşı 2013: 13.

In the Fold of the 'Turkish-Islamic Synthesis'

Muslim Turks' expansion into former Byzantine territories was historically justified and inevitable.[39] The Byzantines are accordingly purged from the medieval history of Anatolia, which thus emerges as entirely Turkish. As Koray Durak recaps, 'A negative image of Byzantium is produced and disseminated in the textbooks through mechanisms of exclusion, exaggeration, and distortion, all of which aim at delegitimising the Byzantine phase of Anatolian history and replacing it with a Turco-Islamic one.'[40] This has proceeded against the background of escalating valorisation of the Ottoman past and a veritable 1453 industry, including the opening of a 1453 museum, which have become hallmarks of the President Tayyip Erdoğan regime.

Although for reasons explained at the start of this book we do not delve here into art-historical or architectural interpretations of Byzantine artefacts, the attitude towards 'cultural heritage' in contemporary Turkey deserves attention, if only because the material remains of Byzantine civilisation in this country exceed Byzantine remains in the rest of the world and are no fewer than those of the Ottomans. For some Turkish art historians, this fact by itself warrants the conclusion that they 'form one of the major parts of the country's cultural heritage'.[41] But if by 'cultural heritage' one means more than the sheer quantity of artefacts on an 'inherited' territory, namely an engagement with their instrumental role in cultural identity building, the observation does not bespeak reality. The mainstream Turkish historiography, which after World War II has been progressively redefining the country's heritage in terms of Turkishness and Islam, is effectively preventing the Byzantine heritage from becoming part of the Turks' cultural self-understanding. Cultural heritage in Turkey, historian Edhem Eldem has forcefully argued, is 'an eminently political matter' – there are few countries, he contends, 'where the issue of cultural heritage has been as constantly and systematically influenced by political concerns as in Turkey' – and explains it with the 'discrepancy between the state's cultural identity, on the one hand, and the "foreign" nature of cultural heritage, on the other'.[42] Referring to the same cleavage, archaeologist Çiğdem Atakuman foregrounds its implications:

> By far the most complex problem is posed by the fact that any presentation of historical continuity and the unity of the Turkish nation based on the heritage found within the territories of the Turkish state is in conflict with the state's ethno-religious postulates framed within Turkish-Islamic

[39] Durak 2014: 259–62.   [40] Durak 2014: 245, 249.   [41] Akyürek 2010: 208–9.
[42] Eldem 2015: 67.

302   In the Fold of the 'Turkish-Islamic Synthesis'

> Synthesis. On the one hand, a land replete with artefacts of thousands of years covering multiplicity of cultural identities; on the other, an official ideology that denies the full inclusion of an important portion of these artefacts and cultural identities they represent in the authorized narratives of Turkishness. A major conflict has been constructed while rather pragmatic attempts have been made to resolve this situation: whereas the Anatolian heritage has been served to the international audience as an important contributor to European civilisation in the hopes of being part of Europe, an innate resistance to western cultural values has been carefully protected in the authorized narratives.[43]

Accordingly, the Turkish state has limited the function of cultural heritage to a matter of prestige building, international diplomacy and touristic display, deliberately removed from the construction of national and universal identities. Under the Islamicist authoritarian regime of Tayyip Erdoğan, cultural policies are demonstrating diminishing concern with disguising the systematic campaign of re-Ottomanisation of Byzantine heritage within claims about diversity and tolerance, especially in Istanbul. A recent collection of articles, seeking to illustrate Turkey's present-day relationship with its Byzantine heritage and the way its material remains are being treated, bears witness to the progressive extinction of Byzantine artefacts from the face of Istanbul, the dilapidated condition or often unprofessional 'restoration' of Byzantine remains and the resultant erasure of the Byzantine from the memory of the modern city. Major palaces and churches, including Hagia Sophia and the Chora Church, declared museums by the Kemalist regime, are being refurbished as Ottoman buildings and mosques. On the level of representation – in education, literature and popular culture, the editors observe – the image of Byzantium emerges as strikingly homogeneous: 'Byzantium is the enemy to be defeated, the woman to be captured; Constantinople is a fortification to be conquered.'[44]

In a longer historical perspective this does not stand out as a Turkish speciality: until the middle of the twentieth century the surviving Roman, Frankish, Venetian and Ottoman buildings in Greece were not considered to be monuments; instead they were generally regarded with indifference or hostility, and a number of buildings constructed by the Venetians in Crete had already been demolished when Greece began to try to assert its European orientation after the end of the Colonels' dictatorship.[45] In the other Balkan countries too, supposedly 'non-national', especially Ottoman

[43] Atakuman 2012: 21–2.   [44] Durak and Vasilakeris 2013: 53.   [45] Gratziou 2008: 209–22.

In the Fold of the 'Turkish-Islamic Synthesis'

remains were subjected to massive destruction. By the same token, instead of a symbol of the Turks' innate talent for cultural synthesis and heed for a multi-cultural heritage, as Özal wanted to advertise it, Istanbul is increasingly becoming a symbol of the Muslim Turks' conquest of the Christian Byzantines.

All in all, mainstream Balkan historiographies after World War II met with little pressure to relinquish their robustly national vantage point in viewing (relations with) Byzantium and its legacy. The emphasis in this body of literature, as far as the representation of Byzantium is concerned, was not so much on the discovery of something as yet unknown in scholarship as on the reinterpretation of what was already known. Allowing for the peculiarity of the Greek case, in all these historiographies a shift of perspective took place from what Byzantium meant for these societies to what these societies meant for Byzantium and its heritage. The major civilisational contribution devolved on Byzantium appeared to be that of having galvanised the proper creative forces of the medieval Balkan nationalities, stirring them to forge cultural values of their own, which they then transmitted to other peoples. Hence the prominence in the scholarly vocabulary of the time of notions like mutual influences, dialogue and symbiosis, but also adaptation, transformation and assimilation of political and cultural transfers. In this respect, the work of G. Ostrogorski was as path-breaking for the Serbs as Duychev's was for the Bulgarians and İnalcık's for the Turks. Other leading medievalists and byzantinists since the 1970s – D. Angelov, V. Gyuzelev, I. Bozhilov in Bulgaria, B. Ferjančić, L. Maksimović and a large group of art historians in Yugoslavia, V. Georgescu, A. Pippidi and N. Ş. Tanaşoca in Romania, Timur and Kafadar in Turkey – devoted the best part of their work to unravelling the originality and creativity involved in the respective 'national' assimilation of the Byzantine paragon. Symptomatic for the period since the 1970s has been the recurrent use of the term 'civilisation' with a national attribution – Bulgarian, Serbian, Romanian and so on – that tacitly merges national and imperial imagination and usually goes hand in hand with assertions of doggedly pursued independence from Byzantium and resistance to Byzantine 'imperialism'. The seminal concept of a 'Byzantine Commonwealth' as devised by Dimitri Obolensky has thus been doubly, even if rarely openly, challenged. First, the national historiographies under study as one rebuffed the notion of mimesis underlying Obolensky's symbolic geography. Second, the idea of a Byzantium not merely exerting multifarious and strong influences but having established commonwealth in the sense of a 'community of states and nations . . . all of which in varying degrees owed allegiance to the Byzantine Church and empire' was not one

304 In the Fold of the 'Turkish-Islamic Synthesis'

that these historiographies espoused.[46] With certain nuances, all of them presented their national cultures and institutional arrangements as drawing upon or bridging 'two worlds' – the Eastern and the Western – yet always remaining true to the essence of their indigenous traditions, so that the outcome, invariably, was a unique Greek, Bulgarian, Serbian, Romanian or Turkish 'civilisation'. Although relative to other historiographic branches engagement with Byzantine history produced fewer (or at least less extravagant and perilous) exaggerations and distortions, as a rule byzantinists in this period remained pliant to the teleology and key tropes of the nationalist versions of history. Those who dared to challenge the historiographic mainstream with studies debunking ethnocentric, anachronistic or politicised approaches to Byzantium remained a small minority, often operating outside their national academic milieu.

[46] Obolensky 1971: 203.

Epilogue and Conclusion

As in the early Renaissance period, when political concerns stimulated interest in the Byzantine world in the first place, write the editors of *The Oxford Handbook of Byzantine Studies* (2008), 'recent and current political and cultural issues in South-East Europe have raised the consciousness of many with regard to the Byzantine past and its contribution to the shaping of the modern world in the Balkan and East Mediterranean region'.[1] With the changes unleashed by the fall of the Berlin Wall and as Cyprus, Romania and Bulgaria entered the political body of the European Union, concepts of 'Europe' have expanded symbolically and materially to include lands with a Byzantine heritage. Byzantium has come to be increasingly seen as a terrain on which to construct a common 'European history'. 'As Europeans seek to define what our continent stands for', the Greek prime minister stated in 2008, 'the study of Byzantium is becoming of paramount importance.'[2]

The rise of interest in Byzantium and its public display during the last few decades has been conspicuous, particularly in countries historically less related to the empire. Starting in 1997, one metropolitan city after another staged blockbuster exhibitions presenting Byzantium as a major, even if somewhat exotic and lavish, 'world civilisation'. Its 'multicultural' profile has become a strong selling point, invariably emphasised at the openings of conferences and exhibitions, at the same time as integrationist post-1989 trends profess to erase East–West divides and peddle awareness of shared cultural roots. A significant shift of emphasis has been taking place away from older narratives of Byzantium, which presented it as an eastern 'Other' in contrast to the Latin West or as Christian in contrast to Islam. Art and architectural historians were among the first to undertake critical re-examination of the essentially orientalist strategies employed to dissociate Byzantine art and architecture from the Western medieval analogues.

---

[1] Jeffreys, Haldon and Cormack 2008: 7.   [2] Cormack and Vassilaki 2008: 11.

306   Epilogue and Conclusion

Seasoned byzantinists pleaded for the integration of Byzantium into general European history, such as Évelyne Patlagean (1932–2008), who insisted that without an understanding of Byzantium there was no understanding of the Middle Ages in the West and vice versa, and that no global picture of the Middle Ages was therefore possible; or Averil Cameron (b.1940), who adds to this argument the impulses coming from the 'new national states attempting to claim their identity by laying claim to Byzantium'.[3] To borrow Gilbert Dagron's memorable phrasing, Byzantium has come to epitomise, in theory at least, 'another way of being and having been European'.[4]

Parallel to such at heart (geo)politically induced changes of perspective, important epistemological shifts are also taking place. Orientation towards cultural history at the expense of the previously prevailing political accounts has become a hallmark of the 'new' Byzantine studies. Subjects already ploughed by medievalists, such as daily life, law and order, rebellion, poverty, state and the economy, art and text or reception, are beginning to exert a pull on byzantinists too. Informed by post-modernist and post-structuralist theory and professing cross-disciplinary methods and comparative thinking, a new generation of byzantinists has been attracted by aspects of Byzantine society that now promise to appeal to rather than repel a large audience, such as non-standard gender behaviours and practices, sexuality, luxury, eunuchs and women in power. In this context, moving from a political narrative to social and cultural history appears less significant than the urge to go beyond the traditional canon of historical subjects by asking new questions of old material and deploying inventive ways to provide answers.

Albeit with some delay, critical (especially post-colonial) theory has spurred reappraisals of the field of Byzantine studies geared towards unmasking its darker undercurrents. The stage was set by Professor of Late Antique and Byzantine History at King's College (London) Averil Cameron's inaugural lecture in 1990, where she undertook to unshroud the long-standing tendency of seeing 'Byzantine studies as a species of orientalism' and the attending 'set of insidious assumptions and attitudes which ... has had a major share in forming attitudes towards Byzantium'.[5] In subsequent writings she discusses how the problematic fit of Byzantium into traditional narratives has led to the 'absence of Byzantium' from contemporary European political and cultural discourse.[6] Dimitar Angelov (b.1972), a Bulgarian-American byzantinist

---

[3] Patlagean 2005: 721–32; 2007; Cameron 2006: 163–78.   [4] Dagron 2007: 158.
[5] Cameron 1992: 9.   [6] Cameron 2008: 4–59.

Epilogue and Conclusion

and the grandson of his namesake, the doyen of the post-war Bulgarian byzantinistics, took up the same thread from the opposite end. He turned his hand to demystifying 'Byzantinism', meaning in this case the stereotypical views of Byzantium and their orientalist undertones, 'as a crippling historical legacy in Europe's backyard, the Balkans', which in the post-communist period appeared in new clothes.[7] In point of fact, notable contributions to this 'genre' were made earlier by scholars coming from another corner of 'Europe's backyard'. Russian byzantinist Alexander Kazhdan and his Ukrainian colleague Ihor Ševčenko believed that, in the words of Kazhdan, 'Byzantium has left us a unique experience of European totalitarianism ... a thousand-year-long experiment in totalitarian practice', which, although not genetically inherited by Russia, was used as a model for its own political ends.[8]

A different strand of critique, one debunking the lack of awareness of the ideologies and historic pressures that created the discipline's conceptual toolkit byzantinists still use, has been levelled, as we have seen, by Anthony Kaldellis. Nationalism and Western-centrism, he asserts, have distorted historical understanding, whereby Byzantium has turned into 'a field colonised by polemical western and nationalist modern Greek claims'.[9] 'The understanding of Byzantium suffers from decades of *idées reçues*', A. Cameron concurs. She bemoans the conspicuous absence of Byzantine history in mainstream narratives of European medieval history and argues against its neglect or 'in-betweenness' in general historiography due to the field's 'continuing association with the competing claims of negativity and exoticism'. She calls for greater theorisation in a discipline that often lags behind developments in related fields, for inserting Byzantine studies into global and transnational history, for comparing the Byzantine empire with other premodern empires and for thinking about Byzantine Christianity from the point of view of the sociology or anthropology of religion.[10]

While the above scholars argue against Byzantine exceptionalism, others see the 'value' of the discipline precisely in laying bare Byzantine 'incomparability' – how different and indeed incompatible the western European and Byzantine political, social and cultural systems were. Byzantium, American byzantinist Warren Treadgold (b.1949) insists, 'was not just another medieval European country, like England or France, but a world of its own'.[11] He looks down at the 'comparative' approach as a fad

[7] Angelov 2003. [8] Kazhdan 2003: 35; Ševčenko 1995: 91. [9] Kaldellis 2014: 208.
[10] Cameron 2014. [11] Treadgold 2010: 16.

308 Epilogue and Conclusion

inapplicable to 'Byzantine uniqueness' and an act of desperation on the part of byzantinists to win the favour of western medievalists.

> Yet few Western medievalists welcome comparisons that, except for basic and obvious similarities, show how much Byzantium differed from the medieval West – especially when they show that Byzantium was more sophisticated than the medieval West. Byzantine exceptionalism ought to make Byzantium seem more interesting and important, not least for understanding how today's Russians and other Eastern Europeans differ from Americans and Western Europeans. Byzantinists, however, seem not to have made that point effectively.[12]

The suggestion that knowledge of Byzantium holds the key to understanding the 'difference' of the eastern Europeans should be read in the light of Treadgold's earlier contentious assertions that 'the general Byzantine disapproval of politics' and Byzantine legacy generally bears at least part of the blame for these people's defective democratic institutions, delayed growth of capitalism and distrust of business people and 'Westerners'.[13]

As these necessarily selected and partial snapshots indicate, there is good reason to argue, together with John Haldon, that in the area of Byzantine studies there are currently some fascinating discussions regarding how byzantinists define their field, where it stands in relation to other historical studies, how they should define their subject matter ('Byzantine' or 'medieval Roman' and so forth) and what it means to describe oneself as a byzantinist.[14] Rehabilitating Byzantium has certainly been *en vogue* during the last twenty-odd years. This usually plays out in the acknowledgement of its complexity, heterogeneity and pluralism, which resonate with post-modern sensitivities. In other respects, the results are less unequivocal. As Paul Stephenson notes, if the geographical frontiers of Europe's past have shifted definitively to the east, the conceptual frontiers have not kept pace.[15] 'Facile orientalisation and fundamental distortion of Byzantium', Greek historian Dimitris Krallis (b.1972) complains, are particularly apparent in works of historians operating outside Byzantine studies, who sidestep the scholarship produced in the field. But he also admits that scholars in other fields 'will be hard pressed to name a single study from the kaleidoscopic array of sub-disciplines that constitute Byzantine studies, that contributes in ground-breaking fashion to theoretical debates on identity, state-formation, and the economy while convincingly situating Byzantium at the very centre of global intellectual trends'.

---

[12] Treadgold 2010: 19.   [13] Treadgold 1998: 88.   [14] Haldon 2016: 5.   [15] Stephenson 2010: 508.

Epilogue and Conclusion   309

A corrective is urgent, he implores, which should be consigned primarily to byzantinists.[16]

As it happens, 'sidestepping' a large corpus of scholarship is not uncommon within the proper field of Byzantine studies. Western handbooks and compendiums of Byzantium, a flourishing genre of late, often include surveys of the historiography in the field; however, they rarely take into account what those in the 'successor states' had or have to say.[17] The language barrier is a predictable but perhaps less decisive explanation. More substantial appears to be the tacit assumption that the expertise of these scholars (save perhaps the Greek) lies not in Byzantium proper, but in their medieval national histories, so whatever contribution they might be able to make will necessarily draw on the particular 'national' material or perspective they can bring to bear. (The omission of Russian scholarship from such state-of-the-art surveys is also symptomatic.) The legitimacy of the national point of view thus appears secured from all sides.

Turning back to southeastern Europe, the political caesura of 1989 entailed less, or at least less fast, change in the national-historiographic mainstreams than one would have expected, especially as regards medieval history-writing and treatments of Byzantium in the grand national narratives. Many of the unstated assumptions of the pre-existent historiographical traditions continue to hold sway over national imaginations. For all that, byzantinists in the region have exerted themselves to diversify their subject matter by including previously unstudied themes – in itself an improvement in that it dissipates the simplistic notion of a monolithic Byzantium. Admittedly, discussing these new themes and the current state of Byzantine studies in the five countries falls outside the focus of the present survey. In what follows, only those stronger new tendencies in the national historiographies which have impacted the thinking about Byzantium will be broached.

In Greece, these tendencies link with a more consistent critical engagement with the construction of national ideology, identity and representations – a current that came about as a reaction to the nationalist upsurge that swept Greek society from the beginning of the 1990s, triggered by the Macedonian issue and Greek-Turkish strife. Informed by advancements in nationalism studies, cultural history and social anthropology, the main thrust came from historians of modern Greece and, soon after, archaeologists. A growing cohort

---

[16] Krallis 2014: 183–99.
[17] A recent example is the otherwise comprehensive survey of Morrisson 2010: 83–104.

310 Epilogue and Conclusion

of scholars, among them the late Elli Skopetea, I. Koubourlis, A. Liakos, C. Koulouri, D. Stamatopoulos and D. Plantzos, to name only a few among the more prolific writers, has ventured into deconstructing Hellenism's partial story. They have demonstrated the fluidity and discursivity of such constructs and problematised the relationship between the present and the past, the Byzantine past included, placing a special emphasis on how modern Greek historical consciousness was shaped regarding Hellenism. Many Greek historians today would contest the concept of 'a continuity of Greek identity': in the words of Peter Mackridge, a sense of realism makes them 'recognise the discontinuities of their cultural history and revel in the rich variety of their heritages, with all its tensions and contradictions, rather than subjecting them to a Procrustean homogeneity'.[18] Although Greek byzantinists on the whole have recoiled from these discussions, they are not impervious to the implications of such critical strands for their study field. To date there is a tendency, in Greek academic writings at least, to bring out Byzantium's complexity and heterogeneity. Sometimes didactically promoted as a model for the present, this representation also abets the desire to write Byzantium into the narrative of Europe and partake in lending the historical underpinnings of the 'European project'. At the same time, a cursory look at the history textbooks currently in use in Greece bears witness to the remarkable stability of the 'Helleno-Christian' formula, bespeaking the traditional Greek understanding of the Eastern Roman empire, which continues to receive endorsement from high academic venues.[19] There is indeed no easy way out of the aporia created by having turned the problem of Byzantine identity into a modern problem for Greek identity. By the same token, and despite the subversive gestures coming from the community of professional historians, the public use of history and the historical culture keep sustaining the Greek historical narrative elaborated over the past two centuries, while the notion of Hellenism continues to function as a powerful ideology for the Greeks. The heavy impact of the historiographic inheritance about Byzantium seems to be deepening the gap between up-to-date scholarship and popular perception.

The Bulgarian grand narrative survived the 1989 watershed unscathed; however, it lost its monopolistic position. At the present time, one witnesses the parallel existence of two asymmetric trends. A minority one, made up of professional byzantinists and art historians, has brought to

[18] Mackridge 2012: 37, 39.
[19] In a recent interview, Hélène Ahrweiler, for example, reiterated that 'Byzantium is the Greek language and Orthodoxy, that is, the two basic components of Greekness' (Burke 2014: 22). See also Saradi 2014: 134–60.

Epilogue and Conclusion 311

completion the radical revision of the purported antinomy between Byzantium and the medieval Bulgarian state. In some recent studies the Bulgarian medieval state of Simeon has been described as 'a state of entirely *"Byzantine"* type', a '*"Byzance à côté de Byzance"*', an '*"Imperium extra Imperium"*' not only in structure, institutions, symbolism and practices but also in terms of art, literature and law. Confronting a long line of medievalists, from V. Zlatarski to I. Bozhilov, such redefinition implicitly cancels the possibility of an ethnic or national character of the Bulgarian medieval state and the existence of a premeditated policy of ethnic unification by the Bulgarian rulers. Shorn of the telos of the Bulgarian nation, medieval Bulgaria is being granted imperial dignity unabashedly replicating the Byzantine paragon.[20] The most innovative research, however, has taken place not in history but in medieval philosophy, philology and art history, which have effectively integrated their subject matter into a broad imperial context. The national-historiographic mainstream, on the other hand, continues to uphold an essentially agonistic view of Byzantium's role in Bulgarian history, to insist on the 'ethnic and political unification of the Bulgarians' as the *spiritus movens* of this history and to emphasise the Bulgarian transformative and creative genius in assimilating Byzantine models. As an adept in Byzantine philosophy described it at an annual ceremony on the occasion of the nationally celebrated Day of the Slavic Script and Culture (24 May),

> Only from the point of view of some anachronistic ideology could the tenacious and conscious gravitation of medieval Bulgaria towards the sphere of byzantinism be seen, in an inferiority-ridden vein, as 'epigonic'. Such is the case with our historiography, which struggles in every way to conceal this 'deficiency' by pushing to the fore the most incredible 'peculiarities' of the Bulgarian.[21]

Such critiques link up with broader critical undercurrents in the regional historiographies. A bold censorious stance on the current state of Byzantine research, not only in Serbia, has been advanced by the aforementioned Serbian byzantinist Vlada Stanković. More poignantly than Averil Cameron, he has taken issue with what he sees as 'anti-innovative tendencies in the field of Byzantine studies', leading to their lagging behind western European medieval and, especially, late-antiquity studies.[22] Stanković is particularly chiding about the way 'the foggy notion of Byzantine Commonwealth' has been put to use. He finds that examples

---

[20] See, for example, Biliarsky 2002: 25–40; 2007: 346. In a different key, Vachkova 2005.
[21] Kapriev 1999.   [22] Stanković 2016–17: 400–1.

312   Epilogue and Conclusion

of misunderstanding the principle of the community of different 'nations',
which abound in the 'national' scholarships of the peripheral regions of
Obolensky's Byzantine commonwealth, tip the scale towards the down-
sides of Obolensky's idea, often seen as an opportunity for a 'national
history' to be included in or connected with Byzantine culture and civilisation. While the local national history narratives have been hindering the
development of the field,

> the superficially understood idea of cultural unity under the cover of the idea
> of commonwealth could do even more damage by subtly bringing the late
> nineteenth-early twentieth century concepts of intellectual colonialism back
> to the scholarly fore ... the emphasis is laid on the cultural aspect of the
> commonwealth idea, which is equated with the Orthodox faith and in that
> sense a priori distinguished from the Western medieval, overwhelmingly
> Catholic European world, an implicit but clear distinction.[23]

Notably, this re-reading 'from the periphery' of the concept of commonwealth,
which heightens its inherent ambiguities, confronts more lenient ones in recent
Western historiography, unfurling mainly in two directions. Some have tried
to emend the concept by arguing that the pull exerted by the Byzantine 'force
field' applied not only to the empire's neighbours but to all medieval kingdoms
in Europe, as they sought to enhance their legitimacy through a link with the
last remnant of the Roman empire – a view that tries to de-provincialise the
eastern European 'commonwealth' as a Byzantinophile fringe and re-envision
the place of Byzantium in the cultural *Weltanschauung* of Europe.[24] The
majority of recent studies, on the other hand, seem to suggest that truly
effective were not any deliberate Byzantine initiatives in the vein of imperialism, tutelage or proselytism, but Byzantium's soft power ('seldom since
matched'), the eager emulation of the 'Byzantine Ideal' as the epitome of the
legacy of Rome and the role of low culture in passing on Byzantine culture to
the 'commonwealth'.[25] Put in the words of Herbert Hunger years ago, 'In some
amazing way, the influence of the Byzantine culture on the Bulgarian and
Serbian states, founded on Byzantine territories, was intensified precisely
during those periods, when they were involved in the fiercest military battles
and political clashes with Byzantium.'[26]

As a way out of what he sees as an ongoing process of marginalisation of
Byzantine studies, Stanković advocates 'a more pronounced inclusion of

---

[23] Stanković 2016–17: 402.   [24] Raffensperger 2012.
[25] Shepard 2006a: 15–55; Ivanov 2014: 207–15; Raffensperger 2012: 3–4, 10–12. For a more favourable
view, see Shepard 2006b: 3–52.
[26] Hunger 1958: 443–4.

Epilogue and Conclusion 313

Byzantine history into the field of Medieval studies, and studies of pre-modern world in general', broadening its temporal and spatial boundaries and disregarding modern national borders when analysing pre-modern, supranational complex societies.[27] Tallying with such prepositions is the work of another Serbian byzantinist, Radivoj Radić (b.1954), who tries to reconceive Byzantium away from its vilified image as oriental, despotic and petrified through uncovering 'the other face of Byzantium', epitomised by the social, everyday and emotional world of *homo Byzantinus*;[28] or editions, such as *Byzantium in (Serbian) Literature and Culture from the Middle to Twenty First Centuries*, which highlight the variety of (sometimes whimsical) avatars and representations of 'the Byzantine' in medieval, modern and post-modern European and Serbian literary culture.[29] And while concentration of work on the later Byzantine period, which was originally triggered by research on relations with Byzantium in this period, persists, it has now largely broken away from this thematic restriction.

For many Romanian historians, 1989 opened the possibility of asserting Romania's intrinsic 'Central Europeanness' and disowning its embedment in the (at the time) loudly decried war-ridden Balkans. Writing in 2010, Dan Ioan Mureşan (b.1974), a French-based medievalist, spoke of a historical amnesia developing in contemporary Romanian historiography that perceives Byzantium as an exotic foreign form, which had mentally and religiously colonised the Romanian people, who actually belonged to the Central European structures. Byzantium, in this vision, appears as the most pernicious factor in the 'orientalisation' of the Romanians and the ultimate cause of their backwardness, 'suddenly forgetting that originally Europe was nothing more than the province around Byzantium'. Mureşan felt obliged to remind the communicators of such views that in the fourteenth century Byzantium was no longer the power that could have sustained such 'protocolonialism' and that 'the massive takeover of the Byzantine influence at that moment was therefore a free and unforced decision by the Romanian side'. Referring to the work of E. Patlagean, whose student he was, he made the prediction that in a unified Europe 'the dominant scientific paradigm will soon take as its starting point for Europe not the moment of Charlemagne, but the era of Constantine the Great and his successors'.[30] A 'nationally engaged' historian, Ioan-Aurel Pop (b.1955) embellished this view with the adage *ex Oriente lux* and the reminder to Western historians that without systematic study of the model of

---

[27] Stanković 2016–17: 403–4.   [28] See, among others, Radic 2002; 2006; 2014.
[29] Bošković 2013.   [30] Ionescu and Iosipescu 2010: 78–9.

314   Epilogue and Conclusion

civilisation that 'Byzantium after Byzantium' represents – 'a model that once expressed the apogee of the European world as a whole' – 'the future of the continent has no meaning and its present life cannot be understood'.[31] Others, however, like the historian and political scientist Daniel Barbu (b.1957), have used Byzantium as a point of departure for an assault on Romania's post-communist present. Contrary to what Iorga intimated, Romanians, Barbu argues, were not at all 'born as post-Byzantine'. All the imports from Byzantium were no more than the expression of a horizon of expectations, maintaining a normative political ideal at variance with the actual social practices – 'forms without substance' – thus generating a latent conflict between the formal 'Byzantium after Byzantium' and the fundamental 'non-Byzantium' or 'Byzantium against Byzantium' (as the title of his book ran). The Romanians took over the political theology and cultural equipment of the Byzantines but remained alien to their underlying meaning and the Byzantine self-understanding connected to it.[32] In effect, Barbu's statement should be read as a subtext to Romania's faulty post-communist transition, reminiscent of P. Mutafchiev's interwar critique of the defective Bulgaria's 'westernisation' as historically foreshadowed by its reckless 'byzantinisation'.

In Turkey, the new developments unleashed by the political turnabouts of the 1990s came to bear with considerable delay on the status of Byzantine studies and the perception of Byzantium. In 1998 an attempt at organising in Istanbul an international event related to Byzantium was cancelled at the last minute 'because of prevailing prejudices against Byzantium, traditionally considered a taboo subject in Turkish society and academia'.[33] It was only in 2001 that a National Committee of 'Byzantine/East Roman Studies' was founded within the Turkish Historical Society, which became the thirty-seventh member of the International Association of Byzantine Studies. In 2015, the first (privately funded) research centre dedicated to Byzantine studies, named The Koç University-Stavros Niarchos Foundation Centre for Late Antique and Byzantine Studies (GABAM), was instituted. Focussing on Byzantine art history and archaeology, it aspires to promote Byzantine civilisation as 'a significant part of Turkey's cultural heritage', knowledge of which 'is important for understanding the Medieval Anatolia, and particularly for understanding the civilisations of the Seljuk, Turkish Principalities and Ottoman periods'.[34] The same year,

---

[31] Ionescu and Iosipescu 2010: 112–13.   [32] Barbu 2001 [1st ed. 1999].

[33] www.boun.edu.tr/en-US/Content/Announcements/Announcements?LoadModule=News&NewsID=1319&Filter=true. See also Necipoğlu 2013: 72–7.

[34] https://gabam.ku.edu.tr/en/about-us/about-gabam.

Epilogue and Conclusion 315

a Byzantine Studies Research Centre was set up at Boğaziçi University – the first Turkish institution attached to a state university that is dedicated to academic research on Byzantine civilisation. On its website modern Turkey is described as 'a geographical, historical, and cultural inheritor of Byzantium' and Byzantium, remarkably, as 'an entity continuously enhancing its traditions with innovative solutions, [which] presented political, religious, and cultural models for other medieval cultures and continues to be a paragon for contemporary multicultural societies faced with the conflict between tradition and modernity'.[35] Published work stemming from the Centre has so far been focussed on Byzantine-Ottoman-Italian relations, trade between Byzantium and the Islamic world and representations of the empire in history education. With these two centres and around a dozen universities that have introduced Byzantine history courses in the last few years, the future of Byzantine studies in Turkey looks brighter. Yet, as Nevra Necipoğlu recently bewailed, against all geographical and historical logic Byzantium continues to be rejected as part of Turkish history and cultural heritage. 'An awareness that Byzantine history and culture cannot be ignored in order for us to understand our own past properly is only just emerging and only in certain circles . . .. A mentality that perceives academic activities in this field as attempts to "revive" Byzantium, although not as widespread as before, still exists in Turkey.'[36]

*

At the end of this journey, there should be little doubt left that in the Balkan historiographic traditions Byzantium is not just a polysemic term laden with diverse connotations, but a heavily loaded subject. The successive waves of exaltation and rejection, identification with and disavowal of Byzantium that the Balkan successors to the empire experienced are due to the fact that Byzantium has always functioned as an agglomerate of ideologically harnessed understandings and a point of reference structuring the national grand narratives. In all these countries, articulations of Byzantium have been tied to articulations of nationhood, authenticity, continuity, independence, orthodoxies and modernity and have thus participated powerfully in the constant redefinition of the collective self.

In a certain sense, therefore, this study may be considered as an object of historical relativism, showing how the ever-shifting present holds up its mirror to the past, which therefore shifts – is altered, transformed,

---

[35] http://byzantinestudies.boun.edu.tr/index.php?page=25.   [36] Necipoğlu 2013: 76–7.

316   Epilogue and Conclusion

reinvented – correspondingly. The diversity of interpretations and instrumentalisations of Byzantium emerged as a result of changing political-ideological and epistemological orientations. Requisites of cultural politics, ethno-history, national emancipation and nation-formation combined with contemporary issues of identity, geopolitical standing and relations with neighbouring states to mould the ways in which Byzantium was studied, represented, appropriated or disowned in the polities that have emerged from its remains. Different, often rival, readings coexisted and competed with each other as parallel scenarios, and some underwent dramatic changes over time. What we are faced with, therefore, is a range of 'competing byzantinisms' and a continuing process of negotiating the place of Byzantium across and within individual historiographical traditions. It has not been my aim to analyse in any depth to what extent the ensuing representations of Byzantium were truthful or universally cogent, or even less divulge the 'true' nature of Byzantium. It has instead been to demonstrate how Byzantium was used to produce alternative views of the past and the present, alternative national self-narrations, and lay bare its potency as an ideological topos and crucial element in the national master narratives, even when, as in the case of Turkish historiography, its influence has been consistently played down. It has been, in other words, to indicate why and how the modern interpretations of Byzantium matter in terms of the scholarly, political and cultural issues that were, and still are, at stake for these societies.

Beneath this volatile surface, still, particular strands of the *longue durée* become apparent. The close connection between history and politics, including revolutionary politics, was as manifest among popularisers of national history during the 'national revival period' as among professional medievalists later on. Preeminent historians, such as Iorga, Lambros, Filov and Köprülü, were also front-rank political leaders. From its modern inception, history-writing was coloured by, and attitudes towards Byzantium changed in accordance with, the given nation's geopolitical standing and current concerns. The concept of 'Byzantium' proved as instrumental in forging a sense of collective identity and legitimising aspirant or newly declared polities in the nineteenth century as it was in burnishing a country's credentials for membership in the European Union in the twenty-first century.

The persistence of the national-Romantic canon is another conspicuous feature across the five historiographical cultures. This is not to suggest that patriotic feelings exerted a more potent soporific action upon the scholarly

Epilogue and Conclusion 317

conscience in 'the (South) East' than they did in 'the West'. Arguably, what makes notions like historical right, ethnic continuity, national unity and pursuit of independence so salient in Balkan history-writing is the protracted process of nation-state-building and the insecurity of the sense of statehood. The paramountcy of the nation-state framework in the production of knowledge is vividly exemplified by Turkish historiography: while late-Ottoman imperial historiography and art history were pluralistic and open to admitting connections to Byzantium on different levels, the Republican historiography, sometimes featuring the same authors, presents a paragon of a parochial, self-centred approach to the past. The professionalisation of history entailed no real break with this tradition. Most historians in the region remained convinced that embracing 'objective' or 'scientific' history did not mean writing 'non-national' history: they saw, and many still see, no discrepancy between history as an academic endeavour and history as a service to the nation. The result obfuscates the significance of a common imperial legacy in conceiving a common history – one shorn of anachronistic retrojection of nationalist classification of human activity into the Byzantine past. Ironically, the Universal Empire and its ecumenical legacy ended up buttressing warring national identities and projects.

The available source repository also abetted such an outcome. The polities and cultures emerging from Byzantium's sphere of operation relied on its sources for information about themselves: the narrative of the early history of all these peoples, which moulded their collective memory, was provided by Byzantine sources. The very lack of such narratives points to the difficulty these polities had in positioning their formation in relation to Byzantium, in that such narratives presuppose a degree of politico-cultural self-sufficiency, in effect rejecting the imperial grand narrative.[37]

The respective national canons of history, on the other hand, display dissimilar dynamics. In Greece after the Enlightenment and in the Turkish Republic, the historical representations of Byzantium demonstrated fundamental stability. Created in the nineteenth century, the Greek master narrative underwent no major changes but 'fleshing out' and expansion by gradually incorporating new spheres (everyday life, law, art, literature, etc.). In Turkey, the confrontation between those allowing for a greater or lesser Byzantine influence and those rejecting it altogether has been uneven enough to guarantee the continued dominance of the latter camp. In Bulgaria, the canon was relatively stable until after World War II, when

---

[37] I am grateful for this observation to an anonymous reader of the manuscript.

318 Epilogue and Conclusion

a gradual but expanding shift began from confrontation with to repossession of Byzantium captured by the concept of 'Byzantino-Slavic culture'. In Serbia and Romania the dynamics unfurled primarily along the changing, and heavily contingent on political conjunctions, balance between Eastern and Western influences and the varying assessments of events or periods considered central to the master narrative – Dušan's empire in the Serbian case and the first centuries of the principalities of Wallachia and Moldavia in the Romanian case. Most of the time, alternative discourses drew their own 'myths' from a repertoire shared with the dominant discourses and as such elicited marginal challenge to the power of the master narratives.

It is at the same time remarkable that these often warring national images were formed in constant dialogue and interaction with each other. Rivalry and cross-fertilisation between historiographical schools were two closely related processes. A common element in the Bulgarian, Serbian, Romanian and Turkish interpretations was their opposition to the 'national imperialism' of the Greeks, which disregarded their 'historical rights' and denied them a share in the making or legacy of the empire. Even when portraying Byzantium as their prime adversary, all contested the Greeks' claim that it belonged to them alone. The competition between Greeks and Slavs, Bulgarians and Romanians, Greeks and Turks over ethnic predominance and imperial 'contribution' was a recurring one, which stoked the flames of historiographic wars. Most of the time, the Bulgarian narratives took shape in response to the Greek ones, and the Romanian interpretations contravened and mirrored the Bulgarian. The Serbian and Turkish scenarios drew on their neighbours' imperial narrations by featuring, respectively, medieval Serbia and the Ottoman empire as both major rivals of Byzantium and the superior – fresh and vibrant – recipients of its power or legacy.

Extra-regional perceptions of Byzantium, which were themselves controversial – treating Byzantium as both part of European civilisation and its cultural opposite – partook with different force at different times in the formation of local images. Western philhellenic thought was decisive for the original estrangement of the Greeks from their Byzantine past; so was Western Romanticism for the discovery of the Greek 'continuity' or the Russian and German byzantinistics for the Bulgarian and Serbian 'Byzantine' perceptions, whereas the Turkish attitude was a direct response to Western and regional deprecations of the state-building capacity of the Turks.

Presently, in both national history-writing and Byzantine studies, one witnesses a bifurcation between revisionist schools, distanced from the ethnocentric paradigm, and the proponents of the historical grand

Epilogue and Conclusion 319

narratives drawing on a long-standing tradition of nationally framed readings of the past. In medieval history-writing, the latter school continues to cultivate the notion of discrete, clearly delineated homogeneous cultures, fighting with each other and for national survival. The former, on the contrary, seeks to flesh out the idea of a large heterogeneous and fluctuating area stretching from the Adriatic to eastern Anatolia, characterised by shared or related cultural and social practices, dynastic alliances and competition, and economic and religious networks – a particular Byzantine phenomenon that cancels the idea of ethnically circumscribed entities and impervious boundaries. Although transnational historiography has gained some terrain in the last couple of decades, the traditionalist school continues to exert considerable influence through institutionalised channels. In history education and public opinion, the impact of non-nationally framed historiography remains limited and its often specialised discourse – a mode of protection against plausible attacks – exerts little effect on the public use of history and the historical culture. (The opening pageant at the 2004 Athens Olympics in which a 5,000-year 'national' heritage was paraded seamlessly before the world is only one among numerous examples.) To some extent, this is also true of diaspora historiography, which shows less inhibition in challenging national taboos and refuting canonical interpretations, but whose 'provocations' are often met with silence at home. An internationally mobile and transnationally trained younger generation of historians seems to forebode an invigorating 'paradigm shift' in the field. Whether this potential will be realised, however, depends on the ability of these scholars to overcome yet another asymmetry by ceasing to act as 'national' resource persons and to devolve the 'impartial' interpretative work and conceptual innovation to their Western peers.

References

Actes du IVe congrès international des études byzantines. 1935. Vol. I. Sofia: Imprimerie de la cour.

Actes du X. congrès international d'études byzantines. 1957 (Istanbul, 15–21.IX.1955). Istanbul: Comité d'organisation du x. congrès international d'études byzantines.

Agapitos, P. 1992. 'Byzantine Literature and Greek Philologists in the Nineteenth Century', *Classica et Medievalia. Revue danoise de philologie et d'histoire* 43: 231-60.

Agapitos, P. 2015. 'Karl Krumbacher and the History of Byzantine Literature', *Byzantinische Zeitschrift* 108/1: 1–52.

Ahrweiler, H. 1975. *L'idéologie politique de l'Empire byzantin*. Paris: P.U.F.

Ahrweiler, H. 2000. *The Making of Europe*. Athens: Livanis Publishing Organization 'Nea Synora'.

Akdağ, M. 1949 [1950]. 'Osmanlı İmparatorluğunun Kuruluş ve İnkişafı Devrinde Türkiye'nin İktisadi Vaziyeti', *Belleten* 13: 497–571 [14: 319–418].

Akdağ, M. 1974. *Türkiye'nin İktisadî ve İçtimaî Tarihi*, 2nd ed., vol. I. Istanbul: Cem Yayınevi.

Akyürek, E. 2010. 'Byzantine Art History in Modern Turkey', in Redford, S. and Ergin, N. (eds.), *Perceptions of the Past in the Turkish Republic: Classical and Byzantine Periods*. Leuven: Peeters, 205–24.

Al-Azmeh, A. 1998. 'Muslim History: Reflections on Periodisation and Categorisation', *The Medieval History Journal* 1/2: 195-231.

Amantos, K. 1923. *Oi Boreioi geitones tis Ellados*. Athens: Ekdotikos oikos 'Eleutheroudakēs'.

Amantos, K. 1969. *Prolegomena to the History of the Byzantine Empire*. Trans. Johnstone, K. Amsterdam: Adolf M. Hekkert.

Anagnosti, M. 1837. *La Valachie et la Moldavie*. Paris: Imprimerie de R. Fournier.

Angelov, B. 1969. 'Za nyakoi obshti cherti v razvitieto na staroslavyanskite literaturi', *Literaturna misăl* 13/3: 51–61.

Angelov, D. 1947. *Bogomilstvoto v Bălgariya. Proizhod, săshtnost i razprostranenie*. Sofia: Bălgarsko istorichesko druzhestvo [revised ed. 1961 and 1980].

Angelov, D. 1948. 'Vizantiyski vliyaniya vărhu srednovekovna Bălgariya', *Istoricheski pregled* 4/4–5: 401–16.

Angelov, D. 1963. 'Kiril i Metodiy i vizantiyskata kultura i politika', in *Hilyada i sto godini slavyanska pismenost 863–1963*. Sofia: BAN, 11–69.

References

Angelov, D. 1971. *Obrazuvane na bălgarskata narodnost.* Sofia: Nauka i izkustvo.

Angelov, D. 1979. 'Vizantiya i Bălgariya (VII–XIV v.)', in *Bălgariya v sveta ot drevnostta do nashi dni*, vol. I. Sofia: Nauka i izkustvo, 190–8.

Angelov, D. 1994. *Vizantiya. Duhovna kultura.* Stara Zagora: Ideya.

Angelov, D. 2003. 'Byzantinism: The Imaginary and Real Heritage of Byzantium in Southeastern Europe', in Keridis, D., Elias–Bursać, E. and Yatromanolakis, N. (eds.), *New Approaches to Balkan Studies.* Herndon, VA: Brassey's, 3–23.

Angold, M. 2014. *The Fall of Constantinople to the Ottomans: Context and Consequences.* London: Routledge.

Argyropoulos, R. 2001. *Les intellectuels grecs à la recherche de Byzance (1860–1912).* Athens: Institut de recherches néohelléniques.

Arnakis, G. 1947. *Hoi protoi othomanoi: symvole eis to provlema tes ptoseos tou Hellenismou tes Mikras Asias (1282–1337).* Athens: n.p.

Arnakis, G. 1963. 'Byzantium and Greece', *Balkan Studies* 4/2: 379–400.

Arnason, J. 2000. 'Approaching Byzantium: Identity, Predicament and Afterlife', *Thesis Eleven* 62: 39–69.

Arseven, C. 1909. *Constantinople, de Byzance á Stamboul.* Paris: Librairie Renouard.

Arseven, C. 1984. *Türk Sanatı.* Istanbul: Yayınevi [1st ed. 1928].

Atakuman, Ç. 2012. 'Heritage As a Matter of Prestige: A Synopsis of the State Heritage Discourse and Practice in Turkey', in Matthews, R. and Curtis, J. (eds.), *Proceedings of the 7th International Congress on the Archaeology of the Ancient Near East - London, 12-16 April 2010*, vol. II. Wiesbaden: Harrassowitz Verlag, 18–24.

Augustinos, G. 1977. *Consciousness and History: Nationalist Critics of Greek Society, 1897–1914.* Boulder, CO: East European Quarterly.

Auzépy, M.-F. 2003. *Byzance en Europe.* Paris: Presses universitaires de Vincennes.

Auzépy, M.-F. and Grélois, J. (eds.) 2001. *Byzance retrouvée. Erudits et voyageur français (XVIᵉ–XVIIIᵉ siècle).* Paris: Publications de la Sorbonne.

Bănescu, N. 1921–2. 'Cele mai vechi ştiri byzantine asupra românilor de la Dunărea de Jos', *Anuarul Institutului de istorie naţională din Cluj I.* Universitatea din Cluj, 138–60.

Bănescu, N. 1923. 'La Roma nuova alle foci del Danubio', *L'Europa Orientale* 3: 580–5.

Barbu, D. 2001. *Bizanţ contra Bizanţ. Explorări în cultura politică românească.* Bucharest: Nemira [1st ed. 1999].

Bariţ, G. 1871. 'Momente din istoria fanarioţilor'. *Transylvania* 4/6: 61–4; 4/7: 73–6; 4/8: 89–92.

Barkan, Ö. 1980. 'Osmanlı İmparatorluğu'nda çiftçi sınıfının hukuki statüsü', in Barkan, Ö. , *Türkiye'de toprak meselesi: Toplu eserler I.* Istanbul: Gözlem Yayınları [1st ed. 1937], as translated in Mishkova, D., Turda, M. and Trencsényi, B. (eds.) 2014. *Discourses of Collective Identity in Central and Southeast Europe (1770–1945): Texts and Commentaries*, vol. IV: *Anti-Modernism – Radical Revisions of Collective Identity.* Budapest: CEU Press, 309–12.

Bayrı, B. 2019. 'The 10th International Congress of Byzantine Studies, Istanbul, September 15–21, 1955', *YILLIK: Annual of Istanbul Studies* 1: 123–44.

Bazzaz, S., Batsaki, Y. and Angelov, D. 2013. 'Introduction: Imperial Geographies in Byzantine and Ottoman Space', in Bazzaz, S., Batsaki, Y. and Angelov, D. (eds.), *Imperial Geographies in Byzantine and Ottoman Space*. Hellenic Studies Series 56. Washington, DC: Center for Hellenic Studies, https://chs .harvard.edu/CHS/article/display/5701.introduction-imperial-geographies-in-byzantine-and-ottoman-space.

Beaton, R. 2009. 'Introduction', in Beaton, R. and Ricks, D. (eds.), *The Making of Modern Greece: Nationalism, Romanticism, and the Uses of the Past (1797–1896)*. Farnham: Ashgate, 1–18.

Beaton, R. 2012. 'Literature and Nation: The "Imagined Community" and the Role of Literature in the Making of Modern Greece', in Dova, S. (ed.), *Classics@10: Historical Poetics in Nineteenth and Twentieth Century Greece: Essays in Honor of Lily Macrakis*. Cambridge, MA: Harvard University Center for Hellenic Studies, https://chs.harvard.edu/CHS/article/display/ 4872.

Belyaev, L. 2000. *Hristianskie drevnosti. Vvedenie v sravnitelynoe izuchenie*. St Petersburg: Aleteiya.

Berktay, A. 2009. *The 'Anti-Nationalist' Liberation of Turkish Historiography*. Saarbrücken: Lambert Academic Publishing.

Berktay, H. 1991. 'Der Aufstieg und die gegenwärtige Krise der nationalistischen Geschichtsschreibung in der Türkei', *Periplus. Jahrbuch für außereuropäische Geschichte* 1: 102–25.

Berlin, I. 1972. 'Foreword', in Meinecke, F., *Historism: The Rise of a New Historical Outlook*. Trans. Anderson, J. London: Routledge and Kegan Paul, ix–xvi.

Berza, M. 1970. 'Problèmes majeurs et orientations de la recherche dans l'étude de l'ancienne culture roumaine', *Revue Roumaine d'Histoire* 9/3: 485–506.

Berza, M. 1972. 'Nicolas Iorga, historien du moyen âge', in Pippidi, D. (ed.), *Nicolas Iorga, L'homme et l'œuvre: à l'occasion du centième anniversaire de sa naissance*. Bucharest: Editions de l'academie RSR, 137–55

Biblioteka 'D-r Iv. Seliminski' 1904, vol. II. 1905, vol. III. 1907, vol. V. Trans. Chilev, P. and Pazheva, E. Sofia: Ministerstvo na narodnoto prosveshtenie.

Bikelas, D. 1890. *Seven Essays on Christian Greece*. London: Alexander Gardner.

Bikić, V. (ed.) 2016. *Byzantine Heritage and Serbian Art – I: Processes of Byzantinisation and Serbian Archaeology*. Belgrade: Serbian National Committee of Byzantine Studies.

Biliarsky, I. 2002. 'Srednovekovna Bălgariya: tsarstvoto i naroda', in *Polihroniya: Sbornik v chest na prof. Ivan Bozhilov*. Sofia: Anubis, 25–40.

Biliarsky, I. 2007. 'Some Observations on the Administrative Terminology of the Second Bulgarian Empire (13th–14th Centuries)', in Shepard, J. (ed.), *The Expansion of Orthodox Europe: Byzantium, the Balkans and Russia*. Aldershot: Ashgate, 327–47.

Bobčev, S. 1925. *Rimsko i vizantiysko pravo v starovremska Bălgaria*. Sofia: Pechatnitsa na Ivan K. Bozhinov.

References

323

Bobčev, S. 1929. 'Bulgaria under Tsar Simeon – I', *Slavonic and East European Review* 7/21: 621–33.

Bobčev, S. 1930. 'Bulgaria under Tsar Simeon – II', *Slavonic and East European Review* 8/22: 99–110.

Bobčev, S. 1934. 'Quelques remarques sur le droit coutumier bulgare pendant l'époque de la domination ottomane', *Revue internationale des études balkaniques* 1/2: 34–45.

Bodin, H. 2016. 'Whose Byzantinism – Ours or Theirs? On the Issue of Byzantinism from a Cultural Semiotic Perspective', in Marciniak, P. and Smythe, D. (eds.), *The Reception of Byzantium in European Culture since 1500.* London: Routledge, 11–42.

Bogdan, I. 1894. *Însemnătatea studiilor slave pentru romînĭ.* Bucharest: Editura Librăriei Socecu.

Bogdan, I. 1895. *Românii şi bulgarii.* Bucharest: Socec.

Boia, L. 2001a. *History and Myth in Romanian Consciousness.* Budapest: CEU Press.

Boia, L. 2001b. *Romania: Borderland of Europe.* London: Reaktion Books.

Bošković, D. (ed.) 2013. *Vizantija u (srpskoj) književnosti i kulturi od srednjeg do dvadeset i prvog veka.* Kragujevac: Filološko-umetnički fakultet.

Botev, H. 1958. *Săbrani săchineniya,* vol. II. Sofia: Bălgarski pisatel.

Bozdoğan, S. 2007. 'Reading Ottoman Architecture through Modernist Lenses: Nationalist Historiography and the "New Architecture" in the Early Republic', in Bozdoğan, S. and Necipoğlu, G. (eds.), *History and Ideology: Architectural Heritage of the 'Lands of Rum'.* Leiden: Brill, 199–221.

Bozdoğan, S. and Necipoğlu, G. 2007. 'Preface: Entangled Discourses – Scrutinizing Orientalist and Nationalist Legacies in the Architectural Historiography of the "Lands of Rum"', in Bozdoğan, S. and Necipoğlu, G. (eds.), *History and Ideology: Architectural Heritage of the 'Lands of Rum'.* Leiden: Brill, 1–6.

Božilov, I. 1975. 'Les Bulgares dans l'empire byzantin', *Godishnik na Sofiyskiya universitet, istoricheski fakultet,* vol. LXIX. Sofia: Universitetska Biblioteka 'Sv. Kliment Ohridski', 143–93.

Bozhilov, I. 1993. 'Preslavskata tsivilizatsiya', in *Sbornik Preslav,* vol. IV. Sofia: Voenno-izdatelski kompleks 'Sv. Georgi Pobedonosets', 33–47.

Bozhilov, I. 1995. 'Razhdaneto na srednovekovna Bălgariya (Nova interpretatsiya)', in Bozhilov, I., *Sedem etyuda po srednovekovna istoriya.* Sofia: Anubis, 11–72.

Bozhilov, I. 2011. 'Byzantium: Finis terrae – Η περατοσ, or the Frontiers of the Byzantine Civilization', in *Proceedings of the 22nd Congress of Byzantine Studies Sofia, 22–27 August, vol. II.* Bulgarian Historical Heritage Foundation: St. Kliment Ohridski University Press, 577–93.

Bozhilov, I. and Gyuzelev, V. 1999. *Istoriya na srednovekovna Bălgariya, VII–XIV vek.* Sofia: Anubis [this edition reproduced vol. I of *Istoriya na Bălgariya v tri toma*].

Brătianu, G. 1937. *Une nouvelle histoire de l'Europe au Moyen Âge.* Bucharest: Fondation Royale Carol I.

324 *References*

Brătianu, G. 1938. *Etudes byzantines d'histoire économique et sociale*. Paris: Libraire Orientaliste Paul Geuthner.

Brătianu, G. 1939. 'Une nouvelle histoire de l'Europe au Moyen-Âge: la fin du Monde antique et le triomphe de l'orient', *Revue belge de philologie et d'histoire* 18/1: 252–66.

Brătianu, G. 1940. *O enigmă și un miracol istoric: poporul român*. Bucharest: Fundația pentru Literatură și Artă 'Regele Carol II'.

Bratianu, G. 1943. *Origines et formation de l'unité roumaine*. Bucharest: Institut d'histoire universelle.

Brătianu, G. 1969. *La mer Noire, des origines à la conquête ottomane*. Munich: Monachii.

Brătianu, G. 1980. *Tradiția istorică despre întemeierea statelor românești*. Bucharest: Eitura Eminescu.

Bréhier, L. 1901. 'Le développement d'études d'histoire byzantine du XVIIe au XXe siècle', *La Revue d'Auvergne*, January–February: 1–36.

Brezeanu, S. 1999. *Romanitatea orientală în evul mediu: de la cetățenii romani la națiunea medievală*. Bucharest: All Educational.

Brown, P. 1976. 'Eastern and Western Christendom in Late Antiquity: A Parting of the Ways', in Baker, D. (ed.), *The Orthodox Churches and the West*. Oxford: Basil Blackwell, 1–24.

Browning, R. 1975. *Byzantium and Bulgaria: A Comparative Study Across the Medieval Frontier*. Berkeley: University of California Press.

Bryer, A. and Lowry, H. (eds.) 1986. *Continuity and Change in Late Byzantine and Early Ottoman Society*. The Centre for Byzantine Studies, University of Birmingham.

Budimir, M. and Skok, P. 1934. 'But et signification des études balkaniques', *Revue internationale des études balkaniques* 1/1: 1–28.

Budimir, M. and Skok, P. 1936. 'Destinées balkaniques', *Revue internationale des études balkaniques* 2/4: 601–13.

Bullen, J. 2003. *Byzantium Rediscovered*. London: Phaidon.

Burckhardt, J. 1943. *Force and Freedom: Reflections on History*. New York: Pantheon Books.

Burckhardt, J. 1949. *The Age of Constantine the Great*. New York: Pantheon Books.

Burke, J. 2014. 'Inventing and Re-inventing Byzantium: Nikephoros Phokas, Byzantine Studies in Greece and "New Rome"', in Nilsson, I. and Stephenson, P. (eds.), *Wanted: Byzantium – The Desire for a Lost Empire*. Uppsala: Uppsala University Press, 9–42.

Burmov, A. 1952. 'Za nachaloto na slavyanskaka pismenost i knizhnina', *Istoricheski pregled* 8/1: 50–9.

Burmov, A. 1957. 'Istoricheskite koreni na Kirilo-Metodievoto delo', *Spisanie na BAN* 1: 63–70.

Calotychos, V. 2003. *Modern Greece: A Cultural Poetics*. Oxford: Berg.

Cameron, A. 1992. *The Use and Abuse of Byzantium: An Essay on Reception*. London: King's College School of Humanities.

Cameron, A. 2006. *The Byzantines*. Oxford: Blackwell.

Cameron, A. 2008. 'The Absence of Byzantium', *Nea Hestia* 82/1: 4–59.

References   325

Cameron, A. 2014. *Byzantine Matters*. Princeton: Princeton University Press.
Cameron, A. 2016. 'Bury, Baynes and Toynbee', in Cormack, R. and Jeffreys, E. (eds.), *Through the Looking Glass: Byzantium through British Eyes*. London: Routledge, 163–75.
Cameron, A. 2019. 'Bitter Furies of Complexity: Did the Byzantines Consider Themselves Roman?' *Times Literary Supplement*, 20 September.
Canat, R. 1951, 1953, 1955. *L'Hellénisme des romantiques*, vols. I–III. Paris: Didier.
Cândea, V. 1971. 'Nicolas Iorga, historien de l'Europe du Sud-Est', in Pippidi, D. (ed.), *Nicolas Iorga: L'homme et l'oeuvr*. Bucharest: eEditions de l'Académie de la R.S.R., 157–249.
Cândea, V. 1972. 'Noi şi Bizanţul', in Popişteănu, C. (ed.), *Lumea Bizanţului*. Bucharest: Institutul de studii istorice si social-politice, 13–22.
Carabott, P. 2003. 'Monumental Visions: The Past in Metaxas' Weltanschauung', in Brown, K. and Hamilakis, Y. (eds.), *The Usable Past: Greek Metahistories*. Lanham, MD: Lexington Books, 23–37.
Çelik, Z. 2011. 'Defining Empire's Patrimony: Late Ottoman Perceptions of Antiquities', in Çelik, Z., Bahrani, Z. and Eldem, E. (eds.), *Scramble for the Past: A Story of Archaeology in the Ottoman Empire, 1753–1914*. Istanbul: Salt, 443–79.
Çetinsaya, G. 1999. 'Rethinking Nationalism and Islam: Some Preliminary Notes on the Roots of "Turkish-Islamic Synthesis" in Modern Turkish Political Thought', *The Muslim World* 89/3–4: 350–76.
Charanis, P. 1949. 'On the Question of the Slavonic Settlements in Greece during the Middle Ages', *Byzantinoslavica* 10: 254–8.
Charanis, P. 1970. 'Observations on the History of Greece During the Early Middle Ages', *Balkan Studies* 11/1: 1–34.
Charanis, P. 1978. 'The Formation of the Greek People', in Vryonis, S., Jr. (ed.), *The 'Past' in Medieval and Modern Greek Culture*. Malibu: Undena Publications, 237–56.
Christodoulou, D. 2010. 'Byzantium in Nineteenth–Century Greek Historiography', in Stephenson, P. (ed.), *The Byzantine World*. London: Routledge, 445–61.
Christodoulou, D. 2013. 'Making Byzantium a Greek Presence: Paparrigopoulos and Koumanoudes Review the Latest History Books', in Delouis, O., Couderc, A. and Guran, P. (eds.), *Héritages de Byzance en Europe du Sud-Est a l'époque moderne et contemporaine*. Athens: Ecole française d'Athènes, 231–47.
Christophilopoulou, A. 1994. 'Oi vyzantines spoudes sto Panepistimio Athinon kata ti diarkeia tou Mesopolemou', *Nea Estia* 1610: 983–91.
Cicance, O. 1971. 'Concepţia lui Nicolae Iorga despre "Byzance après Byzance"', in Stănescu, E. (ed.), *Nicolae Iorga – istoric al Bizanţului*. Bucharest: Editura Academiei R.S.R., 219–28.
Ćirković, S. 1970. *O istoriografiji i metodologiji*. Belgrade: Istorijski institut.
Ćirković, S. 1978. 'Akademik Georgije Ostrogorski u jugoslovenskoj istoriografiji', *Zbornik radova Vizantološkog instituta* 18: 278–81.
Ćirković, S. 1995. *Srbi u srednjem veku*. Belgrade: Idea [first published in Italian (*I Serbi nel medioevo*, 1992) and French (*La Serbie au Moyen âge*, 1992)].

326   References

Ćirković, S. 2004. *The Serbs*. Oxford: Blackwell.

Clogg, R. 1986. *Politics and the Academy: Arnold Toynbee and the Koraes Chair*. London: Routledge.

Clogg, R. 1988. 'The Byzantine Legacy in the Modern Greek World: The Megali Idea', in Clucas, L. (ed.), *The Byzantine Legacy in Eastern Europe*. BoulderCO: East European Monographs, 253–81.

Clucas, L. 1988. *The Byzantine Legacy in Eastern Europe*. BoulderCO: East European Monographs.

Collingwood, R. 1974. *The Idea of History*. London: Oxford University Press.

Cormack, R. and Vassilaki, M. 2008. *Byzantium 330–1453*. London: Royal Academy Publications.

Ćorović, V. 1933. *Istorija Jugoslavije*. Belgrade: Narodno Delo.

Ćorović, V. 1989. *Istorija srpskog naroda*. Belgrade: BIGZ.

Ćurčić, S. 2013. 'Architecture in Byzantium, Serbia and the Balkans Through the Lenses of Modern Historiography', in Angar, M. and Sode, C. (eds.), *Serbia and Byzantium: Proceedings of the International Conference Held on 15 December 2008 at the University of Cologne*. Frankfurt am Main: Peter Lang, 9–31.

Curta, F. 2001. 'Pots, Slavs and "Imagined Communities": Slavic Archaeologies and the History of the Early Slavs', *European Journal of Archaeology* 4/3: 368–84.

Curta, F. 2006. *Southeastern Europe in the Middle Ages, 500–1250*. Cambridge: Cambridge University Press.

Dagron, G. 2007. 'Oublier Byzance: Éclipses et retours de Byzance dans la conscience européenne', *Praktika tes Akademias Athenon* 82: 135–58.

Danforth, N. 2016. 'The Ottoman Empire from 1923 to Today: In Search of a Usable Past', *Mediterranean Quarterly* 27/2: 5–27.

Danilevskiy, N. 1871. *Rossiya i Evropa*. St Petersburg: Obshtestvennaya pol'za.

Danova, N. 1994. *Konstantin Georgiev Fotinov v kulturnoto i ideyno–politicheskoto razvitie na Balkanite prez XIX vek*. Sofia: BAN.

Danova, N. 2003a. 'Obrazi na gărtsi i zapadnoevropeytsi v bălgarskata knizhnina prez XVIII–XIX vek', in Aretov, N. (ed.), *Balkanskite identichnosti v bălgarskata kultura, vol. IV*. Sofia: Kralitsa Mab, 102–23.

Danova, N. 2003b. 'Problemăt za natsionalnata identichnost v uchebnikarskata knizhnina, publitsistikata i istoriografiata prez XVIII–XIX vek', in Aretov, N. (ed.), *Balkanskite identichnosti v bălgarskata kultura, vol. IV*. Sofia: Kralitsa Mab, 69–76.

Daskalov, R. 2018. *Golemite razkazi za bălgarskoto srednovekovie*. Sofia: Riva.

Dedijer, V., Božić, I., Ćirković, S. and Ekmečić, M. 1974. *History of Yugoslavia*. New York: McGraw-Hill [originally published in Serbo-Croatian in 1972].

Delilbaşı, M. 2005. 'The Present and Future of Byzantine Studies in Turkey', in Evangelatou-Notara, F. and Maniati-Kokkini, T. (eds.), *Κλητόριου in memory of Nikos Oikonomides*. Athens: n.p., 63–72.

Delilbaşı, M. 2013. *İki İmparatorluk Tek Coğrafya: Bizans'tan Osmanlı'ya Geçişin Anadolu ve Balkanlar'daki İzleri*. Istanbul: İthaki Yayınları.

Delouis, O., Couderc, A. and Guran, P. (eds.) 2013. *Héritages de Byzance en Europe du Sud-Est à l'époque moderne et contemporaine*. Athens: Ecole française d'Athènes.

References

Derks, T. and Roymans, N. 2009. 'Introduction', in Derks, T. and Roymans, N. (eds.), *Ethnic Constructs in Antiquity: The Role of Power and Tradition*. Amsterdam: Amsterdam University Press, 1–10.

Diehl, C. 1905. 'Les études byzantines en France au XIXe siècle' and 'Les études d'histoire byzantine en 1905', in Diehl, C. , *Etudes byzantines*. Paris: Alphonse Picard et fils, 21–106.

Diehl, C. 1919. *Byzance: grandeur et décadence*. Paris: Flammarion.

Diehl, C. 1957. *Byzantium: Greatness and Decline*. Trans. Walford, N. New Brunswick, NJ: Rutgers University Press [first published as *Byzance, grandeur et décadence* in 1919].

Dimaras, C. 1993. *Neoellēnikos Diafotismos*. Athens: Ermēs.

Dimaras, K. 1982. *Ellinikos Romantismos*. Athens: Ermēs.

Dostoevskiy, F. 1995. *Sobranie sochineniy v 15 tomah*, vol. XIV. St Petersburg: Nauka.

Drinov, M. 1909. *Trudove na M.S. Drinov po bǎlgarska i slavyanska istoriya*. Sofia: Dǎrzhavna pechatnitsa.

Drinov, M. 1915. *Sǎchineniya na M.S. Drinov*, vol. III, Zlatarski, V. (ed.). Sofia: Dǎrzhavna pechatnitsa.

Droysen, J. 1833. *Geschichte Alexanders des Grossen*. Hamburg: Perthes.

Droysen, J. 1836–43. *Geschichte des Hellenismus*, vols. I–II. Hamburg: Perthes.

Dujčev, I. 1960. 'Les Slaves et Byzance', in *Etudes historiques à l'occasion du XIe Congrès international des sciences historiques, Stockholm, aout 1960*, vol. I. Sofia: BAN, 31–71.

Dujčev, I. 1961. 'Il problema delle lingue nazionali nel Medio Evo e gli Slavi', *Ricerche slavistiche* 8: 39–60.

Duychev, I. 1963a. 'Centryi vizantiysko-slavyanskogo obshteniya i sotrudnichestva', *Trudyi Otdela drevneruskoy literaturyi* 19: 107–29.

Dujčev, I. 1963b. 'Les rapports littéraires byzantino-slaves', in *XII Congres international des études byzantines, Ochride 10–16 septembre 1961*, vol. I. Belgrade: Naučno delo, 411–29.

Duychev, I. 1963c. 'Vizantiysko-slavyanska obshtnost v oblastta na narodnoto tvorchestvo', *Izvestiya na etnografskiya institut i muzey* 6: 351–8.

Dujčev, I. 1964. 'Rapporti economici fra Bisanzio e gli Slavi', *Bullettino dell'Istituto Storico Italiano per il Medio Evo e Archivio Muratoriano* 76: 1–30.

Dujčev, I. 1965. 'L'Héritage byzantin chez les Slaves', *Etudes historiques* 2: 131–47.

Dujčev, I. 1966. 'Les études byzantines chez les Slaves méridionaux et occidentaux depuis le XVIIe siècle', *Jahrbuch der Österreichischen Byzantinischen Gesellschaft* 15: 73–88.

Dujčev, I. 1967. 'L'art byzantin du XIIIe siècle', in *Symposium de Sopoćani, 1965*. Belgrade: Filozofski Fakultet. Odeljenje za Istoriju Umetnosti, 103–15.

Dujčev, I. 1972. 'Rapports littéraires entre les Byzantins, les bulgares et les Serbes aux XIVe et XVe siècles', in *Ecole de la Morava et son temps. Symposium Resava, 1968*. Belgrade: Faculté de Philosophie, Département de l'histoire de l'art, 77–100.

Duychev, I. 1998. 'Vizantiya i slavyanskiyat svyat', in Duychev, I., *Izbrani proiz-vedeniya*, vol. I. Sofia: Anubis, 26-45 [originally published as Dujčev, I. 1964.

328 *References*

'Bisanzio e il mondo slavo', in *Settimane di studio del Centro Italiano di studi sull'alto Medioevo. Spoleto 18–23 aprile 1963.* Spoleto: Pr. La Sede del Centro].

Durak, K. 2014. 'The Representation of Byzantine History in High School Textbooks in Turkey', *Byzantine and Modern Greek Studies* 38/2: 245–64.

Durak, K. and Vasilakeris, A. (eds.) 2013. 'Bizans'tan Türkiye'ye Kalan Miras. Tanıdık yabancı', *Toplumsal Tarih* 229: 53–93.

Dvorniković, V. 1939. *Karakterologija Jugoslovena.* Belgrade: Geca Kon.

Eldem, E. 2015. 'Cultural Heritage in Turkey: An Eminently Political Matter', in Haller, D., Lichtenberger, A. and Meerpohl, M. (eds.), *Essays on Heritage, Tourism and Society in the MENA Region.* Paderborn: Ferdinand Schöningh, 67–92.

Elian, A. 1958. 'Les rapports byzantino-roumains', *Byzantinoslavica* 19/2: 212–25.

Elian, A. 1964. 'Moldova şi Bizanţul în secolul al XV-lea', in Berza, M. (ed.), *Cultura moldovenească în timpul lui Ştefan cel Mare.* Bucharest: Editura Academiei R.P.R., 98–179.

Elian, A. 1967. 'Byzance et les Roumains à la fin du Moyen Age', in *Proceedings of the XIIIth International Congress of Byzantine Studies: Oxford, 5– 10 September 1966.* London: Oxford University Press, 195–203.

Erimtan, C. 2008. 'Hittites, Ottomans and Turks: Ağaoğlu Ahmed Bey and the Kemalist Construction of Turkish Nationhood in Anatolia', *Anatolian Studies* 58: 141–71.

Ersanlı, B. 1992. *İktidar ve Tarih, Türkiye'de Resmi Tarih Tezinin Oluşumu, 1929– 1937.* Istanbul: Ada.

Ersanlı, B. 2002. 'The Ottoman Empire in the Historiography of the Kemalsit Era: A Theory of Fatal Decline', in Adanir, F. and Faroqhi, S. (eds.), *The Ottomans and the Balkans: A Discussion of Historiography.* Leiden: Brill, 115–54.

Ersoy, A., Górny, M. and Kechriotis, V. (eds.) 2010. *Discourses of Collective Identity in Central and Southeast Europe (1770–1945): Texts and Commentaries.* Vol. III/1: *Modernism: The Creation of Nation-States.* Vol. III/2: *Modernism – Representations of National Culture.* Budapest: CEU Press.

Fallmerayer, J. 1830–6. *Geschichte der Halbinsel Morea während des Mittelalters,* 2 vols. Stuttgart: Cotta.

Fallmerayer, J. 1990 [1861]. 'Rom und Byzanz', in Fallmerayer, J., *Europa zwischen Rom und Byzanz.* Bozen: Athesia.

Faroqhi, S. 1992. 'In Search of Ottoman History', in Berktay, H. and Faroqhi, S. (eds.), *New Approaches to State and Peasant in Ottoman History.* London: Frank Cass, 211–41.

Faroqhi, S. 2004. *Approaching Ottoman History: An Introduction to the Sources.* Cambridge: Cambridge University Press.

Fassoulakis, S. 1993. 'Gibbon's Influence on Koraes', in Beaton, R. and Roueché, Ch. (eds.), *The Making of Byzantine History: Studies Dedicated to Donald M. Nicol.* Aldershot: Variorum, 169–73.

Ferjančić, B. 1966. *Vizantija i Južni Sloveni.* Belgrade: Zavod za izdavanje udžbenika Socijalističke Republike Srbije.

Ferjančić, B. 1974. *Tesalija u XIII i XIV veku.* Belgrade: Vizantološki institut SANU.

References

329

Ferjančić, B. 1978. 'Akademik Georgije Ostrogorski u svetskoj vizantologiji', *Zbornik radova Vizantološkog instituta* 18: 269–74.

Ferjančić, B. 1994. *Vizantijski i srpski Ser u XIV stoleću*. Belgrade: Srpska akademija nauka i umetnosti.

Ferluga, J. 1976. *Byzantium on the Balkans: Studies on the Byzantine Administration and the Southern Slavs from the VIIth to the XIIth Centuries*. Amsterdam: A. M. Hakkert.

Ferluga, J. 1992. *Untersuchungen zur byzantinischen Provinzverwaltung. VI.–XIII. Jahrhundert*. Amsterdam: A. M. Hakkert.

Filov, B. 1927. 'Vizantiya i Elada', *Bălgarska misăl* 2/1: 32–41; 2/2: 125–35.

Finlay, G. 1877. *A History of Greece from Its Conquest by the Romans to the Present Time B.C. 146 to A.D. 1864*, vol. I. Oxford: Clarendon Press.

Fodac, F. 2006. 'Le premier congrès international d'études byzantines: Prémisses et contexte historique d'organisation', *Etudes byzantines et post-byzantines* 5: 509–22.

Forbes, N., Toynbee, A., Mitrany, D. and Hogarth, D. 1915. *The Balkans: A History of Bulgaria, Serbia, Greece, Rumania, Turkey*. Oxford: Clarendon Press.

Fotinos, D. 1818–19. *History of Ancient Dacia, Present-Day Transylvania, Wallachia and Moldavia*, 3 vols. Vienna: J. B. Zweckius.

Freeman, E. 1879. 'The Byzantine Empire', in Freeman, E., *Historical Essays*. London: Macmillan, 231–77.

Gazi, E. 1998. '"Europe": Writing an Ambivalent Concept in 19th Century Greek Historical Culture', in Heppner, H. and Katsiardi-Hering, O. (eds.), *Die Griechen und Europa* (Zur Kunde Südosteuropa II/25). Vienna: Böhlau, 103–24.

Gazi, E. 2000. *Scientific National History: The Greek Case in Comparative Perspective (1850–1920)*. Frankfurt am Main: Peter Lang.

Geary, P. and Klaniczay, G. (eds.) 2013. *Manufacturing Middle Ages: Entangled History of Medievalism in Nineteenth-Century Europe*. Leiden: Brill.

Georgescu, V. 1974. 'Byzance et les institutions roumaines jusqu'à la fin du XVème siècle', in Berza, M. and Stănescu, E. (eds.), *Actes du XIVe Congrès International des études byzantines, Bucarest, 6–12 septembre, 1971*, vol. I. Bucharest: Editura Academiei RSR, 433–84.

Georgescu, V. 1980. *Bizanțul și instituțiile românești până la mijlocul secolului al XVIII-lea*. Bucharest: Editura Academiei RSR.

Georgescu, V. 1991. *Politică și istorie. Cazul comuniștilor romăni 1944–1977*. Bucharest: Humanitas.

Georgiev, E. 1956. *Kiril i Metodiy. Osnovopolozhnitsi na slavyanskite literaturi*. Sofia: BAN.

Gibbons, H. 1916. *The Foundation of the Ottoman Empire: A History of the Osmanlis Up to the Death of Bayezid I (1300–1403)*. New York: The Century.

Gietzen, A. 2018. 'Bad Byzantines: A Historical Narrative in the Liberal Conception of Vladimir Jovanović', in Alshanskaya, A., Gietzen, A. and Hadjiafxenti, C. (eds.), *Imagining Byzantium: Perception, Patterns, Problems*. Mainz: Verlag des Römisch–Germanischen Zentralmuseums, 101–8.

References

Giurescu, C. 1935. *Istoria românilor, vol. I: Din cele mai vechi timpuri pînă la moartea lui Alexandru cel Bun (1432)*. Bucharest: Editura Fundaţiei pentru Literatură şi Artă.

Giurescu, C. 1943. *Istoria românilor, din cele mai vechi timpuri până la moartea regelui Ferdinand I*. Bucharest: Editura Cugetarea-Georgescu Delafras.

Giuzelev, V. 1981. 'The Bulgarian Medieval State: Seventh through Fourteenth Centuries', *Southeastern Europe* 8/1–2: 19–39.

Gökalp, Z. 1923. *Türkçülüğün Esasları*. Ankara: Matbuat ve İstihbarat Matbaası.

Gounaridis, P. 1994. 'To Vyzantio kai i Diktatoria tou Metaxa', *Ta Historika* 20: 150–7.

Gounaris, B. 2005. 'Constructing and Deconstructing a Common Balkan Past in Nineteenth-Century Greece', in Detrez, R. and Plat, P. (eds.), *Developing Cultural Identity in the Balkans: Convergence vs. Divergence*. Brussels: Peter Lang, 195-211

Gourgouris, S. 1996. *Dream Nation, Enlightenment, Colonization and the Institution of Modern Greece*. Stanford, CA: Stanford University Press.

Grafenauer, B., Petrović, D. and Šidak, J. (eds.) 1953. *Istorija naroda Jugoslavije I*. Belgrade: Prosveta.

Graindor, P. and Grégoire, H. 1924. 'Avant-propos', *Byzantion* 1: v–viii.

Gratziou, O. 2008. 'Venetian Monuments in Crete: A Controversial Heritage', in Damaskis, D. and Plantzos, D. (eds.), *A Singular Antiquity: Archaeology and Hellenic Identity in Twentieth-Century Greece*. Athens: Benaki Museum, 209–22.

Grégoire, H. 1935. 'Le Congrès de Sofia', *Byzantion* 10: 259–81.

Gross, M. 1966. 'Die Jugoslawische Geschichtswissenschaft von heute', *Österreichische Osthefte* 8: 238–45.

Grosul, V. 1996. 'Vizantizm Konstantina Leont'eva', *Revue des Etudes Sud-Est Européennes* 34/3–4: 265–73.

Guillou, A. 1966. 'Le siècle des Lumières', *Jahrbuch der Österreichischen Byzantinischen Gesellschaft* 15: 27–39.

Guran, P. 2018. 'Bizantinistică/Bizantologie şi bizantinism', *Dilema veche* 736. ht tps://dilemaveche.ro/sectiune/din-polul-plus/articol/bizantinisticabizantolo gie-si-bizantinism.

Gürpınar, D. 2013. *Ottoman/Turkish Visions of the Nation, 1860–1950*. Basingstoke: Palgrave Macmillan.

Gyuzelev, V. 1969. *Knyaz Boris I*. Sofia: Nauka i izkustvo.

Gyuzelev, V. 1986. 'Zhivot i nauchno tvorchestvo na Petăr Mutafchiev (1883–1943), in Mutafchiev, P., *Istoriya na bălgarskiya narod (681–1323)*. Sofia: Izdatelstvo na BAN, 6–34.

Gyuzelev, V. 1995. 'Vizantiyskata imperiya i Bălgarskoto tsarstvo v bran i mir', *Arhiv za srednovekovna filosofiya i kultura*, vol. II. Sofia: Universitetsko izdatelstvo 'Sv. Kliment Ohridski', 60–88.

Gyuzelev, V. 2005. 'Bălgariya i Vizantiyskata imperiya', in Gyuzelev, V., Miltenova, A. and Stankova, R. (eds.), *Bălgariya i Sărbiya v konteksta na vizantiyskata tsivilizatsiya*. Sofia: Akademichno izdatelstvo 'Prof. Marin Drinov', 27–46.

References

Gyuzelev, V. 2009. 'Bălgarskoto tsarstvo prez XIII vek: nasoki i faktoki văv vănshnata mu politika', *Zbornik radova Vizantološkog instituta* 66: 119–28.

Gyuzelev, V. 2011. 'Le dialogue Byzantino-Bulgare', in *Proceedings of the 22nd International Congress of Byzantine Studies. Sofia, 22–27 August 2011*, vol. I: *Plenary Papers*. Sofia: Bulgarian Historical Heritage Foundation, 3–15.

Hagen, G. 2006. 'Afterword: Ottoman Understandings of the World in the Seventeenth Century', in Dankoff, R. (ed.), *An Ottoman Mentality: The World of Evliya Çelebi*. Leiden: Brill, 215–56.

Haldon, J. 2016. 'Res publica Byzantina? State Formation and Issues of Identity in Medieval East Rome', *Byzantine and Modern Greek Studies* 40/1: 4–16.

Hamilakis, Y. 2007. *The Nation and Its Ruins: Antiquity, Archaeology, and National Imagination in Greece*. Oxford: Oxford University Press.

Hatzopoulos, M. 2013. 'Receiving Byzantium in Early Modern Greece (1820s–1840s)', in Delouis, O., Couderc, A. and Guran, P. (eds.), *Héritages de Byzance en Europe du Sud-Est à l'époque moderne et contemporaine*. Athens: Ecole française d'Athènes, 219–29.

Hegel, G. 1857. *Lectures on the Philosophy of History*. Trans. Sibree, J. London: Henry G. Bohn.

Heraclides, A. 2013. 'The Essence of the Greek-Turkish Rivalry: National Narrative and Identity', *GreeSE Paper No.51, Hellenic Observatory Papers on Greece and Southeast Europe*. https://dilemaveche.ro/sectiune/din-polul-plus/a rticol/bizantinisticabizantologie-si-bizantinism.

Hering, G. 1980. 'Die Bulgaren in den Schriften griechischer Intellektueller in der ersten Hälfte des 19. Jahrhunderts', *Müncher Zeitschrift für Balkankunde* 3: 47–66.

Hering, G. 1987. 'Die Auseinandersetzungen über die neugriechische Schriftsprache', in Hannick, C. (ed.), *Sprachen und Nationen im Balkan-raum : Die historischen Bedingungen der Entstehung der heutigen Nationalsprachen*. Cologne: Böhlau, 125–94.

Herzfeld, M. 1982. *Ours Once More: Folklore, Ideology and the Making of Modern Greece*. Austin: University of Texas Press.

Hilendarski, P. 1972. *Slavyanobălgarska istoriya*. Sofia: Bălgarski pisatel.

History of Wallachia. 1806. Vienna: Vendoti.

Hunger, H. 1958. 'Byzanz in der Weltpolitik von Bildersturm bis 1453', in Valjavec, F. (ed.), *Historia mundi: Ein Handbuch der Weltgeschichte in zehn Bänden, vol. VI, Hohes und spätes Mittelalter*. Bern: Francke, 386–444.

Ignjatović, A. 2016. *O srpsko–vizantijskom kaleidoskopu: Arhitektura, nacionalizam i imperijalna imaginacija 1878–1941*. Belgrade: Orion Art i Univerzitet u Beogradu.

İnalcık, H. 1954. 'Ottoman Methods of Conquest', *Studia Islamica* 2: 104–29.

İnalcık, H. 1960. 'The Problem of the Relationship between Byzantine and Ottoman Taxation', in Dölger, F. and Beck, H. (eds.), *Akten des XI. Internationalen Byzantinisten-Kongresses 1958*. Munich: C. H. Beck, 237–42.

İnalcık, H. 1973. *The Ottoman Empire: The Classical Age, 1300–1600*. London: Weidenfeld and Nicolson.

332 *References*

İnalcık, H. 1976. 'The Rise of the Ottoman Empire', in Cook, M. (ed.), *A History of the Ottoman Empire to 1730*. Cambridge: Cambridge University Press, 10–54.

İnalcık, H. 1994. 'The Ottoman State: Economy and Society, 1300–1600', in İnalcık, H. and Quataert, D. (eds.), *An Economic and Social History of the Ottoman Empire, 1300–1914*, vol. I. Cambridge: Cambridge University Press, 11–409.

Inan, A. 1941. *L'Anatolie, le pays de la 'race' turque*. Geneva: Publications de la Faculté des sciences économiques et sociales de l'Université de Genève.

Ionescu, M. and Iosipescu, S. (eds.) 2010. *Bizanţ versus Bizanţ: Introducere la o dezbatere privind devenirea românească*. Bucharest: Editura militară.

Ionescu-Nișcov, T. 1974. '*L'époque phanariote dans l'historiographie roumaine et étrangère*', in Symposium *L'époque phanariote (21–25 Octobre 1970)*. Thessaloniki: Institute for Balkan Studies, 145-58

Jorga, N. 1907. *The Byzantine Empire*. London: J. M. Dent.

Iorga, N. 1908. *Geschichte des osmanischen Reiches*, vol. I. Gotha: F. A. Perthes Aktiengesellschaft.

Iorga, N. 1912. *Les Roumains et le nouvel état de choses en Orient*. Vălenii de Munte: Neamul Românesc.

Iorga, N. 1913a. *Două tradiţii istorice în Balcani: a Italiei și a românilor*. Bucharest: Librăriile Socec.

Iorga, N. 1913b. *Istoria statelor balcanice în epoca modernă*. Vălenii de Munte: Neamul Românesc.

Iorga, N. 1913c. *Les bases nécessaires d'une nouvelle histoire du moyen-âge. II. La survivance byzantine dans les pays roumains*. Bucharest: Ed. du Ministère de l'instruction publique.

Iorga, N. 1914. *Histoire des Etats balkaniques à l'époque moderne*. Bucharest: C. Sfetea.

Iorga, N. 1920. *Histoire des Roumains et de leur Civilisation*. Paris: Henry Paulin.

Iorga, N. 1921. *Roumains et Grecs au cours des siècles à l'occasion des mariages princiers de MDCCCCXXI* (Extraits de 'Deux communications au troisième congrès international d'études historiques, à Londres',' par N. Iorga; Bucarest, 1913). Bucharest: Cultura Neamului Românesc.

Iorga, N. 1922a. *Formes byzantines et réalités balkaniques: Leçons faites à la Sorbonne*. Bucharest: H. Champion.

Iorga, N. 1922b. *Influences étrangères sur la nation roumaine: Leçons faites à la Sorbonne*. Paris: Libraire universitaire J. Gamber.

Iorga, N. 1924a. *Choses d'Orient et de Roumanie*. Bucharest: P. Suru.

Iorga, N. 1924b. 'Un Congres la București', *Neamul românesc*, 15 April 1924, 1.

Iorga, N. 1934. *Histoire de la vie byzantine*, vol. III. Bucharest: Édition de l'auteur.

Iorga, N. 1935–6. *La place des Romains dans l'histoire universelle*, 3 vols. Bucharest: Edition de l'Institut d'études byzantines.

Iorga, N. 1939a. *Ce e Bizanţiul*. Bucharest: Institutul de studii bizantine.

Iorga, N. 1939b. *Études byzantines*, 2 vols. Bucharest: Institut d'études byzantines.

Iorga, N. 1940. *Un om, o metodă și o școală*. Bucharest: n.p.

References 333

Iorga, N. 1984. 'Sârbi, bulgari și români în Peninsula Balcanică', in Papacostea, Ș. (ed.), *Nicolae Iorga: Studii asupra Evului Mediu românesc*. Bucharest: Editura Științifică și Enciclopedică.

Iorga, N. 2000. *Byzantium after Byzantium*. Iași: Centre for Romanian Studies [first published as Iorga, N. 1935. *Byzance après Byzance: Continuation de l'Histoire de la vie byzantine*. Bucharest: Édition de l'Institut d'études byzantines].

Irmscher, J. 1976. 'Geschichte der byzantinistischen Studien: Ergebnisse und Aufgaben', *Balkan Studies* 17: 241–68.

Istorija naroda Jugoslavije, vol. I. 1953. Belgrade: Prosveta.

Istorija srpskog naroda, vol. I. 1981. Belgrade: Srpska književna zadruga.

Istoriya na Bălgariya, vol. I. 1954. Sofia: Nauka i izkustvo.

Istoriya na Bălgariya, vol. II. 1981: *Părva bălgarska dărzhava*; vol. III. 1982: *Vtora bălgarska dărzhava*. Sofia: BAN.

Ivanov, S. 2003. 'Byzance rouge: la byzantinologie et les communistes (1928–1948)', in Auzépy, M.-F., *Byzance en Europe*. Paris: Presses Universitaires de Vincennes, 55–60.

Ivanov, S. 2014. 'Byzantium and the Slavs', in Sakel, D. (ed.), *Byzantine Culture: Papers from the Conference 'Byzantine Days of Istanbul'*. Ankara: Türk Tarih Kurumu, 207–15.

Ivanov, S. 2016. 'The Second Rome as Seen by the Third: Russian Debates on "the Byzantine Legacy"', in Marciniak, P. and Smythe, D. (eds.), *The Reception of Byzantium in European Culture Since 1500*. New York: Routledge, 55–79.

Ivanov, Y. 1898. 'Slavyanskata vzaimnost v minaloto i segashnoto', *Bălgarski pregled* 5/4: 99-122.

Ivanov, Y. 1982 [1911]. 'Grătsko-bălgarski otnosheniya predi tsărkovnata borba', in Ivanov, Y. , *Izbrani proizvedeniya*, vol. I. Sofia: Nauka i izkustvo, 157–82.

Janković, D. (ed.) 1975. *The Historiography of Yugoslavia 1965–1975*. Belgrade: Association of the Yugoslav Historical Societies.

Jeffreys, E., Haldon, J. and Cormack, R. 2008. 'Byzantine Studies as an Academic Discipline', in Jeffreys, E., Haldon, J. and Cormack, R. (eds.), *The Oxford Handbook of Byzantine Studies*. Oxford: Oxford University Press, 3–20.

Jenkins, R. 1963. *Byzantium and Byzantinism*. Cincinnati, OH: University of Cincinnati.

Jenkins, R. 1980. *The Victorians and Ancient Greece*. Cambridge, MA: Harvard University Press.

Jireček, K. 1922. *Istorija Srba*, vol. I. Belgrade: Geca Kon [first published in 1911].

Joudiou, B. 1998. 'Les principautés roumaines de Valachie et de Moldavie et leur environnement slavo–byzantin', *Balkanologie* 2/1. https://journals.openedition .org/balkanologie/241.

Jovanović, V. 1863. *The Serbian Nation and the Eastern Question*. London: Bell and Daldy.

Jovanović, V. 1870. *Les Serbes et la mission de la Serbie dans l'Europe d'Orient*. Paris: Librairie internationale.

334   *References*

Kadıoğlu, A. 2009. 'Genos versus Devlet: Conceptions of Citizenship in Greece and Turkey', in Anastasakis, O., Nicolaidis, K. and Öktem, K. (eds.), *In the Long Shadow of Europe: Greeks and Turks in the Era of Postnationalism*. Leiden: Martinus Nijhoff Publishers, 115–42.

Kafadar, C. 1995. *Between Two Worlds: The Construction of the Ottoman State*. Berkeley: University of California Press.

Kaldellis, A. 2007. *Hellenism in Byzantium: The Transformations of Greek Identity and the Reception of the Classical Tradition*. Cambridge: Cambridge University Press.

Kaldellis, A. 2012. 'From Rome to New Rome, from Empire to Nation-State', in Grig, L. and Kelly, G. (eds.), *Two Romes: Rome and Constantinople in Late Antiquity*. Oxford: Oxford University Press, 387–404.

Kaldellis, A. 2014. *New Herodotos: Laonikos Chalkokondyles on the Ottoman Empire, the Fall of Byzantium, and the Emergence of the West*. Cambridge, MA: Harvard University Press.

Kaldellis, A. 2015. *The Byzantine Republic: People and Power in New Rome*. Cambridge, MA: Harvard University Press.

Kaldellis, A. 2019. *Romanland: Ethnicity and Empire in Byzantium*. Cambridge, MA: Harvard University Press.

Kapriev, G. 1999. 'Kulturnata identichnost na srednoekovna Bălgariya', *Kultura* 21 (2346), 28 May. http://newspaper.kultura.bg/bg/article/view/2535.

Karamanolakis, V. 2006. *I sygkrotisi tis istorikis epistimis kai i didaskalia tis istorias sto Panepistimio Athinon (1837–1932)*. Athens: Istoriko Archeio Ellinikis Neolaias, Institouto Neoellinikon Ereunon.

Karavelov, L. 1967. *Săbrani săchineniya*, vols. VI, VII, VIII. Sofia: Bălgarski pisatel.

Katsiamboura, Y. 2005. 'Marxistikes proseggiseis tou Vyzantiou apo tin elliniki istoriografia', *Kritiki epistimi kai ekpaideusi* 1: 71–9.

Kazhdan, A. 2003. '"Trudny put" v Vizantiyu', in Chekalova, A., *Mir Aleksandra Kazhdana*. St Petersburg: Aleteya, 486–502.

Keramopulos, A. 1939. 'Que sont les Koutzovalaques? Un problème ethnologique', *Le Messager d'Athènes*, 5193–200.

Keydar, Ç. 1987. *State and Class in Turkey: A Study in Capitalist Development*. London: Verso.

Kioussopoulou, T. 2013. 'La délégation grecque au IIe Congrès international des études byzantines (Belgrade, 1927)', in Delouis, O., Couderc, A. and Guran, P. (eds.), *Héritages de Byzance en Europe du Sud-Est à l'époque moderne et contemporaine*. Athens: Ecole française d'Athènes, 403–11.

Kitroeff, A. 1989. 'Continuity and Change in Contemporary Greek Historiography', *European History Quarterly* 19: 269–98.

Kitromilides, P. 1979. 'The Dialectic of Intolerance: Ideological Dimensions of Ethnic Conflict', *Journal of the Hellenic Diaspora* 6/4: 5–30.

Kitromilides, P. 1989. '"Imagined Communities" and the Origins of the National Question in the Balkans', *European History Quarterly* 19/2: 149–92.

Kitromilides, P. 1998. 'On the Intellectual Content of Greek Nationalism: Paparrigopoulos, Byzantium and the Great Idea', in Ricks, D. and

References

Magdalino, P. (eds.), *Byzantium and the Modern Greek Identity*. Farnham: Ashgate, 25–33.

Kitsikis, D. 1996. *Türk-Yunan İmparatorluğu: Arabölge Gerçeği Işığında Osmanlı Tarihine Bakış*. Istanbul: İletişim Yayınları.

Kochev, N. (ed.) 1979. *D-r Ivan Seliminski. Izbrani săchineniya*. Sofia: Nauka i izkustvo.

Kokosalakis, N. 1987. 'The Political Significance of Popular Religion in Greece', *Archive des sciences sociales des religions* 64: 37–52.

Kolarov, H. and Gyuzelev, V. 1972. 'Spiridon N. Palaouzov kato istorik na srednovekovna Bălgariya', *Vekove* 1/6: 50–7.

Konstantinova, Y. 2010. 'Myths and Pragmatism in the Political Ideology of Ivan Seliminski', in Kitromilides, P. and Tabaki, A. (eds.), *Greek–Bulgarian Relations in the Age of National Identity Formation*. Athens: Institute of Neohellenic Research, 163–80.

Köprülü, M. 1992. *The Origins of the Ottoman Empire*. Trans. and ed. Leiser, G. Albany: State University of New York Press [originally published as *Les origins de l'Empire Ottoman*. Paris: E. de Boccard (1935)].

Köprülü, M. 1993. *Islam in Anatolia after the Turkish Invasion*. Trans. and ed. Leiser, G. Salt Lake City: University of Utah Press [originally published as M. Fuat Köprülü, 'Anadolu'da yslamiyet: Türk ystilasından Sonra Anadolu Tarih-i Dinisine Bir Nazar ve Bu Tarihin Menba'ları', *Darülfünun Edebiyat Fakültesi Mecmuası* 2 (1922)].

Köprülü, M. 1999. *Some Observations on the Influence of Byzantine Institutions upon Ottoman Institutions*. Trans. and ed. Leiser, G. Ankara: Türk Tarih Kurumu [originally published as *Bizans müesseselerinin osmanlı müesseselerine tesiri hakkında bāzı mülāhazalar* (1931)].

Kordatos, I. 1957. *Istoria tis Neoteras Eladas I*. Athens: Ekdoseis '200s aionas'.

Kostantaras, D. 2015. 'Byzantine Turns in Modern Greek Thought and Historiography, 1767–1874', *The Historical Review/La Revue Historique* 12: 163–98.

Koubourlis, I. 2005. *La formation de l'histoire nationale grecque: L'apport de Spyridon Zambélios (1815–1881)*. Athens: Institut de Recherches Néohelléniques.

Koubourlis, I. 2009. 'European Historiographical Influences upon the Young Konstantinos Paparrigopoulos', in Beaton, R. and Ricks, D. (eds.), *The Making of Modern Greece: Nationalism, Romanticism and the Uses of the Past (1797–1896)*. Farnham: Ashgate, 53–63.

Koubourlis, I. 2010. 'Les Bulgares dans les premiers textes de Constantinos Paparrigopoulos et de Spyridon Zambelios', in Kitromilides, P. and Tabaki, A. (eds.), *Greek–Bulgarian Relations in the Age of National Identity Formation*. Athens: Institute of Neohellenic Research, 133–45.

Koubourlis, I. 2013a. 'Augustin Thierry et l''héllenisation' de l'Empire byzantine jusqu'à 1853: les dettes des historiographes de la Grèce médiévale et moderne à l'école libérale française', in Delouis, O., Couderc, A. and Guran, P. (eds.), *Héritages de Byzance en Europe du Sud-Est à l'époque moderne et contemporaine*. Athens: Ecole française d'Athènes, 249–61.

References

Koubourlis, I. 2013b. 'Liberal and Historicist Views of the Greek War of Independence', *XPONOΣ* 07. www.chronosmag.eu/index.php/ikoubourlis–liberal–and–historicist–views–of–the–greek–war–of–independence.html.

Koufou, A. 2008. 'The Discourse on Hellenicity, Historical Continuity and the Greek Left', in Damaskos, D. and Plantzos, D. (eds.), *A Singular Antiquity: Archeology and Hellenic Identity in Twentieth-Century Greece*. Athens: Mouseio Benaki, 299–307.

Koukoules, P. 1948–57. *Byzantinon bios kai politismos*, 6 vols. Athens: Ekdoseis tou Gallikou Institoutou Athenon.

Koulouri, C. 1991. *Dimensions idéologiques de l'historicité en Grèce (1834–1914)*. Frankfurt am Main: Peter Lang.

Kovačević, L. and Jovanović, L. 1893–4. *Istorija srpskog naroda*, 2 vols. Belgrade: Državna štamparija Kraljevine Srbije.

Krallis, D. 2014. 'The Outsider's Gaze: Reflections on Recent Non-Byzantinist Readings of Byzantine History and on Their Implications for Our Field', *Byzantina Symmeikta* 23: 183–99.

La Grèce byzantine et moderne. Essais historiques. 1893. Paris: Librairies de Firmin-Didot et Cie.

Lambros, S. 1902. *Logoi kai Arthra 1878–1902*. Athens: P. D. Sakellarios.

Langlois, C. and Seignobos, C. 1898. *Introduction aux études historiques*. Paris: Hachette et Cie, 1898.

Laurent, V. 1948. 'Les études byzantines en Roumanie 1939–1946', *Revue des études byzantines* 6: 241–68.

Laurent, V. and Dalleggio, E. 1949. 'Les études byzantines en Grèce (1940–1948)', *Revue des études byzantines* 7: 91–128.

Laurenţiu, V. 2001. *Imagini ale identităţii naţionale: România şi expoziţiile universal de la Paris, 1867–1937*. Bucharest: Editura Meridiane.

Leanca, G. 2013. '"Byzance" et la modernité roumaine: de la négation à la patrimonialisation sous l'influence française', in Delouis, O., Couderc, A. and Guran, P. (eds.), *Héritages de Byzance en Europe du Sud-Est à l'époque moderne et contemporaine*. Athens: Ecole française d'Athènes, 285–300.

Lecky, W. 1896. *A History of European Morals from Augustus to Charlemagne*, vol. II. London: D. Appleton.

Leont'ev, K. 2005. 'Vizantizm i slavyanstvo', in Leont'ev, K., *Polnoe sobranie sochineniy i pisem v 12 tomah*, vols. VII/I. St Petersburg: Vladimir Dal, 300–443 [originally published in 1875].

Levtchenko, M. 1949. *Byzance des origins à 1453*. Paris: Payot [originally published as *Istoriya Vizantii. Kratkiy ocherk*. Moscow: Sotsekgiz (1940)].

Liakos, A. 2004. 'Modern Greek Historiography (1974–2000): The Era of Transition from Dictatorship to Democracy', in Brunnbauer, U. (ed.), *(Re)Writing History: Historiography in Southeastern Europe after Socialism*. Münster: LIT, 351–78.

Liakos, A. 2008. 'Hellenism and the Making of Modern Greece: Time, Language, Space', in Zacharia, K. (ed.), *Hellenisms: Culture, Identity and Ethnicity from Antiquity to Modernity*. Aldershot: Ashgate, 201–36.

References

Lihachov, D. 1969. 'Staroslavyanskite literaturi kato sistema', *Literaturna misăl* 13/1: 3–38.

Lilova, D. 2003. *Văzrozhdenskite znacheniya na natsionalnoto ime.* Sofia: Prosveta.

Lilova, D. 2013. 'L'héritage partagé? Byzance, Fallmerayer et la formation de l'historiographie bulgare au XIXe siècle', in Delouis, O., Couderc, A. and Guran, P. (eds.), *Héritages de Byzance en Europe du Sud-Est à l'époque moderne et contemporaine.* Athens: Ecole française d'Athènes, 319–27.

Lindner, R. 2014. 'Byzantine and Turkish Heritages', in Sakel, D. (ed.), *Byzantine Culture: Papers from the Conference 'Byzantine Days of Istanbul' Held on the Occasion of Istanbul Being European Cultural Capital 2010.* Ankara: n.p., 269–77.

Livanios, D. 2003. 'Christians, Heroes and Barbarians: Serbs and Bulgarians in the Modern Greek Historical Imagination (1602–1950)', in Tziovas, D. (ed.), *Greece and the Balkans: Identities, Perceptions and Cultural Encounters Since the Enlightenment.* Aldershot: Ashgate, 68–83.

Livanios, D. 2008. 'The Quest for Hellenism: Religion, Nationalism, and Collective Identities in Greece, 1453–1913', in Zacharia, K. (ed.), *Hellenisms: Culture, Identity and Ethnicity from Antiquity to Modernity.* Aldershot: Ashgate, 237–69.

Lowry, H. 2003. *The Nature of the Early Ottoman State.* Albany: State University of New York Press.

Lyubenova, L. 1987. 'Lektsionen kurs na prof. Petăr Nikov za istoriyata na bălgarskiya narod pod osmansko vladichestvo', in *Bălgariya prez XV–XVII vek. Istoriografski izsledvaniya.* Sofia: BAN, 253–75.

Mackridge, P. 1998. 'Byzantium and the Greek Language Question in the Nineteenth Century', in Ricks, D. and Magdalino, P. (eds.), *Byzantium and the Modern Greek Identity.* Farnham: Ashgate, 49–61.

Mackridge, P. 2009. *Language and National Identity in Greece 1766–1976.* Oxford: Oxford University Press.

Mackridge, P. 2012. 'The Heritages of the Modern Greeks', *British Academy Review* 19: 33–41.

Magdalino, P. 1992. 'Hellenism and Nationalism in Byzantium', in Burke, J. and Gauntlett. S. (eds.), *Neohellenism.* Canberra: Australian National University, 1–29.

Maksimović, L. 1988. 'Razvoj vizantologije', in *Univerzitet u Beogradu 1838–1988. Zbornik radova.* Belgrade: Univerzitet u Beogradu i Savremena administracija, 655–71.

Maksimović, L. 1995. 'Recepcija vizantijskih državnih institucija u Srbiji i Stojan Novaković', in Stojančević, V. (ed.), *Stojan Novaković – ličnost i delo.* Belgrade: SANU, 267–72.

Maksimović, L. 2003a. 'Srbija i Vizantijsko carstvo', in *Bălgariya i Sărbiya v konteksta na vizantiyskata tsivilizatsiya.* Sofia: Izdatelstvo na BAN 'Marin Drinov', 13–25.

Maksimović, L. 2003b. 'Vuzantijsko nasleđe i Srbi', in Schubert, G., Konstantinović, Z. and Zwiener, U. (eds.), *Serben und Deutsche: Traditionen der Gemeinsamkeit gegen Feindbilder.* Jena: Palm & Enke, 95–106.

338   *References*

Maksimović, L. 2008. *Vizantijski svet i Srbi*. Belgrade: Istorijski institut.
Maksimović, L. and Subotić, G. 2003. 'La Serbie entre Byzance et l'Occident', in *Byzantina-Metabyzantina. La périphérie dans le temps et l'espace*. Paris: EHESS, 169–83.
Malingoudis, P. 1981. '"Die Bulgaren im Byzantinischen Reich" kritische Bemerkungen', *Balkan Studies* 22: 247–67.
Mango, C. 1965. 'Byzantinism and Romantic Hellenism', *Journal of the Warburg and Courtauld Institutes* 28: 29–43.
Mango, C. 1968. 'Review: [Untitled]', *The Journal of Hellenic Studies* 88: 256–8.
Mango, C. 1973. 'The Phanariots and the Byzantine Tradition', in Clogg, R. (ed.), *The Struggle for Greek Independence*. London: Macmillan, 49–55.
Mango, C. 1981. 'Discontinuity with the Classical Past in Byzantium', in Mullett, M. and Scott, R. (eds.), *Byzantium and the Classical Tradition*. Birmingham: Centre for Byzantine Studies, 48–57.
Mango, C. 1984. *Byzantium and Its Image: History and Culture of the Byzantine Empire and Its Heritage*. London: Variorum Reprints.
Mansel, A. 1938. *Mısır ve Ege Tarihi Notları*. Istanbul: Istanbul Üniversitesi Edebiyat Fakültesi Yayınları.
Marciniak, P. and Smythe, D. (eds.) 2016. *The Reception of Byzantium in European Culture Since 1500*. London: Routledge.
Marković, O. 2011. 'Tumačenje istorije Vizantije u sovjetskom modelu udžbenika u Bugarskoj i Jugoslaviji 1945–1953', *Godišnjak za društvenu istoriju* 2: 51–66.
Matalas, P. 2002. *Ethnos kai Orthodoksia: Oi peripeteies mias shesis. Apo to "Elladiko" sto Voulgariko Shisma*. Heraklion: Crete University Press.
Matschke, K.-P. 2002. 'Research Problems Concerning the Transition to Tourkokratia: The Byzantinist Standpoint', in Adanır, F. and Faroqhi, S. (eds.), *The Ottomans and the Balkans: A Discussion of Historiography*. Leiden: Brill, 79–113.
Maufroy, S. 2010. 'Les premiers congrès internationaux des études byzantines: entre nationalisme scientifique et construction internationale d'une discipline', *Revue germanique internationale* 12: 229–40.
Medvedev, I. 2006. *Peterburgskoe vizantinovedenie*. St Petersburg: Aleteya.
Midhat, A. 1885–8. *Mufassal Tarih-i Kurun-i Cedide*, 3 vols. Istanbul: n.p.
Millas, H. 2004. 'National Perception of the "Other" and the Persistence of Some Images', in Aydın, M. and Ifantis, K. (eds.), *Turkish-Greek Relations: The Security Dilemma in the Aegean*. London: Routledge, 53–66.
Millet, G. 1916. *L'école grecque dans l'architecture byzantine*. Paris: Ernest Leroux.
Millet, G. 1919. *L'ancien art serbe. Les églises*. Paris: E. de Boccard.
Mishkova, D. 2004. 'The Uses of Tradition and National Identity in the Balkans', in Todorova, M. (ed.), *Balkan Identities: Nation and Memory*. London: Hurst, 269–93.
Mishkova, D. 2012. 'Liberalism and Tradition in the Nineteenth-Century Balkans: Toward History and Methodology of Political Transfer', *East European Politics and Societies and Cultures* 26/4: 668–92.
Mishkova, D. 2015. 'The Afterlife of a Commonwealth: Narratives of Byzantium in the National Historiographies of Greece, Bulgaria, Serbia and Romania', in

References

Daskalov, R. and Vezenkov, A. (eds.), *Entangled Histories of the Balkans, vol. III: Shared Pasts, Disputed Legacies.* Leiden: Brill, 118–74.

Mishkova, D. 2019. *Beyond Balkanism: The Scholarly Politics of Region Making.* Abingdon: Routledge.

Mishkova, D., Turda, M. and Trencsényi, B. (eds.) 2014. *Discourses of Collective Identity in Central and Southeast Europe (1770–1945): Texts and Commentaries, vol. IV: Anti-Modernism – Radical Revisions of Collective Identity.* Budapest: CEU Press.

Morrisson, C. 2010. 'New Wine in New Bottles: Byzantine Studies Come of Age (c. 1981–c. 2007)', in Harlaftis, G., Karapidakis, N., Sbonias, K. and Vaiopoulos, V. (eds.), *The New Ways of History: Developments in Historiography.* London: I. B. Tauris, 83–104.

Mošin, V. 1937. 'Vizantiski uticaj u Srbiji u XIV veku', *Jugoslovenski istoriski časopis* 3/1–4: 147–60.

Mošin, V. 1939. 'Srednjovekovna Srbija i vizantijska kultura', *Srpski književni glasnik* 56/5: 354–65.

Murnu, G. 1931. 'Românii și grecii', *Revista macedoromână* 3/1–2: 3–9.

Murnu, G. 1938. 'Les roumains de la Bulgarie médiéval', *Balcania* 1: 1–21.

Mutafchiev, P. 1922. 'Gărtsi, vizantiytsi i elini', *Demokratsiya* 3/1: 58–63; 3/4: 84–9.

Mutafchiev, P. 1931. 'Kăm filosofiyata na bălgarskata istoriya. Vizantinizmăt v srednovekovna Bălgariya', Filosofski pregled 3/1: 27–36 [originally published as 'Der Byzantinismus im mittelalterlichen Bulgarien', *Byzantinische Zeitschrift* 30: 387–94 (1929–30)].

Mutafchiev, P. 1934. 'Pop Bogomil i sv. Ivan Rilksi. Duhăt na otritsanieto v nashata istoriya', *Filosofski pregled* 6/2: 97–112.

Mutafchiev, P. 1940. 'Gradăt i seloto', *Prosveta* 5/5: 513–30.

Mutafchiev, P. 1987. *Kniga za bălgarite.* Sofia: BAN.

Mutafchiev, P. 1992. *Istoriya na bălgarskiya narod.* Sofia: BAN [first published in 1943].

Myrogiannis, S. 2012. *The Emergence of a Greek Identity (1700–1821).* Newcastle: Cambridge Scholars.

Năstase, D. 1981. 'L'idée impériale dans les pays Roumains et le "crypto-empire chrétien" sous la domination ottomane. Etat et importance du problème', *Byzantina Symmeikta* 4: 201–50.

Năstase, D. 1988. 'Imperial Claims in the Romanian Principalities from the Fourteenth to the Seventeenth Centuries: New Contributions', in Clucas, L. (ed.), *The Byzantine Legacy in Eastern Europe.* Boulder, CO: East European Monographs, 205–24.

Năsturel, P. 1973. 'Considérations sur l'idée impériale chez les Roumains', *Byzantina* 5: 397–413.

Năsturel, P. 1986. *Le Mont Athos et les Roumains: recherches sur leurs relations du milieu du XIV siècle à 1654.* Rome: Pont. Institutum Studiorum Orientalium.

Necipoğlu, N. 2013. 'Türkiye'de Bizans tarihi çalışmalarına dair gözlemler', *Toplumsal Tarih* 229: 76–7.

References

Neumann, C. 2002. 'Bad Times, Better Self: Definitions of Identity and Strategies for Development in Late Ottoman Historiography, 1850–1900', in Adanır, F. and Faroqhi, S. (eds.), *The Ottomans and the Balkans: A Discussion of Historiography*. Leiden: Brill, 57–78.

Newton, C. 1880. 'Hellenic Studies: An Introductory Address', *Journal of Hellenic Studies* 1: 1–6.

Nicol, D. 1986. 'Byzantium and Greece', in Nicol, D., *Studies in Late Byzantine History and Prosopography*. London: Variorum Reprints, 2–20.

Nikov, P. 1920–1. 'Zadachata na dneshnata bălgarska istoriografiya', *Godishnik na Sofiyskiya universitet, Istoriko-filologicheski fakultet* 17: 289–307.

Nikov, P. 1937. *Vtoro bălgarsko tsarstvo 1186–1396*. Sofia: Istorichesko druzhestvo.

Novaković, S. 1912–13. 'Les problèmes serbes', *Archiv für slavische Philologie* 33: 438–66; 34: 203–33.

Novaković, S. 1966 [1922]. *Iz srpske istorije*. Novi Sad: Budučnost.

Nuri, C. 1912–13. *Tarih-i Tedenniyat-ı Osmaniye, Mukadderat-i Tarihiye*. Istanbul: Yeni Osmanlı Matbaa ve Kütüphansi.

Nuri, C. 1917. *Rum ve Bizans*. Istanbul: Cemiyet Kütübhanesi.

Nystazopoulou-Pelekidou, M. 1994. 'Oi vyzantines istorikes spoudes stin Ellada. Apo ton Spyridona Zambelio ston Dionysio Zakythino', *Symmeikta* 9: 153–76.

Nystazopoulou-Pélékidou, M. 2008. 'L'histoire des congrès internationaux des études byzantines – Première Partie', *Byzantina Symmeikta* 18: 11–33.

Obolensky, D. 1966. 'Modern Russian Attitudes to Byzantium', *Jahrbuch der Österreichischen Byzantinischen Gesellschaft* 15: 61–72.

Obolensky, D. 1971. *The Byzantine Commonwealth: Eastern Europe 500–1453*. London: Weidenfeld and Nicolson.

Obolensky, D. 1982. *The Byzantine Inheritance of Eastern Europe*. London: Variorum Reprints.

Obolensky, D. 1994. *Byzantium and the Slavs*. Crestwood, NY: St. Vladimir's Seminary Press.

Ostrogorski, G. 1934. 'Iz čega je i kako stvorena Vizantija', *Srpski književni glasnik* 41/7: 508–14.

Ostrogorski, G. 1948. 'Uticaj Slovena na društveni preobražaj Vizantije', *Istorijski glasnik* 1: 12–21.

Ostrogorski, G. 1951. *Pronija: Prilog istoriji feudalizma u Vizantiji i u južnoslovenskim zemljama*. Belgrade: Srpska Akademija Nauka.

Ostrogorsky, G. 1954. *Pour l'histoire de la féodalité byzantine*. Brussels: Institut de philologie et d'histoire orientales et slaves.

Ostrogorski, G. 1963. 'Byzantium and the South Slavs', *Slavonic and East European Review* 42/98: 1–14.

Ostrogorski, G. 1965. *Serska oblast posle Dušanove smrti*. Belgrade: Vizantološki institut SANU.

Ostrogorski, G. 1967. 'Problèmes des relations byzantine-serbes au XIVe siècle', in *Proceedings of the XIIIth International Congress of Byzantine Studies. Oxford, 5–10 September 1966*. London: Oxford University Press, 41–55.

References

Ostrogorski, G. 1970. *Vizantija i sloveni*. Belgrade: Prosveta.

Ostrogorsky, G. 1980. *History of the Byzantine State*. Oxford: Basil Blackwell.

Oțetea, A. 1965. 'Nicolae Iorga istoric al românilor', *Studii. Revistă de istorie* 18/6: 1215–25.

Özal, T. 1988. *La Turquie en Europe*. Paris: Plon [revised English edition: *Turkey in Europe and Europe in Turkey*. Nicosia: K. Rustem & Brother (1991)].

Page, G. 2008. *Being Byzantine: Greek Identity Before the Ottomans, 1200–1420*. Cambridge: Cambridge University Press.

Palaouzov, S. 1977. *Izbrani trudove*, vol. II. Sofia: Nauka i izkustvo.

Panaitescu, P. 1944. '"Perioada slavonă" la români și ruperea de cultura Apusului', *Balcania* 7/1: 126–51 [republished in Panaitescu, P. 1971. *Contribuții la istoria culturii românești*. Bucharest: Editura Minerva, 28–49].

Pantelić, B. 2011. 'Memories of a Time Forgotten: The Myth of the Perennial Nation', *Nations and Nationalism* 17/2: 443–64.

Pantelić, B. 2016. 'The Last Byzantines: Perceptions of Identity, Culture, and Heritage in Serbia', *Nationalities Papers* 44/3: 430–55.

Papacostea, Ș. 1996. 'Captive Clio: Romanian Historiography Under Communist Rule', *European History Quarterly* 26: 181–208.

Papacostea, V. 1943. 'La Péninsule Balkanique et le problème des études comparées', *Balcania* 6: iii–xxi.

Paparrigopoulos, K. 1878. *Histoire de la civilisation hellénique*. Paris: Librairie Hachette.

Paparrigopoulo, K. [sic] 1879. *Les évolutions de l'histoire grecque à notre époque*. Athens: Messager d'Athènes.

Paparrigopoulos, K. 1963. *Istoria tou ellinikou ethnous*. 7 vols. [1860–74, revised 1885–8]. Athens: Eleftherodakis.

Park, T. 1975. '*The Life and Writing of Mehmet Fuad Köprülü: The Intellectual and Turkish Cultural Modernization*'. PhD thesis, Johns Hopkins University, Baltimore.

Patlagean, É. 2005. 'Byzance dans le millénaire médiéval', *Annales. Histoire, Sciences Sociales* 4: 721–32.

Patlagean, É. 2007. *Un moyen âge grec: Byzance, IXe–XVe siècle*. Paris: Albin Michel.

Pertusi, A. 1966. 'Le siècle de l'erudition', *Jahrbuch der Österreichischen Byzantinischen Gesellschaft* 15: 3–25.

Pertusi, A. 1967. *Storiografia umanistica e mondo bizantino*. Palermo: Istituto Siciliano di Studi Bizantini e Neoellenici.

Petkanova-Toteva, D. 1969. 'Po povod nyakoi mneniya za starobălgarskata literatura', *Literaturna misăl* 13/5: 24–40.

Petmezas, S. 2009. 'From Privileged Outcasts to Power Players: The "Romantic" Redefinition of the Hellenic Nation in the Mid-Nineteenth Century', in Beaton, R. and Ricks, D. (eds.), *The Making of Modern Greece: Nationalism, Romanticism and the Uses of the Past (1797–1896)*. Farnham: Ashgate, 123–35.

342   *References*

Philippides, D. and Constantas, Gr. 1791. *Geographia Neoteriki*. Vienna: Para tō eugenei Kyriō Thōma tō Trattnern.

Philippidis, D. 1816. *History of Romania*. Leipzig: Tauchnitz.

Pippidi, A. 1983. *Tradiția politică bizantină în țările române în secolele XVI–XVIII*. Bucharest: Editura Academiei RSR.

Pippidi, A. 2004. 'Entre héritage et imitation. La tradition byzantine dans les Pays roumains: Nouvelles réflexions, vingt ans après', in Kitromilides, P. and Tabaki. A. (eds.), *Relations gréco-roumaines: Interculturalité et identité nationale*. Athens: Institut de Recherches Néohelléniques, 23–37.

Pirivatrić, S. 2010. 'A Case Study in the Emergence of Byzantine Studies: Serbia in the Nineteenth and Twentieth Centuries', in Stephenson, P. (ed.), *The Byzantine World*. Abingdon: Routledge, 481–90.

Pirivatrić, S. 2016a. 'The Dynamics of Byzantine-Serbian Political Relations', in Bikić, V. (ed.), *Byzantine Heritage and Serbian Art I: Processes of Byzantinisation and Serbian Archaeology*. Belgrade: Serbian National Committee of Byzantine Studies, 17–35.

Pirivatrić, S. 2016b. 'The Serbs and the Overlapping Authorities of Rome and Constantinople (7th to 16th Century)', in *Proceedings of the 23rd International Congress of Byzantine Studies (Belgrade, 22–27 August, 2016), Plenary Papers*. Belgrade: The Serbian National Committee of AIEB, 223–40.

Politis, A. 1998. 'From Christian Roman Emperors to the Glorious Greek Ancestors', in Ricks, D. and Magdalino, P. (eds.), *Byzantium and the Modern Greek Identity*. Aldershot: Ashgate, 1–14.

Politis, N. 1928. 'Croyances populaires sur le rétablissement de la Nation Hellénique', *La Revue de Grèce* 1: 151–70.

Popescu, C. 2004. *Le style national roumain: Construire une nation à travers l'architecture 1881–1945*. Rennes: Presses universitaires de Rennes.

Prokić, B. 1906. 'Vizantijske istorijske studije u Francuskoj', *Delo* 27: 56–7.

Psichari, J. 1897. *Autour de la Grèce*. Paris: Calmann Lévy.

Radić, R. 1996. 'Georgiy Ostrogorsiy i serbskaya vizantologiya', in *Russkaya emigratsiya v Yugoslavii*. Moscow: Indrik, 200–7.

Radić, R. 2002. *Strah u poznoj Vizantiji 1180–1453*, vols. I–II. Belgrade: Stubovi culture.

Radić, R. 2006. *Vizantija, purpur i pergament*. Belgrade: Evoluta.

Radić, R. 2014. *Drugo lice Vizantije*. Belgrade: Evoluta.

Radojčić, N. 1942. *Razvitak srpske države u srednjem veku*. Belgrade: Državna štamparija.

Radonić, J. 1912. *Prošlost Stare Srbije*. Belgrade: Nova Štampanja 'Davidović'.

Radonić, J. 1938. *Slike iz istorije i književnosti*. Belgrade: n.p.

Rados, L. 2005. *Sub semnul acvilei. Preocupări de bizantinistică în România până la 1918*. Bucharest: Omonia.

Raffensperger, C. 2012. *Reimagining Europe: Kievan Rus' in the Medieval World*. Cambridge, MA: Harvard University Press.

Rambaud, A. 1870. *L'Empire grec au dixième siècle: Constantin Porphyrogénète*. Paris: A. Franck.

References

Rapp, C. 2008. 'Hellenic Identity, Romanitas, and Christianity in Byzantium', in Zacharia, K. (ed.), *Hellenisms: Culture, Identity, and Ethnicity from Antiquity to Modernity*. Aldershot: Ashgate, 127–47.

Refik, A. 1911–12. *Büyük Tarih-i Umumi: Beseriyetin Tekemmülat-ı Medeniye, İçtimaiye, Siyasiye ve Fikriyesi*, vol. IV. Istanbul: Kütübhane-i İslam ve Askeri, İbrahim Hilmi.

Refik, A. 1915. *Bizans İmparatoriçeleri, Bizans Tarihine Medhal, İmparatoriçelerin Tarz-ı Hayatı, Teodora, Atenais, İren, Dindar Teodora, Teofano, Zovi, Anna Comnenus*. Istanbul: Muhtar Halid Kitabhanesi.

Reinsch, D. R. 2010. 'The History of Editing Byzantine Historiographical Texts', in Stephenson, P. (ed.), *The Byzantine World*. London: Routledge, 435–44.

Reinsch, D. R. 2016. 'Hieronymus Wolf as Editor and Translator of Byzantine Texts', in Marciniak, P. and Smythe, D. (eds.), *The Reception of Byzantium in European Culture Since 1500*. New York: Routledge, 43–54.

Runciman, S. 1930. *A History of the First Bulgarian Empire*. London: G. Bell & Sons.

Runciman, S. 1976. 'Gibbon and Byzantium', *Daedalus* 105/3: 103–10.

Russo, D. 1939. *Studii istorice greco-române: opere postume*, 2 vols. Bucharest: Fundația pentru literatură și artă 'Regele Carol II'.

Saradi, H. 2014. 'The Three Fathers of the Greek Orthodox Church: Greek Paideia, Byzantine Innovation and the Formation of Modern Greek Identity', in Nilsson, I. and Stephenson, P. (eds.), *Wanted: Byzantium – The Desire for a Lost Empire*. Uppsala: Uppsala University Press, 134–60.

Schevill, F. 1922. *The History of the Balkan Peninsula: From the Earliest Times to the Present Day*. New York: Harcourt, Brace & Co.

Seton-Watson, R. 1917. *The Rise of Nationality in the Balkans*. London: Constable & Co.

Ševčenko, I. 1956. 'Byzantine Cultural Influences', in Black, C. (ed.), *Rewriting Russian History: Soviet Interpretations of Russia's Past*. New York: Frederick A. Praeger, 143–97.

Ševčenko, I. 1991. *Byzantium and the Slavs in Letters and Culture*. Cambridge, MA: Harvard Ukrainian Research Institute; Naples: Istituto Universitario Orientale.

Ševčenko, I. 1995. 'Was There Totalitarianism in Byzantium? Constantinople's Control Over Its Asiatic Hinterland in the Early Ninth Century', in Mango, C. and Dagron, G. (eds.), *Constantinople and Its Hinterland*. Aldershot: Variorum, 91–105.

Shepard, J. 2006a. 'Byzantium's Overlapping Circles', in *Proceedings of the 21st International Congress of Byzantine Studies*. London: Ashgate, 15–55.

Shepard, J. 2006b. 'The Byzantine Commonwealth 1000–1550', in Angold, M. (ed.), *The Cambridge History of Christianity, vol. V: Eastern Christianity*. Cambridge: Cambridge University Press, 3–52.

Shishmanov, I. 1894–5. 'La Grèce byzantine et moderne: Essais historiques par D. Bikelas', *Bălgarski pregled* 2/4–5: 210–12.

Shishmanov, I. 1928. 'Zapadnoevropeysko i bălgarsko văzrazhdane', in Shishmanov, I. 1965. *Izbrani săchineniya*, vol. I. Sofia: BAN, 74-80.

References

Sigalas, N. 2001. 'Ellēnismos kai exellēnismos: o schēmatismos tēs neo–ellēnikēs ennoias ellēnismos', *Ta Istorika* 34: 3-70.

Slaveykov, P. 1980. *Săchineniya*, vol. VI. Sofia: Bălgarski pisatel.

Solov'ev, V. 1896. 'Vizantizm i Rossiya', *in Sobranie sochineniya*, 2nd ed. St. Petersburg, n.p., 283–325.

Soloviev, V. 1922. *La Russie et l'Eglise Universelle* [1st ed. 1889], 4th ed. Paris: Librairie Stock.

Soloviev, A. 1936. 'Aperçu historique du développement du droit dans les Balkans (jusqu'au XVe siècle)', *Revue Internationale des Etudes Balkaniques* 1–2/3–4: 437–45.

Solovjev, A. 1928a. *Zakonodavstvo Stefana Dušana, cara Srba i Grka*. Skopje: Skopsko naučno društvo.

Solovjev, A. 1928b. *Značaj vizantijskog prava na Balkanu*. Belgrade: Izdanje Čupićeve zadužbine.

Spieser, J.-M. 2016. 'Du Cange and Byzantium', in Cormack, R. and Jeffreys, E. (eds.), *Through the Looking Glass: Byzantium through British Eyes*. London: Routledge, 199–210.

Srećković, P. 1888. *Istorija srpskoga naroda*, vol. II. Belgrade: Kraljevsko–srpska državna štamparija.

Stamatopoulos, D. 2009. *To Vyzantio meta to Ethnos: To provlima tis synecheias stis valkanikes istoriografies*. Athens: Alexandria.

Stănescu, E. (ed.) 1971. *Nicolae Iorga, istoric al Bizanțului*. Bucharest: Editura Academiei RSR.

Stănescu, E. 1974. 'Byzance et les Pays roumains aux IXe–Xv^e siècles', in *Actes du XIVe Congrès International des études byzantines, 6–12 septembre 1971*, vol. I. Bucharest: Editura Academiei RSR, 393–43.

Stanev, N. 1934. *Srednovekovna Bălgariya*. Sofia: St. Atanasov.

Stanković, V. 2012. *Kralj Milutin (1282–1321)*. Belgrade: Freska.

Stanković, V. 2013. 'The Character and Nature of Byzantine Influence in Serbia (from the End of the Eleventh to the End of the Thirteenth Century): Reality – Policy – Ideology', in Angar, M. and Sode, C. (eds.), *Serbia and Byzantium: Proceedings of the International Conference Held on 15 December 2008 at the University of Cologne*. Frankfurt am Main: Peter Lang, 75–93.

Stanković, V. 2016a. 'Introduction: In the Balkans "Without" Constantinople: Questions of Center and Periphery', in Stanković, V. (ed.), *The Balkans and the Byzantine World Before and After the Captures of Constantinople, 1204 and 1453*. Lanham, MD: Lexington Books, xi–xvi.

Stanković, V. 2016b. 'Rethinking the Position of Serbia within Byzantine Oikoumene in the Thirteenth Century', in Stanković, V. (ed.), *The Balkans and the Byzantine World Before and After the Captures of Constantinople, 1204 and 1453*. Lanham, MD: Lexington Books, 91–101.

Stanković, V. 2016–17. 'Putting Byzantium Back on the Map', *Modern Greek Studies Yearbook*. Minneapolis:University of Minnesota, 32/3: 399–405.

Stanojević, S. 1903, 1906. *Vizantija i Srbi*, 2 vols. Novi Sad: Matica Srpska.

References

Stanojević, S. 1908. *Istorija srpskoga naroda*. Belgrade: Štamparija 'Dositije Obradović'.

Stanojević, S. 1922. *Car Dušan*. Belgrade: Izdavačka Knjižara Napredak.

Stanojević, S. 1931. *Ot Velbužda do Kosova*. Belgrade: Naradna štamparija.

Stavrianos, L. 1944. *Balkan Federation: A History of the Movement Toward Balkan Unity in Modern Times*. Northampton, MA: Dept. of History of Smith College.

Ştefănescu, Ş. and Mureşanu, C. (eds.) 2001. *Istoria Românilor*, vol. IV. Bucharest: Editura enciclopedică.

Stephenson, P. 2007. 'E. A. Freeman, a Neglected Commentator on Byzantium and Modern Greece', *La revue historique/Historical Review* 4: 119–56.

Stephenson, P. 2010. 'Byzantium's European Future', in Stephenson, P. (ed.), *The Byzantine World*. London: Routledge, 505–9.

Stouraitis, Y. 2014. 'Roman Identity in Byzantium: A Critical Approach', *Byzantinische Zeitschrift* 107/1: 175–220.

Stouraitis, Y. 2017. 'Reinventing Roman Ethnicity in High and Late Medieval Byzantium', in *Comparative Studies on Medieval Europe*. Vienna: Austrian Academy of Sciences, 70–94.

Stouraitis, Y. 2018. 'Byzantine Romanness: From Geopolitical to Ethnic Conceptions', in Pohl, W., Gantner, C. , Grifoni, C. and Pollheimer-Mohaupt, M. (eds.), *Transformations of Romanness in the Early Middle Ages: Early Medieval Regions and Identities*. Berlin: De Gruyter, 127–35.

Strohmeier, M. 1984. *Seldschukische Geschichte und türkische Geschichtswissenschaft*. Berlin: Klaus Schwarz Verlag.

Svoronos, N. 1953. *Histoire de la Grèce moderne*. Paris: Presses Universitaires de France.

Tabaki, A. 2007. 'Historiographie et identité nationale dans le Sud-Est de l'Europe (XVIIIe siècle–début du XIXe): Antiquité et Byzance dans l'exemple grec', *Etudes balkaniques* 4: 87–96.

Tadić, J. (ed.) 1965. *Historiographie yougoslave 1955–1965*. Belgrade: Federation des Societes Historiques de Yougoslavie.

Tanaşoca, N. 1981. 'De la Vlachie des Assénides au second Empire Bulgare', *Revue des Études Sud-Est Européennes* 19/3: 581–94.

Tanaşoca, N. (ed.) 1984. *Studii istorice privitoare la trecutul românilor de peste Dunăre*. Bucharest: Editura Academiei RSR.

Tanaşoca, N. 1997. 'La construction européenne et le byzantinisme des pays de l'Est: *Le cas de la Roumanie', in New Europe College Yearbook 1994*. Bucharest: Humanitas, 123–41.

Tanaşoca, N. 2001. 'Aperçus of the History of Balkan Romanity', in Theodorescu, R. and Barrows, L. C. (eds.), *Politics and Culture in Southeastern Europe*. Bucharest: UNESCO Studies on Science and Culture, 94–170.

Tanaşoca, N. 2002. 'L'image roumaine de Byzance à l'époque des Lumières', in Theodorescu, R. and Barrows, L. C. (eds.), *South-East Europe: The Ambiguous Definitions of a Space*. Bucharest: UNESCO–CEPES, 47–75.

346 *References*

Tanaşoca, N. 2003. *Bizanţul şi românii: Eseuri, studii, articole*. Bucharest: Editura Fundaţiei Pro.

Tanaşoca, N. 2013. 'Byzance dans la conscience historique des Roumains', in Delouis, O., Couderc, A. and Guran, P. (eds.), *Héritages de Byzance en Europe du Sud-Est à l'époque moderne et contemporaine*. Athens: Ecole française d'Athènes, 263–83.

Tanaşoca, N. 2014. 'Tradiţie bizantină, realitate otomană şi modernitate europeană în epoca brâncovenească', in Chifăr, N., Abrudan, I. and Guran, P. (eds.), *Epoca lui Constantin Brâncoveanu în context Sud-Est European: biserică, societate, geopolitică: simpozion (2014 – Sibiu)*. Sibiu: Andreiana and Astra Museum, 15–48.

Tapkova-Zaimova, V. 1984. '"Grecs" et "Romains" dans la literature bulgare (Contenu d'une réalité médiévale)', *Etudes balkaniques* 1: 51–8.

Tăpkova-Zaimova, V., Dimitrov, D. and Pavlov, P. 2011. *Vizantiya i vizantiyskiyat svyat*. Sofia: Prosveta.

Taranovski, T. 1926. *Dušanov zakonik i Dušanovo carstvo*. Novi Sad: Matica Srpska.

Taranovski, T. 1931–5. *Istorija srpskog prava u Nemanjićkoj državi*, 4 vols. Belgrade: Geca Kon.

Taşkın, Y. 2007. *Milliyetçi Muhafazakar Entelijansiya*. Istanbul: İletişim Yayınları.

Theodor, D. 1981. *Romanitatea carpato-dunăreană şi Bizanţul în veacurile V–XI e. n.* Iaşi: Junimea.

Theodorescu, R. 1974. *Bizanţ, Balcani, Occident la începuturile culturii medievale româneşti (secolele X–XIV)*. Bucharest: Editura ARSR.

Timur, T. 1979. *Osmanlı toplumsal düzeni*. Ankara: Turhan Kitabevi.

Tinnefeld, F. 2011. 'Die Begründung der Byzantinistik als wissenschaftliche Disziplin', in Schreiner, P. and Vogt, E. (eds.), *Karl Krumbacher: Leben und Werk*. Munich: Verlag der Bayerischen Akademie der Wissenschaften, 27–38.

Treadgold, W. 1998. 'The Persistence of Byzantium', *The Wilson Quarterly* 22/4: 66–9.

Treadgold, W. 2010. 'Byzantine Exceptionalism and Some Recent Books on Byzantium', *Historically Speaking* 11/5: 16–19.

Tsoukalas, C. 1999. 'European Modernity and Greek National Identity', *Journal of Southern Europe and the Balkans* 1/1: 7–14.

Turan, O. 1970. 'Anatolia in the Period of the Seljuks and the Beyliks', in Holt, P., Lambton, A. and Lewis, B. (eds.), *The Cambridge History of Islam*, vol. I. Cambridge: Cambridge University Press, 231–62.

Turan, O. 1980. *Tarihi akışı içinde din ve medeniyet*. Istanbul: Nakışlar Yayınevi.

Tziovas, D. (ed.) 2014. *Re-imagining the Past Antiquity and Modern Greek Culture*. Oxford: Oxford University Press.

Ubavkić, M. 1886. *Istorija Srba*, vol. I. Belgrade: Kraljevsko–srpska državna štamparija.

Ubavkić, M. 1887–9. *Istorija Srba*, 2 vols. Belgrade: Prosveta.

Üre, P. 2014. *'Byzantine Heritage, Archaeology, and Politics between Russia and the Ottoman Empire: Russian Archaeological Institute in Constantinople (1894–*

References 347

1914)', unpublished PhD thesis, London School of Economics and Political Science.

Ursinus, M. 1986. 'Byzantine History in Late Ottoman Turkish Historiography', *Byzantine and Modern Greek Studies* 10/1: 211–22.

Ursinus, M. 1987. '"Der schlechteste Staat": Ahmed Midhat Efendi (1844–1913) on Byzantine Institutions', *Byzantine and Modern Greek Studies* 11/1: 237–44.

Ursinus, M. 1988. 'From Süleyman Pasha to Mehmet Köprülü: Roman and Byzantine History in Late Ottoman Historiography', *Byzantine and Modern Greek Studies* 12/1: 305–14.

Vachkova, V. 2005. *Simeon Veliki – pătyat kăm koronata na Zapada*. Sofia: Kama.

Vakalopoulos, A. 1961. *Istoria tou Neou Ellenismou, vol. I. Arches kai diamorphose tou*. Thessaloniki: N. Nikolaide [rev. ed. Thessaloniki: n.p., 1974].

Vakalopoulos, A. 1968. 'Byzantinism and Hellenism: Remarks on the Racial Origin and the Intellectual Continuity of the Greek Nation', *Balkan Studies* 9/1: 101–26.

Vakalopoulos, A. 1970. *Origins of the Greek Nation: The Byzantine Period, 1204–1461*. New Brunswick, NJ: Rutgers University Press.

Vasiliev, A. 1927. 'Byzantine Studies in Russia, Past and Present', *The American Historical Review* 32/3: 539–45.

Vasiliev, A. 1952. *History of the Byzantine Empire, 324–1453*. Madison: The University of Wisconsin Press.

Velestinlis, R. 1976. 'Revolutionary Proclamation (1797)', in Clogg, R. (ed. and trans.), *The Movement for Greek Independence, 1770–1821: A Collection of Documents*. London: Macmillan, 149–50.

Veloudis, G. 1970. 'Jakob Philipp Fallmerayer und die Entstehung des neugrie-chischen Historismus', *Südost–Forschungen* 29: 43–90.

Veloudis, G. 1982. *O Jakob Fallmerayer kai i genesi tou ellinikou istorismou*. Athens: E.M.N.E.–Mnimon.

Vikelas, D. 1885. *Le rôle et les aspirations de la Grèce dans la question d'Orient*. Paris: Cercle Saint-Simon.

Vrbavac, D. 1900. *Nemanjići i Obrenovići ili upoređenje dva svetla perioda u našoj prošlosti*. Kragujevac: Štamparija Radivoja Jovanovića.

Vryonis, S., Jr. 1967. *Byzantium and Europe*. New York: Harcourt, Brace and World.

Vryonis, S., Jr. 1969–70. 'The Byzantine Legacy and Ottoman Forms', *Dumbarton Oaks Papers*, 23/4: 251–308.

Vryonis, S., Jr. 1971. *The Decline of Medieval Hellenism in Asia Minor and the Process of Islamization from the Eleventh through the Fifteenth Century*. Berkeley: University of California Press.

Vryonis, S., Jr.1978. 'Recent Scholarship on Continuity and Discontinuity of Culture: Classical Greeks, Byzantines, Modern Greeks', in Vryonis, S., Jr. (ed.), *The 'Past' in Medieval and Modern Greek Culture*. Malibu, CA: Undena Publications, 237–56.

Vryonis, S., Jr.1991. 'The Byzantine Legacy in the Formal Culture of the Balkan Peoples', in Yiannias, J. (ed.), *The Byzantine Tradition After the Fall of Constantinople*. Charlottesville: University Press of Virginia, 17–44.

Vryonis, S., Jr. 1992. 'Byzantine Civilization, a World Civilization', in Laiou, A. and Maguire, H. (eds.), *Byzantium: A World Civilization*. Washington, DC: Dumbarton Oaks, 19–36.

Vryonis, S., Jr. 1999. 'Greek Identity in the Middle Ages', in *Byzantium and Hellenism: Proceedings of an International Conference Held at Trieste on 1–3 Oct, 1997* [=*Etudes balkaniques* 6, 21–36].

Xenopol, A. 1925. *Istoria românilor din Dacia Traiană, vol. III: Primii domni și vechile așezăminte: 1290–1457* (3rd ed.). Bucharest: Editura 'Cartea Românească'.

Yerasimos, S. 1990. *Légendes d'Empire: La fondation de Constantinople et de Ste-Sophie dans les traditions turques*. Paris: Maisonneuve.

Yiannias, J. J. 1991. *The Byzantine Tradition After the Fall of Constantinople*. Charlottesville: University Press of Virginia.

Yıldız, Ş. 2011. 'A Review of Byzantine Studies and Architectural Historiography in Turkey Today', *METU Journal of the Faculty of Architecture* 28/2: 63–80.

Yıldız, Ş. 2013. '*Byzantium Between "East" and "West": Perceptions and Architectural Historiography of the Byzantine Heritage*' (unpublished PhD thesis). Ankara: Middle East Technical University.

Yıldız, Ş. 2014. 'Osmanlı'dan Cumhuriyet'e Entelektüellerin Gözüyle Bizans İstanbul'u', *Doğu Batı Dergisi* 68: 103–26.

Zakythinos, D. 1966. 'Le point de vue des épigones', *Jahrbuch der Österreichischen Byzantinischen Gesellschaft* 15: 89–96.

Zakythinos, D. 1967. 'Byzance et les peuples de l'Europe du Sud-Est: La synthèse byzantine', *Actes du Premier Congrès International des Etudes Balkaniques et Sud-Est Européennes*, vol. III. Sofia: Academie Bulgare des Sciences, 7–26.

Zakythinos, D. 1976. *The Making of Modern Greece: From Byzantium to Independence*. Oxford: Basil Blackwell.

Zakythinos, D. 1980–1. 'Byzance état national ou multi-national?', *Deltion XAE* 10: 29–52.

Zambelios, S. 1856. 'La poésie populaire en Grèce', *Le Spectateur de l'Orient* 6: 229–39.

Zane, G. (ed.) 1940. *Nicolae Bălcescu. Opere I. Scrieri istorice, politice și economice, 1844–1847*. Bucharest: Fundația pentru literatură și artă 'Regele Carol II'.

Zelepos, I. 2002. *Die Ethnisierung griechischer Identität 1870–1912*. Munich: Oldenbourg.

Zinkeisen, J. 1832. *Geschichte Griechenlands vom Anfange geschichtlicher Kunde bis auf unsere Tage*. Leipzig: Barth.

Živković, M. 2007. 'Inverted Perspective and Serbian Peasants: Antiquities and the Byzantine Revival in Serbia', in Gow, A. (ed.), *Hyphenated Histories: Articulations of Central European Bildung and Slavic Studies in the Contemporary Academy*. Leiden: Brill, 141–66.

Ziya, İ. 1937. *İstanbul ve Boğaziçi: Bizans ve Türk Medeniyetinin Eserleri*. Istanbul: Dârü't-tıbâ'ati'l-amire [1st ed. 1920].

Zlatarski, V. 1895. *Glavnite periodi v bălraskata istoria*. Sofia: n.p.

References

Zlatarski, V. 1920. 'Istoricheskoto znachenie na Bălgaria s ogled kăm neynoto mezhdudărzhavno polozhenie', *Slavianska biblioteka* 1: 30–56.

Zlatarski, V. 1971–2. *Istoriya na bălgarskata dărzhava prez srednite vekove*, 2 vols. Sofia: Nauka i izkustvo [1st ed., 1918 – vol. I; 2nd ed., 1927 – vol. II].

Zlatarski, V. 1972. *Istoria na bălgarskata dărzhava prez srednite vekove*, vol. II. Sofia: Nauka i izkustvo [1st ed., 1934].

Index

Adamantiou, Adamantios, 127
Ahrweiler, Hélène, 211, 310
Akdağ, Mustafa, 297–8
Amantos, Konstantinos, 128–30, 131, 132
Angelov, Dimităr, 222–6, 303
   development synchronicity thesis, 225–6
   on Bulgarian feudalism as forerunner of the
      Byzantine, 222–3
   on 'byzantinism' in medieval Bulgaria,
      224, 225
Angelov, Dimităr (Jr.), 306, 307
Arnakis, George, 204–5, 298
Arseven, Celal Esad, 179–80, 192, 286
Athos, Mount, 236, 256, 269

Bălcescu, Nicolae, 72
Balkan wars (1912–13), 83, 117, 118, 124, 172, 174, 175
Balkans
   'Aromanian question', 160
   and orientalism, 307
   liberal narrative of, 79
   national awakening, 1, 18
   nationalism in, 84
   Ottoman expansion in, 188, 297, 300
   Romanian migration from, 110
   Romania's role in, 113, 117
   Serbian plans for expansion in, 68
   Slavic invasion and settlement, 221
Bănescu, Nicolae, 158–9, 265, 266
Barbu, Daniel, 314
Bariţ, George, 73
Barkan, Ömer Lütfi, 194–5, 286, 291
Baynes, Norman, 79
Berza, Mihai, 265, 270, 273, 280
   on 'Slavo-Romanian culture', 270–1
Bobchev, Stefan, 141, 153, 232
Bogdan, Ioan, 111, 113, 116, 161
Boia, Lucian, 71, 283
Botev, Hristo, 58, 136
Bozhilov, Ivan, 238–41, 283, 303, 311
   'pax Symeonica', 239–40

'Preslav civilisation', 240–1
Brătianu, Gheorghe I, 164–5
Brezeanu, Stelian, 283, 285
Bulgaria
   liberation from Ottoman rule, 64
   nationalism, 49, 63, 132
   nationalist 'revival' under communism, 226
   struggle against 'Hellenism' and the 'Greek
      Church', 26, 27, 56–7
   the great loser of World War I, 132
Bulgaria, medieval
   Boris I, prince of Bulgaria, 24
   Christianisation, 24. See also Bulgarian
      historiography/on (the impact of)
      Christianisation
   First Bulgarian Kingdom, 24, 27, 33, 58, 70, 94,
      95, 97, 136, 140, 142, 159, 284
   impact of proximity to Byzantium, 18, 24–5
   Ivan Alexander, tsar of Bulgaria, 234
   Ivan Asen II, tsar of Bulgaria, 65, 284
   Ivan Shishman, tsar of Bulgaria, 234
   Second Bulgarian Kingdom, 25, 74, 94, 96, 97,
      120, 136, 141, 161, 236, 268, 284
   Simeon, tsar of Bulgaria, 24. See also Bulgarian
      historiography/on Simeon's empire
Bulgarian historiography
   and nationalism, 251
   'Byzantino-Slavic culture', 231–4, 237–8, 318
   developmental synchronicity between
      medieval Bulgaria and Byzantium, 225–6
   during communist rule, 220–41
      nationalist turn, 226–7
      the late-socialist version of *History of
         Bulgaria*, 227
      the Stalinist version of *History of Bulgaria*,
         221–2
   during the interwar period, 132–43
   early modern narrative, 26–7
   national-Romantic renditions of Byzantium,
      55–64
   mirroring the Greek narrative, 61–2

Index

on (the impact of) Christianisation, 58, 59, 94, 140, 223, 225, 227, 233, 237

on Bogomilism, 93, 95, 137–8, 221, 223, 224, 226, 232

  in the mirror of iconoclasm, 93

on 'byzantinism', 60, 61, 92, 93, 96, 136–9, 141, 224, 225, 232–3, 239

on Simeon's empire, 26, 58, 59, 95, 138, 140–1, 221, 239–40

on the adoption of the Slavic alphabet, 57, 92, 95, 140, 224, 227–8, 237

on the character of Old Slavonic literature, 228–9

on the 'denationalising' policy of Byzantium, 95–6, 141

on the Patriarchate of Constantinople, 57, 62, 96, 231

on the 'Slavs of the Bulgarian group', 239

positivist turn, 92–8

post-1989, 310–11

Bulgarians

  as lacking 'national spirit', 63

  as 'liberators' of the Slavs, 94, 227

Bulgars (proto-Bulgarians), 24, 33, 94, 106, 137, 142, 221, 223

Burckhardt, Jacob, 35

Bury, John, 77, 78, 79

Byzance après Byzance, 1, 117, 156–7, 269, 270, 271, 276, 314. *See also* Iorga, Nicolae

Byzantine Commonwealth, 2, 70, 235, 241, 266, 303, 311–12

  as 'the product of a modern Slavic bias', 215

Byzantine studies, 1, *13*, 115

  and the 'war of faculties', 203

  as dependent on nationalist historiographical traditions, 213

  as national medieval histories, 1

  in early modern Italy, *12*

  in France, 13

    related to French imperial visions, *13*

  in Germany, 114

    early modern period, *12*

    nineteenth century, *17*

  in Russia, 3, 13, 17, 80–2

    impact on Balkan Slavic historiographies, 39, 83

    Stalinist period, 219–20

  in southeastern Europe

    during the Enlightenment, 18–19

    early modern period, 14

    in the frame of interwar 'balkanology', 167–9

    national-Romantic renditions, 74–5

    professionalisation, 83–4, 91, 123–4

  in Turkey, 193, 314–15

in western Europe, 3

  (and the USA) after the fall of the Berlin Wall, 305–9

  as complicit in the Hellenisation of Byzantium, 213

  Graecophile perspective on Byzantium, 79–80

  the 'Age of Erudition', 11–13

institutionalisation

  Bulgaria, 84, 133

  Greece, 84, 125–6, 128

  Romania, 84

  Russia, 80–1

  Serbia/Yugoslavia, 84, 242

  Turkey, 314–15

  western Europe, 76–7

international congresses, 123, 127, 155, 165–7, 239, 271, 287

politics of, 4

Byzantinische Zeitschrift, 76, 81, 98, 123, 164

'byzantinism', 15, 41. *See also* Bulgarian historiography

'byzantism'. *See* Leont'ev, Konstantin

Byzantium

  an elusive phenomenon, 4

  as a dystopian mirror for the 'enlightened West', 15

  as antagonistic to Western civilisation, 201

  as common Balkan patrimony, 135

  as conduit for classical culture, 11, 16, 36, 53, 126

  as different from the Roman empire, 11, 13

  as 'Greek state', 18, 26, 32, 48, 51–2, 54, 61, 129, 206, 208, 209

    instrumentalisation in the Bulgarian narrative, 62–3

  as 'Hellenic *Kulturnation*', 210

  as incompatible with the idea of nationality, 104, 135, 155

  as positive alternative to Western culture, 41

  as synthesis of Roman statehood, Greek culture and Christianity, 152

  as the cause of the Ottoman decline, 175

  as the evil demiurge of Bulgarian history, 136, 139

  as 'the nation-state of the Romans', 213, 214–15

  excluded from Turkey's historical heritage, 193

  fall to the Ottomans (1453), 11, 16, 115, 155, 170, 288, 301

    Western responsibility, *88*, 114

  reception studies, 4–5

Cameron, Averil, 306, 307, 311

Cândea, Virgil, 271

Cantemir, Dimitrie, 30

Catherine the Great's 'Greek Plan' (1782), 17

Index

Catholic Church, catholicism, 14, 19, 31, 76, 134, 216, 257, 278
Çelebi, Katip, 171
Chaadaev, Pyotr, 39
Charanis, Peter, 207
Ćirković, Sima, 250–2
  on nationalism in historiography, 250–1
Constantin (Cyril) and Methodius
  as 'Bulgarian apostles', 57, 95
  as Slav enlighteners, 221
Constantinople
  and Megali Idea, 43, 49, 54, 84
  as centre of Byzantine semiosphere, 3
  as New Rome, 31, 78, 121, 158, 162
  capture by the Crusaders (1204), 28, *88*, *90*, 165, 170, 217, 236, 240, 260, 261
  Russian aspirations for, 40
  the city of Rhomaiōn genos, 218
Ćorović, Vladimir, 144–7, 148
critical ('scientific') historiography. *See also under* historiographies of individual countries and nationalism, 122, 317

Danilevskiy, Nikolay, 40
Delilbaşı, Melek, 300
Diehl, Charles, 77, 78, 152, 179, 185, 187
diffusion, theory of, 103
Drinov, Marin, 92, 136
Droysen, Johann Gustav, 50
Du Cange, Charles Du Fresne, 12
Duychev, Ivan, 224, 226, 229–35, 236, 283
  approach to Byzantine-Slavic relations, 229–30
  'Slavia Orthodoxa' concept, 229, 231–4, 241
Dvorniković, Vladimir, 150–1

Eastern (Orthodox) Church, 13, 14, 16, 20, 46, 47, 56, 155, 189, 236, 278. *See also* Patriarchate of Constantinople
  in Bulgaria, 24, 236
  in Romania, 110, 111, 112, 157, 268, 280–1
  in Serbia, 28, 65, 66, 101, 145, 254
  nationalisation, 56, 57, 66, 145, 154, 192
'Eastern Question', 40, 44, 63, 82
Eastern Rumelia, 63
Elian, Alexandru, 265, 266–9, 275
  on the 'Byzantine-Slavonic synthesis' as the transmitter of Byzantine influence to the Romanians, 268–9
  on the ethnic indistinctness of the north-Danubian populations before the fourteenth century, 267
Emerson, James, 37
Enlightenment, 6
  concern with 'revivalism', 18
  'neo-Hellenic', 19

view of the Middle Ages, 14
views of Byzantium, 14–17
Erbiceanu, Constantin, 74

Fallmerayer, Jakob Philipp, 43–4, 49, 89, 90, 92, 110, 135, 201
  Greek rebuttal of, 44–5
  his Bulgarian reception, 56, 60, 62
Fauriel, Claude, 37
Ferjančić, Božidar, 247, 249, 303
Ferluga, Jadran, 247, 249
feudalism
  in Byzantium, 104, 195, 221, 243, 247, 291
  role of the Slavs, 245
  in medieval Bulgaria, 222–3, 226, 246
  in medieval Serbia, 248
  in the Seljuk state, 292
  'progressive Slavic', 228
  Western, 134, 149, 162
Filov, Bogdan, 142–3, 316
Finlay, George, 38, 50
Fotinov, Konstantin, 57
Freeman, Edward, 76, 78

Georgescu, Valentin, 281, 303
  on the 'imperial ideology' of the Romanian princes, 276
  'Romanian' adaptation of Byzantine institutions, 275
Geršić, Grigorije, 65
Gibbon, Edward, 14, 15, 22, 49, 73, 88, 97, 114, 173
Gibbons, Herbert, 184–5, 187, 289, 290
Giurescu, Constantin, 161–2, 264
Glück, Heinrich, 193
Gökalp, Ziya, 184
Graikoi, 22
Granovsky, Timofei, 39
Greece
  and the Patriarchate of Constantinople, 57
  civil war, 199
  language question, 85–7, 128
  Metaxas regime, 131
  military dictatorship, 199
  nationalism, 32, 36, 43, 91, 202
    Enlightenment, 22, 24
  war of independence, 1, 21, 22, 37, 55
Greece, ancient, 3, 16, 19, 22, 23, 36, 37, 39, 42, 47, 48, 80, 90, 114, 115, 127, 131, 132, 142, 143, 166, 200, 201, 205, 218
Greek historiography
  after 1989, 309–10
  after World War II, 199–218
  and nationalism, 212, 216
  and the Greek Left, 130, 131, 199–200, 211
  debate on the Byzantine 'nation-state', 214–15

Index

'external' challenges to Hellenic continuity (after World War II), 200–4. *See also* Jenkins, Romilly; Mango, Cyril; Nicol, Donald
'Helleno-Christianity', 48, 57, 88, 199
in the wake of the 1922 debacle, 124–32
neo-Hellenic Enlightenment views, 21–4
new currents after 1974, 212
on Byzantine-Ottoman continuity, 298–9
pre-modern phase, 19
reassertions of Hellenic continuity (after World War II), 204–12
'scientific' turn, 87–92
shift from political to cultural history, 87–8
the national-Romantic paradigm shift, 42–54
Byzantium as the telos of modern Greece, 52
impact of German historicism, 46, 50
Greeks
as descendants of Slavs and Albanians, 44
as the arch-enemies of the Bulgarians. *See* Bulgarian historiography/national-Romantic renditions of Byzantium
as usurpers of the Roman empire, 33
pre-modern identity, 20
'racial continuity', 38, 89, 129, 131, 201, 205, 206, 207, 212
Greek-Turkish war (1919–22), 176
Grégoire, Henri, 124, 167, 287
Guizot, François, 16
Gyuzelev, Vasil, 235–8, 283, 303
'Bulgarian-Byzantine cultural dialogue', 237
on the essence of Byzantine-Bulgarian relations, 235

Habsburg empire, 12, 70, 99, 257, 258
Hamilakis, Yannis, 50, 131
Hasdeu, Bogdan, 72, 73, 74
Hatzidakis, Georgios, 128
Hegel, Georg Wilhelm Friedrich, 15
Heisenberg, August, 123, 133
Hellenism
and the Western model of cultural history, 23–4
as a Western colonial imposition and diasporic construct, 216
as constructing the unity of Greek history, 50–1, 79, 83, 86, 211
as discursively constructed Greek identity, 215–16
as imported from the West, 202
'Byzantine', 46, 53, 63, 85, 88, 89, 157, 202, 210, 215
Indigenous versus Western, 53
'neo-Hellenism', 205, 216
product of the Renaissance, 19

Hezarfen, Hüseyin, 171
historical rights, 1, 318
Bulgaria, 146
Greece, 44, 51, 127
Serbia, 68, 105
historicism, 35, 37, 46

iconoclasm, 93
Ignjatović, Aleksandar, 69, 103
İnalcık, Halil, 289–91, 297
on (spheres of) Byzantine-Ottoman continuity, 290–1
on the nature of the early Ottoman state, 289–90
Iorga, Nicolae, 1, 116–21, 135, 147, 155–8, 163, 166, 185, 187, 230, 265, 266, 268, 269, 273, 276, 280, 314, 316
'new Romanian Byzantium', 156
eastern Romanity as bearer of Roman imperial tradition, 120
Romanii populare, 119
Italy
émigré Byzantine scholars, 11, 19
Ivanov, Yurdan, 98

Jenkins, Romilly, 200–1, 204, 205
Jireček, Konstantin, 99, 147
Jovanović, Vladimir, 67

Kafadar, Cemal, 294, 303
Kaldellis, Anthony, 216, 307
critique of the state of Byzantine scholarship, 213–14
on Byzantium as nation-state, 213, 214
on Hellenism in Byzantium, 215–16
on language and Orthodoxy in Byzantine identity, 214–15
Karavelov, Lyuben, 58, 62
Karolidis, Pavlos, 84
Katartzis, Dimitrios, 20
Kemal, Mustafa (Atatürk), 124, 181, 183, 286
Keydar, Çağlar, 293
Khomyakov, Aleksey, 40
Kitromilides, Paschalis, 52
Kogălniceanu, Mihail, 72
Kolettis, Ioannis, 43, 50, 84, 87
Kondakov, Nikodim, 81
Köprülü, Mehmet Fuat, 186–90, 194, 286, 289
and the pure Turkish-Islamic nature of the Ottoman state, 187–8
reception of his views, 190–2
Korais Chair of Modern Greek and Byzantine History, Language and Literature, 200
Korais, Adamantios, 21–2
Kordatos, Ioannis, 130–1

354   *Index*

Koukoules, Phaedon, 126
Kovačević, Ljubomir, 99
Krug, Johann Philipp, 17
Krumbacher, Karl, 76, 79, 100, 113, 123, 147

Lamanskiy, Vladimir, 81, 93
Lambros, Spyridon, 45, 84, 89–91, 98, 113, 126, 127, 316
Lecky, William, 35
Leont'ev, Konstantin, 40–1
Liakos, Antonis, 51, 85, 203, 310
Lihachov, Dmitriy, 228, 230, 233
Litzica, Constantin, 113, 122
Louis XIV, king of France, 11

'Macedonian question', 64, 74, 130
Maior, Petru, 31, 33
Maksimović, Ljubomir, 247, 252–5, 261, 262, 303
    Serbia as a 'specific phenomenon of civilisation', 255
Mango, Cyril, 201–3, 205, 216
Manousis, Theodoros, 45, 52
Manzikert, battle of, 176, 193, 288, 298
Megali Idea, 43, 49, 50, 61, *84–5*, 131, 176, 202, 205, 207, 211
    debacle, 124, 125
Mehmed Murad Mizancı, 175, 178
Mehmed Ziya İhtifalci, 179, 180–1
Micu, Samuil, 31, 33
Midhat, Ahmet, 173–4, 177, 194
Millet, Gabriel, 164, 167, 256
Millet-i-Rum (Rum Millet), 19, 195
Milošević, Slobodan, 255, 258
Montesquieu, Charles de, *11*, 14, 21, 47, 88, 97, 114, 172
Mošin, Vladimir, 154
Mureşan, Dan Ioan, 313
Murnu, George, 159–61, 282
Mutafchiev, Petăr, 62, 133–9, 150, 151, 220, **222**, 223, 226, 232, 233, 235, 236, 240, 283
    on Simeon's 'Golden Age', 138
    on the destructive role of Byzantine influence on the Bulgarians, 136–8, 139
    rehabilitation of Byzantium, 134

Năstase, Dumitru, 273–5, 276, 277
    'the Christian Crypto-empire' of the Romanian princes, 274
Năsturel, Petre, 273, 283
nationalism
    cultural versus racial, 49, 182, 186
    irrelevance of the 'national principle' in the Middle Ages, 103–5, 141
    neo-Hellenic, 45
    Romantic, 35, 122

theories of, 250
Necipoğlu, Nevra, 288, 315
Neroulos Rizos, Iakovos, 22
Nicol, Donald, 203–4
Niebuhr, Georg, 16
Nikov, Petăr, 140–1
Novaković, Stojan, 99, 102, 103–8, 109, 135, 146, 147
Nuri, Celal, 174–5

Obolensky, Dimitri, 2, 13, 70, 80, 230, 235, 241, 303
Old (Church) Slavonic
    as official language in the Romanian principalities, 70
    as old-Bulgarian, 229
    as supranational language, 228
orientalism, 16, 190
    and philhellenism, 24
    Byzantine studies as a species of, 306
    views of Byzantium, 201, 282, 305, 307, 308
Orthodoxy, 65, 107, 118, 135, 152, 210, 253, 254, 271, 281
    as defining identity under the Ottomans, 19
Osman I, founder of the Ottoman dynasty, 297
Ostrogorski, Georgiy, 151–3, 232, 242–7, 258
    historical-materialist views, 246
    on Stefan Dušan's empire, 244–5, 246–7
    on the Balkan Slavs' contribution to Byzantine society, 244–5
Ottoman empire
    as 'Frontier Empire', 290
    as heir to the Byzantine empire, 177–8
    as liberator from Byzantine (feudal) oppression, 195, 297
    as 'paradise of cultural pluralism', 195
    attitude to cultural heritage, 178–9
    Ottoman culture as part of Western culture, 295
    Tanzimat era, 171
    Turkification of, 188
    upsurge of Turkish nationalism in, 178–9
    Young Ottomans, 171
    Young Turk revolution, 172
Ottoman historiography
    during the *Tanzimat* era, 171–2
    impact of modern Greek-Turkish relations on, 176
    in search of new sources of identity, 172–81
    incipient engagement with Byzantine artistic legacy, 179–81
Ottomans
    as heirs of the Byzantines, 177
    as infected by the 'Greek disease', 175
    as the moral opposite of the Byzantines, 173–5

Index

355

Paisiy Hilendarski, 26–7, 55, 62
Palaouzov, Spiridon, 60
Panaitescu, Petre, 162–4, 264, 280
Pantelić, Bratislav, 256–9
  critique of 'Serbian Byzantium', 256–8
Papacostea, Victor, 168
Paparrigopoulos, Konstantinos, 45, 63, 88, 89, 91,
    93, 98, 130, 192
  and Megali Idea, 49
  creation of the Greek grand narrative, 48–53
  nationalisation of Byzantium, 51–2
  shift from racial to cultural continuity, 49–50
Patlagean, Évelyne, 306, 313
Patriarchate of Constantinople, 22, 25, 39, 56, 57,
    145, 156, 267, 303
  transformation under the Ottomans, 18,
    25, 234
Pavlovich, Christaki, 55
Peter the Great's view of Byzantium, 17
Phanariots, 19, 21, 60, 157
philhellenism
  and formation of the Greek historical canon,
    23–4, 37–9
Phillipides, Dimitrie (Daniel), 20
Pippidi, Andrei, 275, 276–9, 303
  Byzantium as myth and 'idée-force' for
    Romanian culture, 277–8
Pirivatrić, Srđan, 261–2
Politis, Nikolaos, 84
Pop, Ioan-Aurel, 313
positivism, 6, 83, 84, 92, 173
Psycharis, Ioannis, 86

Radić, Radivoj, 247, 313
Radojčić, Nikola, 144, 147–8, 149
Radonić, Jovan, 99, 101–2, 144
Rajić, Jovan, 29
Rakovski, Georgi, 58, 136
Rambaud, Alfred, 77, 185, 187
Ranke, Leopold von, 16
Refik, Ahmet, 176–8, 186
Romaioi, 20, 21, 22, 86, 135, 214, 217
Romania
  as the real Byzance après Byzance, 157
  cultural politics under Ceauşescu's regime, 265
  Greater Romania, 155, 164, 165
  nationalism, 155, 266
    Enlightenment, 31
Romanian historiography
  and nationalism, 117, 251, 276
  during communist rule, 264–79
    de-Stalinisation, 264–5
    national-communist discourse, 270
    'cultural revolution' under Ceauşescu's
      regime, 265

grecismul, 111, 112, 158
  interwar narratives in, 155–65
  Latinist School, 31–4, 70, 71, 72, 73, 75,
    279
  national-Romantic phase, 70–4
  on the 'imperial ideology' of the Romanian
    princes, 274, 277–8, 281
  on the Patriarchate of Constantinople, 111
  on Phanariot Greeks, 32, 73, 74, 111, 269,
    275, 281
  post-communist, 264–79, 313–14
  post-Romantic, 109–22
  seventeenth-century humanist tradition
    in, 30–1
  Slav influence on Romania, 110–12, 115, 161,
    162–4, 270–1, 275, 280
  Vlachs, 33–4, 119, 121, 159–60, 266, 283–5
    role in the Second Bulgarian Kingdom, 74,
      120, 161, 268, 284
Romanians
  as the 'Eastern Romans', 30, 71
  ethnogenesis, 113, 159, 264, 270, 280
Romanticism. *See under* historiographies of
  individual countries
Rome, ancient, 16, 21, 30, 31, 38, 40, 46, 47, 114,
    121, 157, 158, 166, 168, 172, 217, 218, 272,
    279, 292
Romiosyne, 86
Rozanov, Vasiliy Rozanov, 41
Runciman, Steven, 142, 286
Russia
  links with the Balkan Slavs, 81
  nationalism, 41
  Panslav designs for recreating Byzantium, 40
  Slavophile and Westernizer attitudes to
    Byzantium, 39–40
  underpinnings of interest in Byzantium, 17, 80
Russian Archaeological Institute in
    Constantinople, 82, 100
Russo, Demostene, 110–12, 113–16, 134, 163, 266
Ruvarac, Ilarion, 99, 103

Sathas, Konstantinos, 91, 98
Schevill, Ferdinand, 78
Schlözer, August Ludwig von, 14, 17
Seliminski, Ivan, 55–6
Serbia. *See also* Yugoslavia/Kingdom of the Serbs,
  Croats and Slovenes
  nationalism, 99, 143, 255, 257
  political emancipation, 64
Serbia, medieval
  Christianisation, 27
  Stefan Dušan, tsar of Serbia, 28, 64, 234,
    256, 259
  early state-building, 28

Index

Serbia, medieval (cont.)
Stefan Milutin, king of Serbia, 154, 252, 253, 256, 261
Nemanjić dynasty, 28, 64, 108, 255
Stefan Nemanja, prince of Serbia, 65, 108, 145, 246, 253
Stefan the First-Crowned, king of Serbia, 28, 150
Serbian historiography
'Belgrade School of Byzantine Studies', 247, 248–50, 252, 262
in First Yugoslavia, 143–51
Russian émigré scholars' contribution, 151–4
in socialist Yugoslavia, 242–52
History of the Peoples of Yugoslavia, 247–8
national-Romantic matrix, 64–8
on Stefan Dušan's empire, 252, 254
post-communist, 252–63
methodological and institutional cleavages, 261
pre-World War I critical school, 99–109
recent developments in, 311–13
'Serbo-Byzantinism', 68, 101, 144, 149, 154
critique of, 256–8
Stefan Dušan's empire, 29, 64, 65, 66, 67, 75, 102, 108, 109, 144, 148–50
Shishmanov, Ivan, 105, 114, 115, 134
Şincai, Gheorghe, 31
Slaveykov, Petko, 57, 59
Slavs
as 'imitators' of Byzantium, 118
as inherently democratic, 93
as lacking ethnic sentiment and sense of community, 106
as mediators of Byzantine influences to the Romanians, 70
as the autochthonous population of Eastern Europe, 55
Hellenisation, 49, 89
Solov'ev, Aleksandar, 153
Solov'ev, Vladimir, 41
Srećković, Pantelija, 66, 67–8, 99, 103
Stănescu, Eugen, 272–3
Stanev, Nikola, 140
Stanković, Vlada, 259–61, 311, 312
challenging the 'centre–periphery discourse', 261
irrelevance of the notion of 'independent polities' in the late-medieval Balkans, 259–60
Stanojević, Stanoje, 99, 100–1, 109, 144, 146, 148, 244
Stouraitis, Ioannis, 217–18
critique of the notion of nation-state in medieval context, 217
on Hellenic ethnicity in late Byzantium, 218

Stritter, Johann, 17
Strzygowski, Josef, 193
Svetosavlje, 257
Svoronos, Nikos, 200, 210–11

Taeschner, Franz, 190
Tanaşoca, Nicolae Şerban, 279–83, 303
on Byzantine hostility to Romanian identity, 279–80
on Romanian Orthodoxy and Church, 281–2
on the Balkan Vlachs, 283–4
Taranovskiy, Teodor, 153
Theodor, Dan Gh., 270
Theotokas, Giorgos, 125
Therianos, Dionyssios, 53
Timur, Taner, 291–3, 303
'Turkish-Byzantine synthesis' in the Seljuk sultanate, 291–3
translatio imperii
from the West to the East, 217, 218
to 'Imperium Bulgarorum et Graecorum', 240
to post-Byzantine Romanian principalities, 274, 276, 277
to Serbia, 69
to the 'Vlacho-Bulgarian Kingdom', 34
transnational history, 167, 307, 319
Transylvania, 31, 73, 110, 265
Treaty of Kuchuk Kainarji (1774), 17, 40
Turan, Osman, 287, 296–7
Turgut Özal's *Turkey in Europe*, 294–5
Turkey
Kemalism, 181, 183, 192, 289
nationalism, 181, 193, 286, 288, 289
promulgation of the Republic, 181
war of independence, 181, 288
Turkish historiography
after World War II, 303
Anatolianism, 182, 190
denial of Byzantine influence on Ottoman institutions and art, 187–90, 192–3, 296–7
dissociation from the Ottoman-Islamic past, 183–4
during the early Republic, 181–93
on Byzantine-Ottoman continuities, 290–1, 293, 294
on Byzantium's 'oppressive feudalism', 195
rehabilitation of the Ottoman past, 194
'Sun Language Theory', 182, 183
treatment of cultural heritage, 301–3
Turkification of Ottoman imperial history, 192, 289. *See also* Köprülü, Mehmet Fuat
'Turkish History Thesis', 182–3, 186, 190, 286, 288, 295
'Turkish-Islamic synthesis', 287–8, 296, 302

Index

Turks
  as having similar 'relations of production' and 'political superstructure' to Byzantium, 292
  as incapable of empire-building, 184–5
  as promoters of religious freedom and just administration, 296
  Seljuk Turks/Seljuks, 170, 176, 189, 291–3, 296, 299

Ubavkić, Milan, 66, 69
Uspenskiy, Fyodor, 81, 100

Vakalopoulos, Apostolos, 205–7
Vasil'evskiy, Vasiliy G., 77, 80, 81, 93
Veis, Nicos, 125, 128
Velestinlis, Rigas (Feraios), 20, 21
Vikelas, Dimitrios, 84, 88–9, 91, 93, 97, 114, 115, 126, 129, 134
Vizantiyskiy vremennik, 80, 98, 220
Vlachs/Aromanians, 113, 265. *See also* Romanian historiography/on Vlachs/Aromanians
Voltaire, François, 14, 15, 17, 114
Vryonis, Speros Jr., 191, 207–8, 298

Wallachia and Moldavia, 30, 31, 33, 70, 71, 277
  (medieval) state formation, 265, 267
  establishment of metropolitan seats in, 70, 267, 280
  medieval heralds of the modern nation-state, 121

Phanariot regime in, 32, 71
  union (1859), 110
Western semiosphere, 3
Wolf, Hieronymus, 12, 171

Xenopol, Alexandru, 74, 110–13, 115, 116

Young Turks, 177
Yugoslavia/Kingdom of the Serbs, Croats and Slovenes, 144
  geopolitical and international position after World War II, 242
  integral Yugoslavism and/versus Serbian nationalism, 144
  nationalism, 247
  'Serbian Byzantium' in post-1990 identity politics, 255
  Wars of Yugoslav Succession (1990–9), 255

Zahariadis, Nikos, 131
Zakythinos, Dionysios, 48, 208–10
Zambelios, Spyridon, 45, 46–8, 50, 63, 89, 98
Zinkeisen, Johann Wilhelm
Zlatarski, Vasil, 93–7, 106, 107, 112, 121, 136, 140, 142, 192, 220, 240, 284, 311
  on the Christianisation of the Bulgarians, 94
  on the creation of the Bulgarian state, 94
  on the 'denationalising' policy of Byzantium, 95–6
  on the reign of Tsar Simeon, 95